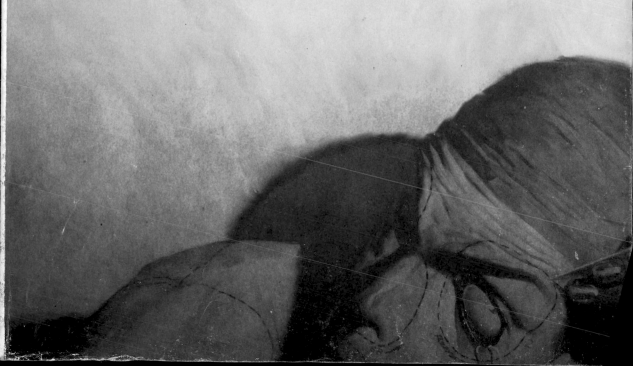

the vertigo *HORROR* anthology

# flinch

**BOOK ONE**

# WRITERS

BRIAN **AZZARELLO** / RICHARD **BRUNING** / SCOTT **CUNNINGHAM** / GARTH **ENNIS** / BOB **FINGERMAN** / DEVIN **GRAYSON**
PHIL **HESTER** / BRUCE **JONES** / JOHN **KURAMOTO** / JOE R. **LANSDALE** / WILLIAM **MESSNER-LOEBS** / DEAN **MOTTER** / COLIN **RAFF**
ROBERT **RODI** / JOHN **ROZUM** / GREG **RUCKA** / TY **TEMPLETON** / JEN **VAN METER** / IVAN **VELEZ JR.** / MARK **WHEATLEY**
KENT **WILLIAMS** / BILL **WILLINGHAM** / JIM **WOODRING**

# ARTISTS

HO CHE **ANDERSON** / RICK **BURCHETT** / RICHARD **CORBEN** / RANDY **DUBURKE** / KIERON **DWYER** / DUNCAN **FEGREDO**
MARCELO **FRUSIN** / PAUL **GULACY** / MARC **HEMPEL** / PHIL **HESTER** / PHIL **JIMENEZ** / KELLEY **JONES** / JIM **LEE** / RICK **MAGYAR**
PAT **MCEOWN** / JON **J MUTH** / ANDE **PARKS** / FRANK **QUITELY** / EDUARDO **RISSO** / JAMES **ROMBERGER** / BILL **SIENKIEWICZ**
TY **TEMPLETON** / KENT **WILLIAMS** / BILL **WILLINGHAM**

# the vertigo *HORROR* anthology
# flinch
## BOOK ONE

# COLORISTS

TAD **EHRLICH** / NOELLE **GIDDINGS** / GRANT **GOLEASH** / BJARNE **HANSEN** / MATT **HOLLINGSWORTH** / JOHN **KURAMOTO**
LEE **LOUGHRIDGE** / MAXIMILLIAN **MIRTH** / PATRICIA **MULVIHILL** / PAMELA **RAMBO** / SHERILYN **VAN VALKENBURGH**
JOSÉ **VILLARRUBIA** / DANIEL **VOZZO** / JASON **WRIGHT** / ZYLONOL

# LETTERERS

RICHARD **BRUNING** / JOHN **COSTANZA** / JOHN **HEEBINK** / MARC **HEMPEL** / TODD **KLEIN** / JACK **MORELLI** / TOM **ORZECHOWSKI**
CLEM **ROBINS** / WILLIE **SCHUBERT** / TY **TEMPLETON** / ELLIE **DE VILLE** / JOHN **WORKMAN**

# COVER ART

PHIL **HALE**

# ORIGINAL SERIES COVERS

PHIL **HALE** (ISSUE #1) / RICHARD **CORBEN** (ISSUE #2) / SUE **COE** (ISSUE #3) / STEPHEN JOHN **PHILLIPS** AND JOSÉ **VILLARRUBIA**
(ISSUE #4) / TIM **SALE** (ISSUE #5) / KENT **WILLIAMS** (ISSUE #6) / JOHN **MUELLER** (ISSUE #7)
JAE **LEE** AND JOSÉ **VILLARRUBIA** (ISSUE #8)

**FLINCH BOOK ONE**

Published by DC Comics. Compilation Copyright © 2015 DC Comics. All Rights Reserved.

Originally published in single magazine form as FLINCH 1-8. Copyright © 1999, 2000 DC
Comics. All Rights Reserved. VERTIGO and all characters, their distinctive likenesses and
related elements featured in this publication are trademarks of DC Comics.
The stories, characters and incidents featured in this publication are entirely fictional.
DC Comics does not read or accept unsolicited submissions of ideas, stories or artwork.

DC Comics
2900 West Alameda Avenue
Burbank, CA 91505
Printed in the USA. First Printing.
ISBN: 978-1-4012-5812-2

Library of Congress Cataloging-in-Publication Data

Flinch book one / Brian Azzarello, Jim Lee, Eduardo Risso.
   pages cm
   ISBN 978-1-4012-5812-2 (paperback)
 1.  Graphic novels.  I. Azzarello, Brian. II. Lee, Jim, 1964- III. Risso, Eduardo.
PN6728.F568F57 2015
741.5'973—dc23

                          2015031184

**PEFC Certified**

Printed on paper from
sustainably managed
forests and controlled
sources

**PEFC**
PEFC/29-31-75    www.pefc.org

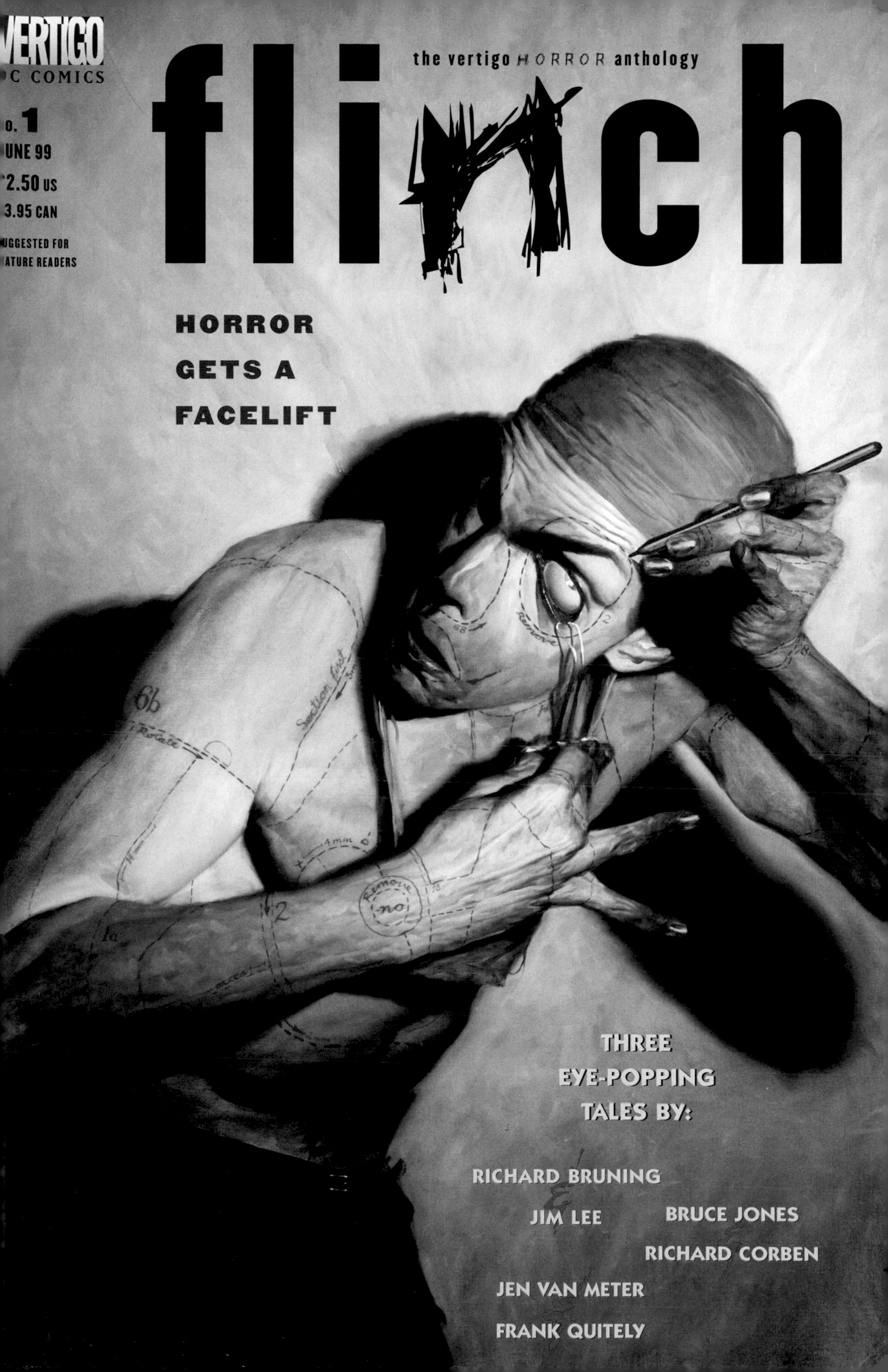
ERTIGO
C COMICS
o. 1
UNE 99
2.50 US
3.95 CAN
UGGESTED FOR
ATURE READERS
the vertigo HORROR anthology
flinch
HORROR
GETS A
FACELIFT
THREE
EYE-POPPING
TALES BY:
RICHARD BRUNING
&
JIM LEE
BRUCE JONES
&
RICHARD CORBEN
JEN VAN METER
&
FRANK QUITELY

the vertigo *HORROR* anthology

# flinch

## BOOK ONE

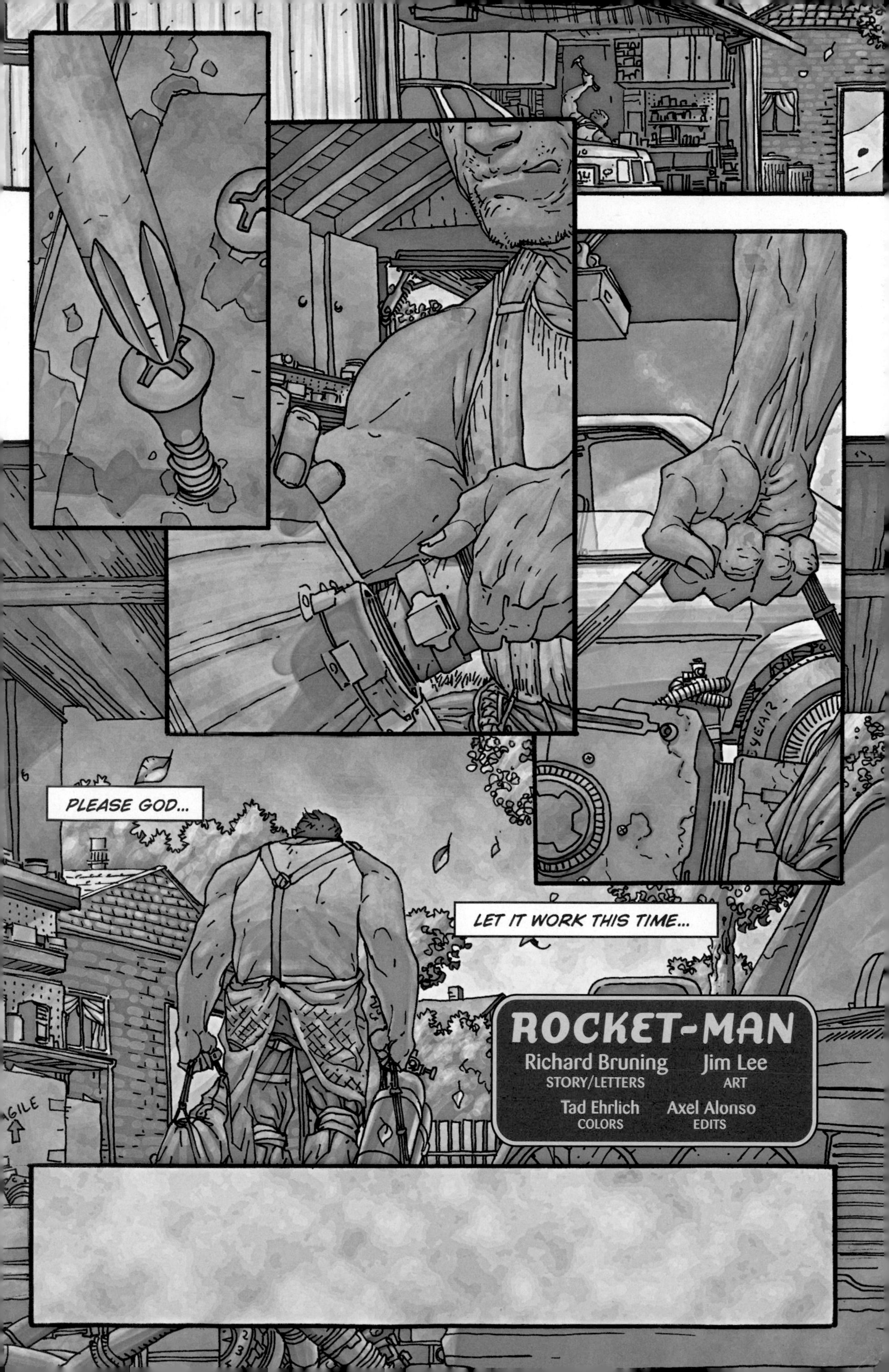
PLEASE GOD...
LET IT WORK THIS TIME...
ROCKET-MAN
Richard Bruning
STORY/LETTERS
Jim Lee
ART
Tad Ehrlich
COLORS
Axel Alonso
EDITS

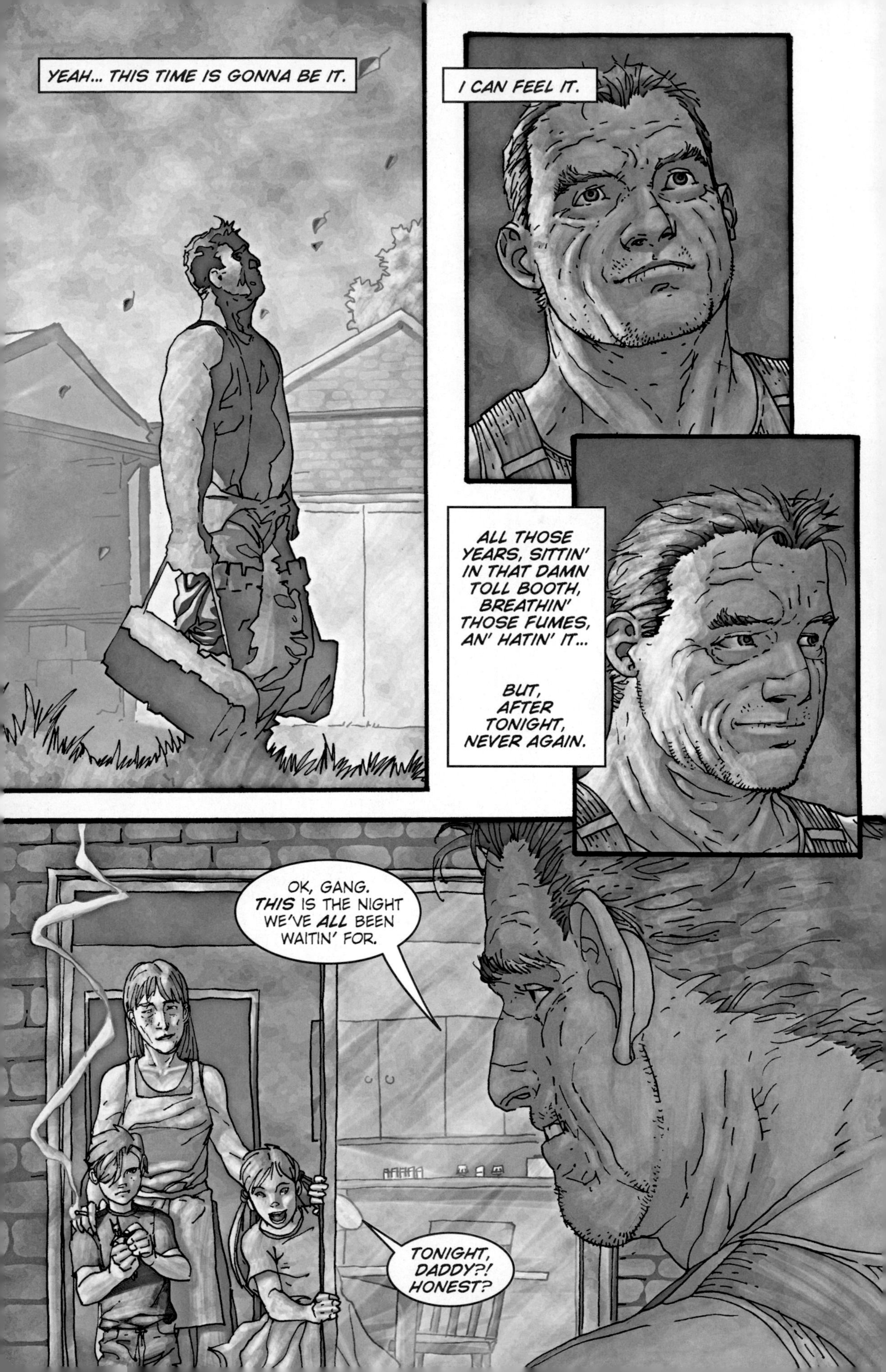
YEAH... THIS TIME IS GONNA BE IT.
I CAN FEEL IT.
ALL THOSE YEARS, SITTIN' IN THAT DAMN TOLL BOOTH, BREATHIN' THOSE FUMES, AN' HATIN' IT...
BUT, AFTER TONIGHT, NEVER AGAIN.
OK, GANG. THIS IS THE NIGHT WE'VE ALL BEEN WAITIN' FOR.
TONIGHT, DADDY?! HONEST?

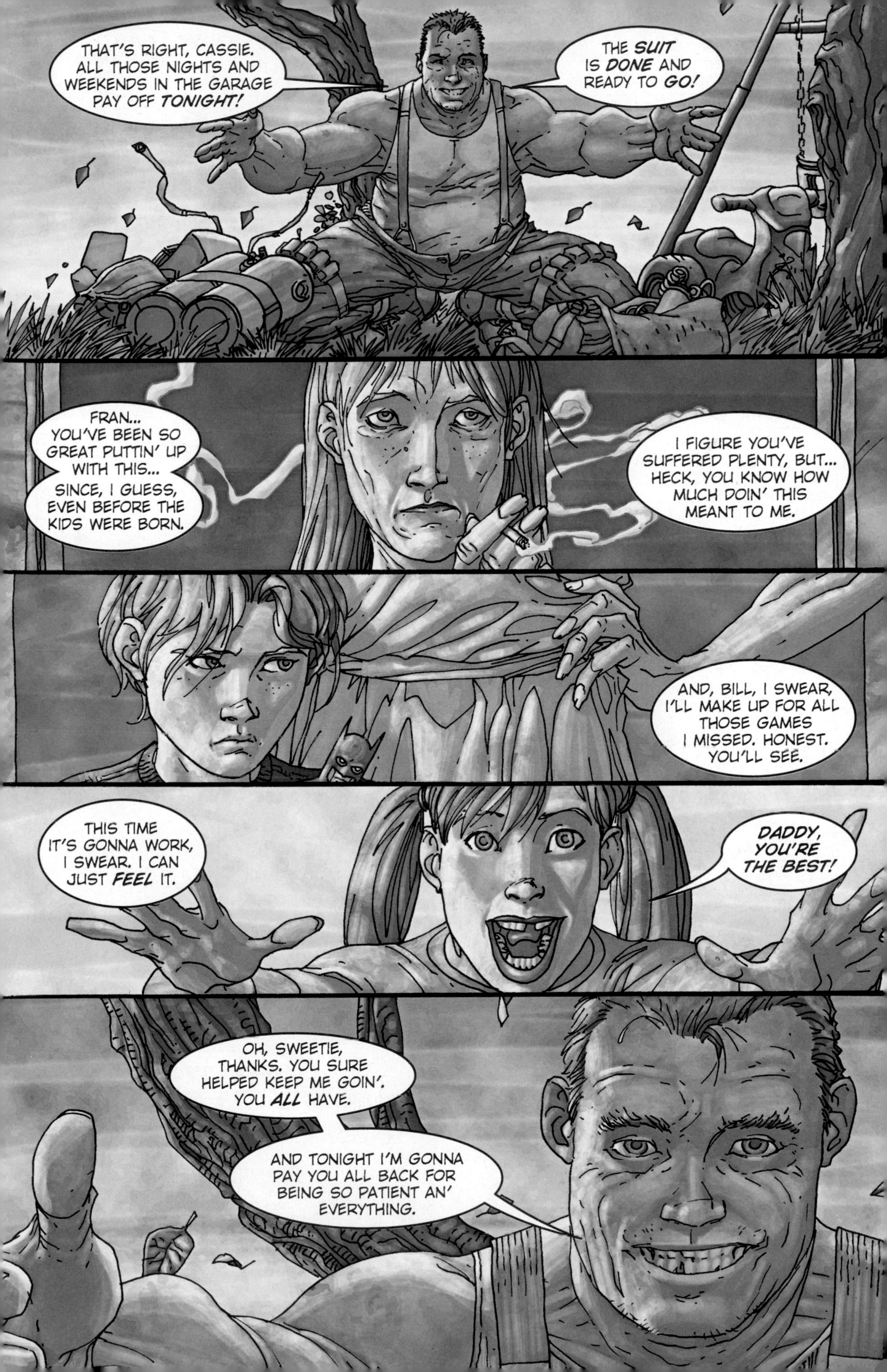
THAT'S RIGHT, CASSIE. ALL THOSE NIGHTS AND WEEKENDS IN THE GARAGE PAY OFF TONIGHT!
THE SUIT IS DONE AND READY TO GO!
FRAN... YOU'VE BEEN SO GREAT PUTTIN' UP WITH THIS...
SINCE, I GUESS, EVEN BEFORE THE KIDS WERE BORN.
I FIGURE YOU'VE SUFFERED PLENTY, BUT... HECK, YOU KNOW HOW MUCH DOIN' THIS MEANT TO ME.
AND, BILL, I SWEAR, I'LL MAKE UP FOR ALL THOSE GAMES I MISSED. HONEST. YOU'LL SEE.
THIS TIME IT'S GONNA WORK, I SWEAR. I CAN JUST FEEL IT.
DADDY, YOU'RE THE BEST!
OH, SWEETIE, THANKS. YOU SURE HELPED KEEP ME GOIN'. YOU ALL HAVE.
AND TONIGHT I'M GONNA PAY YOU ALL BACK FOR BEING SO PATIENT AN' EVERYTHING.

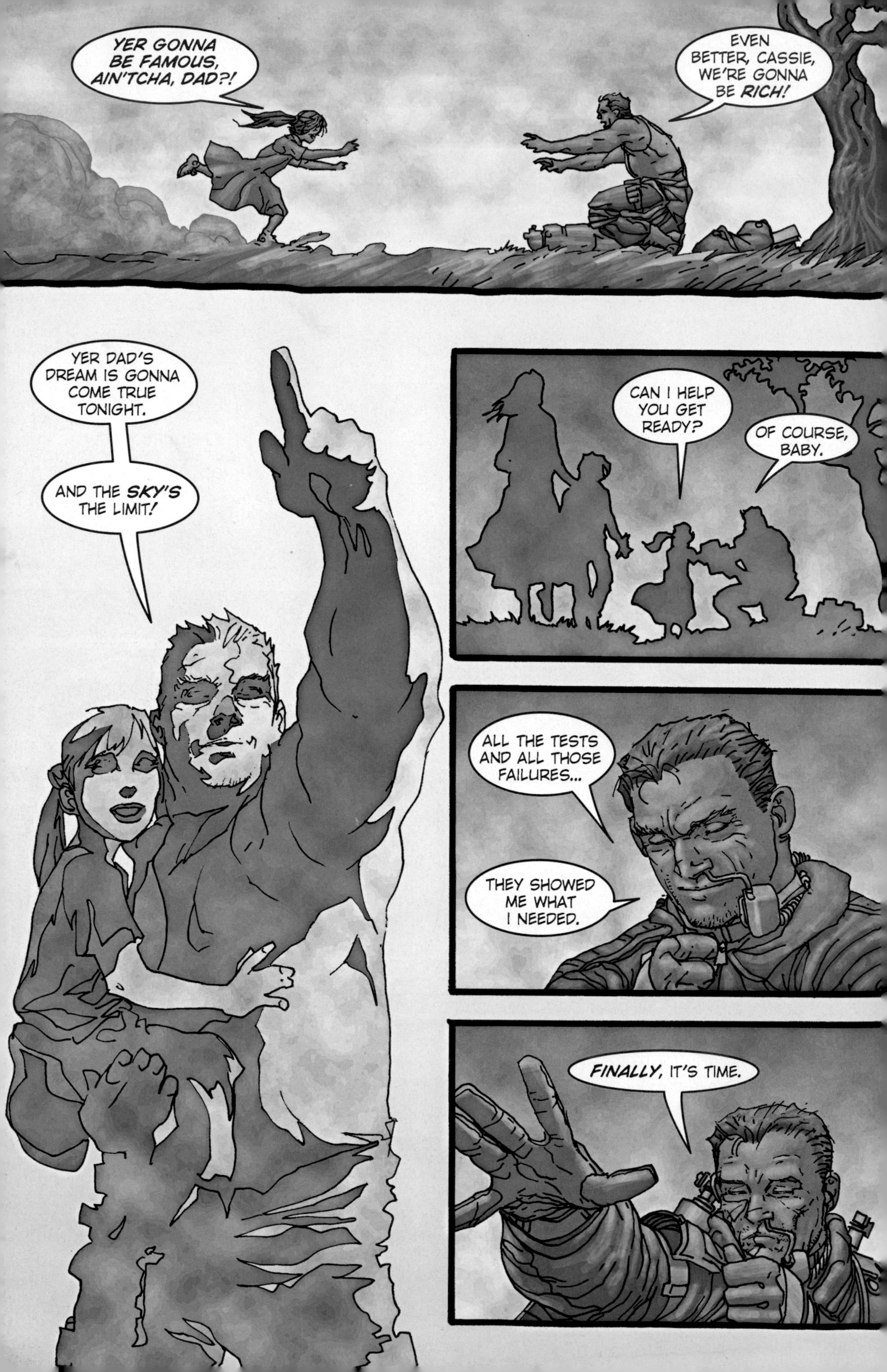
YER GONNA BE FAMOUS, AIN'TCHA, DAD?!
EVEN BETTER, CASSIE, WE'RE GONNA BE RICH!
YER DAD'S DREAM IS GONNA COME TRUE TONIGHT.
AND THE SKY'S THE LIMIT!
CAN I HELP YOU GET READY?
OF COURSE, BABY.
ALL THE TESTS AND ALL THOSE FAILURES...
THEY SHOWED ME WHAT I NEEDED.
FINALLY, IT'S TIME.

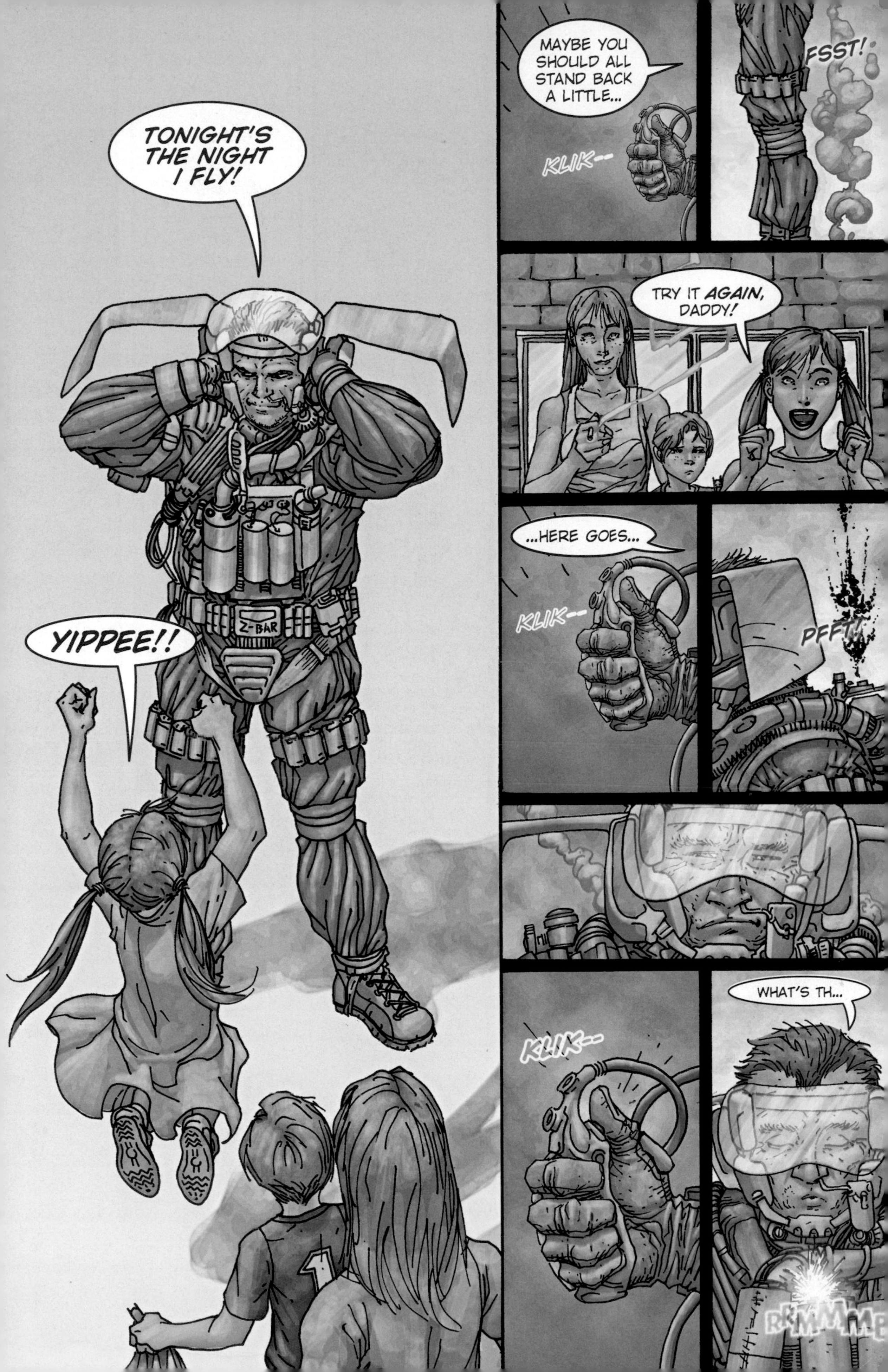
TONIGHT'S THE NIGHT I FLY!
YIPPEE!!
MAYBE YOU SHOULD ALL STAND BACK A LITTLE...
KLIK--
FSST!
TRY IT AGAIN, DADDY!
...HERE GOES...
KLIK--
PFFT!
KLIK--
WHAT'S TH...
Z-BAR

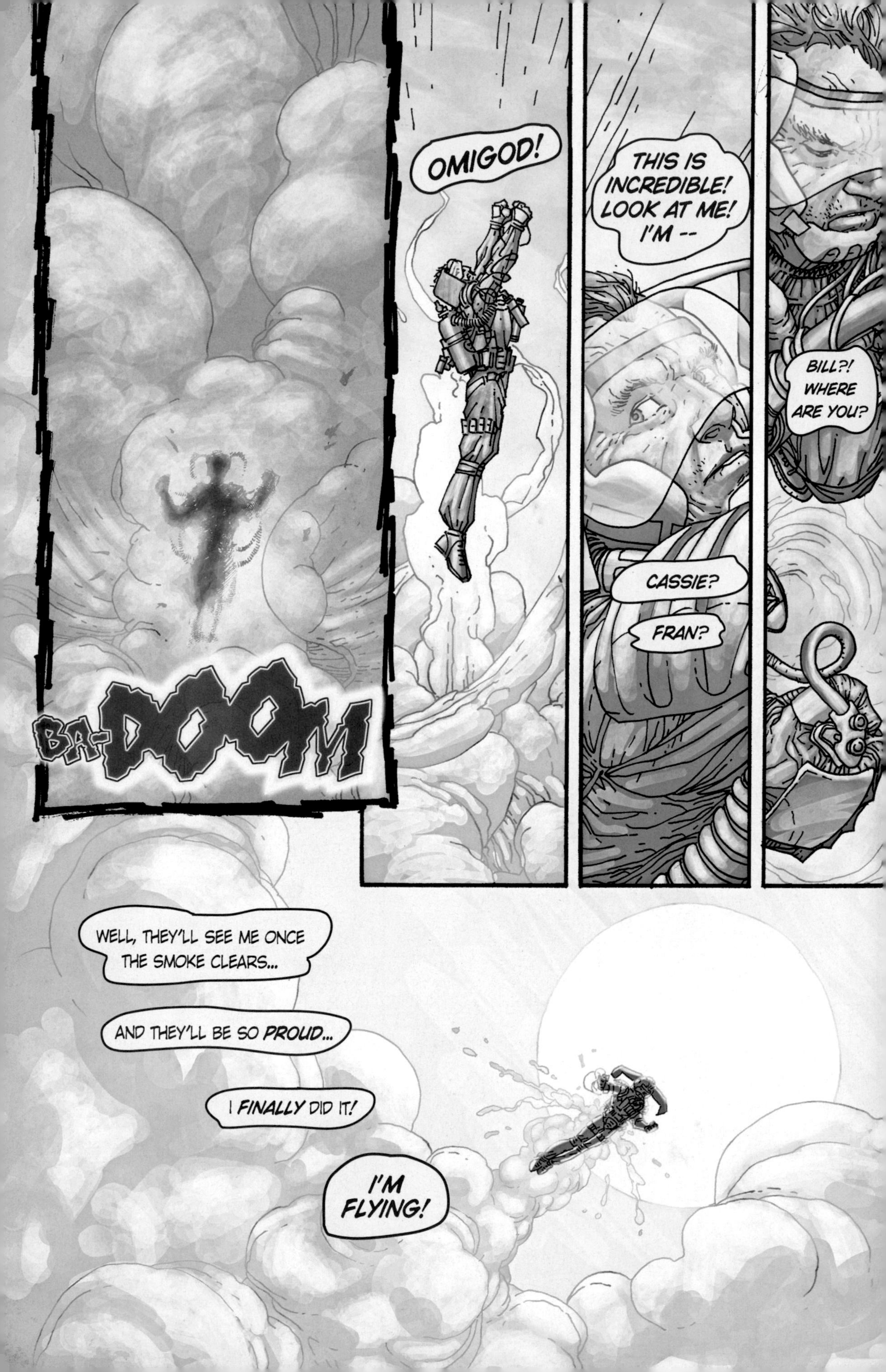
BA-DOOM
OMIGOD!
THIS IS INCREDIBLE! LOOK AT ME! I'M --
CASSIE?
FRAN?
BILL?! WHERE ARE YOU?
WELL, THEY'LL SEE ME ONCE THE SMOKE CLEARS...
AND THEY'LL BE SO PROUD...
I FINALLY DID IT!
I'M FLYING!

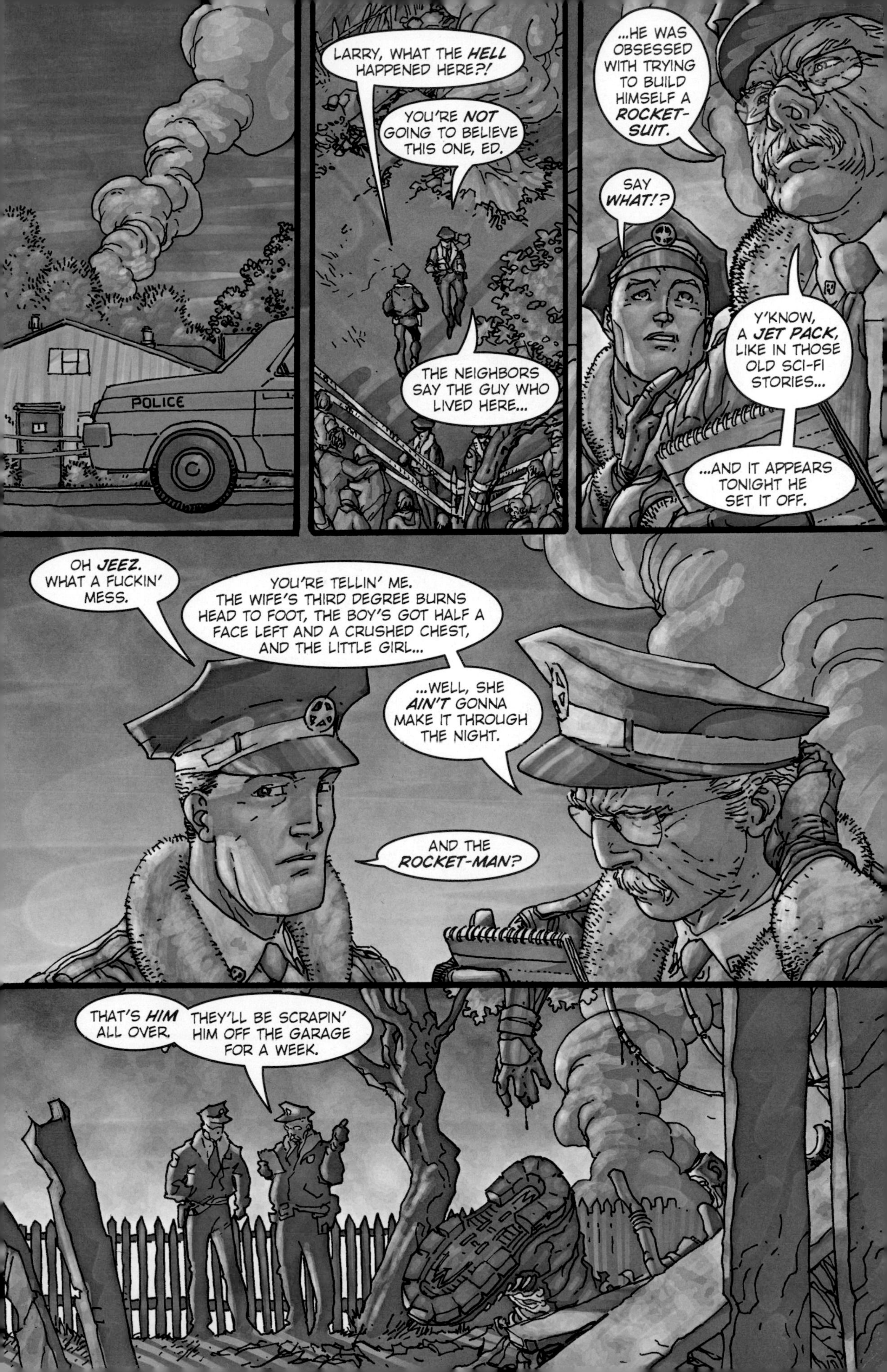

POLICE
LARRY, WHAT THE HELL HAPPENED HERE?!
YOU'RE NOT GOING TO BELIEVE THIS ONE, ED.
THE NEIGHBORS SAY THE GUY WHO LIVED HERE...
...HE WAS OBSESSED WITH TRYING TO BUILD HIMSELF A ROCKET-SUIT.
SAY WHAT!?
Y'KNOW, A JET PACK, LIKE IN THOSE OLD SCI-FI STORIES...
...AND IT APPEARS TONIGHT HE SET IT OFF.
OH JEEZ. WHAT A FUCKIN' MESS.
YOU'RE TELLIN' ME. THE WIFE'S THIRD DEGREE BURNS HEAD TO FOOT, THE BOY'S GOT HALF A FACE LEFT AND A CRUSHED CHEST, AND THE LITTLE GIRL...
...WELL, SHE AIN'T GONNA MAKE IT THROUGH THE NIGHT.
AND THE ROCKET-MAN?
THAT'S HIM ALL OVER.
THEY'LL BE SCRAPIN' HIM OFF THE GARAGE FOR A WEEK.

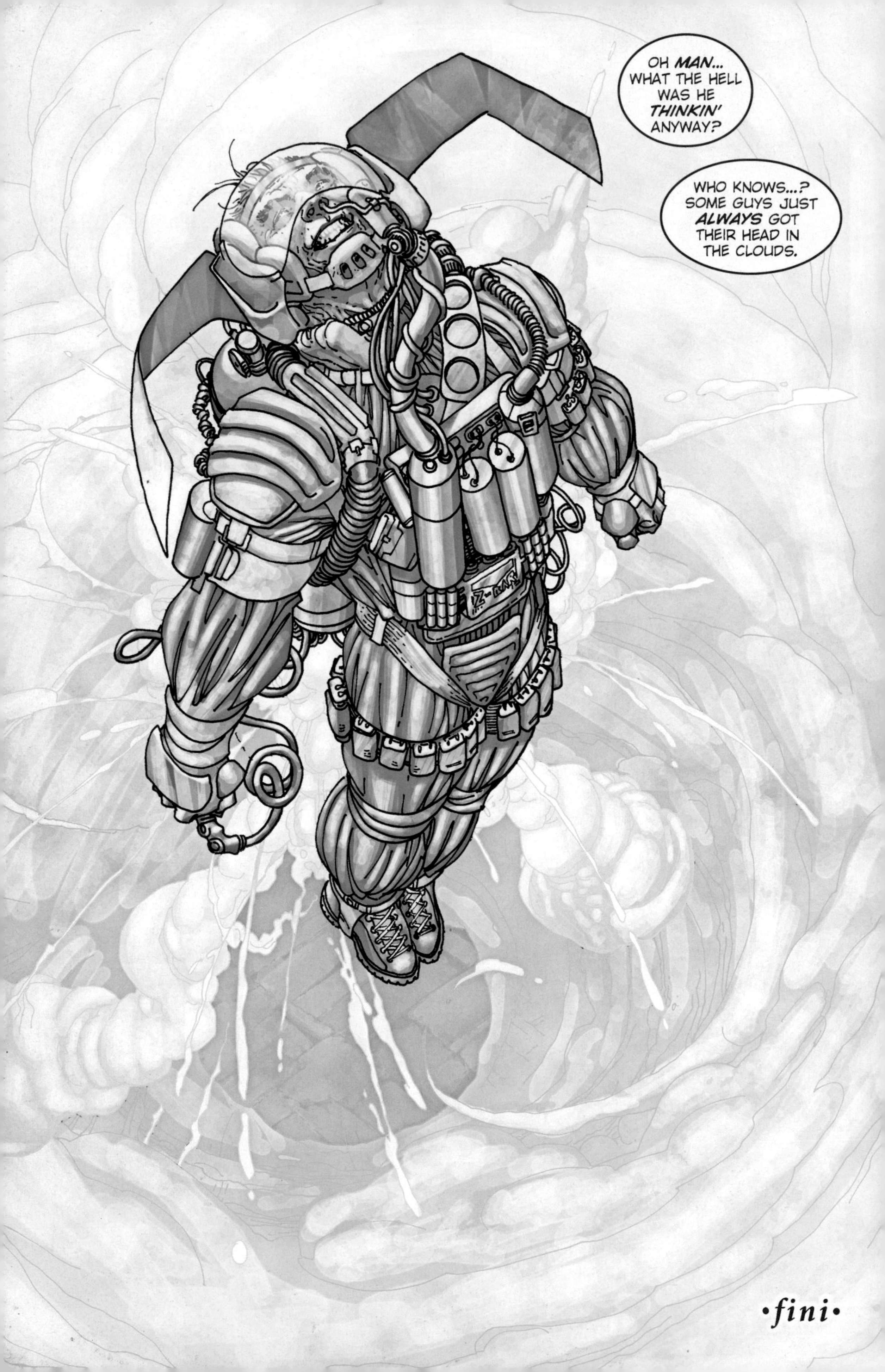
OH *MAN*... WHAT THE HELL WAS HE *THINKIN'* ANYWAY?
WHO KNOWS...? SOME GUYS JUST *ALWAYS* GOT THEIR HEAD IN THE CLOUDS.
•fini•

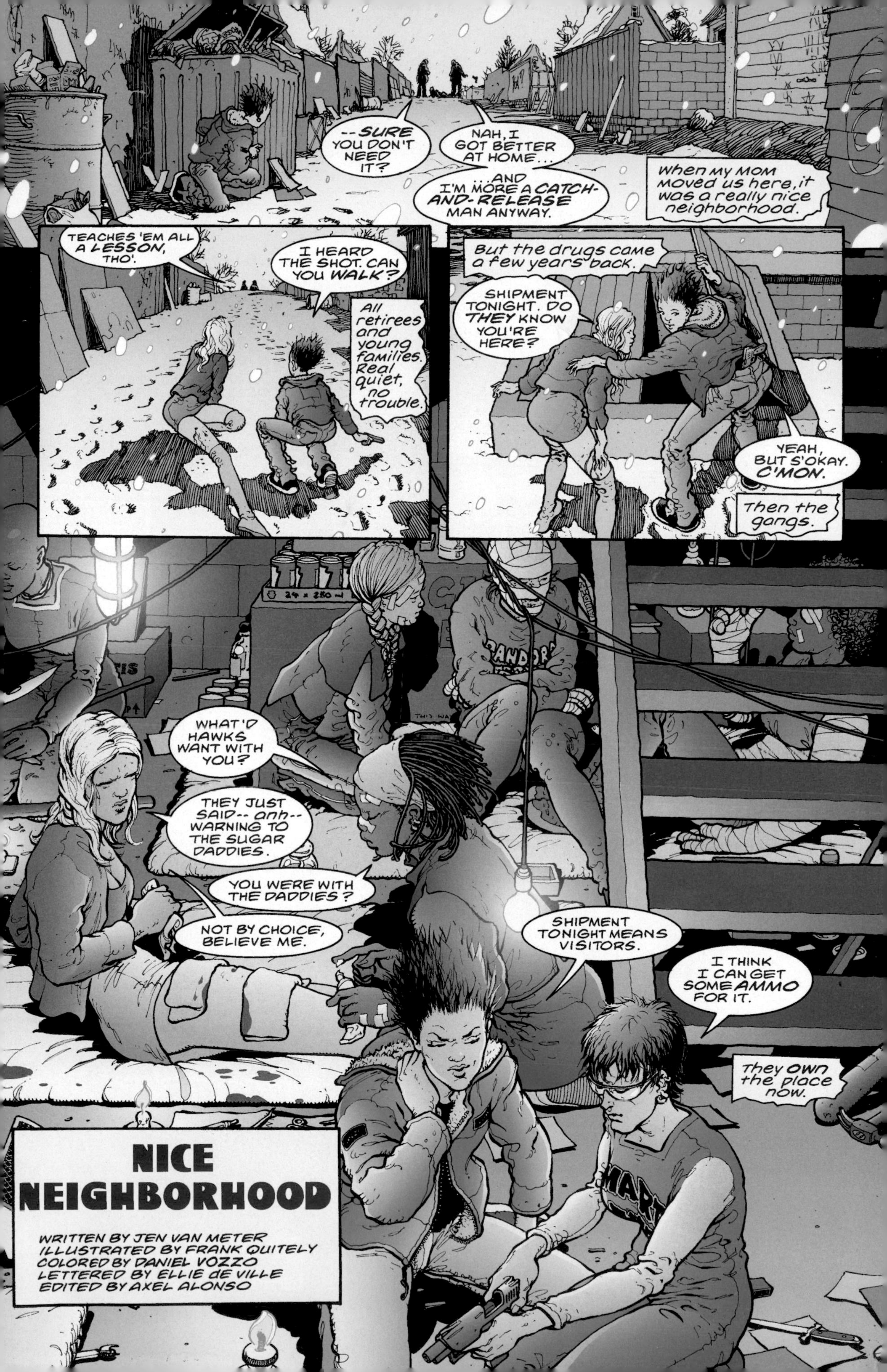
--SURE YOU DON'T NEED IT?
NAH, I GOT BETTER AT HOME...
...AND I'M MORE A CATCH-AND-RELEASE MAN ANYWAY.
When my MOM moved us here, it was a really nice neighborhood.
TEACHES 'EM ALL A LESSON, THO'.
I HEARD THE SHOT. CAN YOU WALK?
All retirees and young families. Real quiet, no trouble.
But the drugs came a few years back.
SHIPMENT TONIGHT. DO THEY KNOW YOU'RE HERE?
YEAH, BUT S'OKAY. C'MON.
Then the gangs.
WHAT'D HAWKS WANT WITH YOU?
THEY JUST SAID-- anh-- WARNING TO THE SUGAR DADDIES.
YOU WERE WITH THE DADDIES?
NOT BY CHOICE, BELIEVE ME.
SHIPMENT TONIGHT MEANS VISITORS.
I THINK I CAN GET SOME AMMO FOR IT.
They OWN the place now.
NICE NEIGHBORHOOD
WRITTEN BY JEN VAN METER
ILLUSTRATED BY FRANK QUITELY
COLORED BY DANIEL VOZZO
LETTERED BY ELLIE DE VILLE
EDITED BY AXEL ALONSO

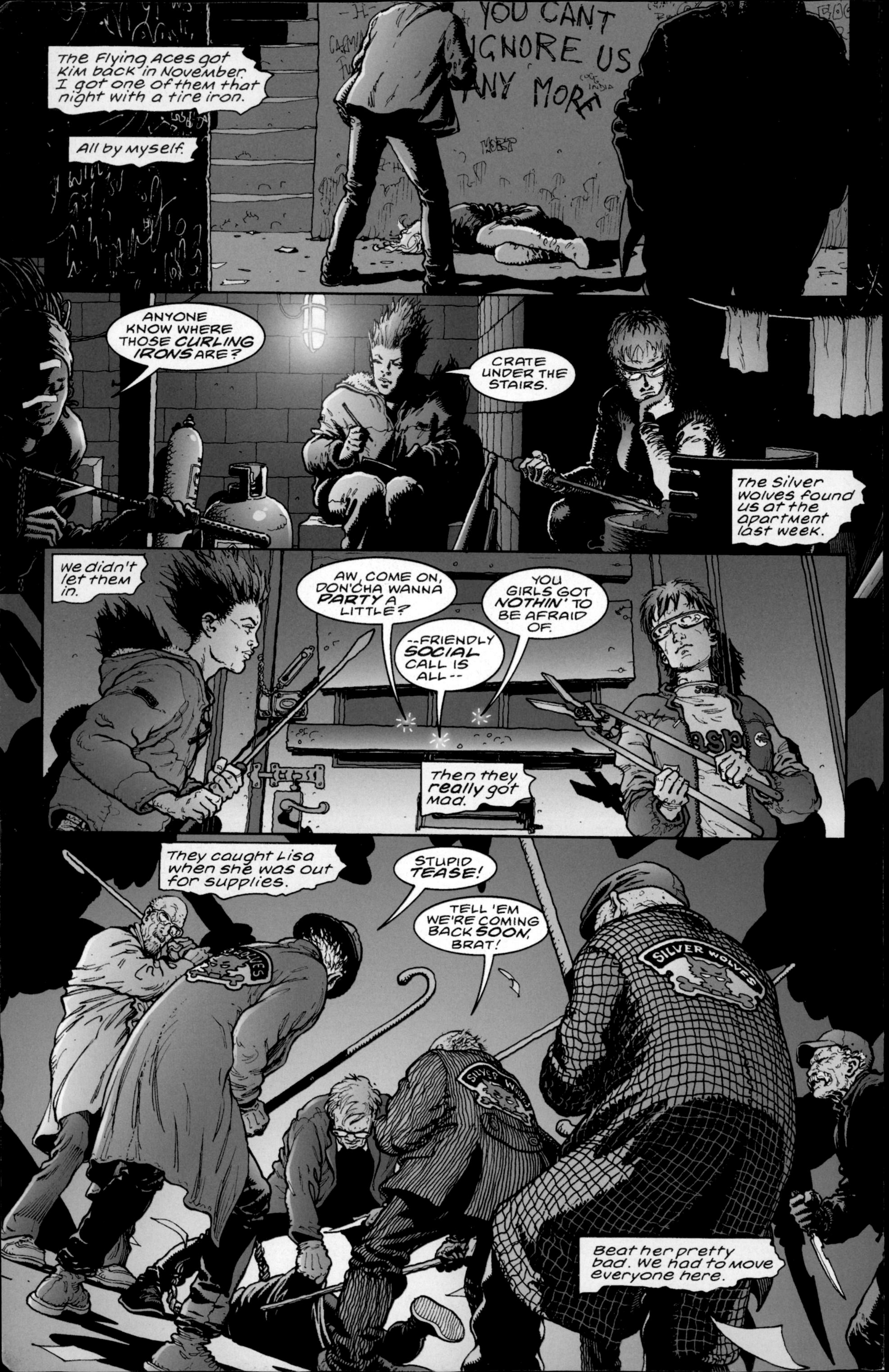
YOU CANT IGNORE US ANY MORE
The Flying Aces got Kim back in November. I got one of them that night with a tire iron.
All by myself.
ANYONE KNOW WHERE THOSE CURLING IRONS ARE?
CRATE UNDER THE STAIRS.
The Silver wolves found us at the apartment last week.
We didn't let them in.
AW, COME ON, DON'CHA WANNA PARTY A LITTLE?
--FRIENDLY SOCIAL CALL IS ALL--
YOU GIRLS GOT NOTHIN' TO BE AFRAID OF.
Then they really got mad.
They caught Lisa when she was out for supplies.
STUPID TEASE!
TELL 'EM WE'RE COMING BACK SOON, BRAT!
SILVER WOLVES
Beat her pretty bad. We had to move everyone here.

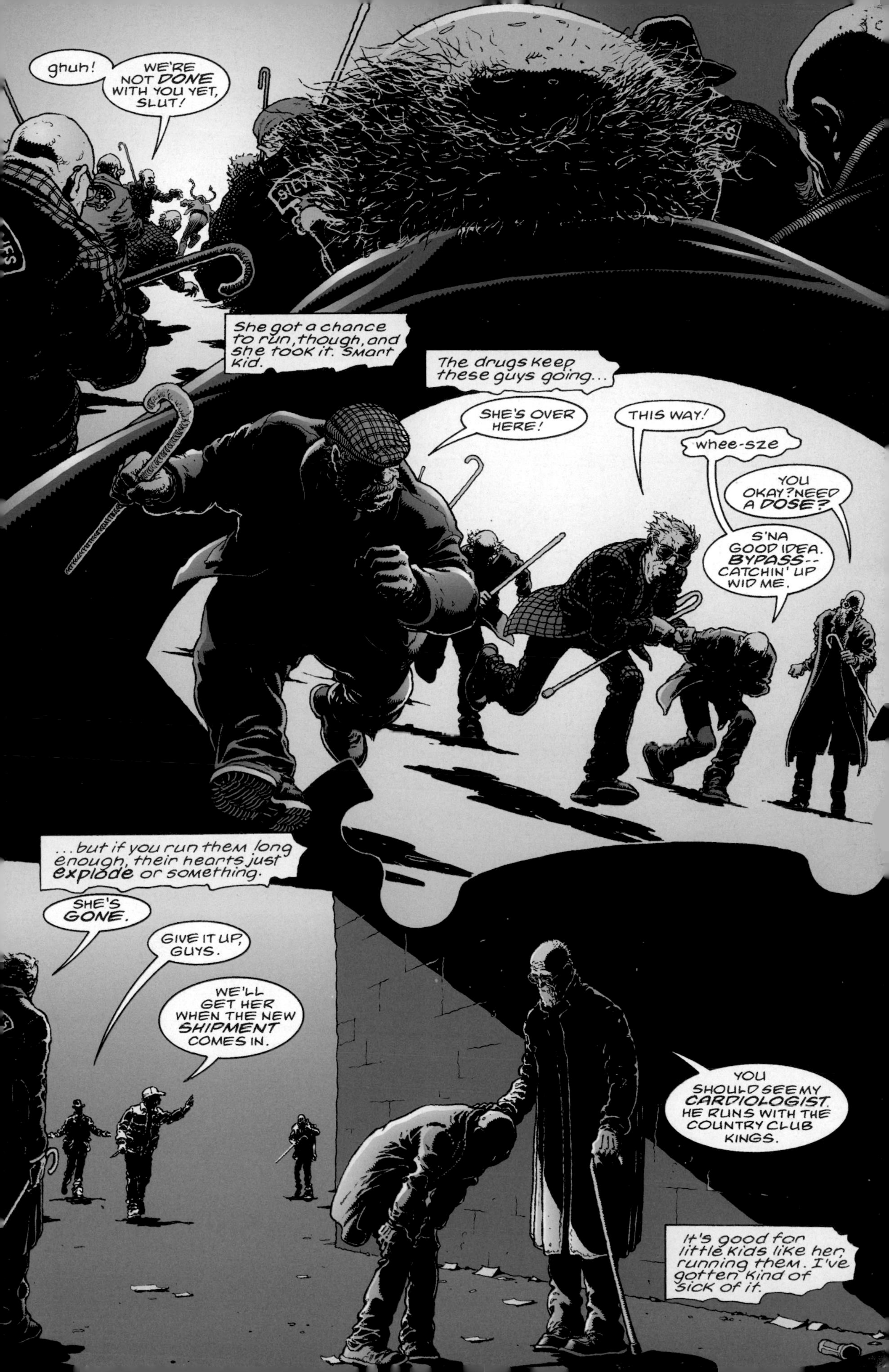
ghuh!
WE'RE NOT DONE WITH YOU YET, SLUT!
She got a chance to run, though, and she took it. Smart kid.
The drugs keep these guys going...
SHE'S OVER HERE!
THIS WAY!
whee-sze
YOU OKAY? NEED A DOSE?
S'NA GOOD IDEA. BYPASS-- CATCHIN' UP WID ME.
...but if you run them long enough, their hearts just explode or something.
SHE'S GONE.
GIVE IT UP, GUYS.
WE'LL GET HER WHEN THE NEW SHIPMENT COMES IN.
YOU SHOULD SEE MY CARDIOLOGIST. HE RUNS WITH THE COUNTRY CLUB KINGS.
It's good for little kids like her, running them. I've gotten kind of sick of it.

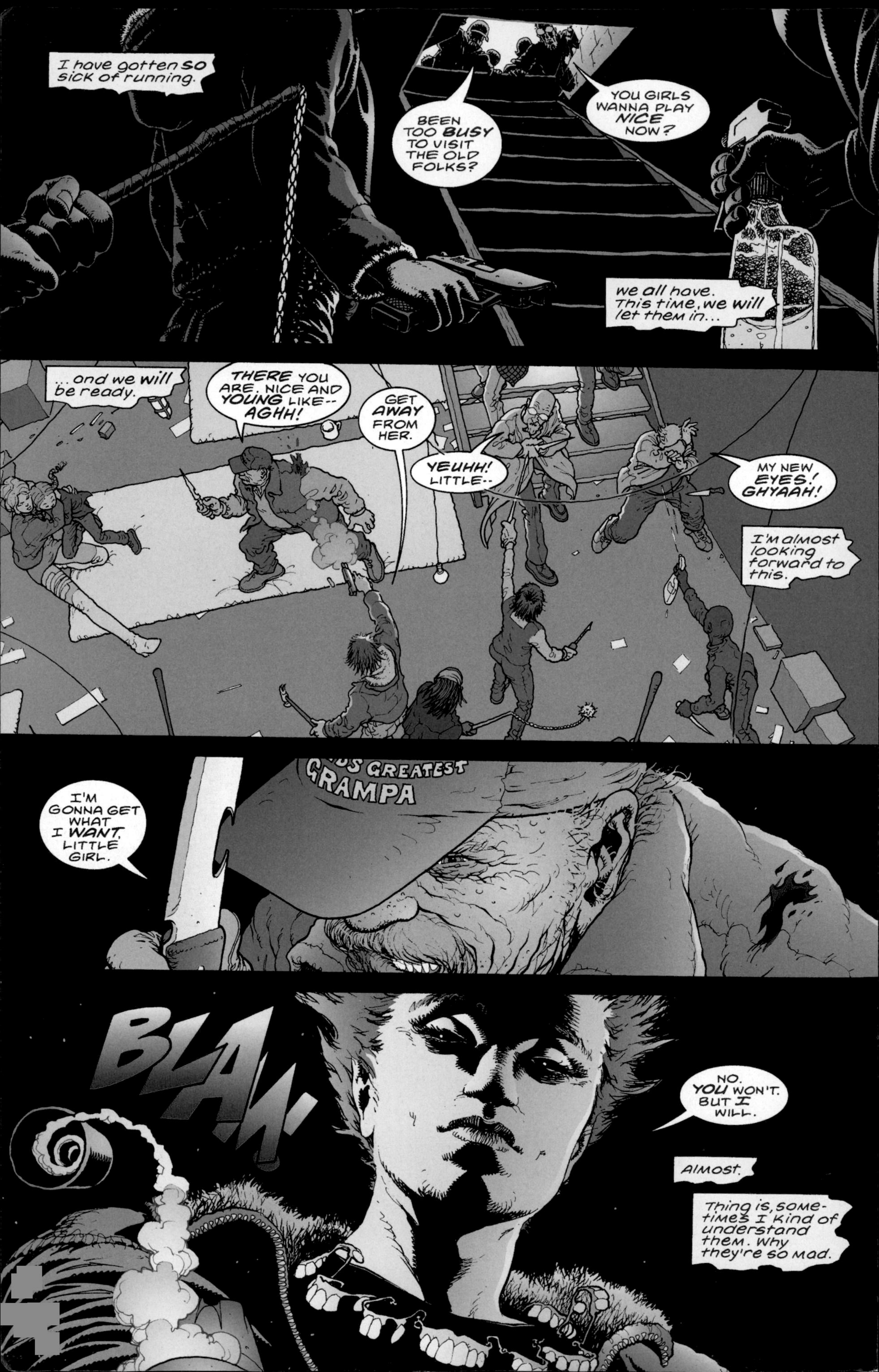

I have gotten SO sick of running.
BEEN TOO BUSY TO VISIT THE OLD FOLKS?
YOU GIRLS WANNA PLAY NICE NOW?
we all have. This time, we will let them in...
...and we will be ready.
THERE YOU ARE. NICE AND YOUNG LIKE-- AGHH!
GET AWAY FROM HER.
YEUHH! LITTLE--
MY NEW EYES! GHYAAH!
I'm almost looking forward to this.
GRAMPA
I'M GONNA GET WHAT I WANT, LITTLE GIRL.
BLAM!
NO. YOU WON'T. BUT I WILL.
Almost.
Thing is, some-times I kind of understand them. Why they're so mad.

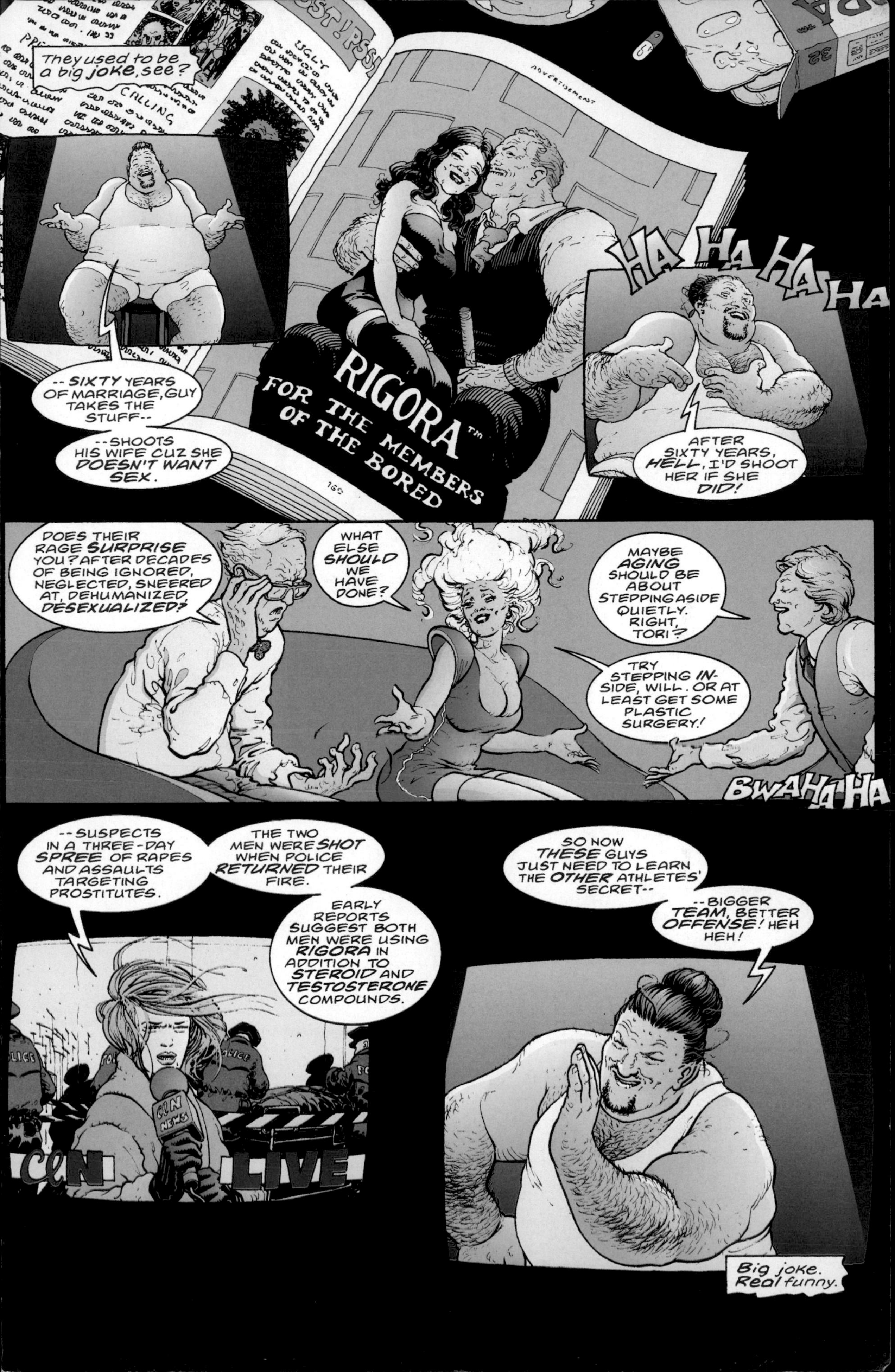
They used to be a big joke, see?
-- SIXTY YEARS OF MARRIAGE, GUY TAKES THE STUFF--
--SHOOTS HIS WIFE CUZ SHE DOESN'T WANT SEX.
RIGORA™ FOR THE MEMBERS OF THE BORED
HA HA HA HA HA
AFTER SIXTY YEARS, HELL, I'D SHOOT HER IF SHE DID!
DOES THEIR RAGE SURPRISE YOU? AFTER DECADES OF BEING IGNORED, NEGLECTED, SNEERED AT, DEHUMANIZED, DESEXUALIZED?
WHAT ELSE SHOULD WE HAVE DONE?
MAYBE AGING SHOULD BE ABOUT STEPPING ASIDE QUIETLY. RIGHT, TORI?
TRY STEPPING INSIDE, WILL. OR AT LEAST GET SOME PLASTIC SURGERY!
BWAHAHA HA
-- SUSPECTS IN A THREE-DAY SPREE OF RAPES AND ASSAULTS TARGETING PROSTITUTES.
THE TWO MEN WERE SHOT WHEN POLICE RETURNED THEIR FIRE.
EARLY REPORTS SUGGEST BOTH MEN WERE USING RIGORA IN ADDITION TO STEROID AND TESTOSTERONE COMPOUNDS.
POLICE
CCN LIVE
SO NOW THESE GUYS JUST NEED TO LEARN THE OTHER ATHLETES' SECRET--
--BIGGER TEAM, BETTER OFFENSE! HEH HEH!
Big joke. Real funny.

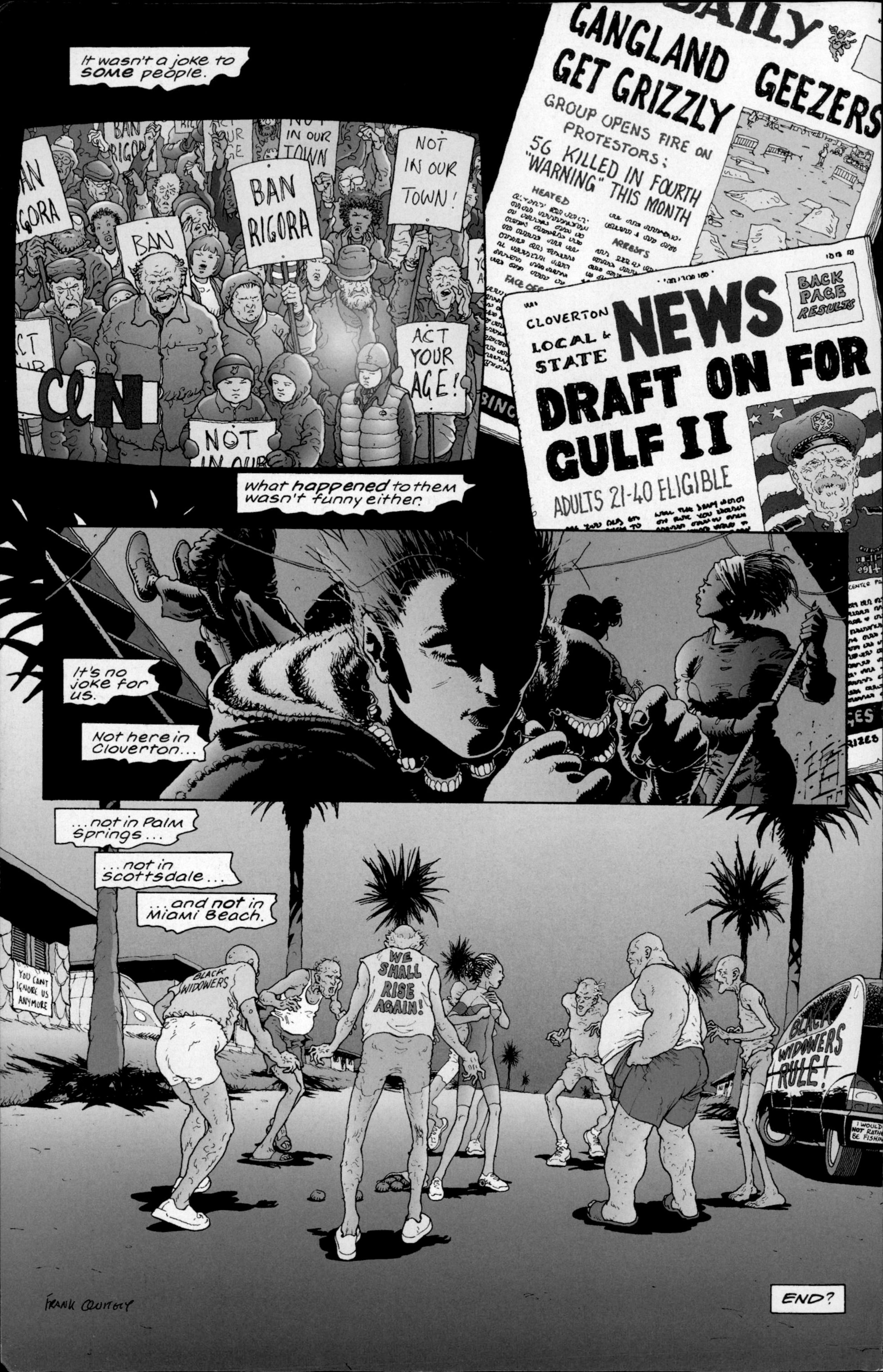

It wasn't a joke to some people.
BAN RIGORA
BAN
NOT IN OUR TOWN!
ACT YOUR AGE!
NOT IN OUR
CCN
GANGLAND GEEZERS GET GRIZZLY
GROUP OPENS FIRE ON PROTESTORS: 56 KILLED IN FOURTH "WARNING" THIS MONTH
HEATED
ARRESTS
CLOVERTON LOCAL & STATE NEWS
BACK PAGE RESULTS
DRAFT ON FOR GULF II
ADULTS 21-40 ELIGIBLE
what happened to them wasn't funny either.
It's no joke for us.
Not here in Cloverton...
...not in Palm Springs...
...not in Scottsdale...
...and not in Miami Beach.
YOU CAN'T IGNORE US ANYMORE
BLACK WIDOWERS
WE SHALL RISE AGAIN!
BLACK WIDOWERS RULE!
I WOULD NOT RATHER BE FISHING
FRANK QUITELY
END?

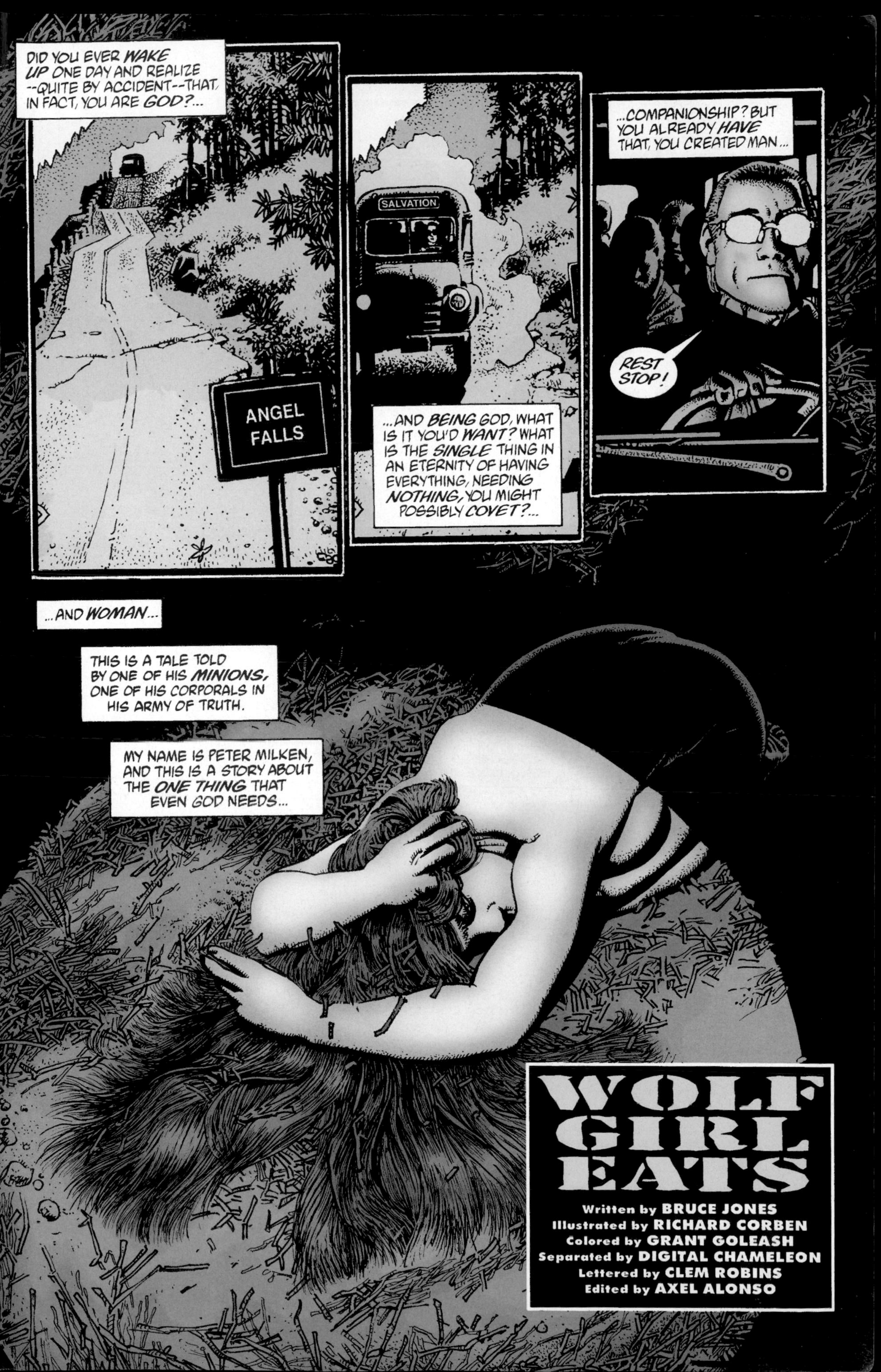

DID YOU EVER WAKE UP ONE DAY AND REALIZE --QUITE BY ACCIDENT--THAT, IN FACT, YOU ARE GOD?...
ANGEL FALLS
SALVATION
...AND BEING GOD, WHAT IS IT YOU'D WANT? WHAT IS THE SINGLE THING IN AN ETERNITY OF HAVING EVERYTHING, NEEDING NOTHING, YOU MIGHT POSSIBLY COVET?...
...COMPANIONSHIP? BUT YOU ALREADY HAVE THAT, YOU CREATED MAN...
REST STOP!
...AND WOMAN...
THIS IS A TALE TOLD BY ONE OF HIS MINIONS, ONE OF HIS CORPORALS IN HIS ARMY OF TRUTH.
MY NAME IS PETER MILKEN, AND THIS IS A STORY ABOUT THE ONE THING THAT EVEN GOD NEEDS...
WOLF GIRL EATS
Written by BRUCE JONES
Illustrated by RICHARD CORBEN
Colored by GRANT GOLEASH
Separated by DIGITAL CHAMELEON
Lettered by CLEM ROBINS
Edited by AXEL ALONSO

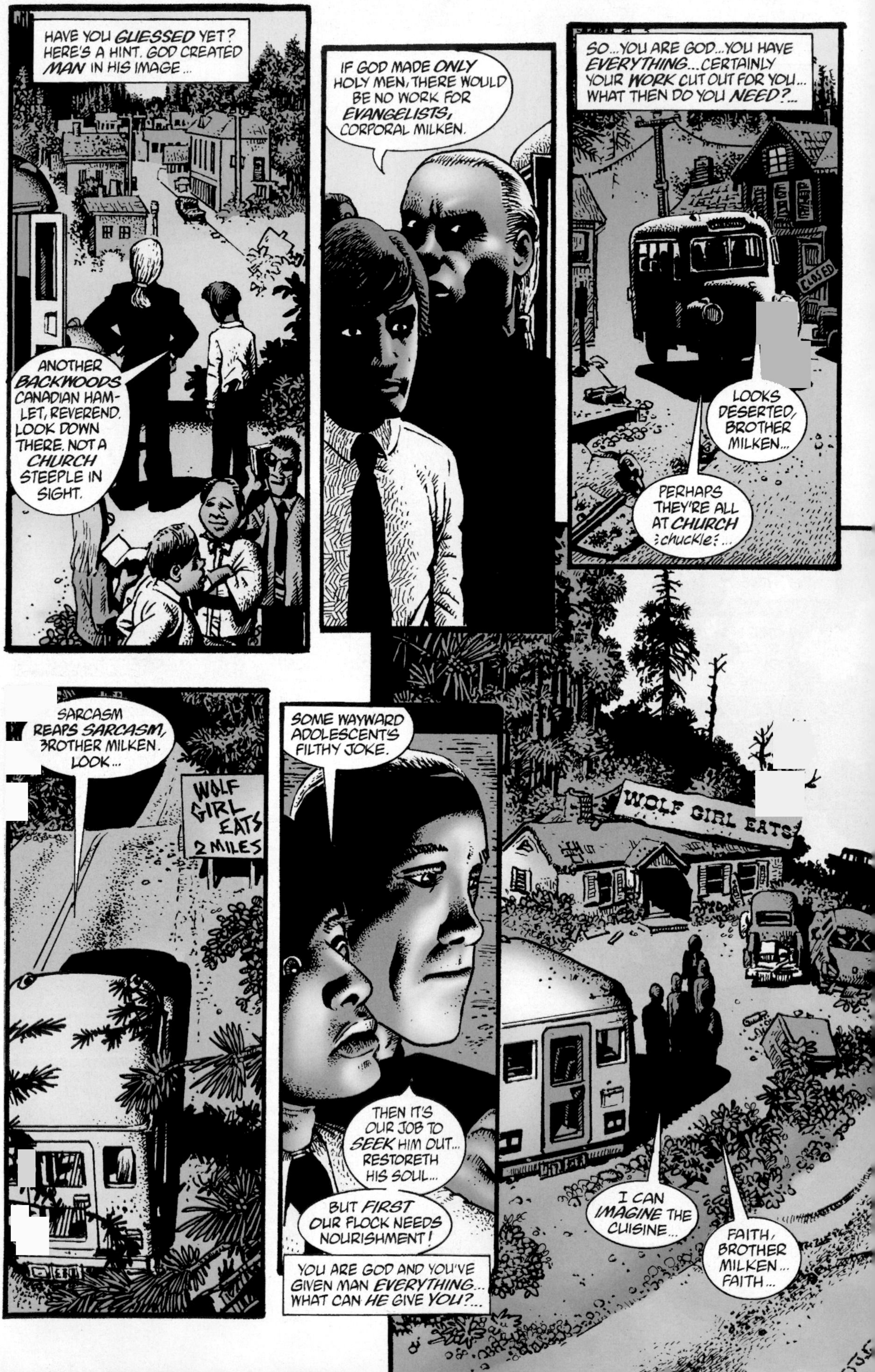
HAVE YOU GUESSED YET? HERE'S A HINT. GOD CREATED MAN IN HIS IMAGE...
ANOTHER BACKWOODS CANADIAN HAMLET, REVEREND. LOOK DOWN THERE. NOT A CHURCH STEEPLE IN SIGHT.
IF GOD MADE ONLY HOLY MEN, THERE WOULD BE NO WORK FOR EVANGELISTS, CORPORAL MILKEN.
SO...YOU ARE GOD...YOU HAVE EVERYTHING...CERTAINLY YOUR WORK CUT OUT FOR YOU... WHAT THEN DO YOU NEED?...
CLOSED
LOOKS DESERTED, BROTHER MILKEN...
PERHAPS THEY'RE ALL AT CHURCH :chuckle:...
SARCASM REAPS SARCASM, BROTHER MILKEN. LOOK...
WOLF GIRL EATS 2 MILES
SOME WAYWARD ADOLESCENT'S FILTHY JOKE.
THEN IT'S OUR JOB TO SEEK HIM OUT... RESTORETH HIS SOUL...
BUT FIRST OUR FLOCK NEEDS NOURISHMENT!
YOU ARE GOD AND YOU'VE GIVEN MAN EVERYTHING... WHAT CAN HE GIVE YOU?...
WOLF GIRL EATS
I CAN IMAGINE THE CUISINE...
FAITH, BROTHER MILKEN... FAITH...

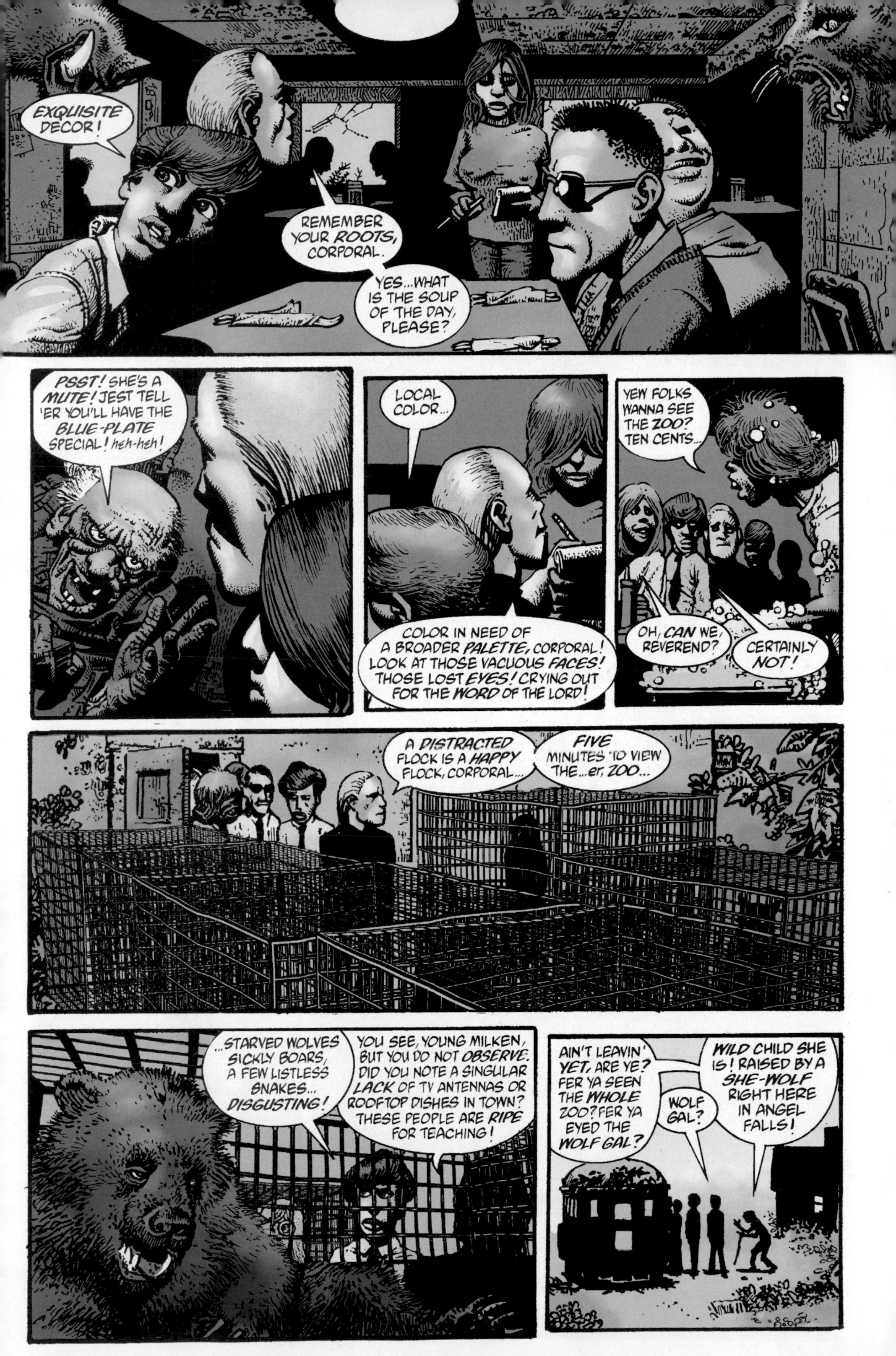
EXQUISITE DECOR!
REMEMBER YOUR ROOTS, CORPORAL.
YES...WHAT IS THE SOUP OF THE DAY, PLEASE?
PSST! SHE'S A MUTE! JEST TELL 'ER YOU'LL HAVE THE BLUE-PLATE SPECIAL! heh-heh!
LOCAL COLOR...
COLOR IN NEED OF A BROADER PALETTE, CORPORAL! LOOK AT THOSE VACUOUS FACES! THOSE LOST EYES! CRYING OUT FOR THE WORD OF THE LORD!
YEW FOLKS WANNA SEE THE ZOO? TEN CENTS...
OH, CAN WE, REVEREND?
CERTAINLY NOT!
A DISTRACTED FLOCK IS A HAPPY FLOCK, CORPORAL...
FIVE MINUTES TO VIEW THE...er, ZOO...
...STARVED WOLVES SICKLY BOARS, A FEW LISTLESS SNAKES... DISGUSTING!
YOU SEE, YOUNG MILKEN, BUT YOU DO NOT OBSERVE. DID YOU NOTE A SINGULAR LACK OF TV ANTENNAS OR ROOFTOP DISHES IN TOWN? THESE PEOPLE ARE RIPE FOR TEACHING!
AIN'T LEAVIN' YET, ARE YE? FER YA SEEN THE WHOLE ZOO? FER YA EYED THE WOLF GAL?
WOLF GAL?
WILD CHILD SHE IS! RAISED BY A SHE-WOLF RIGHT HERE IN ANGEL FALLS!

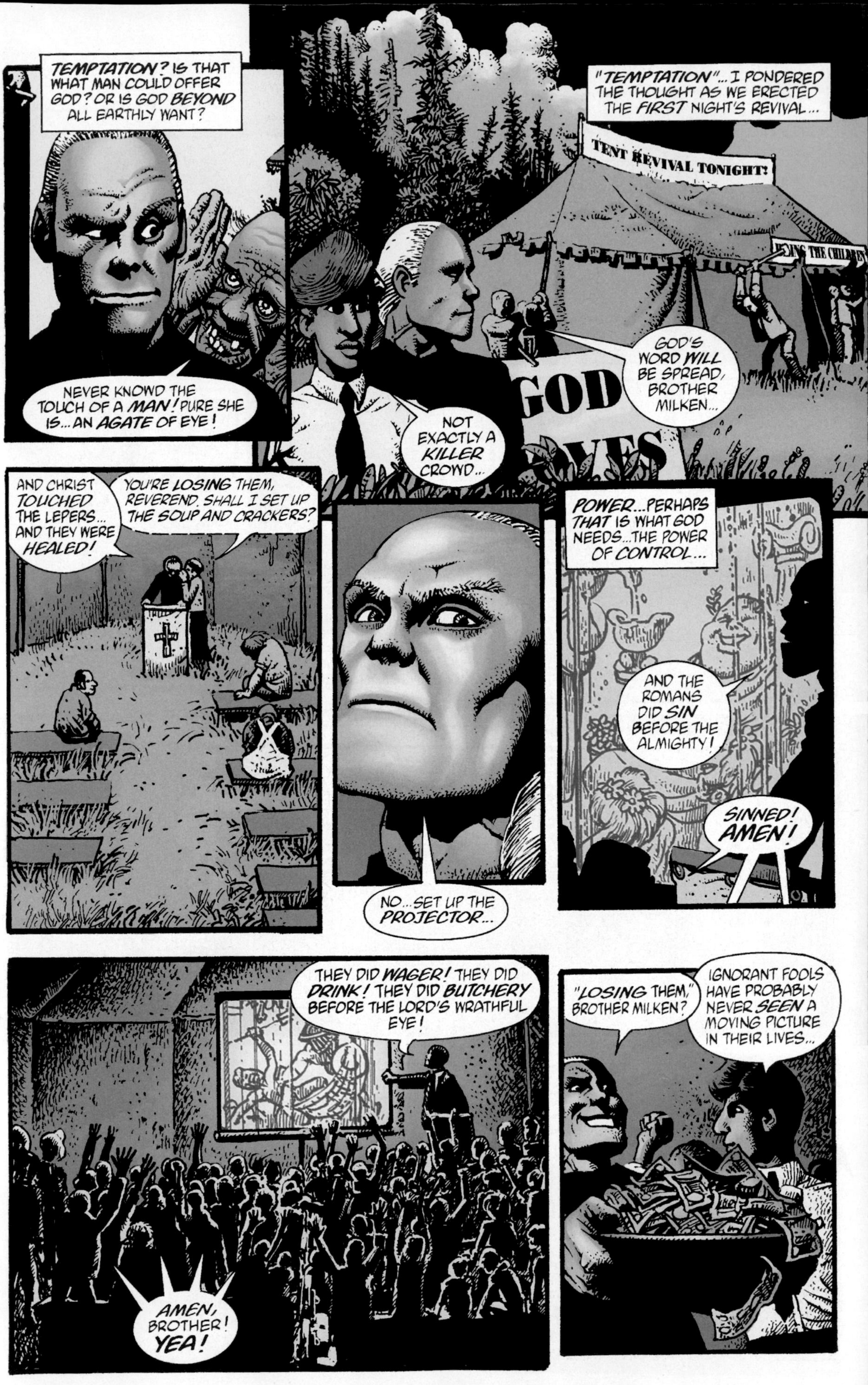
TEMPTATION? IS THAT WHAT MAN COULD OFFER GOD? OR IS GOD BEYOND ALL EARTHLY WANT?
NEVER KNOWD THE TOUCH OF A MAN! PURE SHE IS... AN AGATE OF EYE!
"TEMPTATION"... I PONDERED THE THOUGHT AS WE ERECTED THE FIRST NIGHT'S REVIVAL...
TENT REVIVAL TONIGHT!
GOD
GOD'S WORD WILL BE SPREAD, BROTHER MILKEN...
NOT EXACTLY A KILLER CROWD...
AND CHRIST TOUCHED THE LEPERS... AND THEY WERE HEALED!
YOU'RE LOSING THEM, REVEREND. SHALL I SET UP THE SOUP AND CRACKERS?
NO... SET UP THE PROJECTOR...
POWER... PERHAPS THAT IS WHAT GOD NEEDS... THE POWER OF CONTROL...
AND THE ROMANS DID SIN BEFORE THE ALMIGHTY!
SINNED! AMEN!
THEY DID WAGER! THEY DID DRINK! THEY DID BUTCHERY BEFORE THE LORD'S WRATHFUL EYE!
AMEN, BROTHER! YEA!
"LOSING THEM," BROTHER MILKEN?
IGNORANT FOOLS HAVE PROBABLY NEVER SEEN A MOVING PICTURE IN THEIR LIVES...

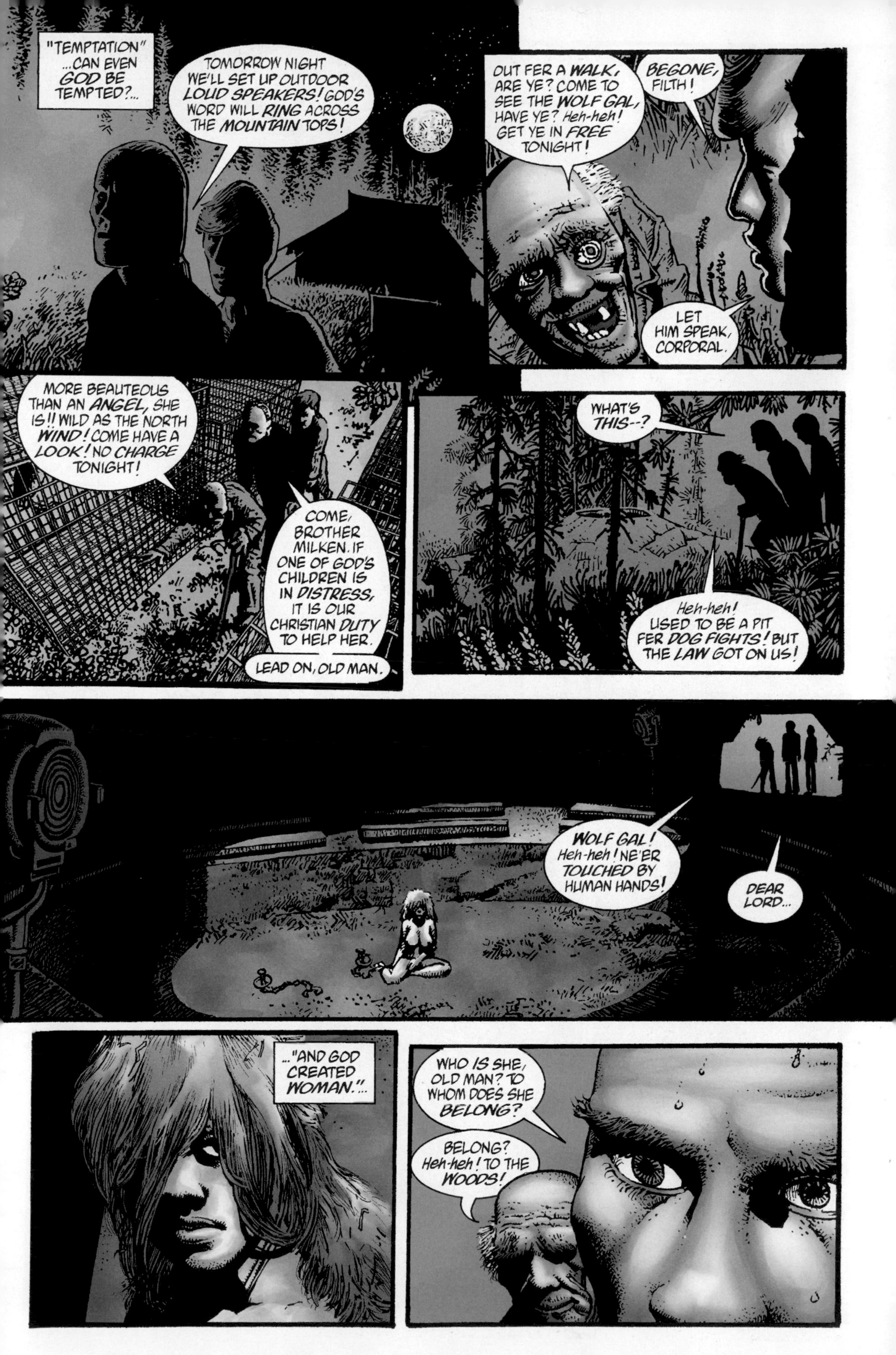
"TEMPTATION" ...CAN EVEN GOD BE TEMPTED?...
TOMORROW NIGHT WE'LL SET UP OUTDOOR LOUD SPEAKERS! GOD'S WORD WILL RING ACROSS THE MOUNTAIN TOPS!
OUT FER A WALK, ARE YE? COME TO SEE THE WOLF GAL, HAVE YE? Heh-heh! GET YE IN FREE TONIGHT!
BEGONE, FILTH!
LET HIM SPEAK, CORPORAL.
MORE BEAUTEOUS THAN AN ANGEL, SHE IS!! WILD AS THE NORTH WIND! COME HAVE A LOOK! NO CHARGE TONIGHT!
COME, BROTHER MILKEN. IF ONE OF GOD'S CHILDREN IS IN DISTRESS, IT IS OUR CHRISTIAN DUTY TO HELP HER.
LEAD ON, OLD MAN.
WHAT'S THIS--?
Heh-heh! USED TO BE A PIT FER DOG FIGHTS! BUT THE LAW GOT ON US!
WOLF GAL! Heh-heh! NE'ER TOUCHED BY HUMAN HANDS!
DEAR LORD...
..."AND GOD CREATED WOMAN."...
WHO IS SHE, OLD MAN? TO WHOM DOES SHE BELONG?
BELONG? Heh-heh! TO THE WOODS!

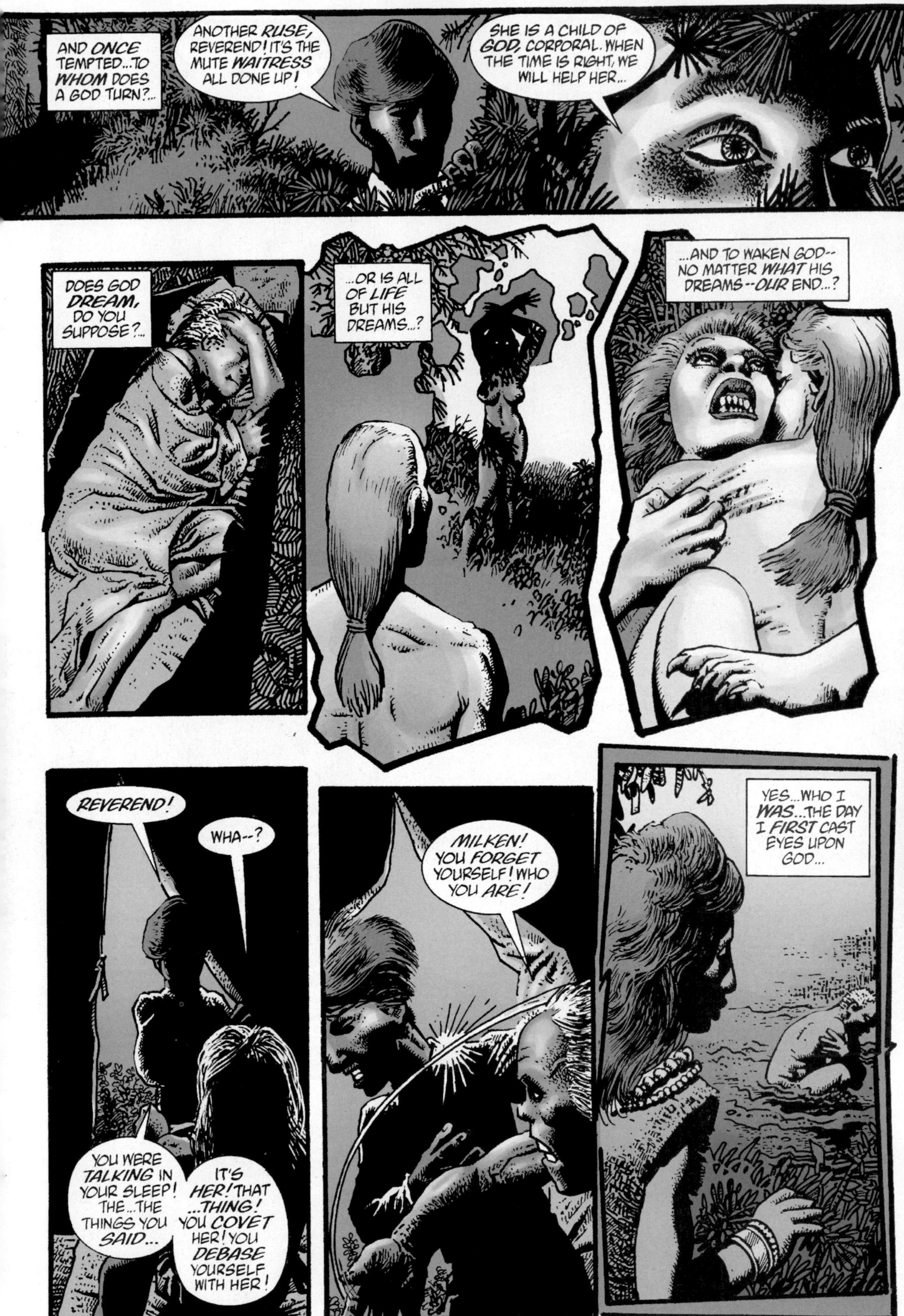

AND ONCE TEMPTED...TO WHOM DOES A GOD TURN?...
ANOTHER RUSE, REVEREND! IT'S THE MUTE WAITRESS ALL DONE UP!
SHE IS A CHILD OF GOD, CORPORAL. WHEN THE TIME IS RIGHT, WE WILL HELP HER...
DOES GOD DREAM, DO YOU SUPPOSE?...
...OR IS ALL OF LIFE BUT HIS DREAMS...?
...AND TO WAKEN GOD-- NO MATTER WHAT HIS DREAMS--OUR END...?
REVEREND!
WHA--?
YOU WERE TALKING IN YOUR SLEEP! THE...THE THINGS YOU SAID...
IT'S HER! THAT ...THING! YOU COVET HER! YOU DEBASE YOURSELF WITH HER!
MILKEN! YOU FORGET YOURSELF! WHO YOU ARE!
YES...WHO I WAS...THE DAY I FIRST CAST EYES UPON GOD...

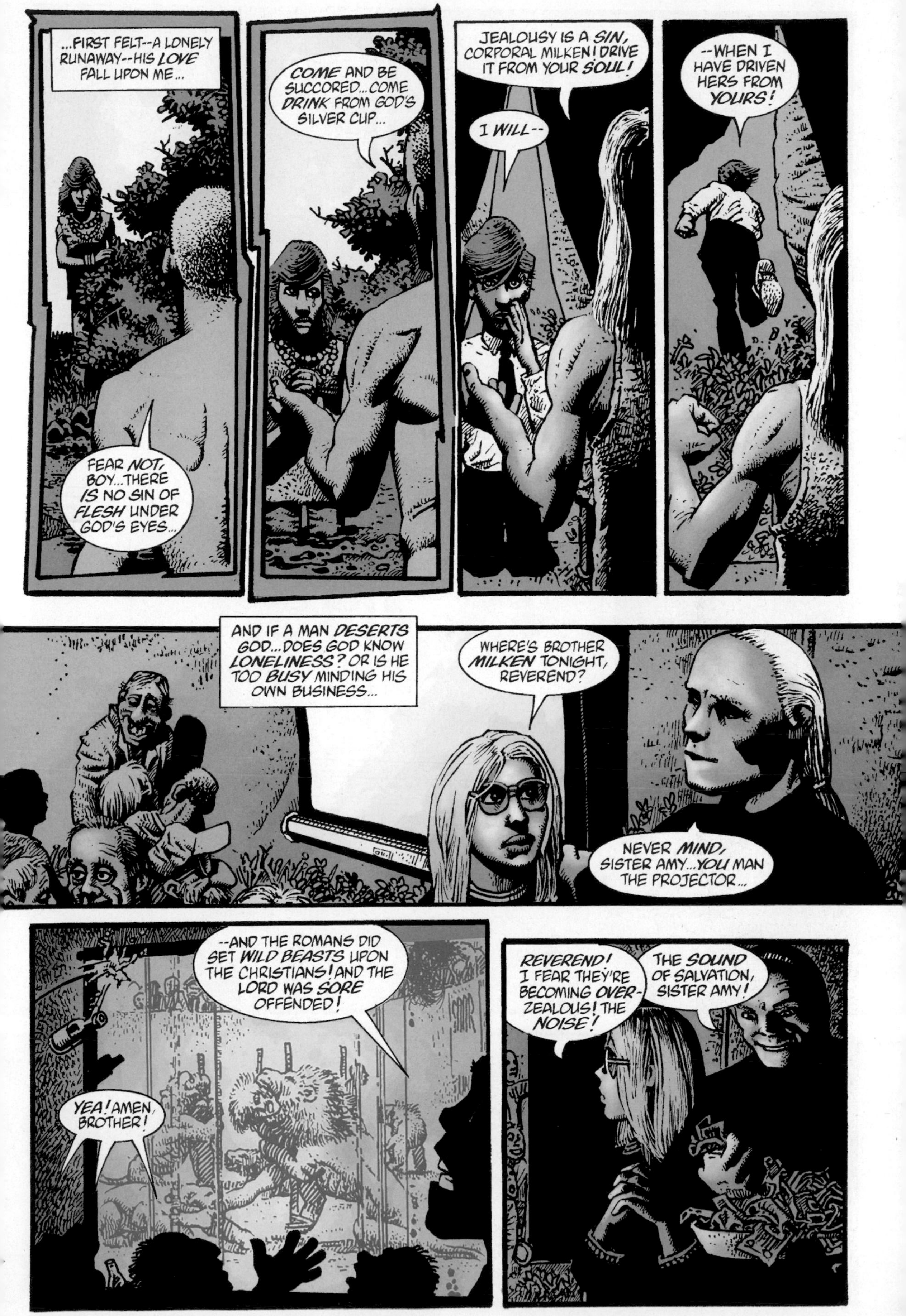
...FIRST FELT--A LONELY RUNAWAY--HIS LOVE FALL UPON ME...
FEAR NOT, BOY...THERE IS NO SIN OF FLESH UNDER GOD'S EYES...
COME AND BE SUCCORED...COME DRINK FROM GOD'S SILVER CUP...
JEALOUSY IS A SIN, CORPORAL MILKEN! DRIVE IT FROM YOUR SOUL!
I WILL--
--WHEN I HAVE DRIVEN HERS FROM YOURS!
AND IF A MAN DESERTS GOD...DOES GOD KNOW LONELINESS? OR IS HE TOO BUSY MINDING HIS OWN BUSINESS...
WHERE'S BROTHER MILKEN TONIGHT, REVEREND?
NEVER MIND, SISTER AMY...YOU MAN THE PROJECTOR...
--AND THE ROMANS DID SET WILD BEASTS UPON THE CHRISTIANS! AND THE LORD WAS SORE OFFENDED!
YEA! AMEN, BROTHER!
REVEREND! I FEAR THEY'RE BECOMING OVER-ZEALOUS! THE NOISE!
THE SOUND OF SALVATION, SISTER AMY!

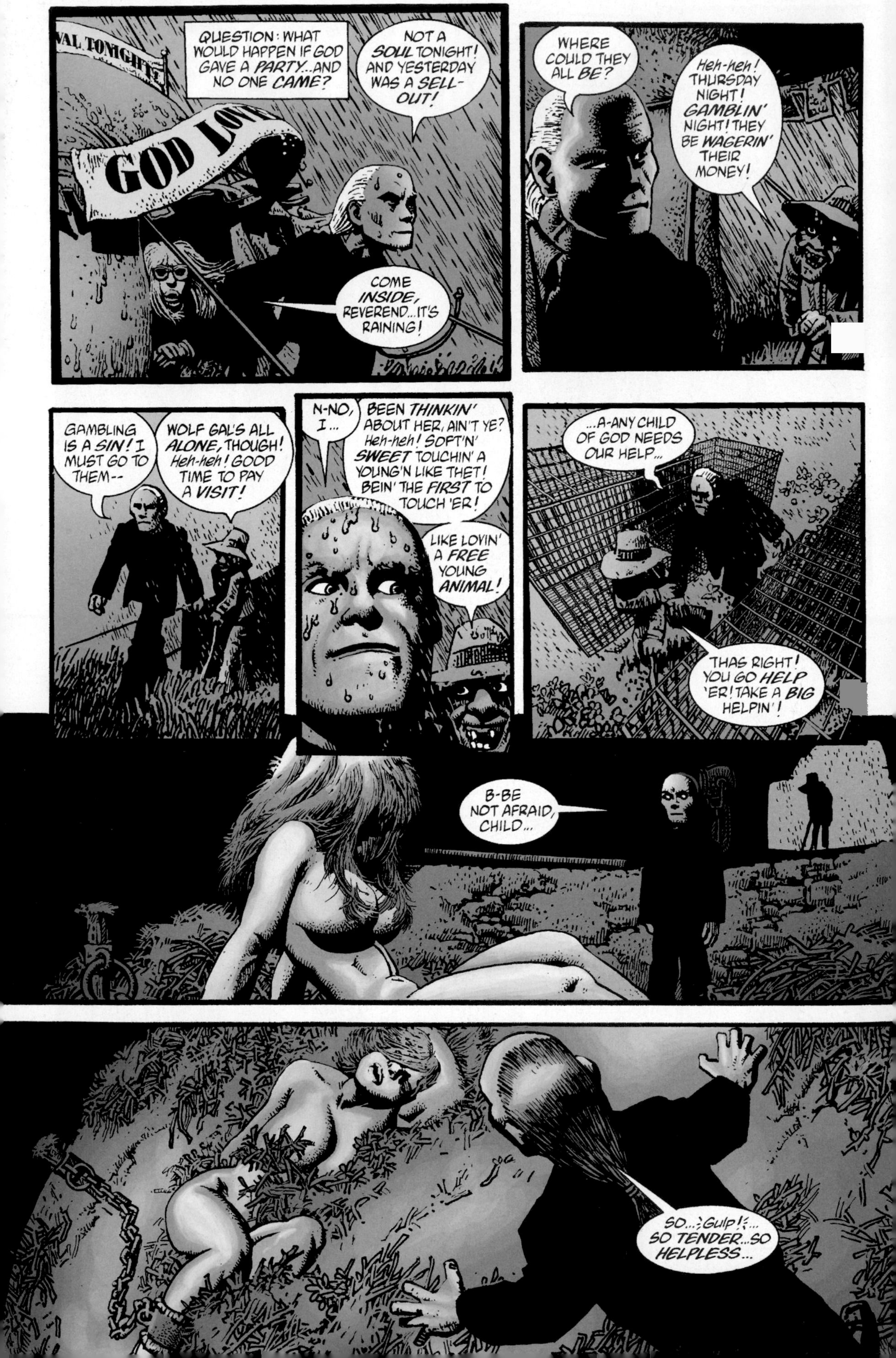
VAL TONIGHT
GOD LOV
QUESTION: WHAT WOULD HAPPEN IF GOD GAVE A PARTY...AND NO ONE CAME?
NOT A SOUL TONIGHT! AND YESTERDAY WAS A SELL-OUT!
COME INSIDE, REVEREND...IT'S RAINING!
WHERE COULD THEY ALL BE?
Heh-heh! THURSDAY NIGHT! GAMBLIN' NIGHT! THEY BE WAGERIN' THEIR MONEY!
GAMBLING IS A SIN! I MUST GO TO THEM--
WOLF GAL'S ALL ALONE, THOUGH! Heh-heh! GOOD TIME TO PAY A VISIT!
N-NO, I...
BEEN THINKIN' ABOUT HER, AIN'T YE? Heh-heh! SOFT'N' SWEET TOUCHIN' A YOUNG'N LIKE THET! BEIN' THE FIRST TO TOUCH 'ER!
LIKE LOVIN' A FREE YOUNG ANIMAL!
...A-ANY CHILD OF GOD NEEDS OUR HELP...
THAS RIGHT! YOU GO HELP 'ER! TAKE A BIG HELPIN'!
B-BE NOT AFRAID, CHILD...
SO...;Gulp!;... SO TENDER...SO HELPLESS...

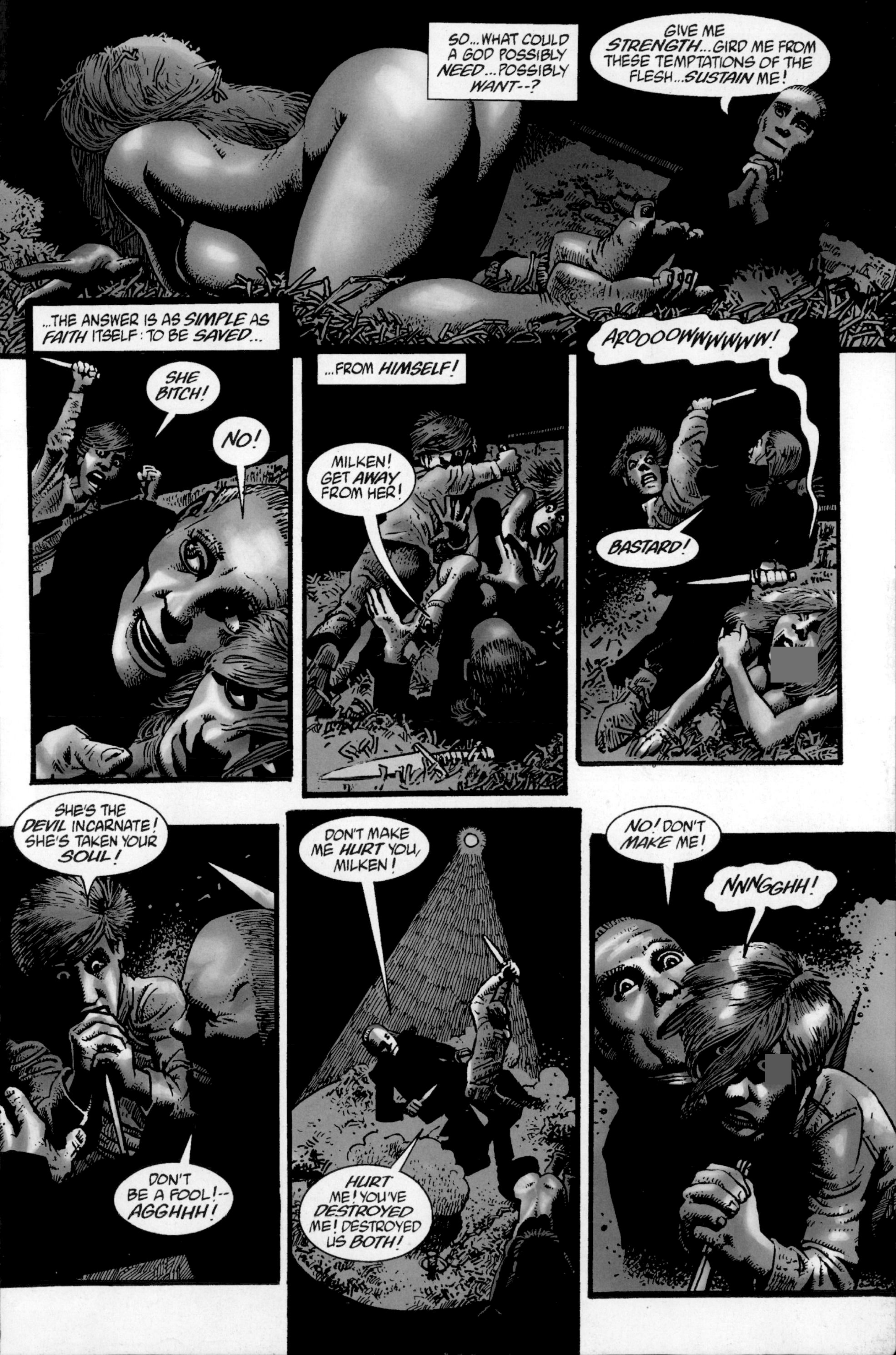
SO...WHAT COULD A GOD POSSIBLY NEED...POSSIBLY WANT--?
GIVE ME STRENGTH...GIRD ME FROM THESE TEMPTATIONS OF THE FLESH...SUSTAIN ME!
...THE ANSWER IS AS SIMPLE AS FAITH ITSELF: TO BE SAVED...
SHE BITCH!
NO!
...FROM HIMSELF!
MILKEN! GET AWAY FROM HER!
AROOOOWWWWWW!
BASTARD!
SHE'S THE DEVIL INCARNATE! SHE'S TAKEN YOUR SOUL!
DON'T BE A FOOL!--AGGHHH!
DON'T MAKE ME HURT YOU, MILKEN!
HURT ME! YOU'VE DESTROYED ME! DESTROYED US BOTH!
NO! DON'T MAKE ME!
NNNGGHH!

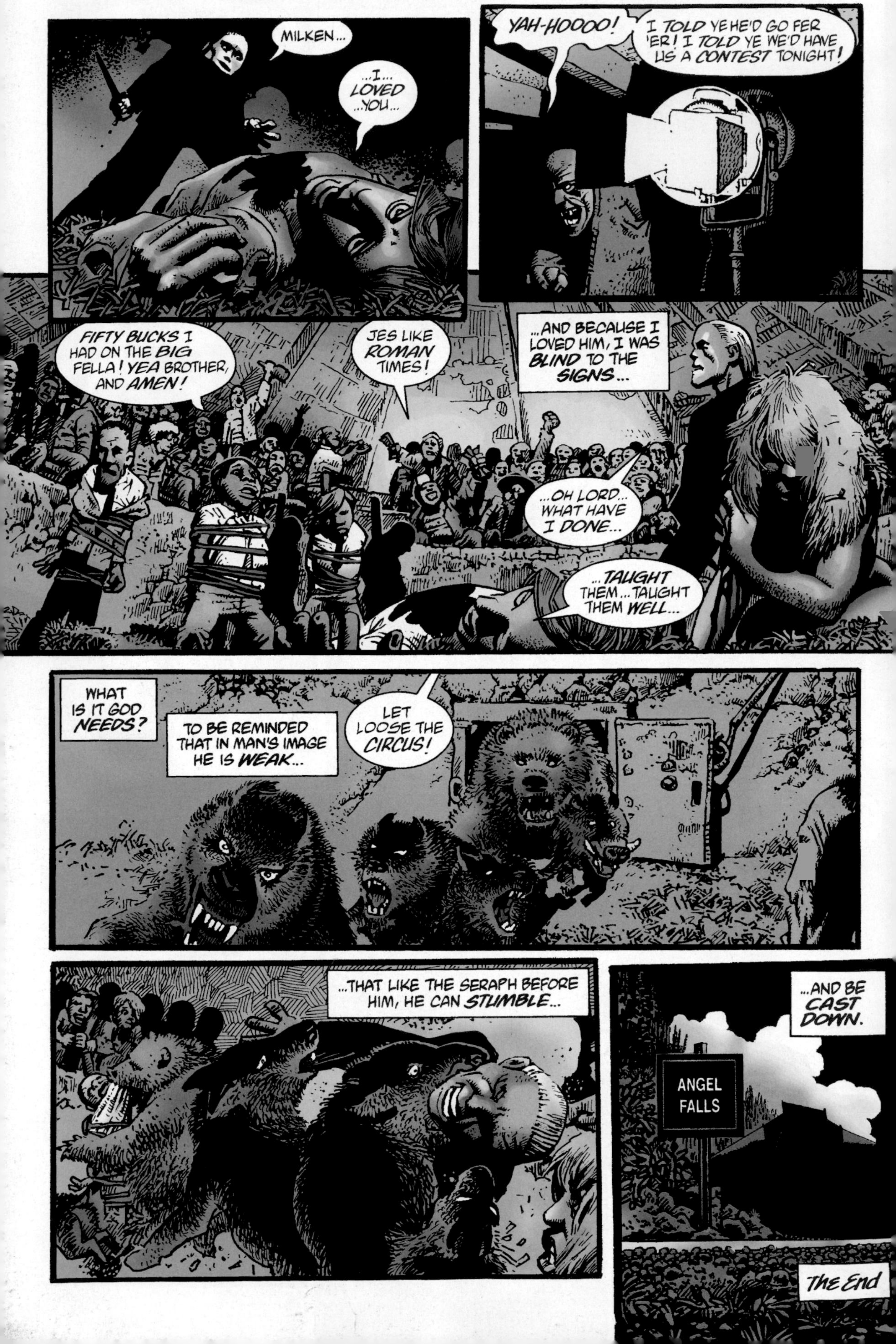
MILKEN...
...I... LOVED ...YOU...
YAH-HOOOO!
I TOLD YE HE'D GO FER 'ER! I TOLD YE WE'D HAVE US A CONTEST TONIGHT!
FIFTY BUCKS I HAD ON THE BIG FELLA! YEA BROTHER, AND AMEN!
JES LIKE ROMAN TIMES!
...AND BECAUSE I LOVED HIM, I WAS BLIND TO THE SIGNS...
...OH LORD... WHAT HAVE I DONE...
...TAUGHT THEM... TAUGHT THEM WELL...
WHAT IS IT GOD NEEDS?
TO BE REMINDED THAT IN MAN'S IMAGE HE IS WEAK...
LET LOOSE THE CIRCUS!
...THAT LIKE THE SERAPH BEFORE HIM, HE CAN STUMBLE...
...AND BE CAST DOWN.
ANGEL FALLS
THE End

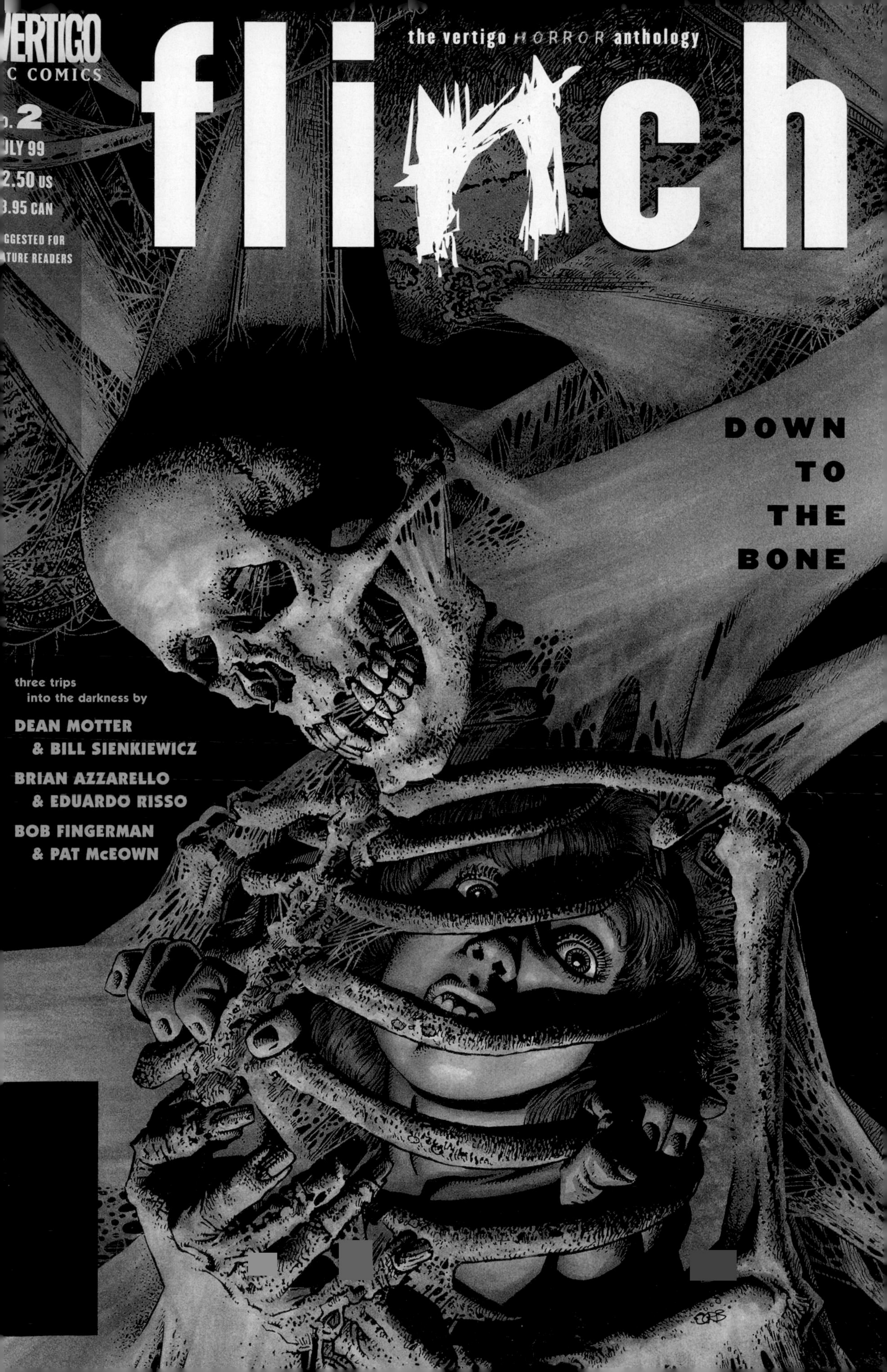

ERTIGO
C COMICS
flinch
the vertigo HORROR anthology
.2
JLY 99
2.50 US
.95 CAN
GGESTED FOR
TURE READERS
DOWN
TO
THE
BONE
three trips
into the darkness by
DEAN MOTTER
& BILL SIENKIEWICZ
BRIAN AZZARELLO
& EDUARDO RISSO
BOB FINGERMAN
& PAT McEOWN

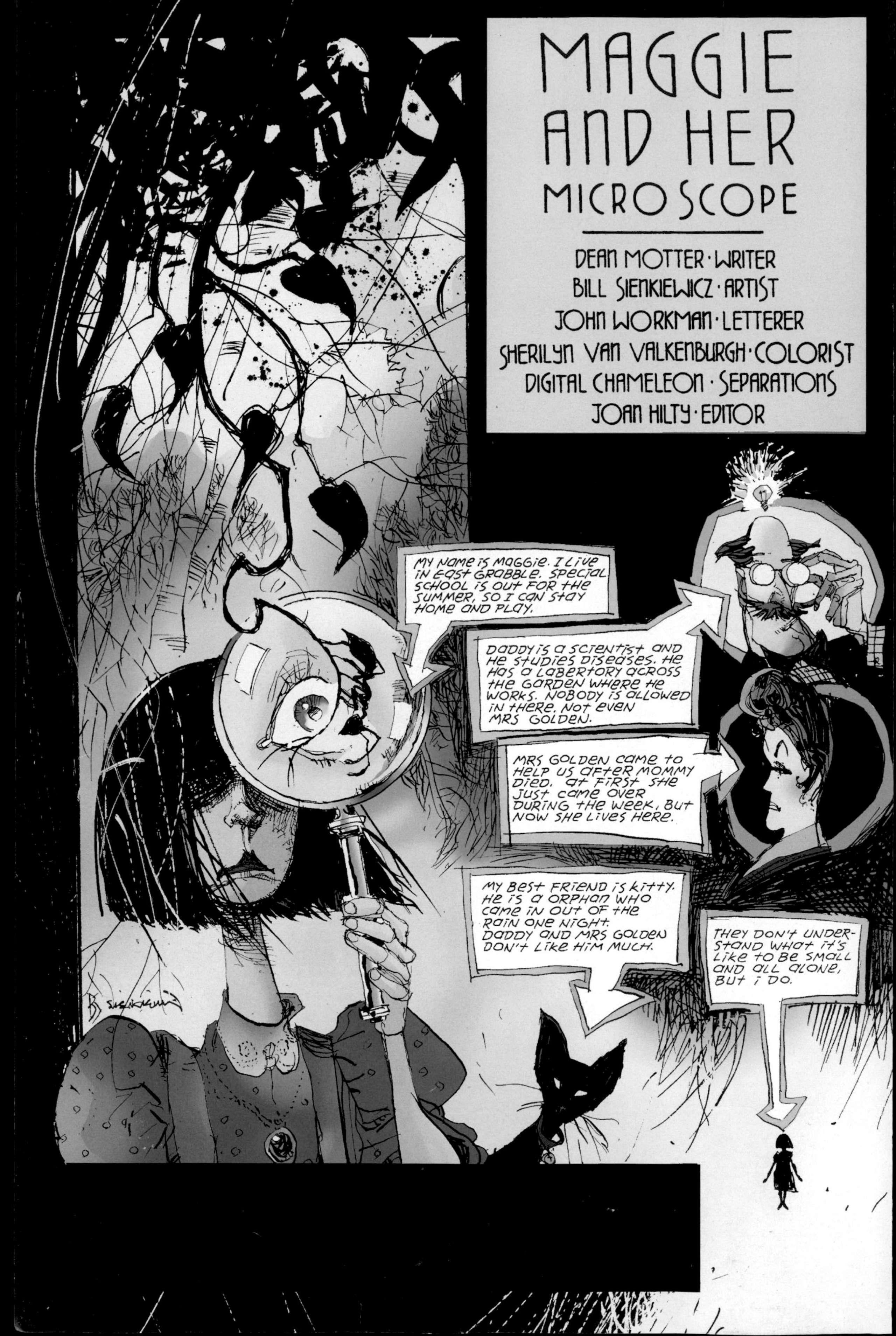
MAGGIE AND HER MICROSCOPE
DEAN MOTTER · WRITER
BILL SIENKIEWICZ · ARTIST
JOHN WORKMAN · LETTERER
SHERILYN VAN VALKENBURGH · COLORIST
DIGITAL CHAMELEON · SEPARATIONS
JOAN HILTY · EDITOR
MY NAME IS MAGGIE. I LIVE IN EAST GRABBLE. SPECIAL SCHOOL IS OUT FOR THE SUMMER, SO I CAN STAY HOME AND PLAY.
DADDY IS A SCIENTIST AND HE STUDIES DISEASES. HE HAS A LABERTORY ACROSS THE GARDEN WHERE HE WORKS. NOBODY IS ALLOWED IN THERE. NOT EVEN MRS GOLDEN.
MRS GOLDEN CAME TO HELP US AFTER MOMMY DIED. AT FIRST SHE JUST CAME OVER DURING THE WEEK, BUT NOW SHE LIVES HERE.
MY BEST FRIEND IS KITTY. HE IS A ORPHAN WHO CAME IN OUT OF THE RAIN ONE NIGHT. DADDY AND MRS GOLDEN DON'T LIKE HIM MUCH.
THEY DON'T UNDERSTAND WHAT IT'S LIKE TO BE SMALL AND ALL ALONE, BUT I DO.

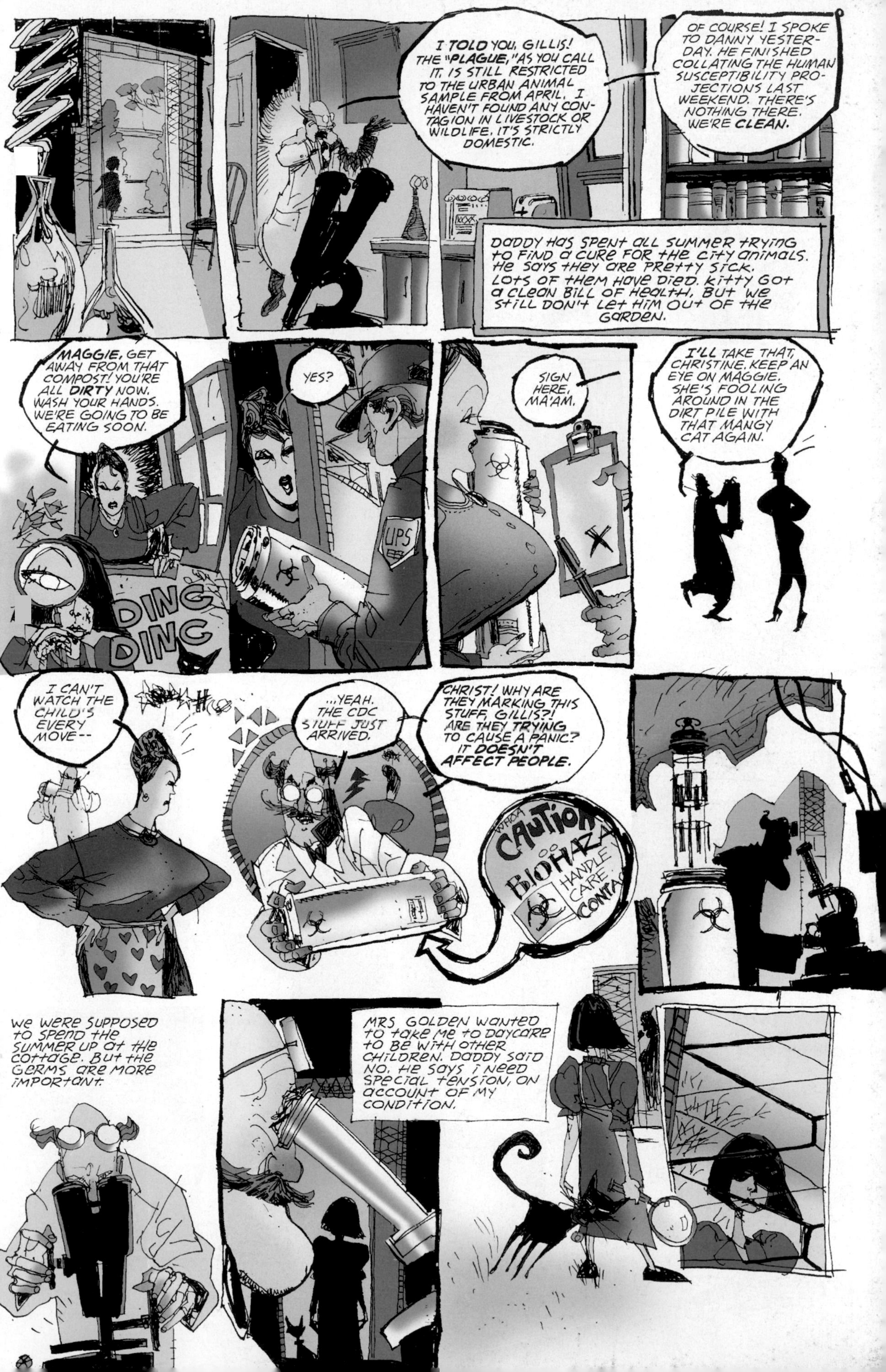
I TOLD YOU, GILLIS! THE "PLAGUE," AS YOU CALL IT, IS STILL RESTRICTED TO THE URBAN ANIMAL SAMPLE FROM APRIL. I HAVEN'T FOUND ANY CONTAGION IN LIVESTOCK OR WILDLIFE. IT'S STRICTLY DOMESTIC.
OF COURSE! I SPOKE TO DANNY YESTERDAY. HE FINISHED COLLATING THE HUMAN SUSCEPTIBILITY PROJECTIONS LAST WEEKEND. THERE'S NOTHING THERE. WE'RE CLEAN.
DADDY HAS SPENT ALL SUMMER TRYING TO FIND A CURE FOR THE CITY ANIMALS. HE SAYS THEY ARE PRETTY SICK. LOTS OF THEM HAVE DIED. KITTY GOT A CLEAN BILL OF HEALTH. BUT WE STILL DON'T LET HIM OUT OF THE GARDEN.
MAGGIE, GET AWAY FROM THAT COMPOST! YOU'RE ALL DIRTY NOW. WASH YOUR HANDS. WE'RE GOING TO BE EATING SOON.
DING DING
YES?
UPS
SIGN HERE, MA'AM.
I'LL TAKE THAT, CHRISTINE. KEEP AN EYE ON MAGGIE. SHE'S FOOLING AROUND IN THE DIRT PILE WITH THAT MANGY CAT AGAIN.
I CAN'T WATCH THE CHILD'S EVERY MOVE--
...YEAH. THE CDC STUFF JUST ARRIVED.
CHRIST! WHY ARE THEY MARKING THIS STUFF, GILLIS?! ARE THEY TRYING TO CAUSE A PANIC? IT DOESN'T AFFECT PEOPLE.
WHOA CAUTION BIOHAZA HANDLE CARE CONTAC
WE WERE SUPPOSED TO SPEND THE SUMMER UP AT THE COTTAGE. BUT THE GERMS ARE MORE IMPORTANT.
MRS GOLDEN WANTED TO TAKE ME TO DAYCARE TO BE WITH OTHER CHILDREN. DADDY SAID NO. HE SAYS I NEED SPECIAL TENSION, ON ACCOUNT OF MY CONDITION.

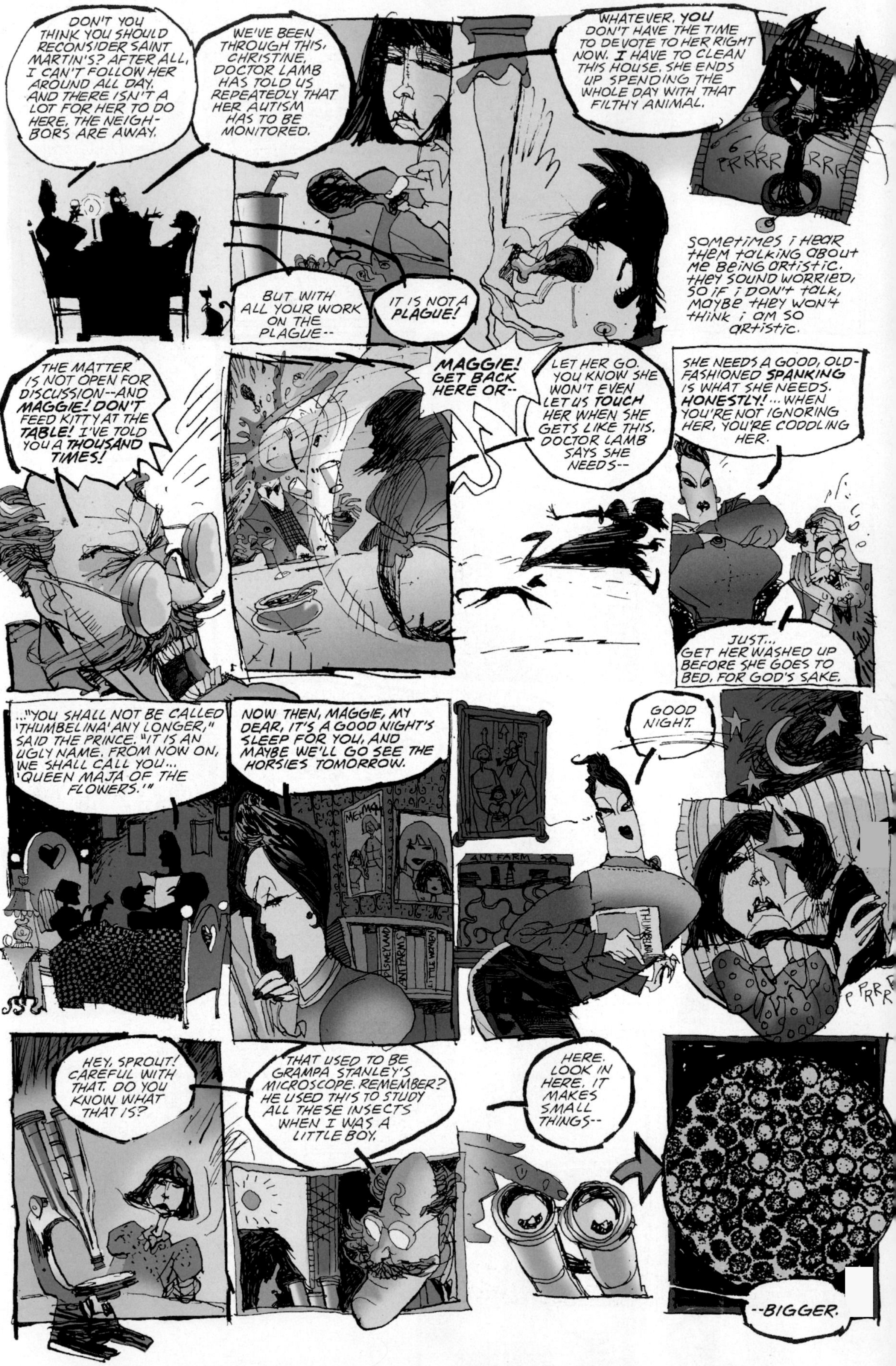
DON'T YOU THINK YOU SHOULD RECONSIDER SAINT MARTIN'S? AFTER ALL, I CAN'T FOLLOW HER AROUND ALL DAY. AND THERE ISN'T A LOT FOR HER TO DO HERE. THE NEIGHBORS ARE AWAY.
WE'VE BEEN THROUGH THIS, CHRISTINE. DOCTOR LAMB HAS TOLD US REPEATEDLY THAT HER AUTISM HAS TO BE MONITORED.
BUT WITH ALL YOUR WORK ON THE PLAGUE--
IT IS NOT A PLAGUE!
WHATEVER. YOU DON'T HAVE THE TIME TO DEVOTE TO HER RIGHT NOW. I HAVE TO CLEAN THIS HOUSE. SHE ENDS UP SPENDING THE WHOLE DAY WITH THAT FILTHY ANIMAL.
PRRRR RRRR
sometimes i hear them talking about me being artistic. they sound worried, so if i don't talk, maybe they won't think i am so artistic.
THE MATTER IS NOT OPEN FOR DISCUSSION--AND MAGGIE! DON'T FEED KITTY AT THE TABLE! I'VE TOLD YOU A THOUSAND TIMES!
MAGGIE! GET BACK HERE OR--
LET HER GO. YOU KNOW SHE WON'T EVEN LET US TOUCH HER WHEN SHE GETS LIKE THIS. DOCTOR LAMB SAYS SHE NEEDS--
SHE NEEDS A GOOD, OLD-FASHIONED SPANKING IS WHAT SHE NEEDS. HONESTLY! ...WHEN YOU'RE NOT IGNORING HER, YOU'RE CODDLING HER.
JUST... GET HER WASHED UP BEFORE SHE GOES TO BED, FOR GOD'S SAKE.
..."YOU SHALL NOT BE CALLED 'THUMBELINA' ANY LONGER," SAID THE PRINCE. "IT IS AN UGLY NAME. FROM NOW ON, WE SHALL CALL YOU... 'QUEEN MAJA OF THE FLOWERS.'"
NOW THEN, MAGGIE, MY DEAR, IT'S A GOOD NIGHT'S SLEEP FOR YOU, AND MAYBE WE'LL GO SEE THE HORSIES TOMORROW.
DISNEYLAND
ANT FARMS
LITTLE WOMEN
GOOD NIGHT.
ANT FARM
PPRRR
HEY, SPROUT! CAREFUL WITH THAT. DO YOU KNOW WHAT THAT IS?
THAT USED TO BE GRAMPA STANLEY'S MICROSCOPE. REMEMBER? HE USED THIS TO STUDY ALL THESE INSECTS WHEN I WAS A LITTLE BOY.
HERE. LOOK IN HERE. IT MAKES SMALL THINGS--
--BIGGER.

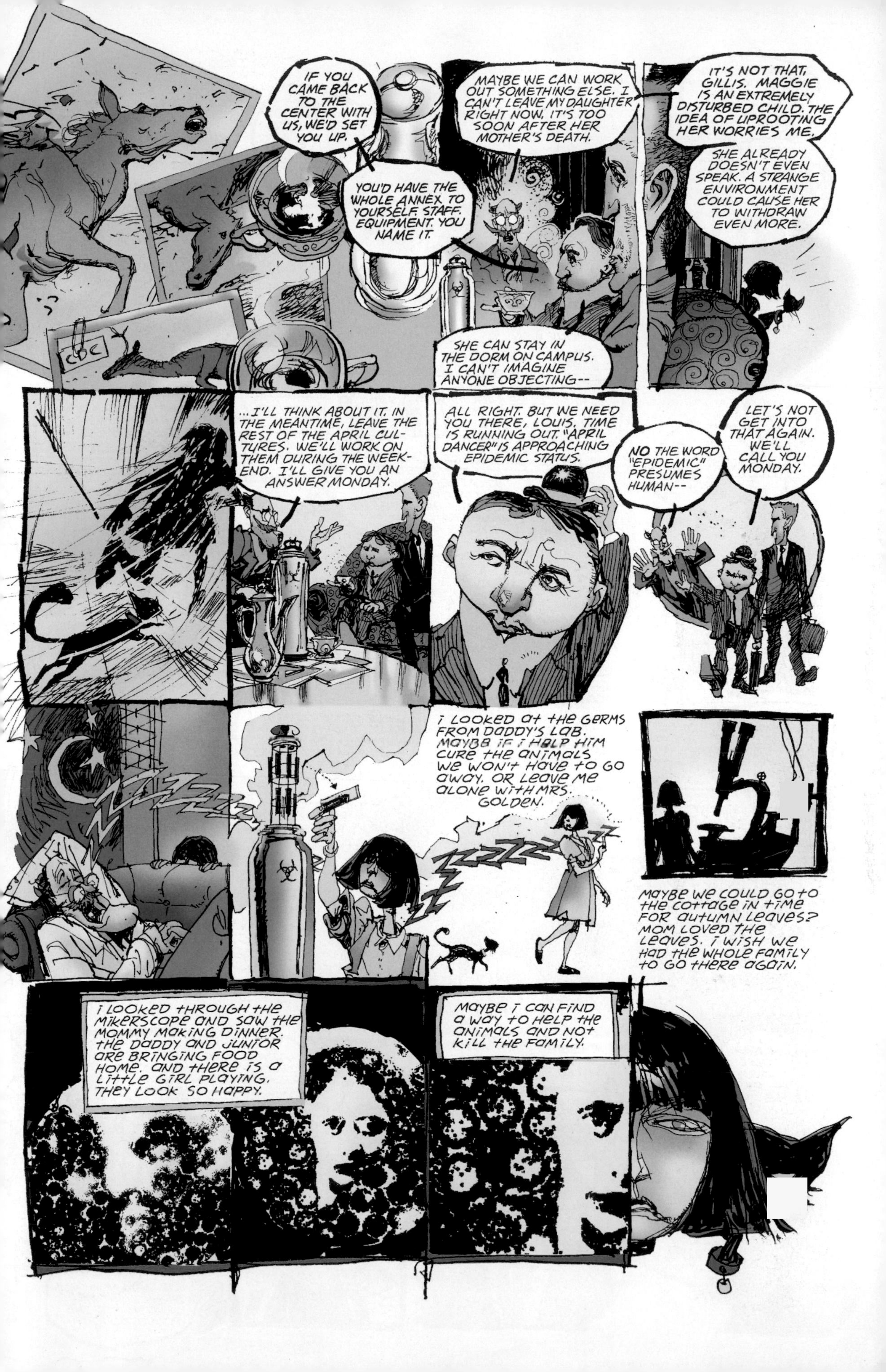
IF YOU CAME BACK TO THE CENTER WITH US, WE'D SET YOU UP.
YOU'D HAVE THE WHOLE ANNEX TO YOURSELF. STAFF. EQUIPMENT. YOU NAME IT.
MAYBE WE CAN WORK OUT SOMETHING ELSE. I CAN'T LEAVE MY DAUGHTER RIGHT NOW. IT'S TOO SOON AFTER HER MOTHER'S DEATH.
SHE CAN STAY IN THE DORM ON CAMPUS. I CAN'T IMAGINE ANYONE OBJECTING--
IT'S NOT THAT, GILLIS. MAGGIE IS AN EXTREMELY DISTURBED CHILD. THE IDEA OF UPROOTING HER WORRIES ME.
SHE ALREADY DOESN'T EVEN SPEAK. A STRANGE ENVIRONMENT COULD CAUSE HER TO WITHDRAW EVEN MORE.
...I'LL THINK ABOUT IT. IN THE MEANTIME, LEAVE THE REST OF THE APRIL CULTURES. WE'LL WORK ON THEM DURING THE WEEKEND. I'LL GIVE YOU AN ANSWER MONDAY.
ALL RIGHT. BUT WE NEED YOU THERE, LOUIS. TIME IS RUNNING OUT. "APRIL DANCER" IS APPROACHING EPIDEMIC STATUS.
NO THE WORD "EPIDEMIC" PRESUMES HUMAN--
LET'S NOT GET INTO THAT AGAIN. WE'LL CALL YOU MONDAY.
i looked at the germs from daddy's lab. maybe if i help him cure the animals we won't have to go away. or leave me alone with mrs. golden.
maybe we could go to the cottage in time for autumn leaves? mom loved the leaves. i wish we had the whole family to go there again.
i looked through the mikerscope and saw the mommy making dinner. the daddy and junior are bringing food home. and there is a little girl playing. they look so happy.
maybe i can find a way to help the animals and not kill the family.

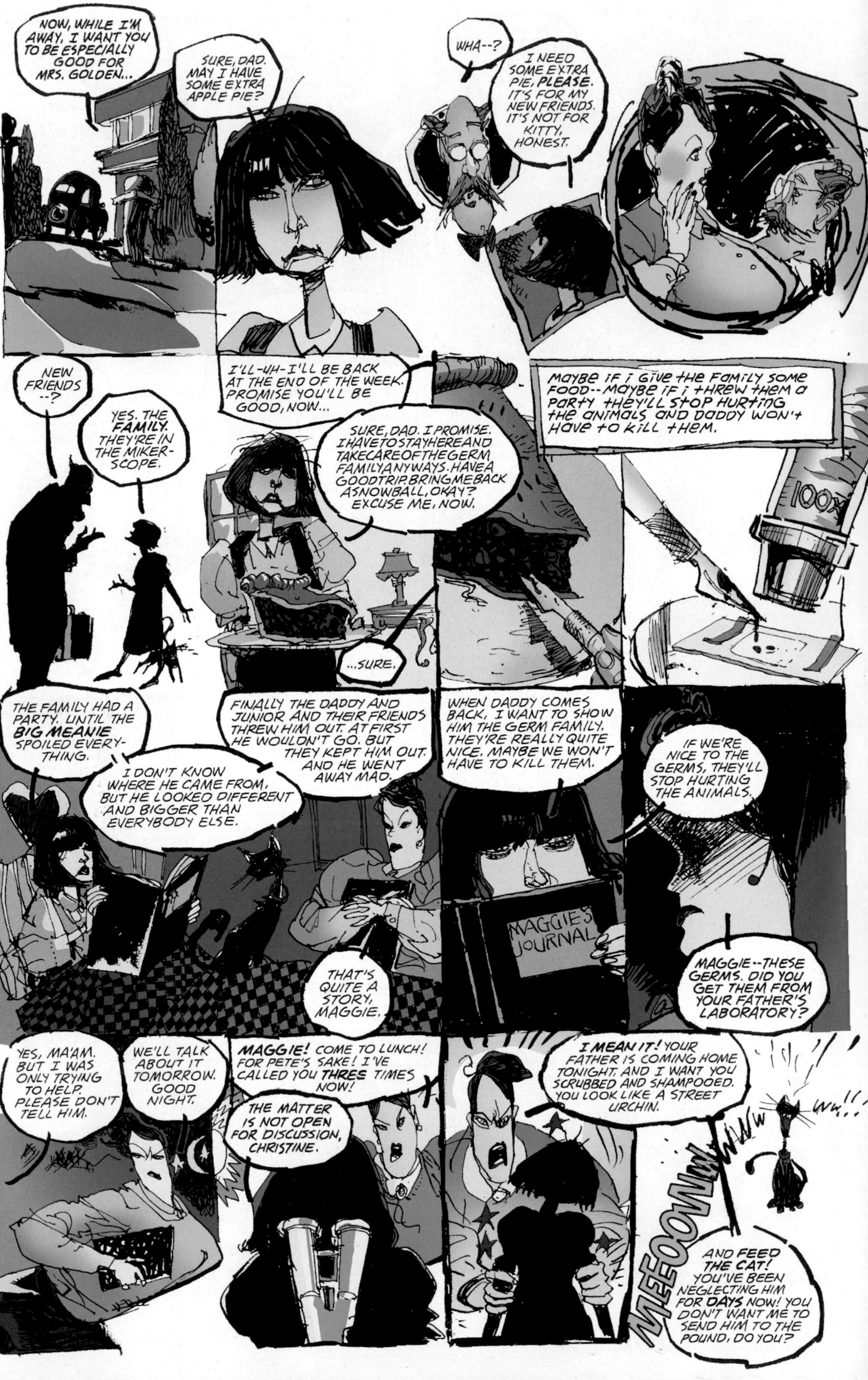
NOW, WHILE I'M AWAY, I WANT YOU TO BE ESPECIALLY GOOD FOR MRS. GOLDEN...
SURE, DAD. MAY I HAVE SOME EXTRA APPLE PIE?
WHA--?
I NEED SOME EXTRA PIE, PLEASE. IT'S FOR MY NEW FRIENDS. IT'S NOT FOR KITTY, HONEST.
NEW FRIENDS--?
YES. THE FAMILY. THEY'RE IN THE MIKER-SCOPE.
I'LL--UH--I'LL BE BACK AT THE END OF THE WEEK. PROMISE YOU'LL BE GOOD, NOW...
SURE, DAD. I PROMISE. IHAVETOSTAYHEREAND TAKECAREOFTHEGERM FAMILYANYWAYS. HAVEA GOODTRIP. BRINGMEBACK ASNOWBALL, OKAY? EXCUSE ME, NOW.
...SURE.
Maybe if i give the family some food--maybe if i threw them a party they'll stop hurting the animals and daddy won't have to kill them.
100X
THE FAMILY HAD A PARTY. UNTIL THE BIG MEANIE SPOILED EVERYTHING.
I DON'T KNOW WHERE HE CAME FROM, BUT HE LOOKED DIFFERENT AND BIGGER THAN EVERYBODY ELSE.
FINALLY THE DADDY AND JUNIOR AND THEIR FRIENDS THREW HIM OUT. AT FIRST HE WOULDN'T GO. BUT THEY KEPT HIM OUT. AND HE WENT AWAY MAD.
THAT'S QUITE A STORY, MAGGIE.
WHEN DADDY COMES BACK, I WANT TO SHOW HIM THE GERM FAMILY. THEY'RE REALLY QUITE NICE. MAYBE WE WON'T HAVE TO KILL THEM.
MAGGIE'S JOURNAL
IF WE'RE NICE TO THE GERMS, THEY'LL STOP HURTING THE ANIMALS.
MAGGIE--THESE GERMS. DID YOU GET THEM FROM YOUR FATHER'S LABORATORY?
YES, MA'AM. BUT I WAS ONLY TRYING TO HELP. PLEASE DON'T TELL HIM.
WE'LL TALK ABOUT IT TOMORROW. GOOD NIGHT.
MAGGIE! COME TO LUNCH! FOR PETE'S SAKE! I'VE CALLED YOU THREE TIMES NOW!
THE MATTER IS NOT OPEN FOR DISCUSSION, CHRISTINE.
I MEAN IT! YOUR FATHER IS COMING HOME TONIGHT, AND I WANT YOU SCRUBBED AND SHAMPOOED. YOU LOOK LIKE A STREET URCHIN.
MEEOOWWWWWWW!!
AND FEED THE CAT! YOU'VE BEEN NEGLECTING HIM FOR DAYS NOW! YOU DON'T WANT ME TO SEND HIM TO THE POUND, DO YOU?

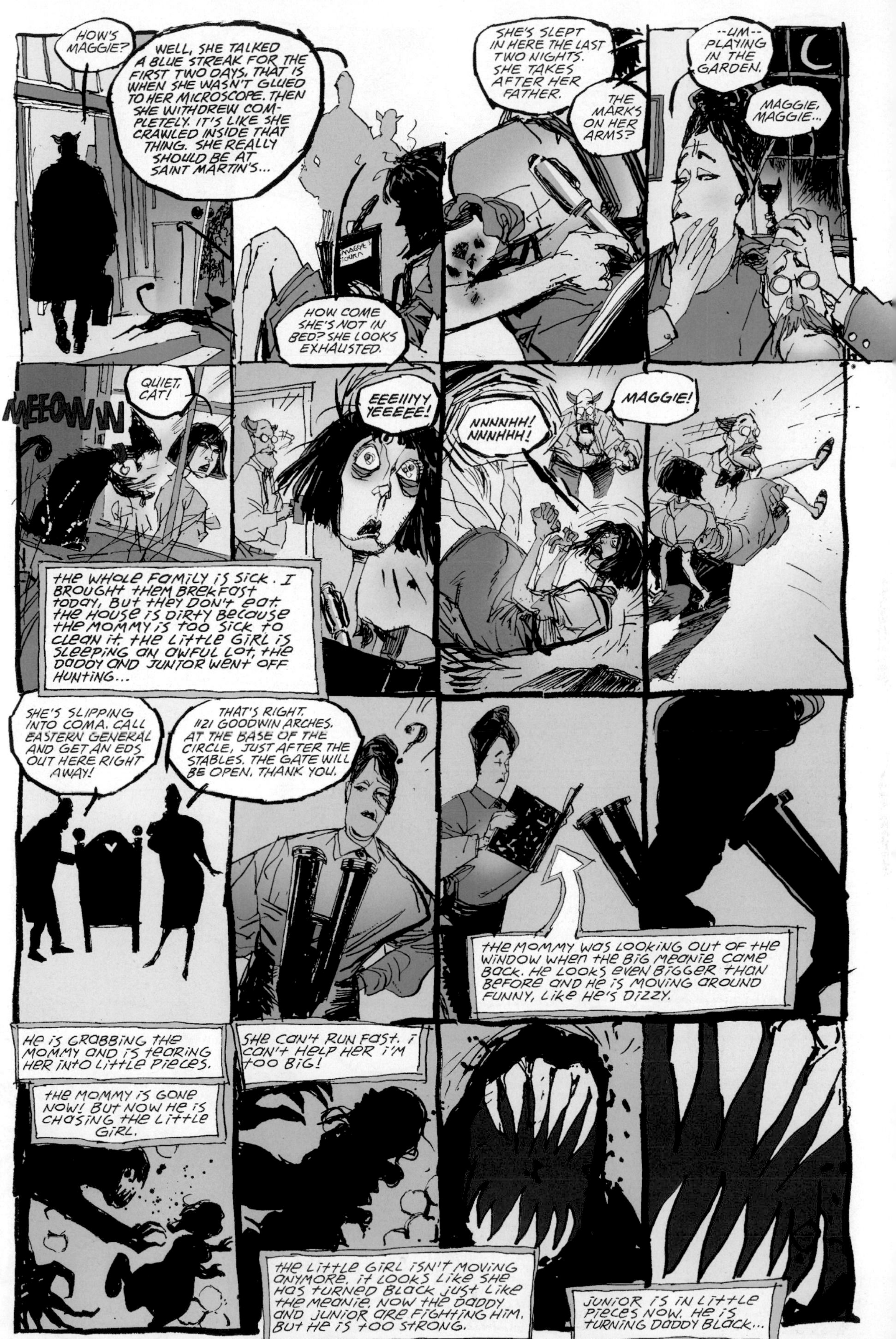
HOW'S MAGGIE?
WELL, SHE TALKED A BLUE STREAK FOR THE FIRST TWO DAYS, THAT IS WHEN SHE WASN'T GLUED TO HER MICROSCOPE. THEN SHE WITHDREW COMPLETELY. IT'S LIKE SHE CRAWLED INSIDE THAT THING. SHE REALLY SHOULD BE AT SAINT MARTIN'S...
HOW COME SHE'S NOT IN BED? SHE LOOKS EXHAUSTED.
SHE'S SLEPT IN HERE THE LAST TWO NIGHTS. SHE TAKES AFTER HER FATHER.
THE MARKS ON HER ARMS?
--UM-- PLAYING IN THE GARDEN.
MAGGIE, MAGGIE...
MEEOWWW
QUIET, CAT!
EEEIIIYY YEEEEEE!
NNNNHH! NNNHHH!
MAGGIE!
the whole family is sick. I brought them brekfast today, But they Don't eat. the house is dirty because the mommy is too sick to clean it. the little girl is sleeping an awful lot, the daddy and junior went off hunting...
SHE'S SLIPPING INTO COMA. CALL EASTERN GENERAL AND GET AN EDS OUT HERE RIGHT AWAY!
THAT'S RIGHT. 1121 GOODWIN ARCHES. AT THE BASE OF THE CIRCLE, JUST AFTER THE STABLES. THE GATE WILL BE OPEN. THANK YOU.
the mommy was looking out of the window when the big meanie came back. He looks even bigger than before and he is moving around funny, like he's dizzy.
He is grabbing the mommy and is tearing her into little pieces.
She can't run fast. i can't help her i'm too big!
the mommy is gone now! But now he is chasing the little girl.
the little girl isn't moving anymore. it looks like she has turned black just like the meanie. now the daddy and junior are fighting him. But he is too strong.
junior is in little pieces now. he is turning daddy black...

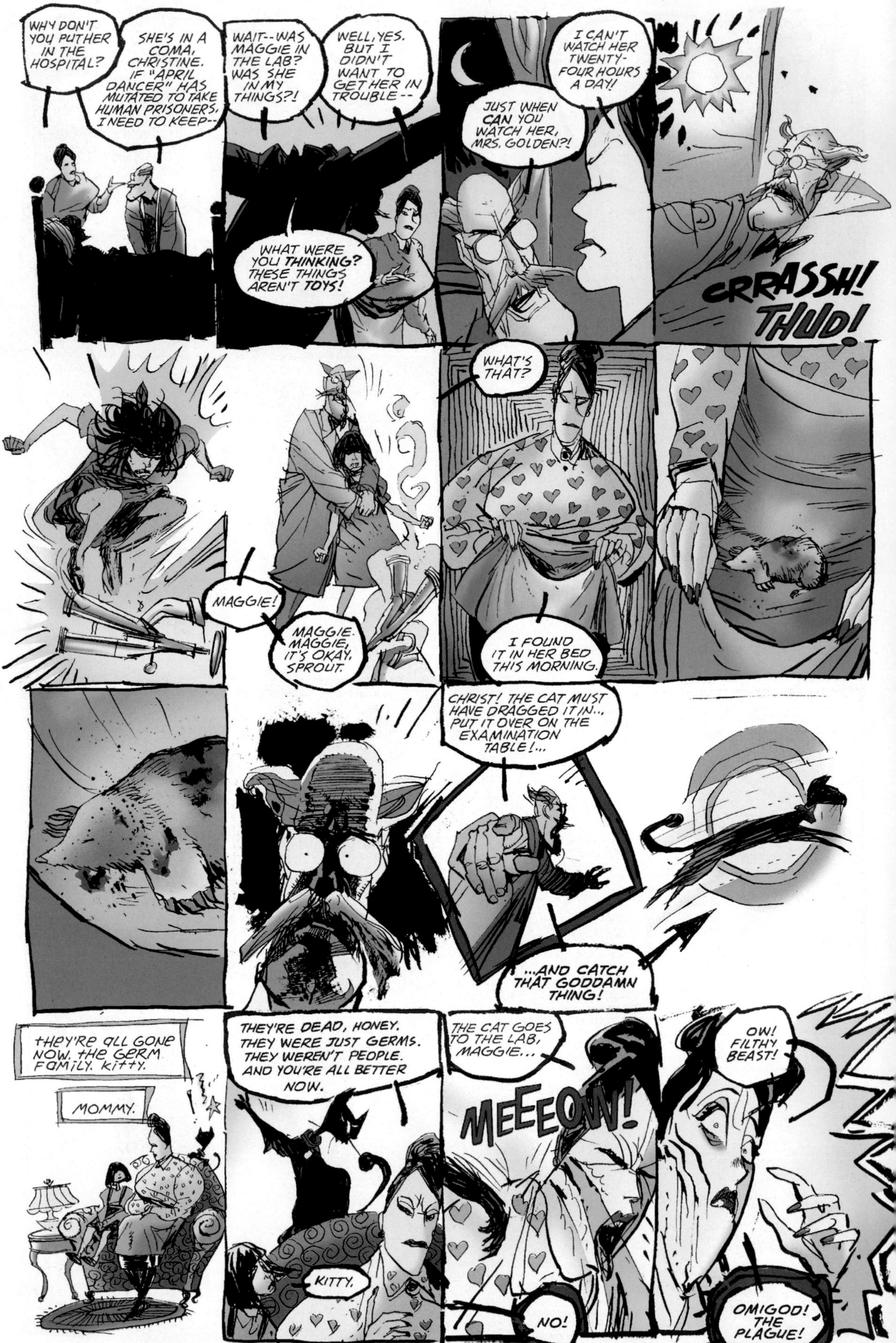
WHY DON'T YOU PUT HER IN THE HOSPITAL?
SHE'S IN A COMA, CHRISTINE. IF "APRIL DANCER" HAS MUTATED TO TAKE HUMAN PRISONERS, I NEED TO KEEP--
WAIT--WAS MAGGIE IN THE LAB? WAS SHE IN MY THINGS?!
WELL, YES. BUT I DIDN'T WANT TO GET HER IN TROUBLE--
WHAT WERE YOU THINKING? THESE THINGS AREN'T TOYS!
I CAN'T WATCH HER TWENTY-FOUR HOURS A DAY!
JUST WHEN CAN YOU WATCH HER, MRS. GOLDEN?!
CRRASSH!
THUD!
MAGGIE!
MAGGIE. MAGGIE, IT'S OKAY, SPROUT.
WHAT'S THAT?
I FOUND IT IN HER BED THIS MORNING.
CHRIST! THE CAT MUST HAVE DRAGGED IT IN.. PUT IT OVER ON THE EXAMINATION TABLE!...
...AND CATCH THAT GODDAMN THING!
they're all gone now. the germ family. kitty.
MOMMY.
THEY'RE DEAD, HONEY. THEY WERE JUST GERMS. THEY WEREN'T PEOPLE. AND YOU'RE ALL BETTER NOW.
KITTY.
THE CAT GOES TO THE LAB, MAGGIE...
MEEEOW!
NO!
OW! FILTHY BEAST!
OMIGOD! THE PLAGUE!

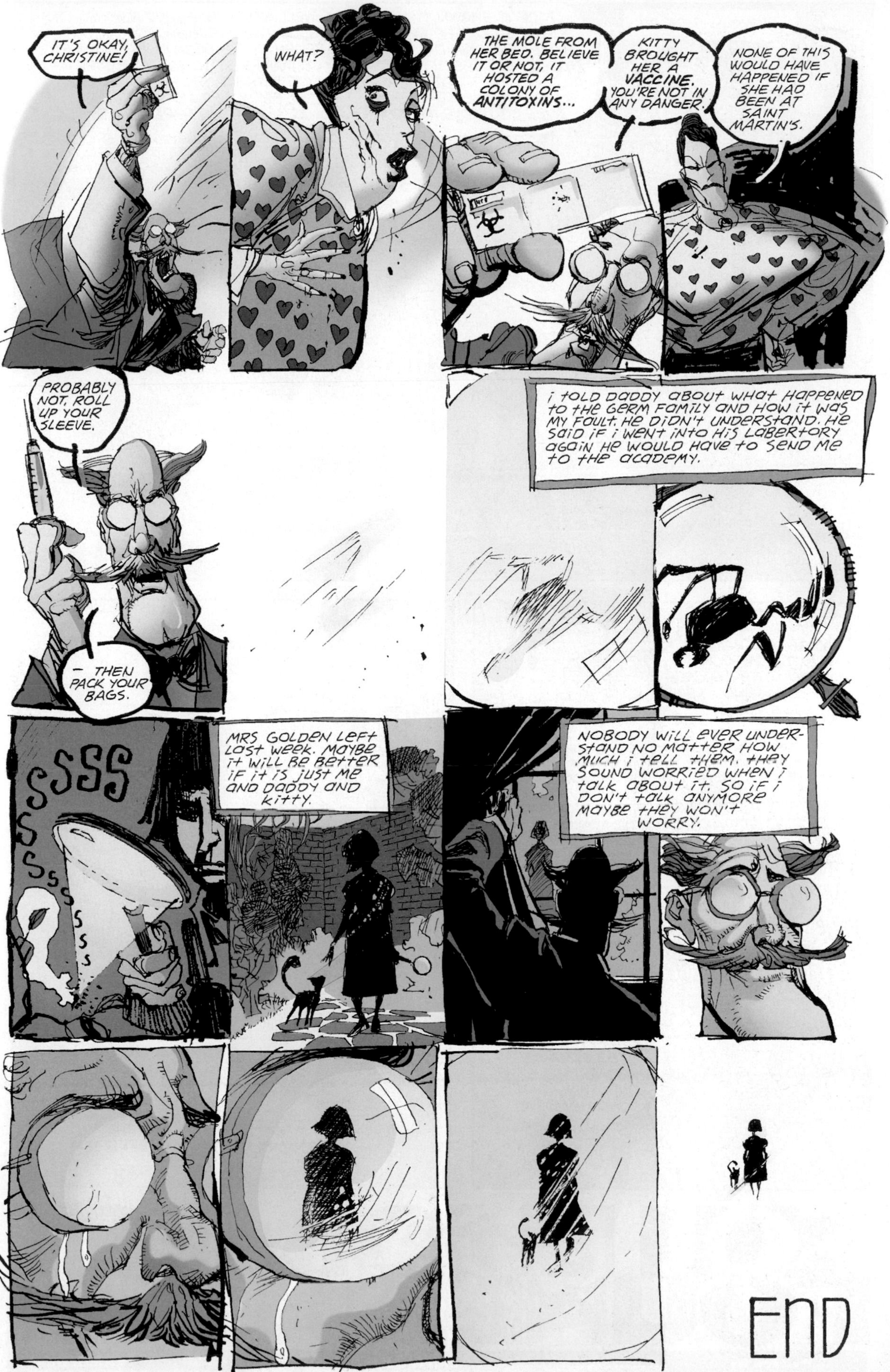

IT'S OKAY, CHRISTINE!
WHAT?
THE MOLE FROM HER BED. BELIEVE IT OR NOT, IT HOSTED A COLONY OF **ANTITOXINS**...
KITTY BROUGHT HER A **VACCINE**. YOU'RE NOT IN ANY DANGER.
NONE OF THIS WOULD HAVE HAPPENED IF SHE HAD BEEN AT SAINT MARTIN'S.
PROBABLY NOT. ROLL UP YOUR SLEEVE.
– THEN PACK YOUR BAGS.
i told daddy about what happened to the germ family and how it was my fault. he didn't understand. he said if i went into his labertory again he would have to send me to the academy.
SSS SSSSSSSS
MRS GOLDEN LEFT LAST WEEK. MAYBE IT WILL BE BETTER IF IT IS JUST ME AND DADDY AND KITTY.
NOBODY WILL EVER UNDERSTAND NO MATTER HOW MUCH i TELL THEM. THEY SOUND WORRIED WHEN i TALK ABOUT IT. SO IF i DON'T TALK ANYMORE MAYBE THEY WON'T WORRY.
END

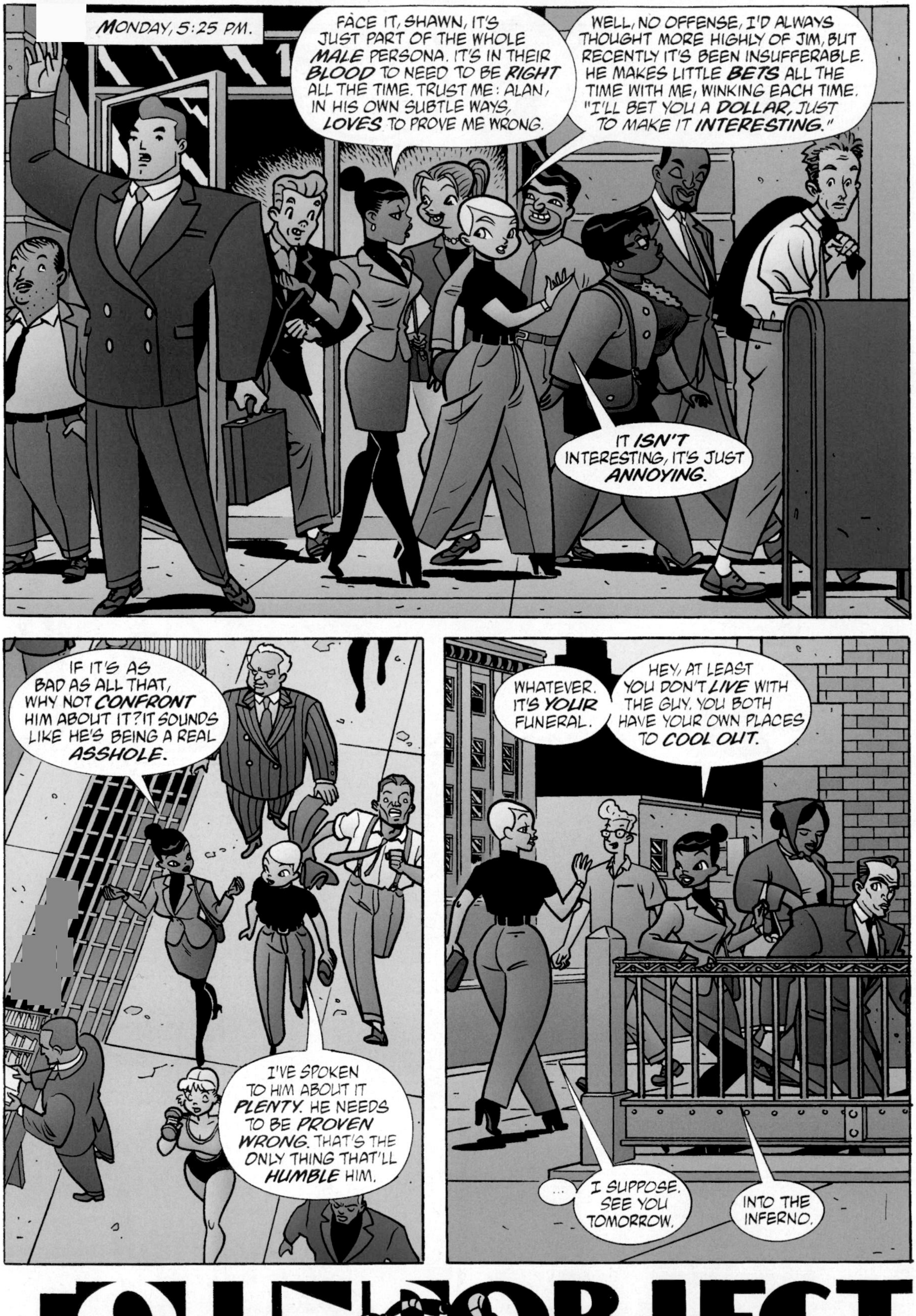
MONDAY, 5:25 PM.
FACE IT, SHAWN, IT'S JUST PART OF THE WHOLE MALE PERSONA. IT'S IN THEIR BLOOD TO NEED TO BE RIGHT ALL THE TIME. TRUST ME: ALAN, IN HIS OWN SUBTLE WAYS, LOVES TO PROVE ME WRONG.
WELL, NO OFFENSE, I'D ALWAYS THOUGHT MORE HIGHLY OF JIM, BUT RECENTLY IT'S BEEN INSUFFERABLE. HE MAKES LITTLE BETS ALL THE TIME WITH ME, WINKING EACH TIME. "I'LL BET YOU A DOLLAR, JUST TO MAKE IT INTERESTING."
IT ISN'T INTERESTING, IT'S JUST ANNOYING.
IF IT'S AS BAD AS ALL THAT, WHY NOT CONFRONT HIM ABOUT IT? IT SOUNDS LIKE HE'S BEING A REAL ASSHOLE.
I'VE SPOKEN TO HIM ABOUT IT PLENTY. HE NEEDS TO BE PROVEN WRONG. THAT'S THE ONLY THING THAT'LL HUMBLE HIM.
WHATEVER. IT'S YOUR FUNERAL.
HEY, AT LEAST YOU DON'T LIVE WITH THE GUY. YOU BOTH HAVE YOUR OWN PLACES TO COOL OUT.
...
I SUPPOSE. SEE YOU TOMORROW.
INTO THE INFERNO.

# FOUND OBJECT

Written by OB FINGERMAN | Illustrated by PAT McEOWN | Colored by MATT HOLLINGSWORTH | Lettered by CLEM ROBINS | Edited by AXEL ALONSO

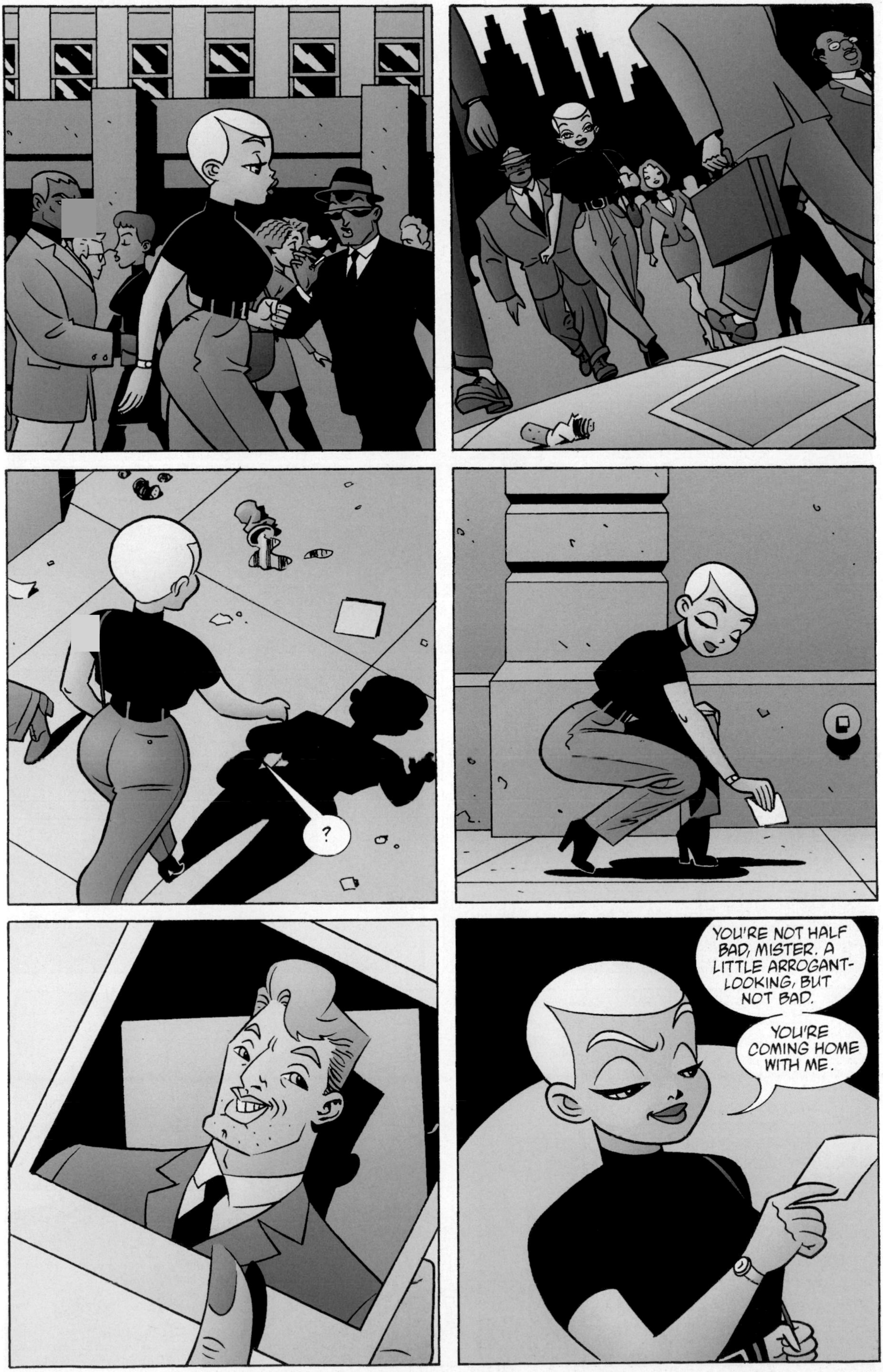
?
YOU'RE NOT HALF BAD, MISTER. A LITTLE ARROGANT-LOOKING, BUT NOT BAD.
YOU'RE COMING HOME WITH ME.

HERE'S YOUR *NEW* HOME.

TUESDAY, 5:21 P.M.

HANG IN THERE BABY

SO, YOU AND JIM SETTLE YOUR *DIFFERENCES?*

NOT QUITE YET. WE'VE GOT A *WAGER* GOING AND IF I WIN, THAT'LL BE THAT.

HEY, QUITTING TIME!

YOU ARE *SO* LUCKY YOU GET TO *WALK* TO WORK. THE SUBWAY IS *KILLING* ME.

MAÑANA, BABY.

MM-HMM.

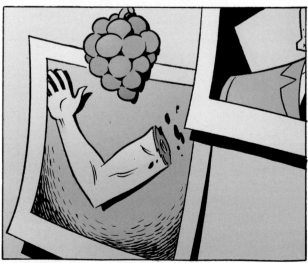

HMMM.

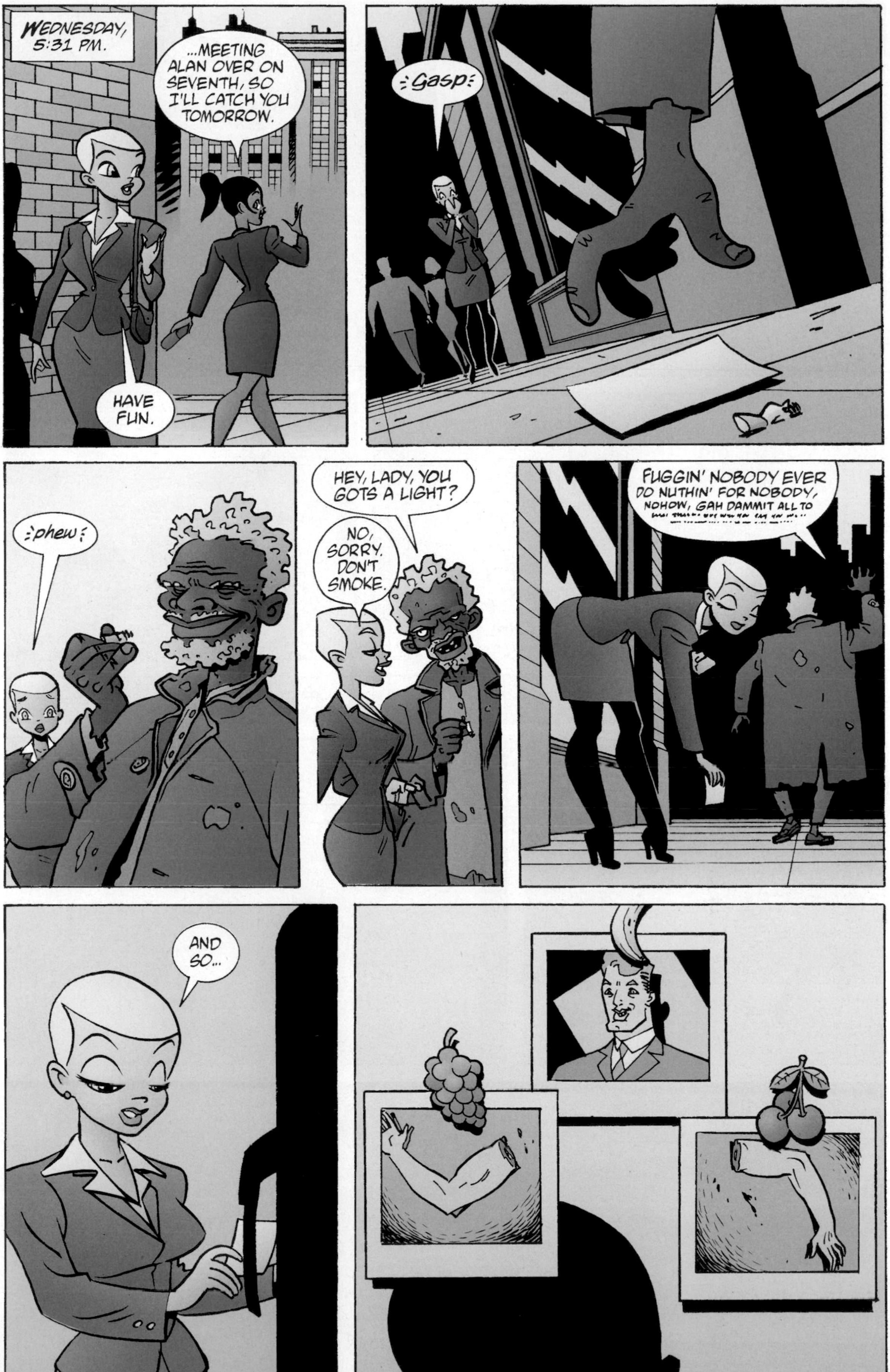
WEDNESDAY, 5:31 PM.
...MEETING ALAN OVER ON SEVENTH, SO I'LL CATCH YOU TOMORROW.
HAVE FUN.
Gasp
phew
HEY, LADY, YOU GOTS A LIGHT?
NO, SORRY. DON'T SMOKE.
FUGGIN' NOBODY EVER DO NUTHIN' FOR NOBODY, NOHOW, GAH DAMMIT ALL TO
AND SO...

THURSDAY, 5:29 P.M.

YOU ALL RIGHT, SHAWN?

YEAH, I'VE JUST GOT TO HURRY HOME TODAY. NOTHING MAJOR, JUST GOTTA SCOOT.

OKAY, BE GOOD!

YES!

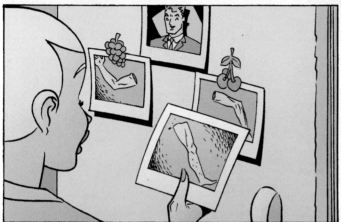

FRIDAY, 5:27 P.M.

...IT'S HER MESS AND I GOTTA STRAIGHTEN IT OUT? I DON'T HAVE TO DO THAT. NOT MY JOB.

Uh-huh. HEY, QUITTING TIME, CHICA! GOTTA MOTOR!

AWESOME!

SATURDAY, 5:30 P.M.

NO ONE.

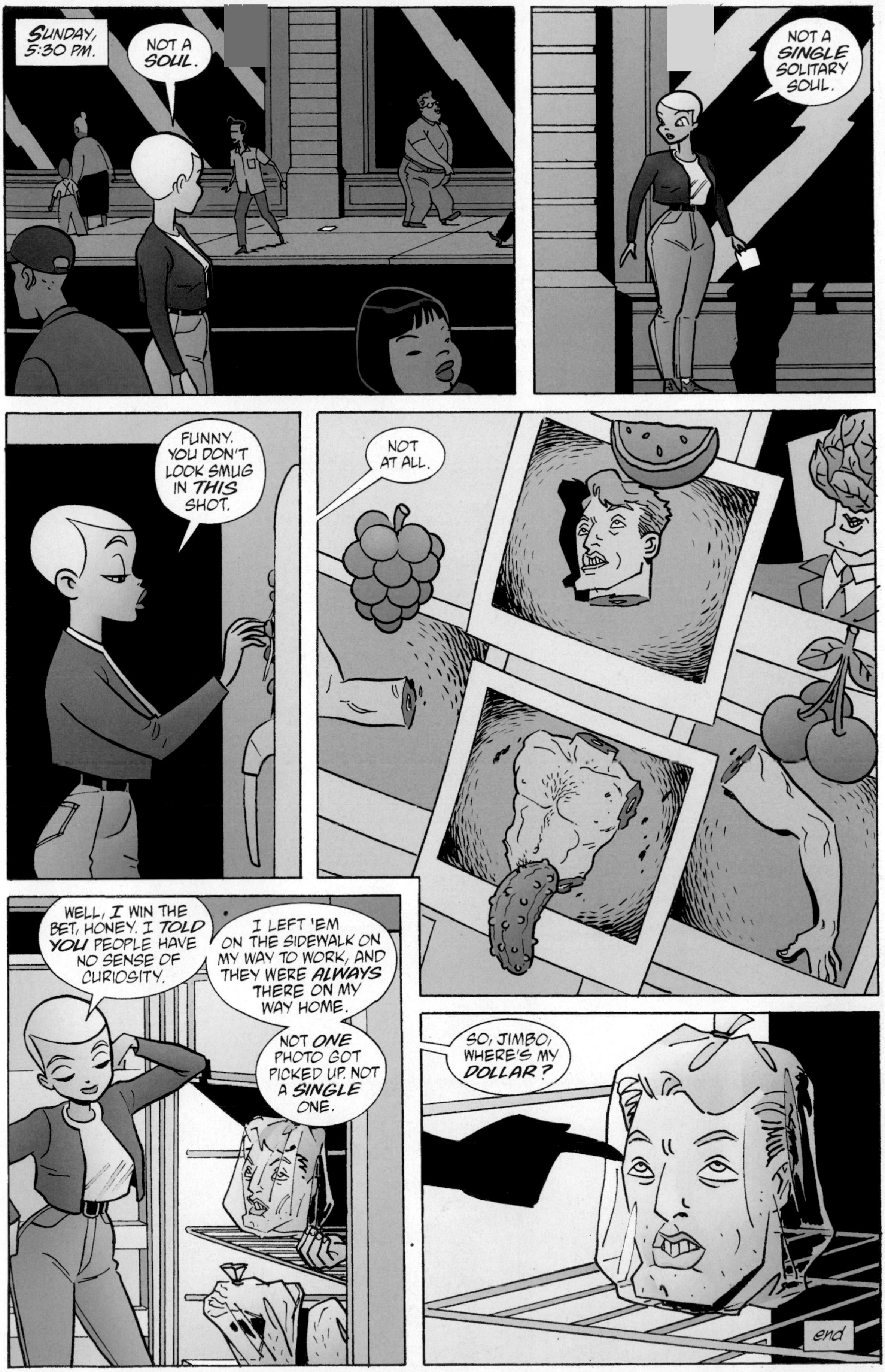

SUNDAY, 5:30 PM.
NOT A SOUL.
NOT A SINGLE SOLITARY SOUL.
FUNNY. YOU DON'T LOOK SMUG IN THIS SHOT.
NOT AT ALL.
WELL, I WIN THE BET, HONEY. I TOLD YOU PEOPLE HAVE NO SENSE OF CURIOSITY.
I LEFT 'EM ON THE SIDEWALK ON MY WAY TO WORK, AND THEY WERE ALWAYS THERE ON MY WAY HOME.
NOT ONE PHOTO GOT PICKED UP. NOT A SINGLE ONE.
SO, JIMBO, WHERE'S MY DOLLAR?
end

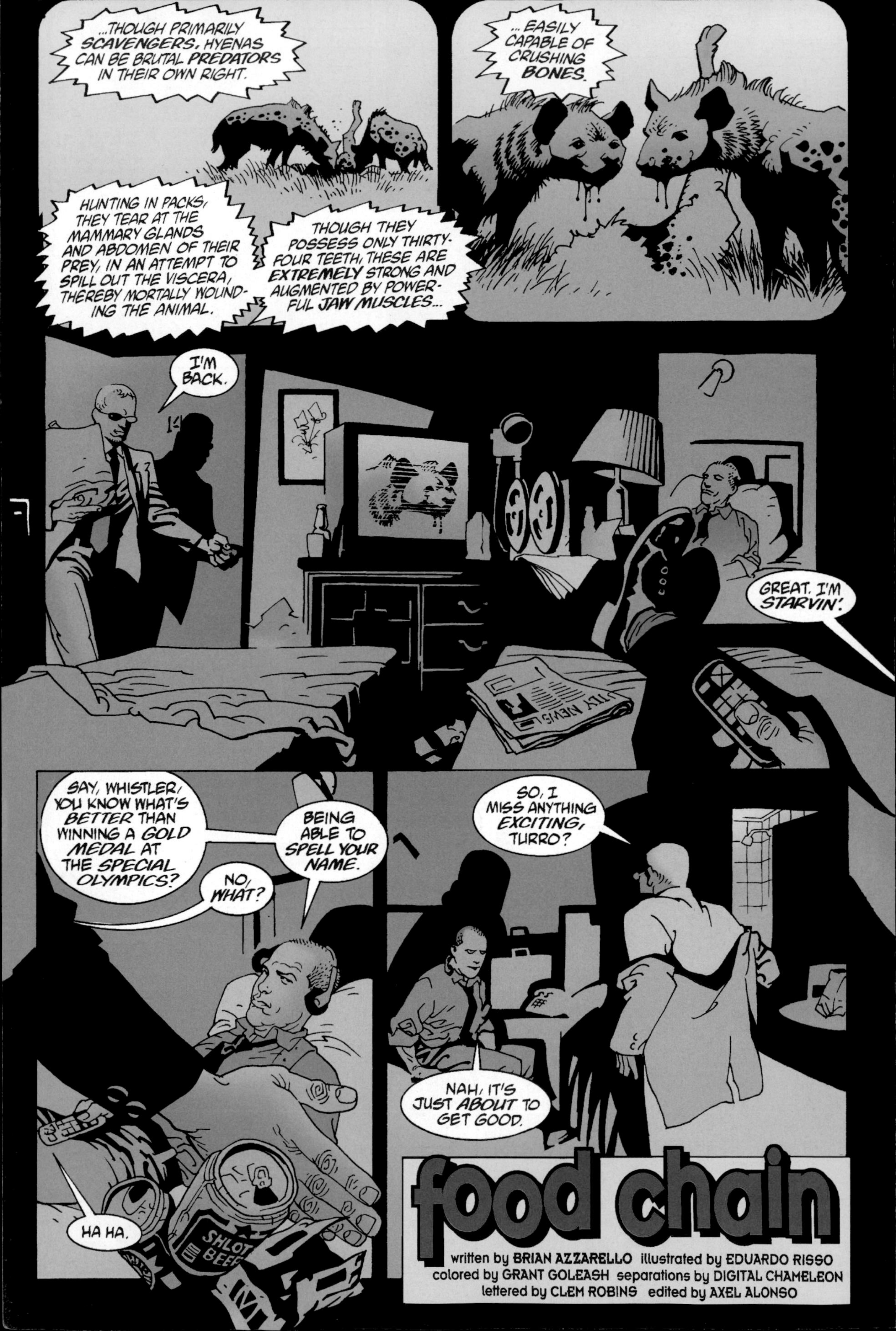
...THOUGH PRIMARILY SCAVENGERS, HYENAS CAN BE BRUTAL PREDATORS IN THEIR OWN RIGHT.
HUNTING IN PACKS, THEY TEAR AT THE MAMMARY GLANDS AND ABDOMEN OF THEIR PREY, IN AN ATTEMPT TO SPILL OUT THE VISCERA, THEREBY MORTALLY WOUNDING THE ANIMAL.
THOUGH THEY POSSESS ONLY THIRTY-FOUR TEETH, THESE ARE EXTREMELY STRONG AND AUGMENTED BY POWERFUL JAW MUSCLES...
... EASILY CAPABLE OF CRUSHING BONES.
I'M BACK.
GREAT. I'M STARVIN'.
CITY NEWS
SAY, WHISTLER, YOU KNOW WHAT'S BETTER THAN WINNING A GOLD MEDAL AT THE SPECIAL OLYMPICS?
NO, WHAT?
BEING ABLE TO SPELL YOUR NAME.
HA HA.
SHLOTZ BEER
SO, I MISS ANYTHING EXCITING, TURRO?
NAH, IT'S JUST ABOUT TO GET GOOD.
food chain
written by BRIAN AZZARELLO illustrated by EDUARDO RISSO
colored by GRANT GOLEASH separations by DIGITAL CHAMELEON
lettered by CLEM ROBINS edited by AXEL ALONSO

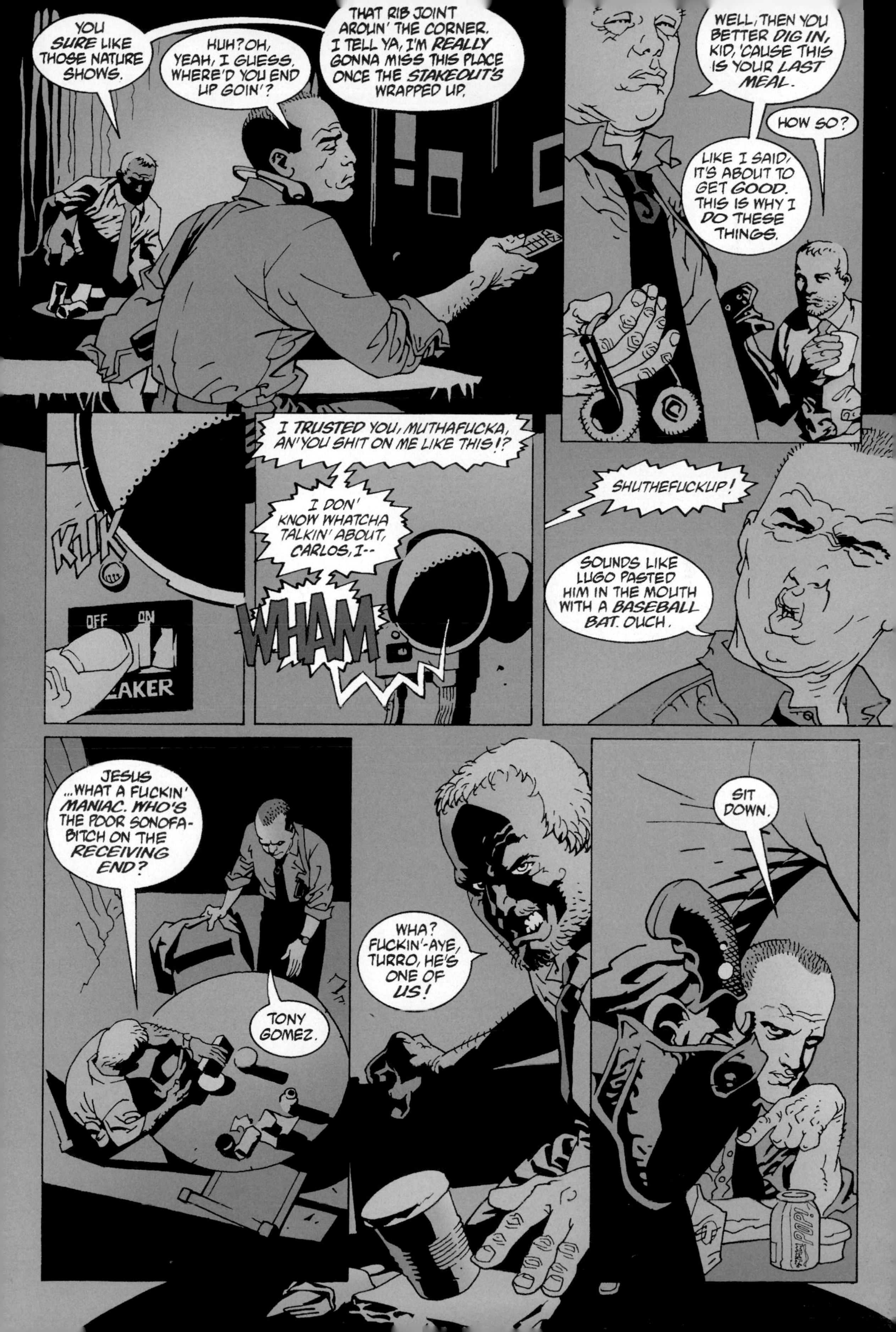
YOU SURE LIKE THOSE NATURE SHOWS.
HUH? OH, YEAH, I GUESS. WHERE'D YOU END UP GOIN'?
THAT RIB JOINT AROUN' THE CORNER. I TELL YA, I'M REALLY GONNA MISS THIS PLACE ONCE THE STAKEOUT'S WRAPPED UP.
WELL, THEN YOU BETTER DIG IN, KID, 'CAUSE THIS IS YOUR LAST MEAL.
HOW SO?
LIKE I SAID, IT'S ABOUT TO GET GOOD. THIS IS WHY I DO THESE THINGS.
KLIK
OFF ON
EAKER
I TRUSTED YOU, MUTHAFUCKA, AN' YOU SHIT ON ME LIKE THIS!?
I DON' KNOW WHATCHA TALKIN' ABOUT, CARLOS, I--
WHAM
SHUTHEFUCKUP!
SOUNDS LIKE LUGO PASTED HIM IN THE MOUTH WITH A BASEBALL BAT. OUCH.
JESUS ...WHAT A FUCKIN' MANIAC. WHO'S THE POOR SONOFA-BITCH ON THE RECEIVING END?
TONY GOMEZ.
WHA? FUCKIN'-AYE, TURRO, HE'S ONE OF US!
SIT DOWN.

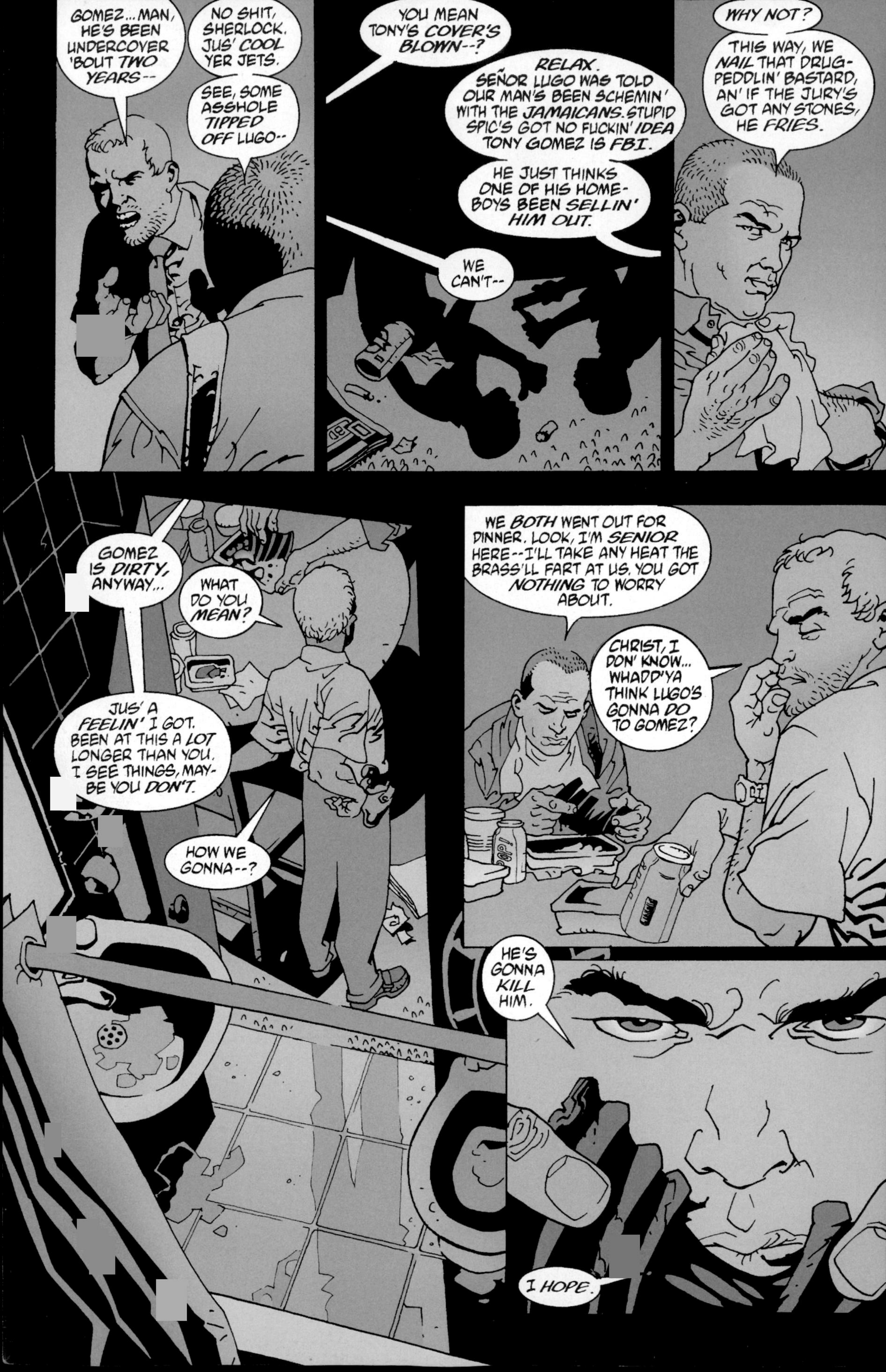
GOMEZ... MAN, HE'S BEEN UNDERCOVER 'BOUT TWO YEARS--
NO SHIT, SHERLOCK. JUS' COOL YER JETS.
SEE, SOME ASSHOLE TIPPED OFF LUGO--
YOU MEAN TONY'S COVER'S BLOWN--?
RELAX. SEÑOR LUGO WAS TOLD OUR MAN'S BEEN SCHEMIN' WITH THE JAMAICANS. STUPID SPIC'S GOT NO FUCKIN' IDEA TONY GOMEZ IS FBI.
HE JUST THINKS ONE OF HIS HOME-BOYS BEEN SELLIN' HIM OUT.
WE CAN'T--
WHY NOT?
THIS WAY, WE NAIL THAT DRUG-PEDDLIN' BASTARD, AN' IF THE JURY'S GOT ANY STONES, HE FRIES.
GOMEZ IS DIRTY, ANYWAY...
WHAT DO YOU MEAN?
JUS' A FEELIN' I GOT. BEEN AT THIS A LOT LONGER THAN YOU. I SEE THINGS, MAY-BE YOU DON'T.
HOW WE GONNA--?
WE BOTH WENT OUT FOR DINNER. LOOK, I'M SENIOR HERE--I'LL TAKE ANY HEAT THE BRASS'LL FART AT US. YOU GOT NOTHING TO WORRY ABOUT.
CHRIST, I DON' KNOW... WHADD'YA THINK LUGO'S GONNA DO TO GOMEZ?
HE'S GONNA KILL HIM.
I HOPE.

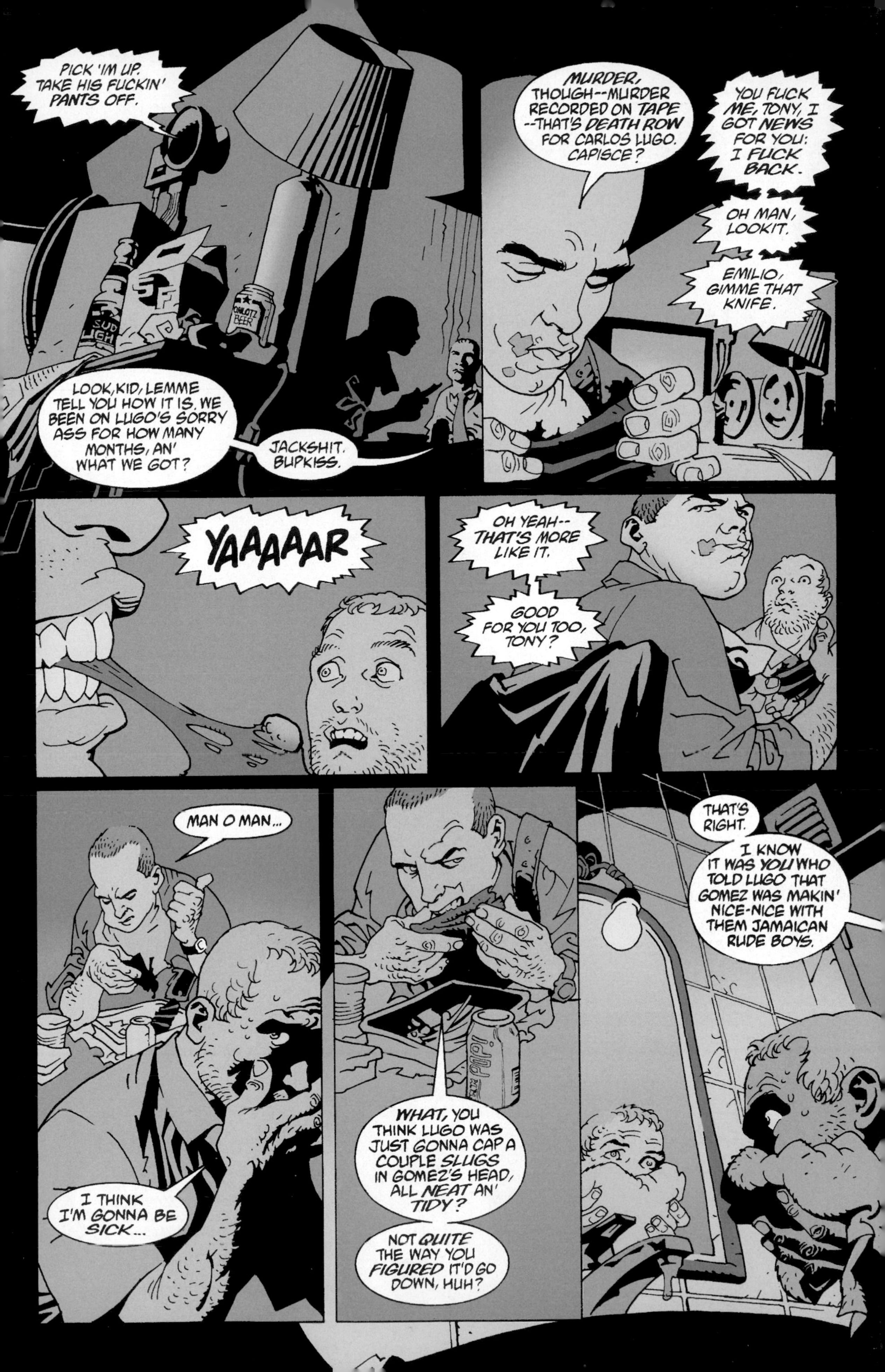
PICK 'IM UP. TAKE HIS FUCKIN' PANTS OFF.
LOOK, KID, LEMME TELL YOU HOW IT IS. WE BEEN ON LUGO'S SORRY ASS FOR HOW MANY MONTHS, AN' WHAT WE GOT?
JACKSHIT. BUPKISS.
SUD LIGHT
CARLOTZ BEER
MURDER, THOUGH--MURDER RECORDED ON TAPE--THAT'S DEATH ROW FOR CARLOS LUGO. CAPISCE?
YOU FUCK ME, TONY, I GOT NEWS FOR YOU: I FUCK BACK.
OH MAN, LOOKIT.
EMILIO, GIMME THAT KNIFE.
YAAAAAR
OH YEAH--THAT'S MORE LIKE IT.
GOOD FOR YOU TOO, TONY?
MAN O MAN...
I THINK I'M GONNA BE SICK...
WHAT, YOU THINK LUGO WAS JUST GONNA CAP A COUPLE SLUGS IN GOMEZ'S HEAD, ALL NEAT AN' TIDY?
NOT QUITE THE WAY YOU FIGURED IT'D GO DOWN, HUH?
THAT'S RIGHT.
I KNOW IT WAS YOU WHO TOLD LUGO THAT GOMEZ WAS MAKIN' NICE-NICE WITH THEM JAMAICAN RUDE BOYS.

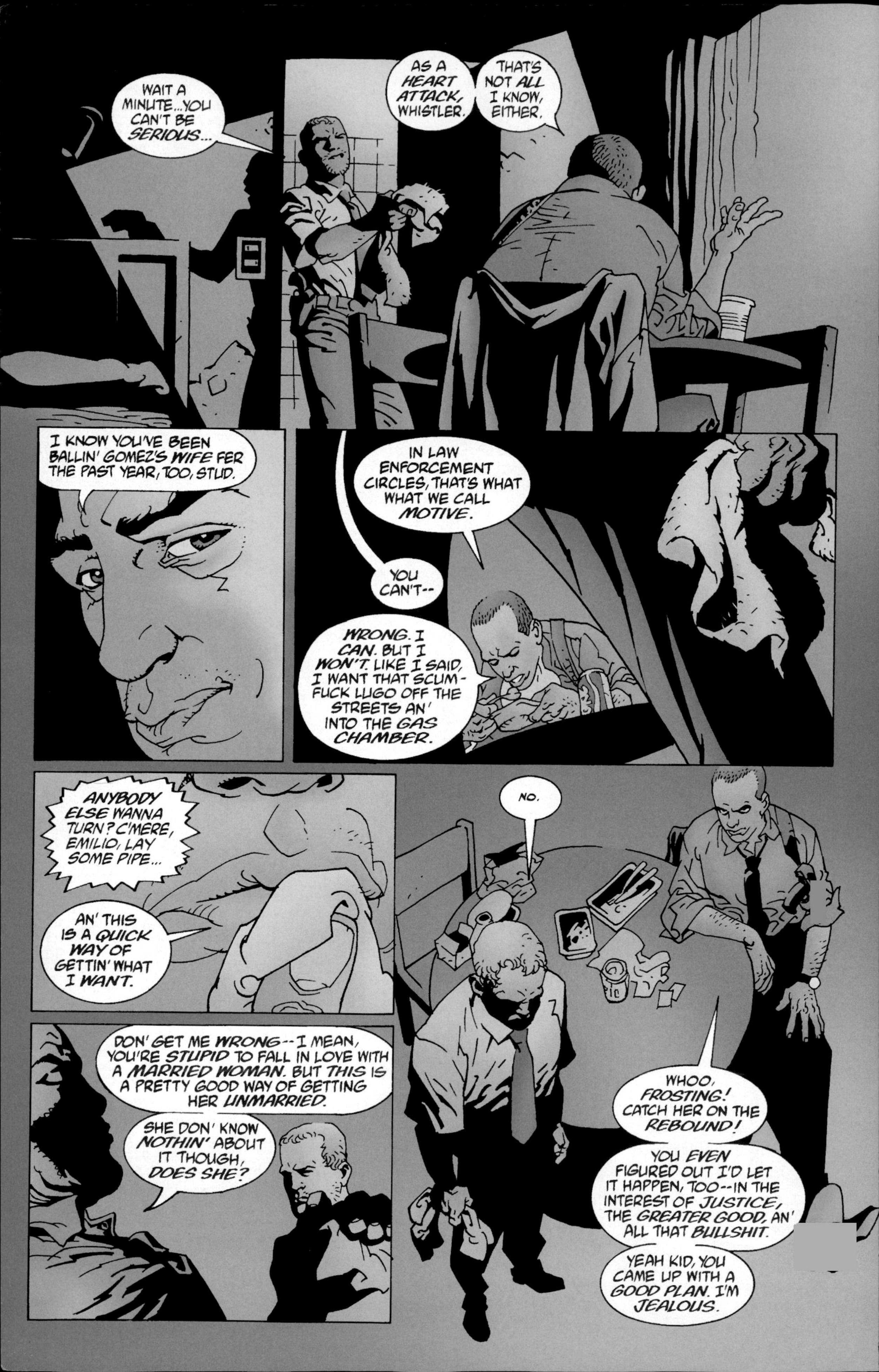
WAIT A MINUTE...YOU CAN'T BE SERIOUS...
AS A HEART ATTACK, WHISTLER.
THAT'S NOT ALL I KNOW, EITHER.
I KNOW YOU'VE BEEN BALLIN' GOMEZ'S WIFE FER THE PAST YEAR, TOO, STUD.
IN LAW ENFORCEMENT CIRCLES, THAT'S WHAT WHAT WE CALL MOTIVE.
YOU CAN'T--
WRONG. I CAN. BUT I WON'T. LIKE I SAID, I WANT THAT SCUM-FUCK LUGO OFF THE STREETS AN' INTO THE GAS CHAMBER.
ANYBODY ELSE WANNA TURN? C'MERE, EMILIO, LAY SOME PIPE...
AN' THIS IS A QUICK WAY OF GETTIN' WHAT I WANT.
NO.
DON' GET ME WRONG--I MEAN, YOU'RE STUPID TO FALL IN LOVE WITH A MARRIED WOMAN. BUT THIS IS A PRETTY GOOD WAY OF GETTING HER UNMARRIED.
SHE DON' KNOW NOTHIN' ABOUT IT THOUGH, DOES SHE?
WHOO, FROSTING! CATCH HER ON THE REBOUND!
YOU EVEN FIGURED OUT I'D LET IT HAPPEN, TOO--IN THE INTEREST OF JUSTICE, THE GREATER GOOD, AN' ALL THAT BULLSHIT.
YEAH KID, YOU CAME UP WITH A GOOD PLAN. I'M JEALOUS.

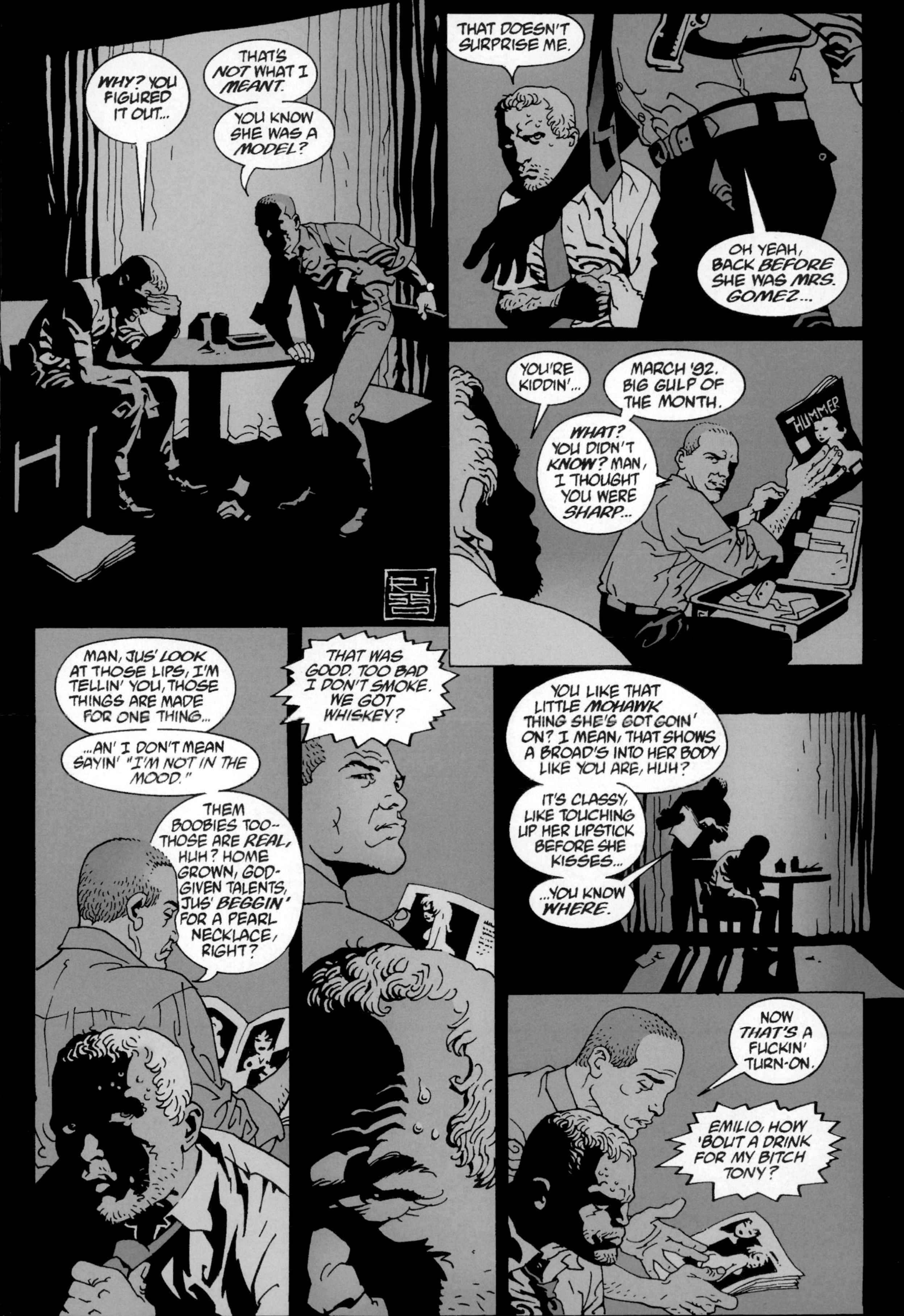

WHY? YOU FIGURED IT OUT...
THAT'S NOT WHAT I MEANT.
YOU KNOW SHE WAS A MODEL?
THAT DOESN'T SURPRISE ME.
OH YEAH, BACK BEFORE SHE WAS MRS. GOMEZ...
YOU'RE KIDDIN'...
MARCH '92. BIG GULP OF THE MONTH.
WHAT? YOU DIDN'T KNOW? MAN, I THOUGHT YOU WERE SHARP...
HUMMER
MAN, JUS' LOOK AT THOSE LIPS, I'M TELLIN' YOU, THOSE THINGS ARE MADE FOR ONE THING...
...AN' I DON'T MEAN SAYIN' "I'M NOT IN THE MOOD."
THEM BOOBIES TOO-- THOSE ARE REAL, HUH? HOME GROWN, GOD-GIVEN TALENTS, JUS' BEGGIN' FOR A PEARL NECKLACE, RIGHT?
THAT WAS GOOD. TOO BAD I DON'T SMOKE. WE GOT WHISKEY?
YOU LIKE THAT LITTLE MOHAWK THING SHE'S GOT GOIN' ON? I MEAN, THAT SHOWS A BROAD'S INTO HER BODY LIKE YOU ARE, HUH?
IT'S CLASSY, LIKE TOUCHING UP HER LIPSTICK BEFORE SHE KISSES...
...YOU KNOW WHERE.
NOW THAT'S A FUCKIN' TURN-ON.
EMILIO, HOW 'BOUT A DRINK FOR MY BITCH TONY?

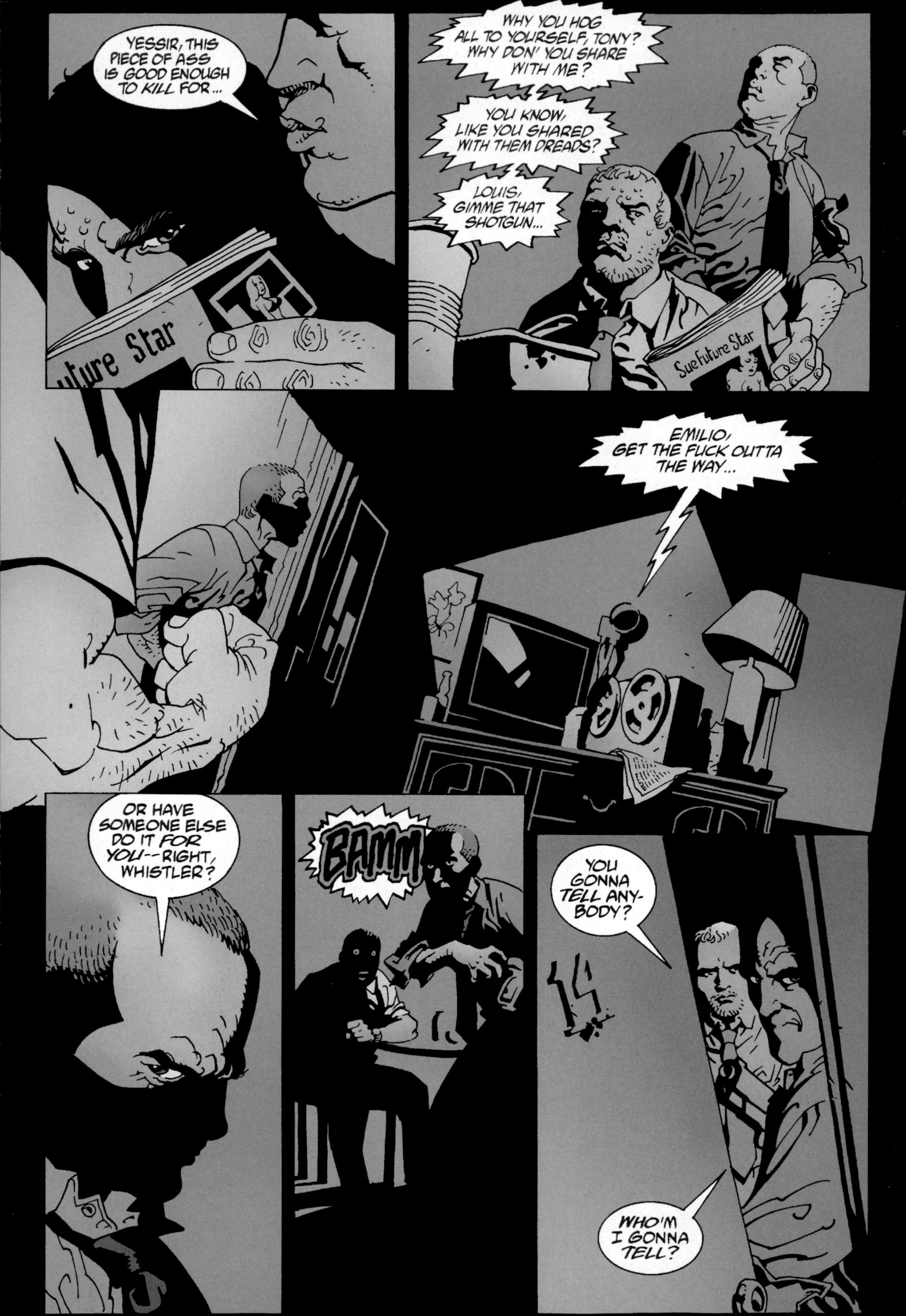
YESSIR, THIS PIECE OF ASS IS GOOD ENOUGH TO KILL FOR...
uture Star
WHY YOU HOG ALL TO YOURSELF, TONY? WHY DON' YOU SHARE WITH ME?
YOU KNOW, LIKE YOU SHARED WITH THEM DREADS?
LOUIS, GIMME THAT SHOTGUN...
Sue Future Star
EMILIO, GET THE FUCK OUTTA THE WAY...
OR HAVE SOMEONE ELSE DO IT FOR YOU--RIGHT, WHISTLER?
BAMM
YOU GONNA TELL ANY-BODY?
WHO'M I GONNA TELL?

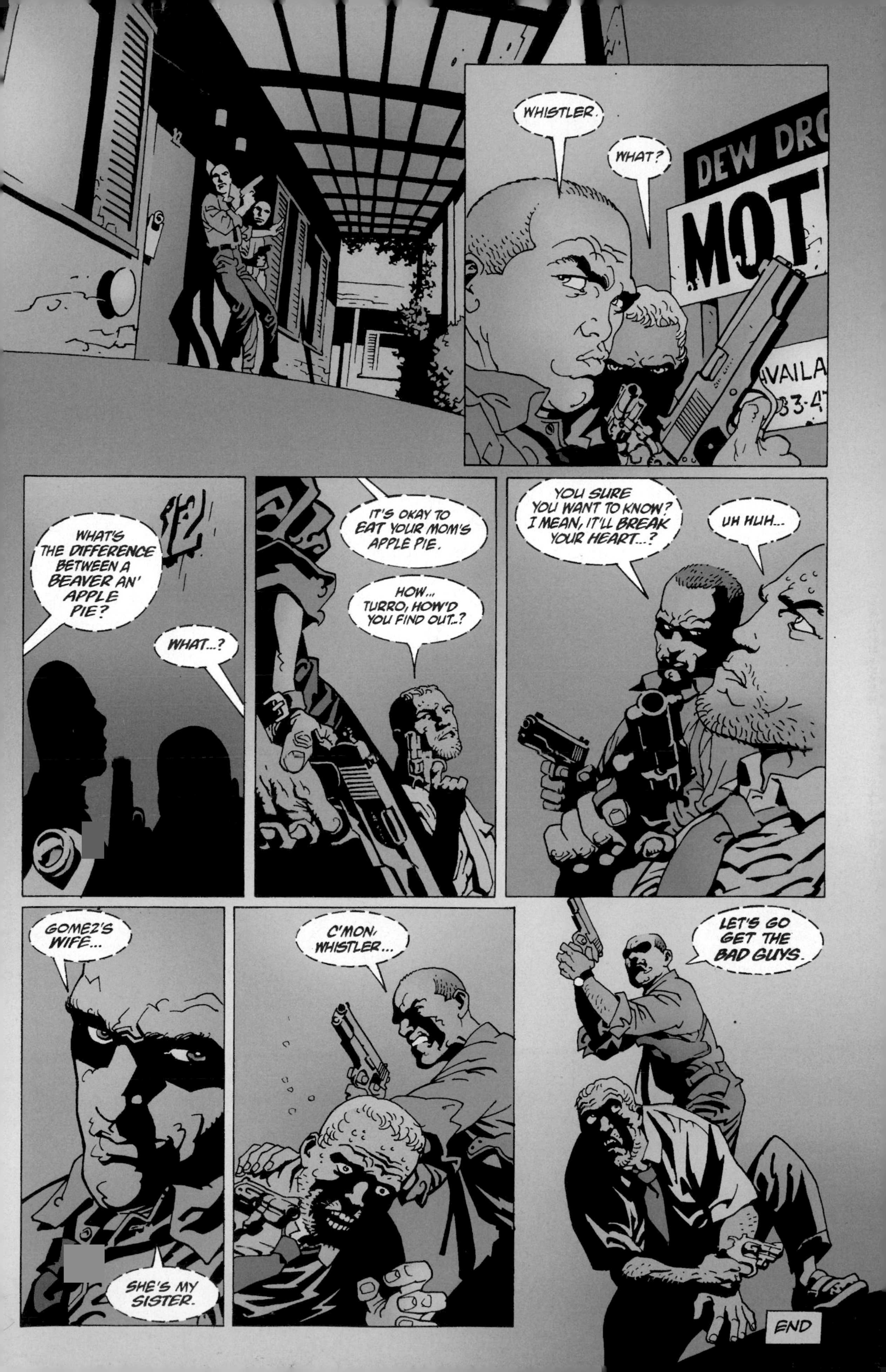
WHISTLER.
WHAT?
DEW DRO
MOT
AVAILA
WHAT'S THE DIFFERENCE BETWEEN A BEAVER AN' APPLE PIE?
WHAT...?
IT'S OKAY TO EAT YOUR MOM'S APPLE PIE.
HOW... TURRO, HOW'D YOU FIND OUT...?
YOU SURE YOU WANT TO KNOW? I MEAN, IT'LL BREAK YOUR HEART...?
UH HUH...
GOMEZ'S WIFE...
SHE'S MY SISTER.
C'MON, WHISTLER...
LET'S GO GET THE BAD GUYS.
END

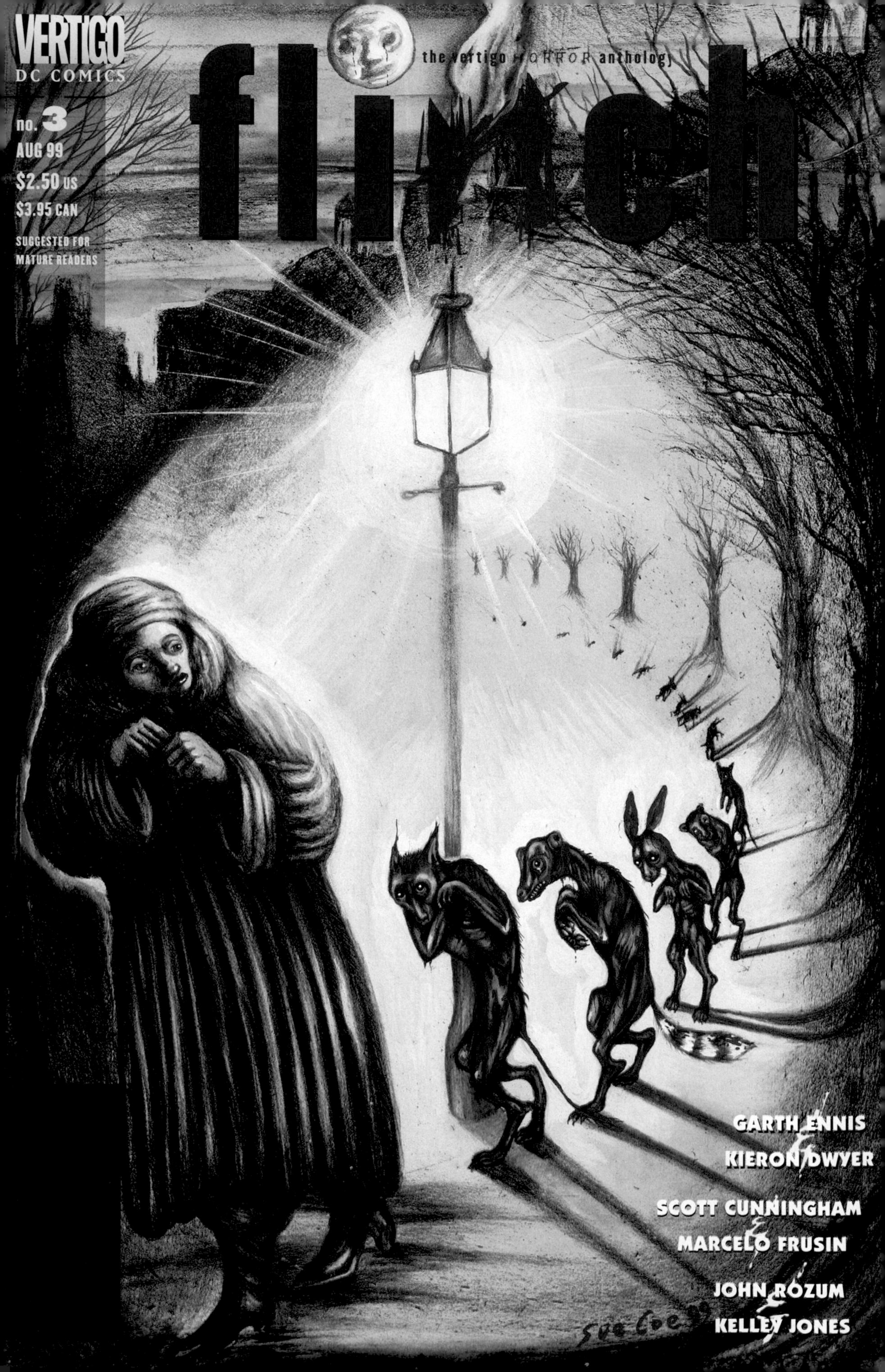
VERTIGO
DC COMICS
flinch
the vertigo HORROR anthology
no. 3
AUG 99
$2.50 US
$3.95 CAN
SUGGESTED FOR MATURE READERS
GARTH ENNIS & KIERON DWYER
SCOTT CUNNINGHAM & MARCELO FRUSIN
JOHN ROZUM & KELLEY JONES

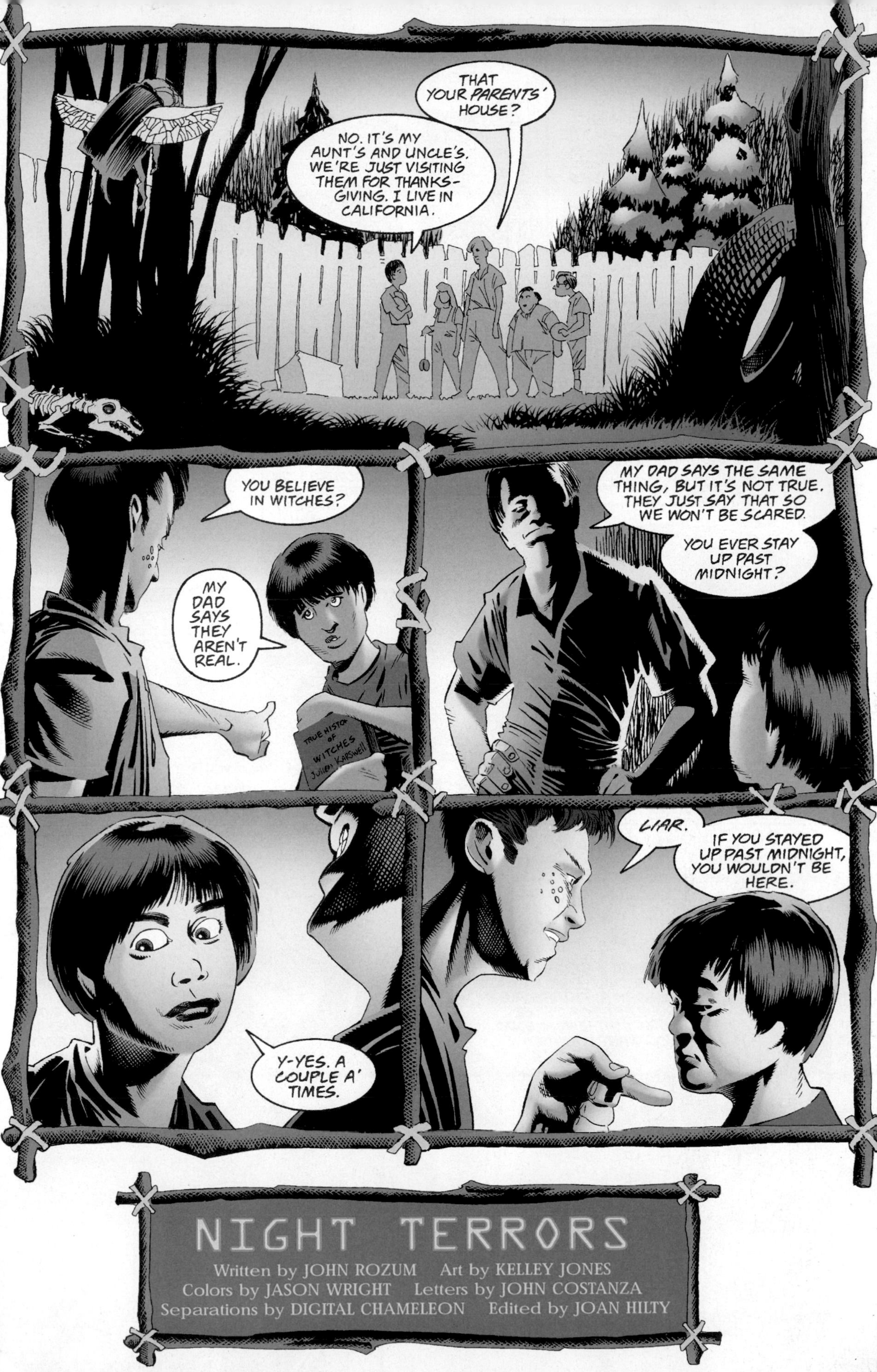
THAT YOUR PARENTS' HOUSE?
NO. IT'S MY AUNT'S AND UNCLE'S. WE'RE JUST VISITING THEM FOR THANKS-GIVING. I LIVE IN CALIFORNIA.
YOU BELIEVE IN WITCHES?
MY DAD SAYS THEY AREN'T REAL.
WITCHES
Julian Karswell
MY DAD SAYS THE SAME THING, BUT IT'S NOT TRUE. THEY JUST SAY THAT SO WE WON'T BE SCARED.
YOU EVER STAY UP PAST MIDNIGHT?
Y-YES. A COUPLE A' TIMES.
LIAR.
IF YOU STAYED UP PAST MIDNIGHT, YOU WOULDN'T BE HERE.

# NIGHT TERRORS

Written by JOHN ROZUM Art by KELLEY JONES
Colors by JASON WRIGHT Letters by JOHN COSTANZA
Separations by DIGITAL CHAMELEON Edited by JOAN HILTY

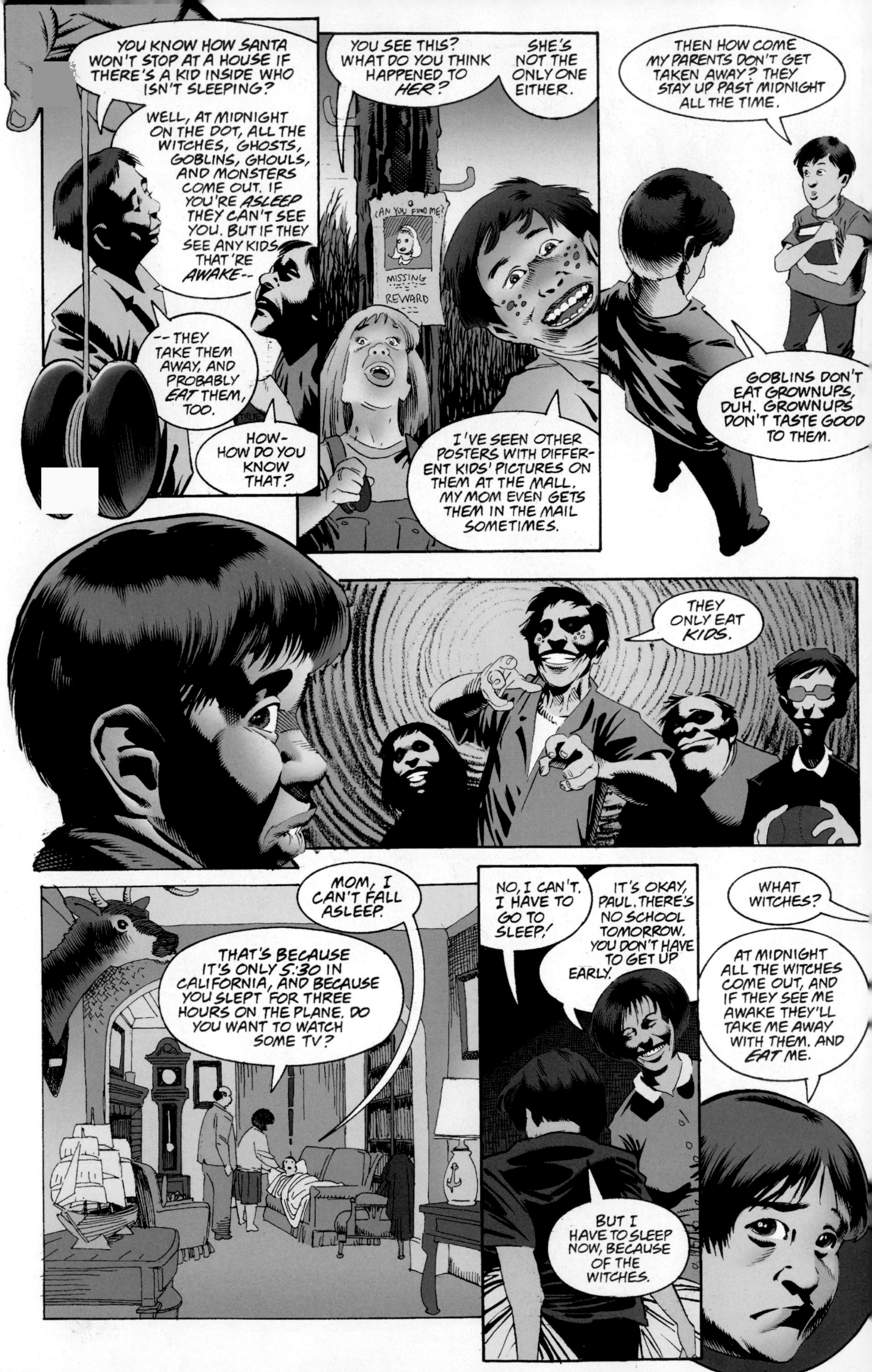
YOU KNOW HOW SANTA WON'T STOP AT A HOUSE IF THERE'S A KID INSIDE WHO ISN'T SLEEPING?
WELL, AT MIDNIGHT ON THE DOT, ALL THE WITCHES, GHOSTS, GOBLINS, GHOULS, AND MONSTERS COME OUT. IF YOU'RE ASLEEP THEY CAN'T SEE YOU. BUT IF THEY SEE ANY KIDS THAT'RE AWAKE--
--THEY TAKE THEM AWAY, AND PROBABLY EAT THEM, TOO.
HOW-HOW DO YOU KNOW THAT?
YOU SEE THIS? WHAT DO YOU THINK HAPPENED TO HER?
CAN YOU FIND ME?
MISSING
REWARD
SHE'S NOT THE ONLY ONE EITHER.
I'VE SEEN OTHER POSTERS WITH DIFFERENT KIDS' PICTURES ON THEM AT THE MALL. MY MOM EVEN GETS THEM IN THE MAIL SOMETIMES.
THEN HOW COME MY PARENTS DON'T GET TAKEN AWAY? THEY STAY UP PAST MIDNIGHT ALL THE TIME.
GOBLINS DON'T EAT GROWNUPS, DUH. GROWNUPS DON'T TASTE GOOD TO THEM.
THEY ONLY EAT KIDS.
MOM, I CAN'T FALL ASLEEP.
THAT'S BECAUSE IT'S ONLY 5:30 IN CALIFORNIA, AND BECAUSE YOU SLEPT FOR THREE HOURS ON THE PLANE. DO YOU WANT TO WATCH SOME TV?
NO, I CAN'T. I HAVE TO GO TO SLEEP!
IT'S OKAY, PAUL. THERE'S NO SCHOOL TOMORROW. YOU DON'T HAVE TO GET UP EARLY.
BUT I HAVE TO SLEEP NOW, BECAUSE OF THE WITCHES.
WHAT WITCHES?
AT MIDNIGHT ALL THE WITCHES COME OUT, AND IF THEY SEE ME AWAKE THEY'LL TAKE ME AWAY WITH THEM. AND EAT ME.

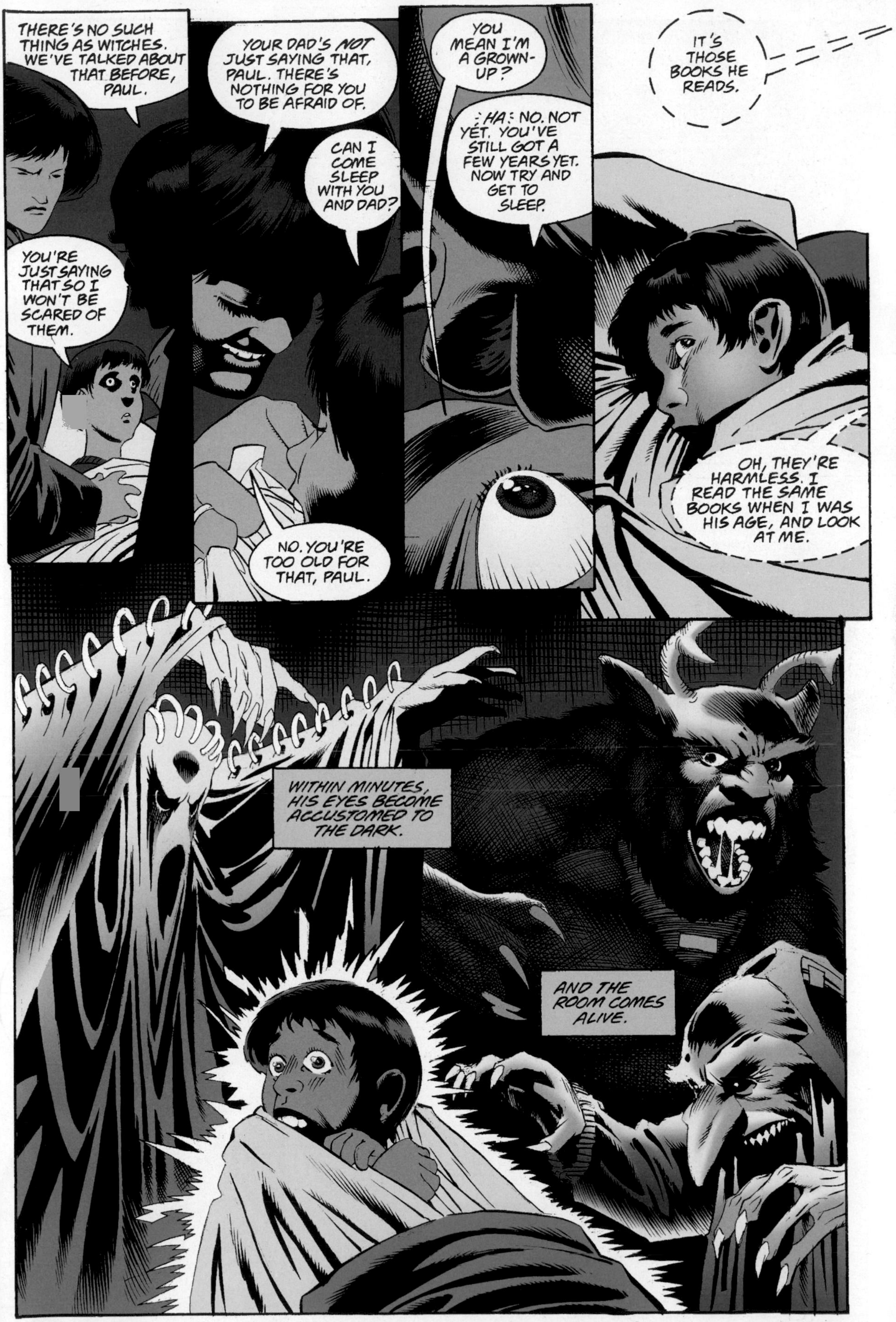
THERE'S NO SUCH THING AS WITCHES. WE'VE TALKED ABOUT THAT BEFORE, PAUL.
YOU'RE JUST SAYING THAT SO I WON'T BE SCARED OF THEM.
YOUR DAD'S NOT JUST SAYING THAT, PAUL. THERE'S NOTHING FOR YOU TO BE AFRAID OF.
CAN I COME SLEEP WITH YOU AND DAD?
NO. YOU'RE TOO OLD FOR THAT, PAUL.
YOU MEAN I'M A GROWN-UP?
:HA: NO. NOT YET. YOU'VE STILL GOT A FEW YEARS YET. NOW TRY AND GET TO SLEEP.
IT'S THOSE BOOKS HE READS.
OH, THEY'RE HARMLESS. I READ THE SAME BOOKS WHEN I WAS HIS AGE, AND LOOK AT ME.
WITHIN MINUTES, HIS EYES BECOME ACCUSTOMED TO THE DARK.
AND THE ROOM COMES ALIVE.

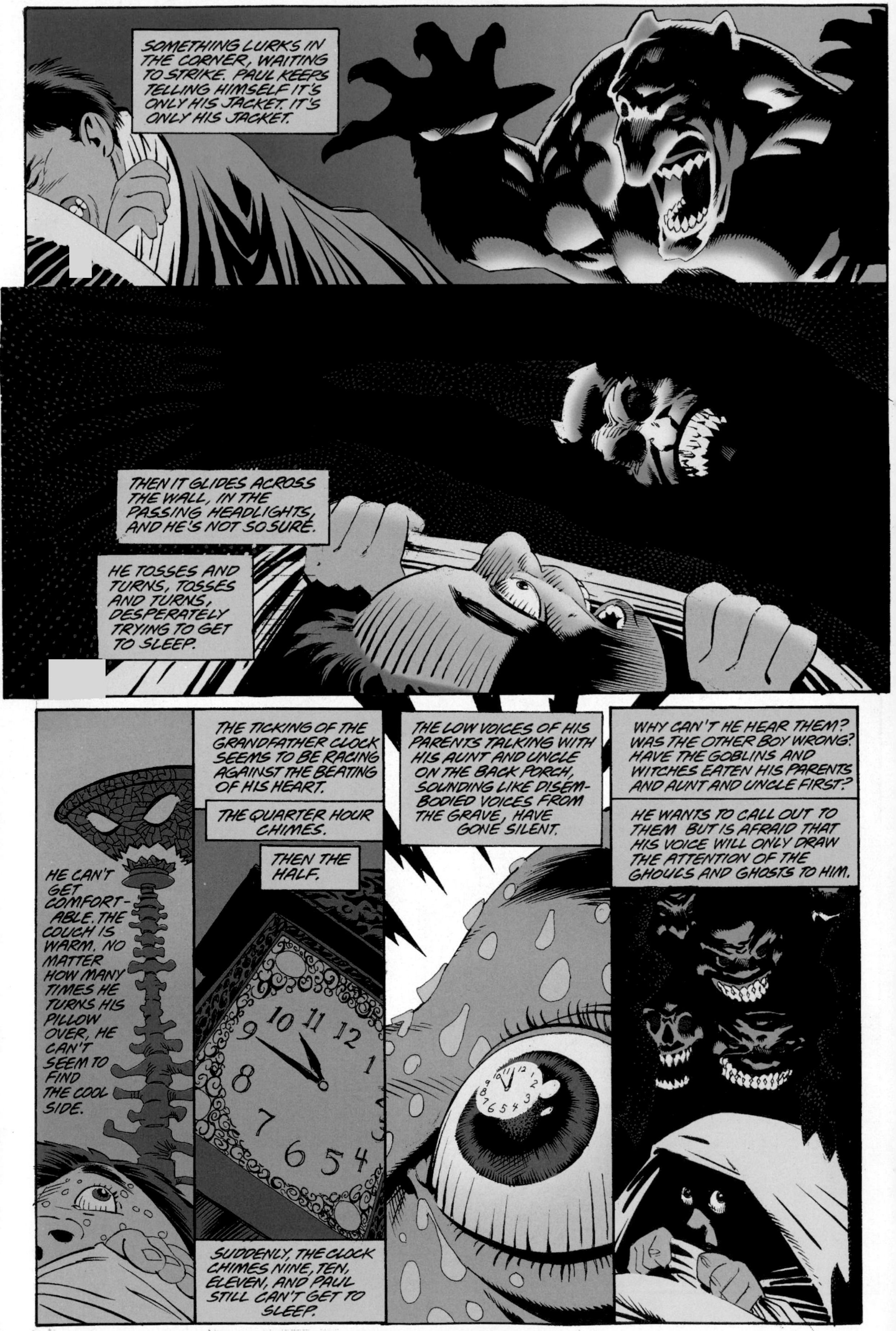
SOMETHING LURKS IN THE CORNER, WAITING TO STRIKE. PAUL KEEPS TELLING HIMSELF IT'S ONLY HIS JACKET. IT'S ONLY HIS JACKET.
THEN IT GLIDES ACROSS THE WALL, IN THE PASSING HEADLIGHTS, AND HE'S NOT SO SURE.
HE TOSSES AND TURNS, TOSSES AND TURNS, DESPERATELY TRYING TO GET TO SLEEP.
HE CAN'T GET COMFORT-ABLE. THE COUCH IS WARM. NO MATTER HOW MANY TIMES HE TURNS HIS PILLOW OVER, HE CAN'T SEEM TO FIND THE COOL SIDE.
THE TICKING OF THE GRANDFATHER CLOCK SEEMS TO BE RACING AGAINST THE BEATING OF HIS HEART.
THE QUARTER HOUR CHIMES.
THEN THE HALF.
SUDDENLY, THE CLOCK CHIMES NINE, TEN, ELEVEN, AND PAUL STILL CAN'T GET TO SLEEP.
THE LOW VOICES OF HIS PARENTS TALKING WITH HIS AUNT AND UNCLE ON THE BACK PORCH, SOUNDING LIKE DISEM-BODIED VOICES FROM THE GRAVE, HAVE GONE SILENT.
WHY CAN'T HE HEAR THEM? WAS THE OTHER BOY WRONG? HAVE THE GOBLINS AND WITCHES EATEN HIS PARENTS AND AUNT AND UNCLE FIRST?
HE WANTS TO CALL OUT TO THEM BUT IS AFRAID THAT HIS VOICE WILL ONLY DRAW THE ATTENTION OF THE GHOULS AND GHOSTS TO HIM.

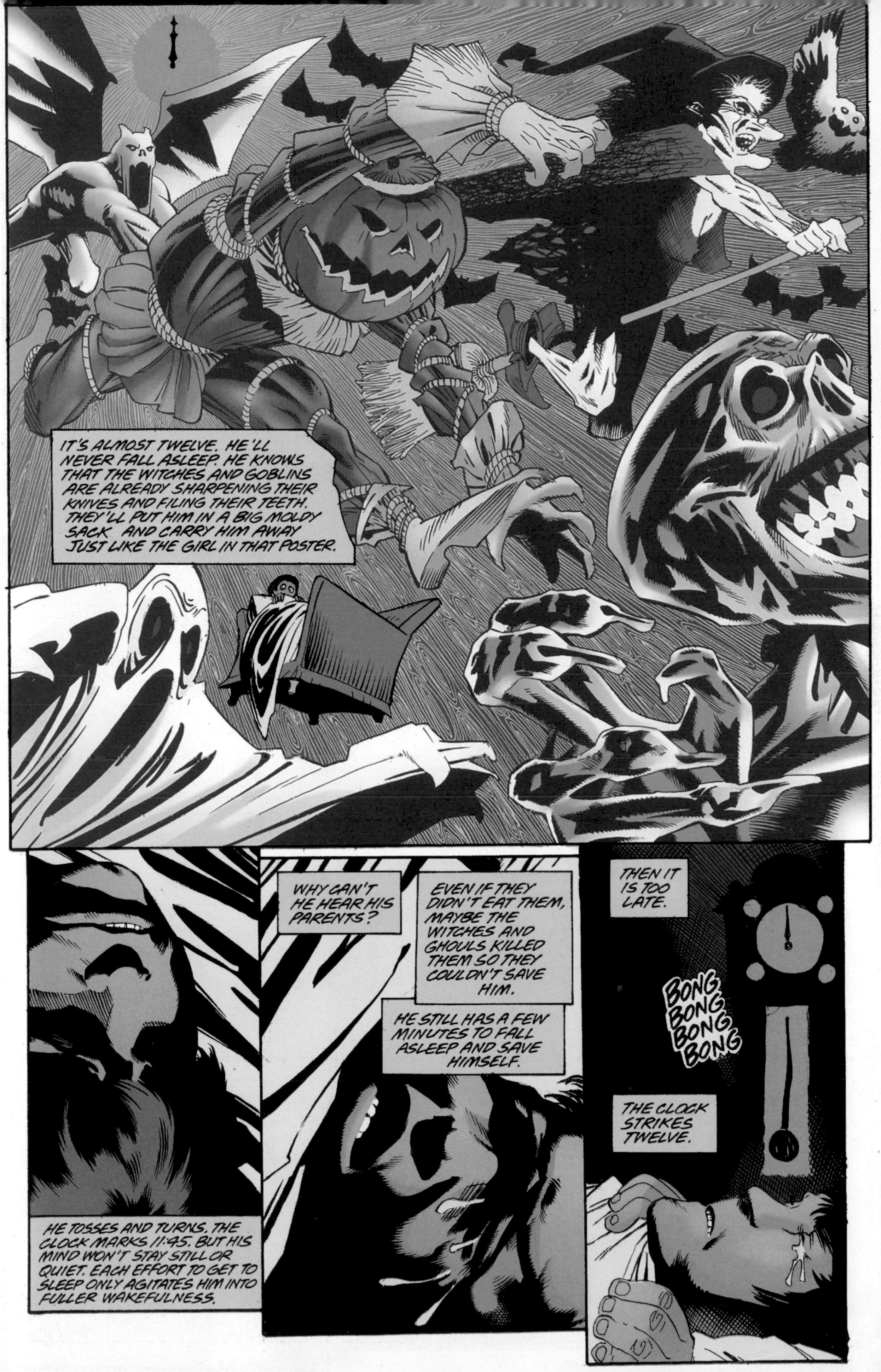
IT'S ALMOST TWELVE. HE'LL NEVER FALL ASLEEP. HE KNOWS THAT THE WITCHES AND GOBLINS ARE ALREADY SHARPENING THEIR KNIVES AND FILING THEIR TEETH. THEY'LL PUT HIM IN A BIG MOLDY SACK AND CARRY HIM AWAY JUST LIKE THE GIRL IN THAT POSTER.
HE TOSSES AND TURNS. THE CLOCK MARKS 11:45. BUT HIS MIND WON'T STAY STILL OR QUIET. EACH EFFORT TO GET TO SLEEP ONLY AGITATES HIM INTO FULLER WAKEFULNESS.
WHY CAN'T HE HEAR HIS PARENTS?
EVEN IF THEY DIDN'T EAT THEM, MAYBE THE WITCHES AND GHOULS KILLED THEM SO THEY COULDN'T SAVE HIM.
HE STILL HAS A FEW MINUTES TO FALL ASLEEP AND SAVE HIMSELF.
THEN IT IS TOO LATE.
BONG BONG BONG BONG
THE CLOCK STRIKES TWELVE.

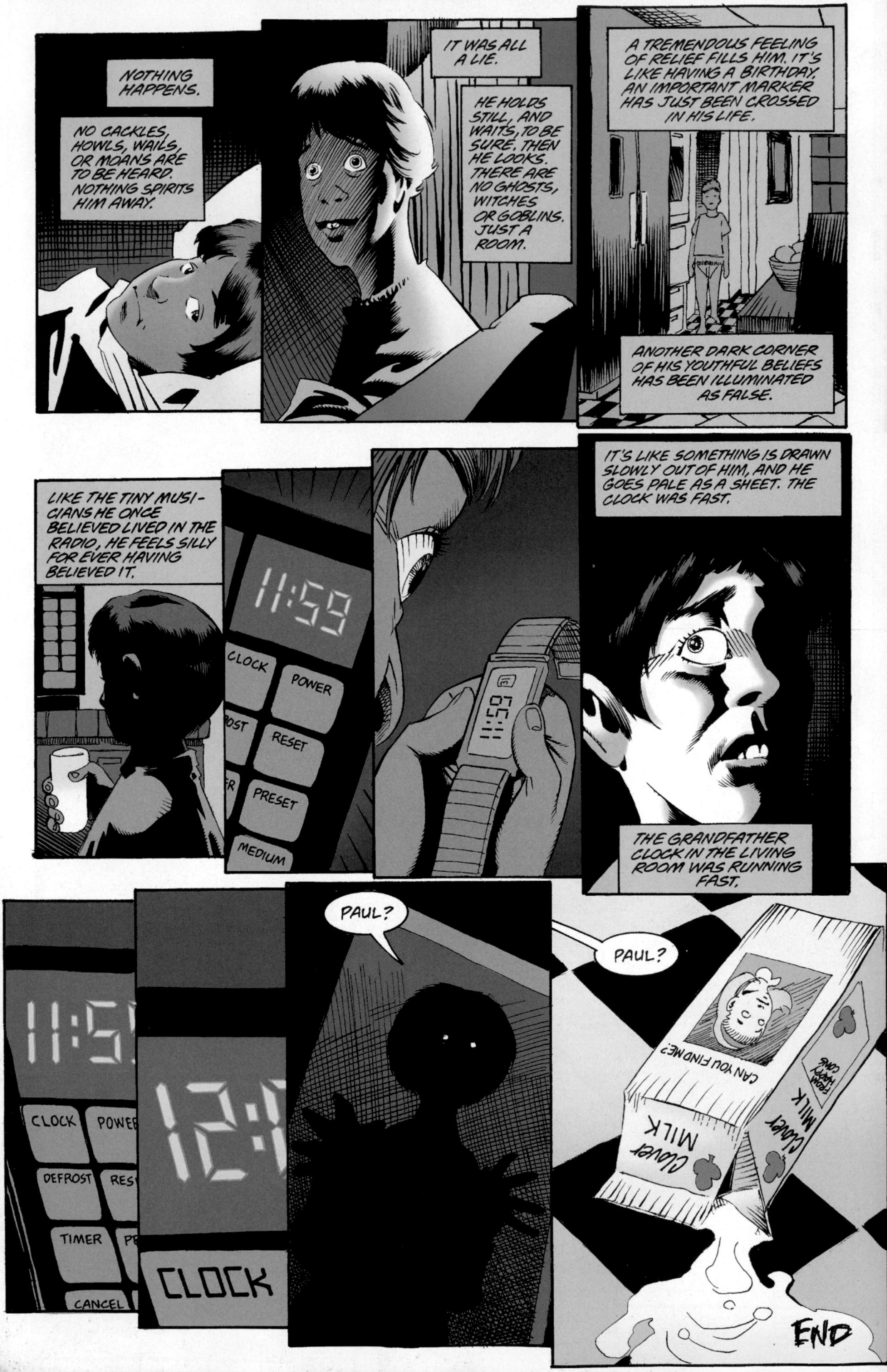
NOTHING HAPPENS.
NO CACKLES, HOWLS, WAILS, OR MOANS ARE TO BE HEARD. NOTHING SPIRITS HIM AWAY.
IT WAS ALL A LIE.
HE HOLDS STILL, AND WAITS, TO BE SURE. THEN HE LOOKS. THERE ARE NO GHOSTS, WITCHES OR GOBLINS. JUST A ROOM.
A TREMENDOUS FEELING OF RELIEF FILLS HIM. IT'S LIKE HAVING A BIRTHDAY. AN IMPORTANT MARKER HAS JUST BEEN CROSSED IN HIS LIFE.
ANOTHER DARK CORNER OF HIS YOUTHFUL BELIEFS HAS BEEN ILLUMINATED AS FALSE.
LIKE THE TINY MUSI-CIANS HE ONCE BELIEVED LIVED IN THE RADIO, HE FEELS SILLY FOR EVER HAVING BELIEVED IT.
11:59
CLOCK
POWER
RESET
PRESET
MEDIUM
11:59
IT'S LIKE SOMETHING IS DRAWN SLOWLY OUT OF HIM, AND HE GOES PALE AS A SHEET. THE CLOCK WAS FAST.
THE GRANDFATHER CLOCK IN THE LIVING ROOM WAS RUNNING FAST.
CLOCK
DEFROST
TIMER
CANCEL
CLOCK
PAUL?
PAUL?
CAN YOU FIND ME?
Clover MILK
Clover MILK
END

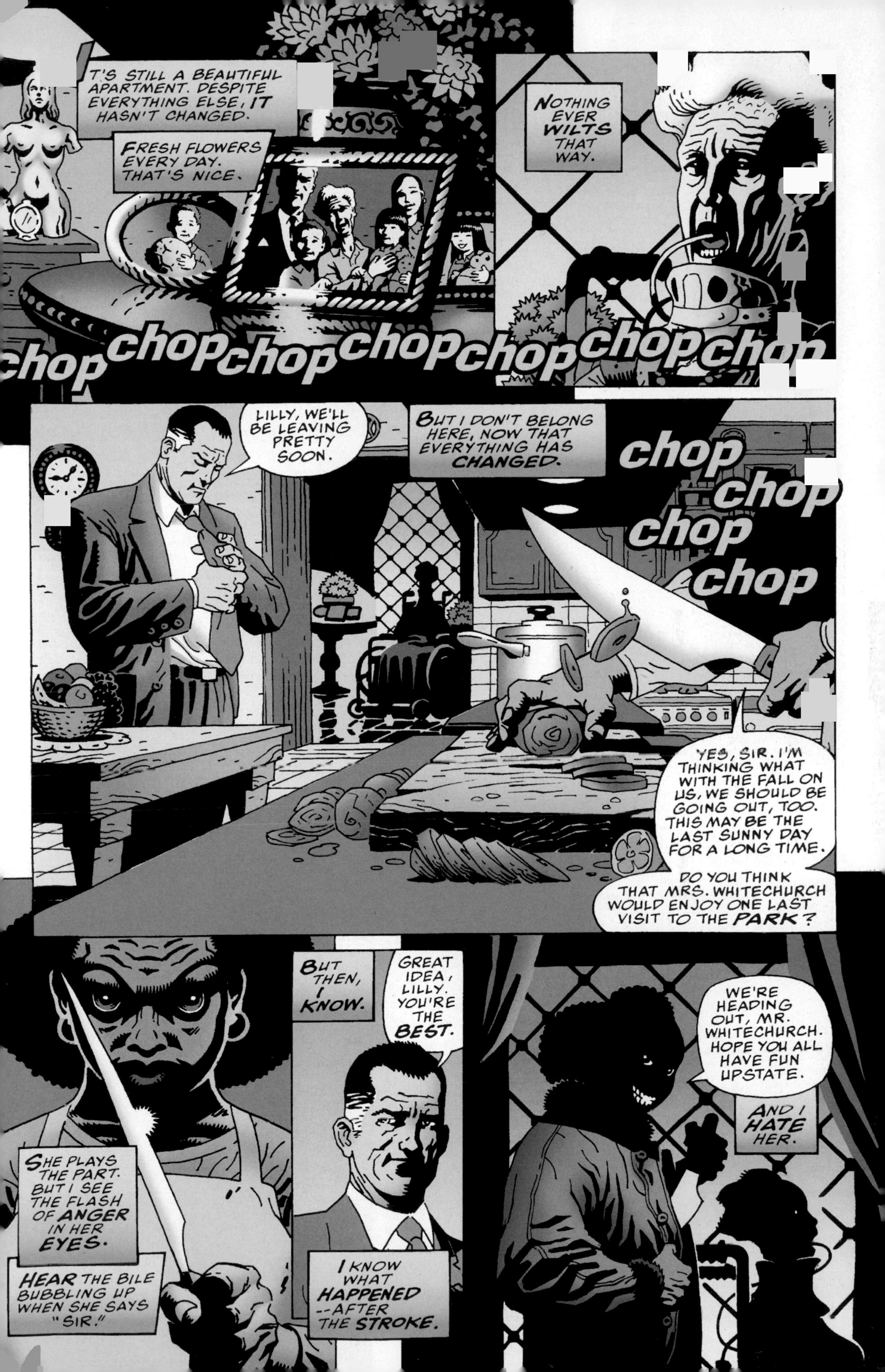
T'S STILL A BEAUTIFUL APARTMENT. DESPITE EVERYTHING ELSE, IT HASN'T CHANGED.
FRESH FLOWERS EVERY DAY. THAT'S NICE.
NOTHING EVER WILTS THAT WAY.
chop chop chop chop chop chop chop
LILLY, WE'LL BE LEAVING PRETTY SOON.
BUT I DON'T BELONG HERE, NOW THAT EVERYTHING HAS CHANGED.
chop chop chop chop
YES, SIR. I'M THINKING WHAT WITH THE FALL ON US, WE SHOULD BE GOING OUT, TOO. THIS MAY BE THE LAST SUNNY DAY FOR A LONG TIME.
DO YOU THINK THAT MRS. WHITECHURCH WOULD ENJOY ONE LAST VISIT TO THE PARK?
SHE PLAYS THE PART. BUT I SEE THE FLASH OF ANGER IN HER EYES.
HEAR THE BILE BUBBLING UP WHEN SHE SAYS "SIR."
BUT THEN, I KNOW.
GREAT IDEA, LILLY. YOU'RE THE BEST.
I KNOW WHAT HAPPENED --AFTER THE STROKE.
WE'RE HEADING OUT, MR. WHITECHURCH. HOPE YOU ALL HAVE FUN UPSTATE.
AND I HATE HER.

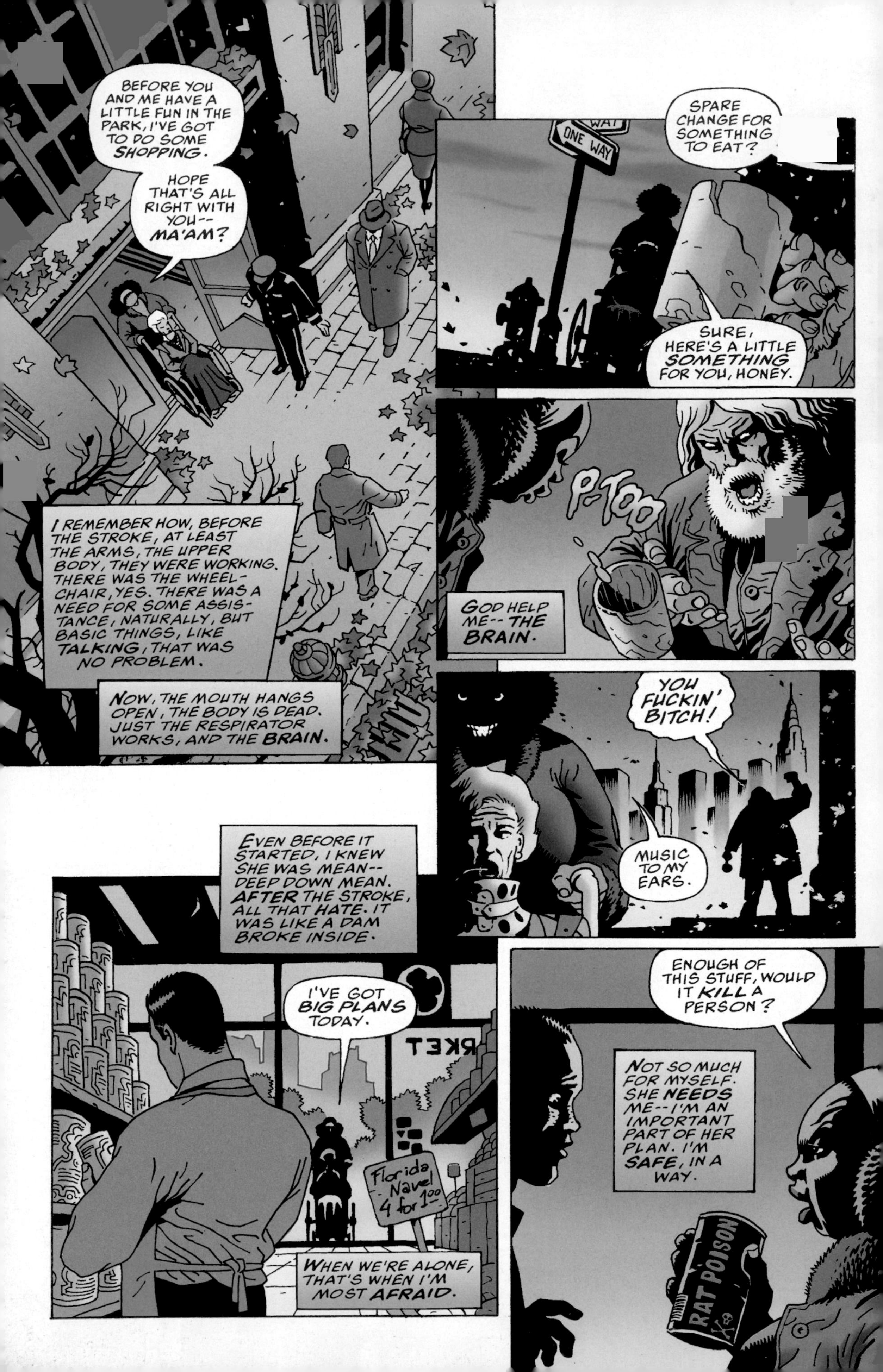
BEFORE YOU AND ME HAVE A LITTLE FUN IN THE PARK, I'VE GOT TO DO SOME SHOPPING.
HOPE THAT'S ALL RIGHT WITH YOU-- MA'AM?
I REMEMBER HOW, BEFORE THE STROKE, AT LEAST THE ARMS, THE UPPER BODY, THEY WERE WORKING. THERE WAS THE WHEEL-CHAIR, YES. THERE WAS A NEED FOR SOME ASSIS-TANCE, NATURALLY, BUT BASIC THINGS, LIKE TALKING, THAT WAS NO PROBLEM.
NOW, THE MOUTH HANGS OPEN, THE BODY IS DEAD. JUST THE RESPIRATOR WORKS, AND THE BRAIN.
ONE WAY
SPARE CHANGE FOR SOMETHING TO EAT?
SURE, HERE'S A LITTLE SOMETHING FOR YOU, HONEY.
P-TOO
GOD HELP ME-- THE BRAIN.
YOU FUCKIN' BITCH!
MUSIC TO MY EARS.
EVEN BEFORE IT STARTED, I KNEW SHE WAS MEAN-- DEEP DOWN MEAN. AFTER THE STROKE, ALL THAT HATE. IT WAS LIKE A DAM BROKE INSIDE.
I'VE GOT BIG PLANS TODAY.
RKET
Florida Navel 4 for 1.00
WHEN WE'RE ALONE, THAT'S WHEN I'M MOST AFRAID.
ENOUGH OF THIS STUFF, WOULD IT KILL A PERSON?
NOT SO MUCH FOR MYSELF. SHE NEEDS ME-- I'M AN IMPORTANT PART OF HER PLAN. I'M SAFE, IN A WAY.
RAT POISON

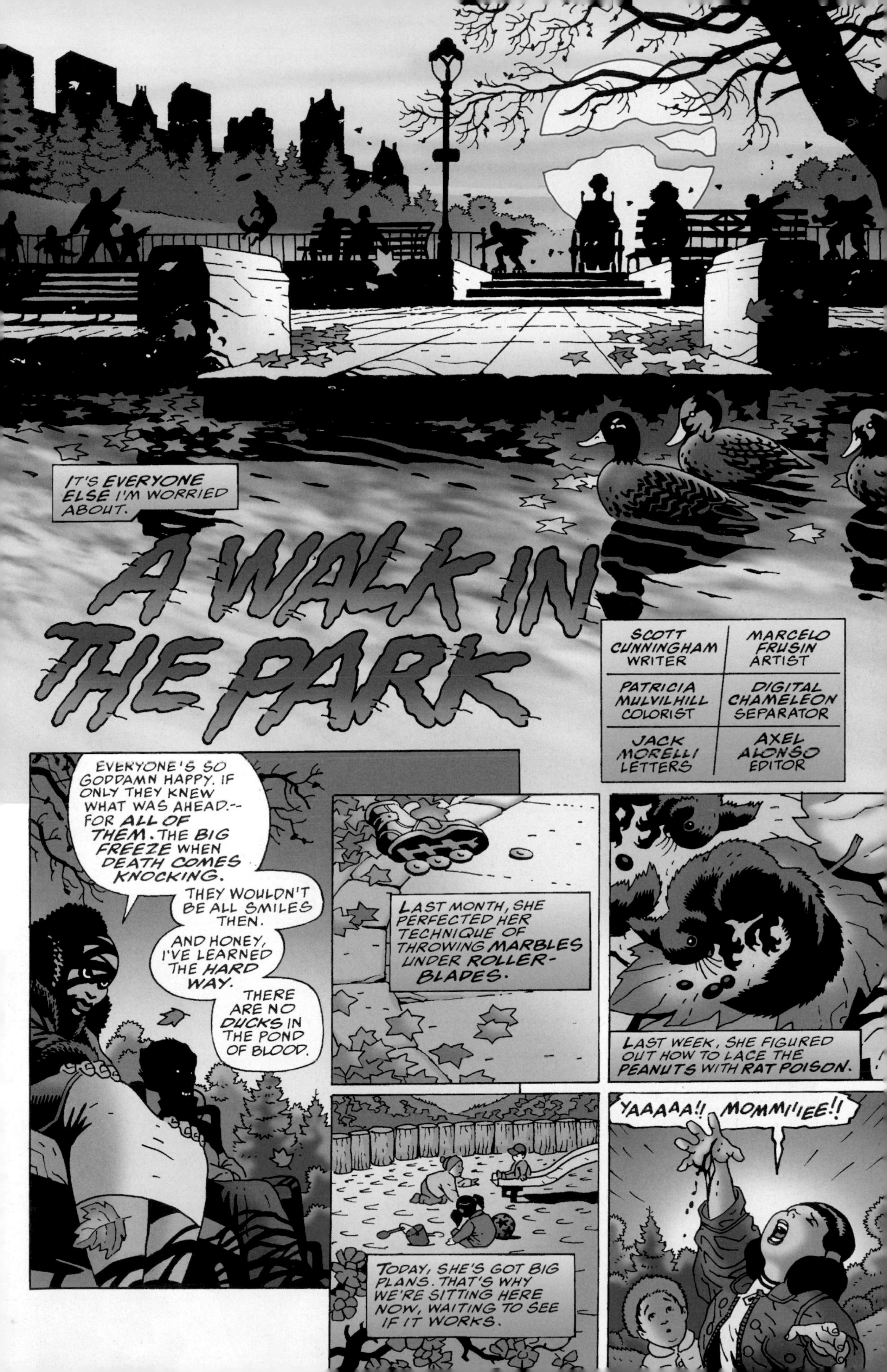

IT'S EVERYONE ELSE I'M WORRIED ABOUT.
A WALK IN THE PARK
SCOTT CUNNINGHAM WRITER
MARCELO FRUSIN ARTIST
PATRICIA MULVILHILL COLORIST
DIGITAL CHAMELEON SEPARATOR
JACK MORELLI LETTERS
AXEL ALONSO EDITOR
EVERYONE'S SO GODDAMN HAPPY. IF ONLY THEY KNEW WHAT WAS AHEAD.-- FOR ALL OF THEM. THE BIG FREEZE WHEN DEATH COMES KNOCKING.
THEY WOULDN'T BE ALL SMILES THEN.
AND HONEY, I'VE LEARNED THE HARD WAY.
THERE ARE NO DUCKS IN THE POND OF BLOOD.
LAST MONTH, SHE PERFECTED HER TECHNIQUE OF THROWING MARBLES UNDER ROLLER-BLADES.
LAST WEEK, SHE FIGURED OUT HOW TO LACE THE PEANUTS WITH RAT POISON.
TODAY, SHE'S GOT BIG PLANS. THAT'S WHY WE'RE SITTING HERE NOW, WAITING TO SEE IF IT WORKS.
YAAAAA!! MOMMIIEE!!

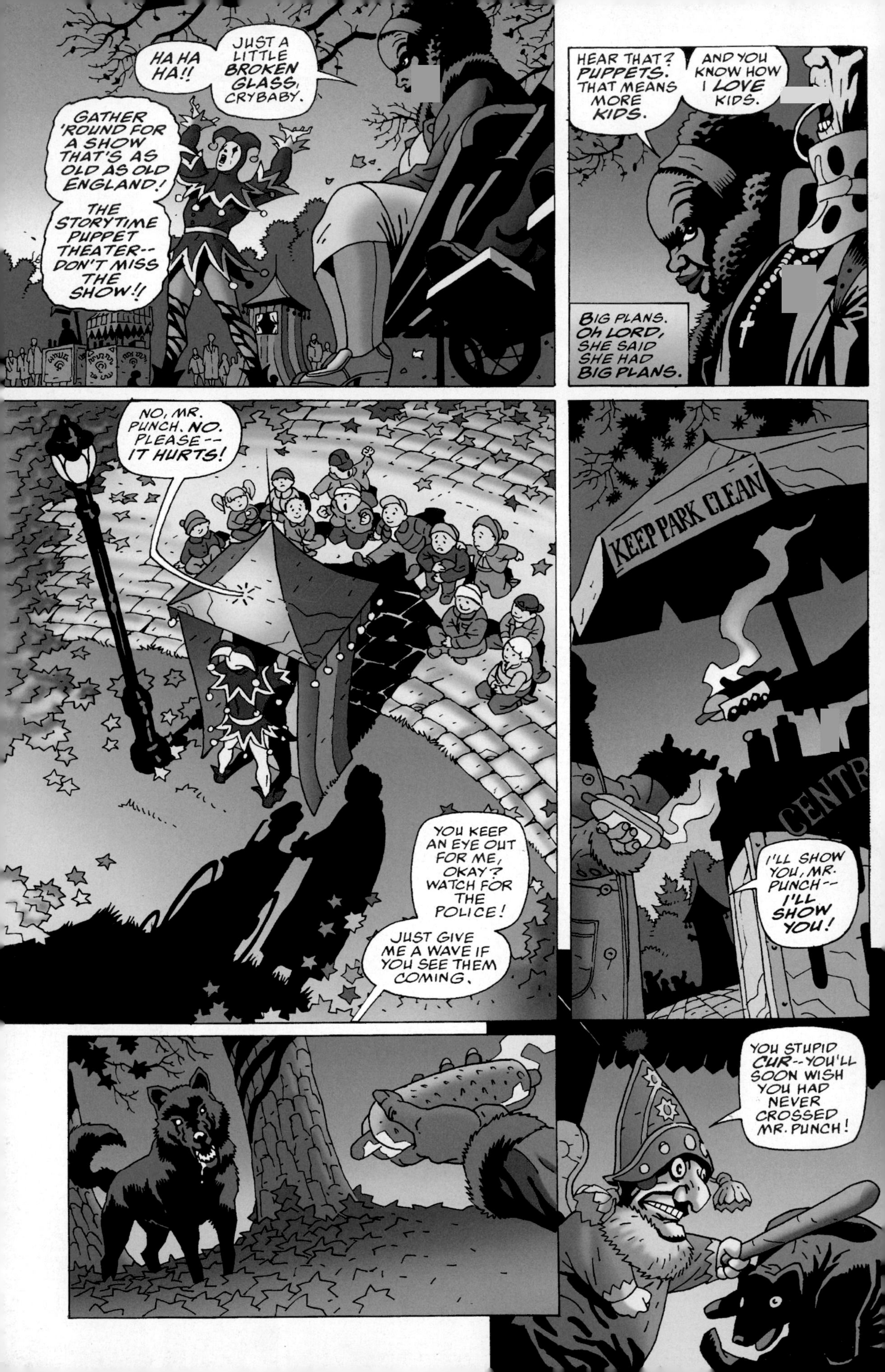
HA HA HA!!
JUST A LITTLE BROKEN GLASS, CRYBABY.
GATHER 'ROUND FOR A SHOW THAT'S AS OLD AS OLD ENGLAND!
THE STORYTIME PUPPET THEATER-- DON'T MISS THE SHOW!!
HEAR THAT? PUPPETS. THAT MEANS MORE KIDS.
AND YOU KNOW HOW I LOVE KIDS.
BIG PLANS. Oh LORD, SHE SAID SHE HAD BIG PLANS.
NO, MR. PUNCH. NO. PLEASE-- IT HURTS!
YOU KEEP AN EYE OUT FOR ME, OKAY? WATCH FOR THE POLICE!
JUST GIVE ME A WAVE IF YOU SEE THEM COMING.
KEEP PARK CLEAN
CENTR
I'LL SHOW YOU, MR. PUNCH-- I'LL SHOW YOU!
YOU STUPID CUR--YOU'LL SOON WISH YOU HAD NEVER CROSSED MR. PUNCH!

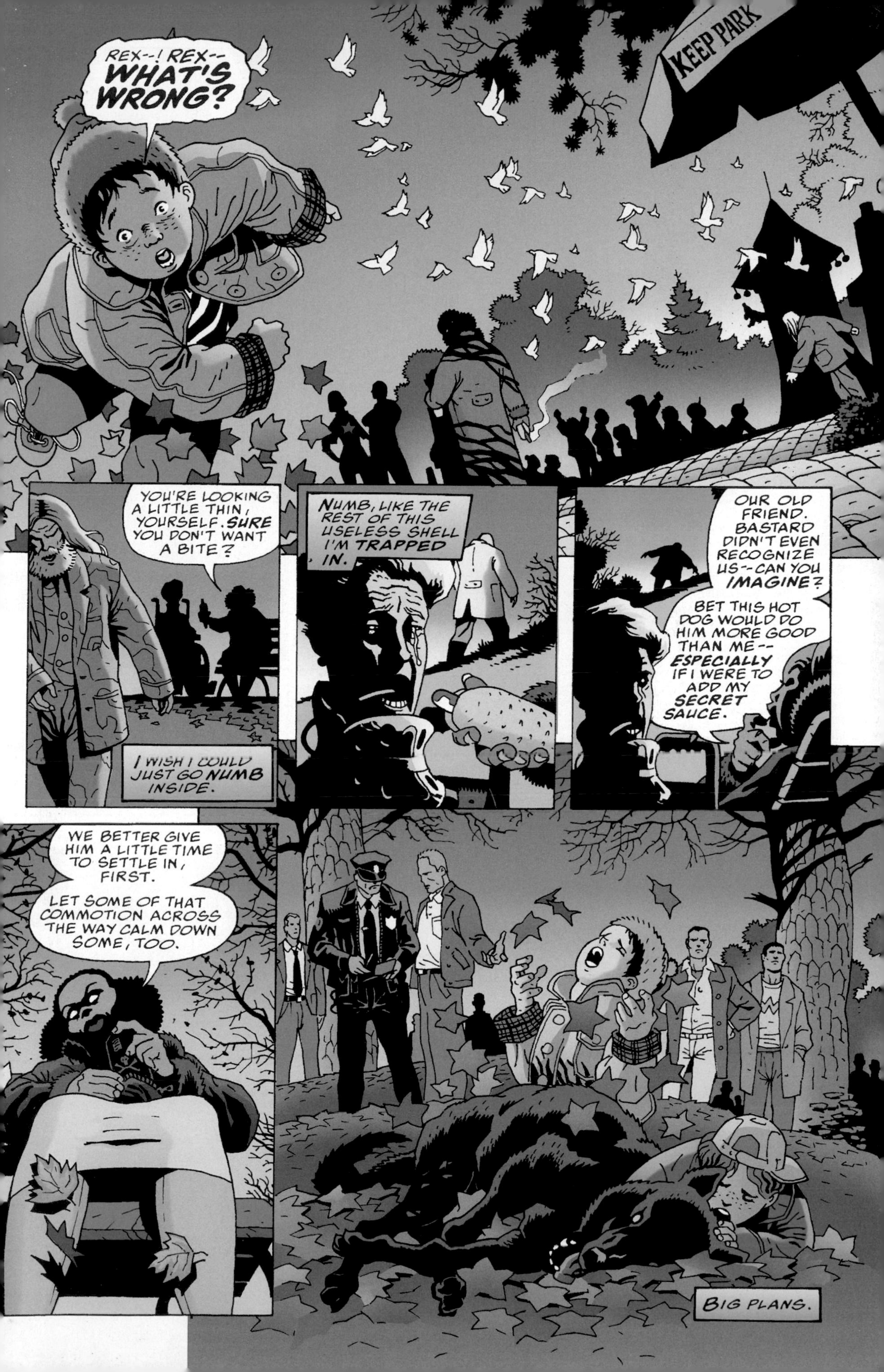
REX--! REX-- WHAT'S WRONG?
KEEP PARK
YOU'RE LOOKING A LITTLE THIN, YOURSELF. SURE YOU DON'T WANT A BITE?
I WISH I COULD JUST GO NUMB INSIDE.
NUMB, LIKE THE REST OF THIS USELESS SHELL I'M TRAPPED IN.
OUR OLD FRIEND. BASTARD DIDN'T EVEN RECOGNIZE US--CAN YOU IMAGINE?
BET THIS HOT DOG WOULD DO HIM MORE GOOD THAN ME--ESPECIALLY IF I WERE TO ADD MY SECRET SAUCE.
WE BETTER GIVE HIM A LITTLE TIME TO SETTLE IN, FIRST.
LET SOME OF THAT COMMOTION ACROSS THE WAY CALM DOWN SOME, TOO.
BIG PLANS.

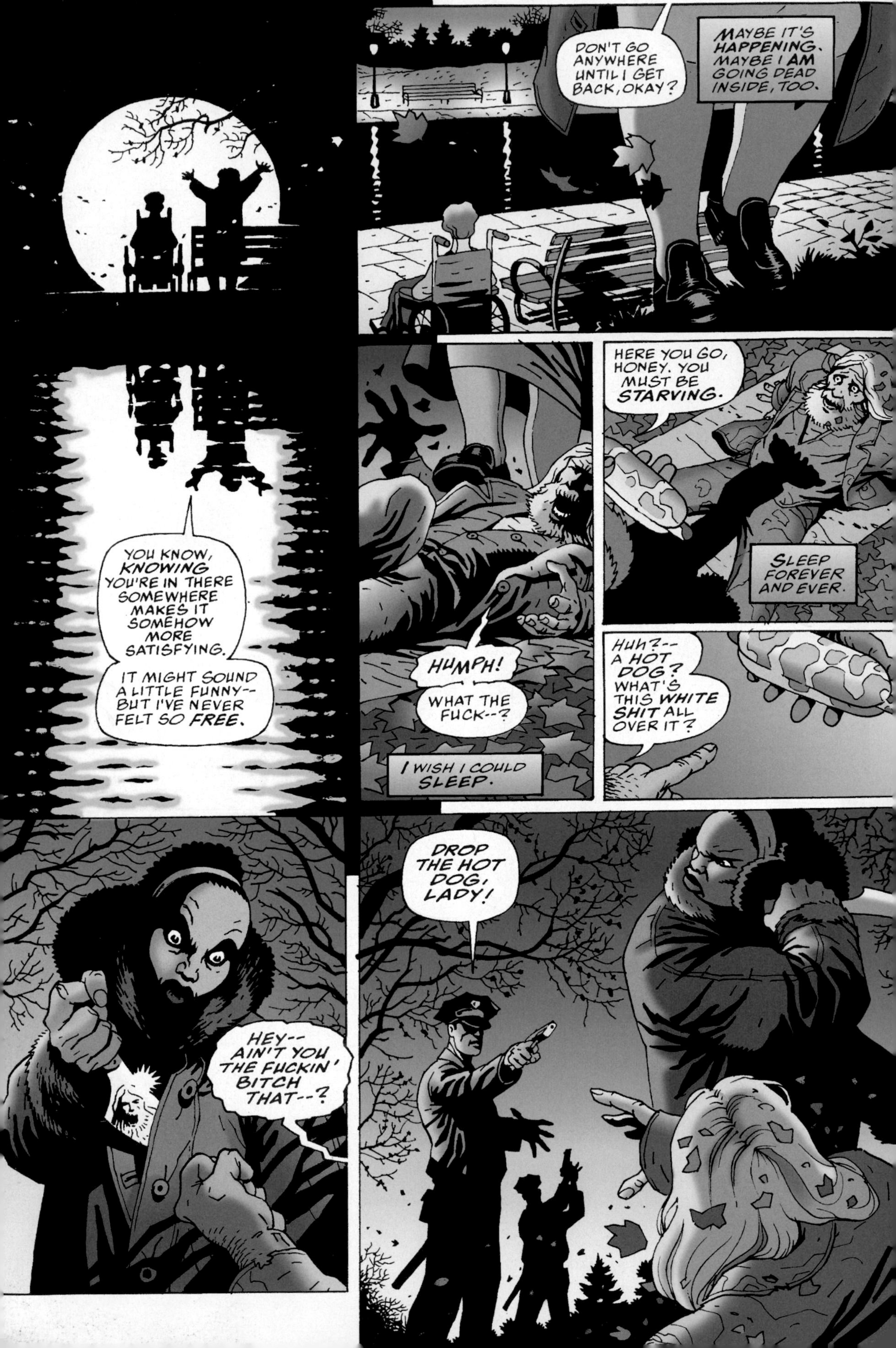
DON'T GO ANYWHERE UNTIL I GET BACK, OKAY?
MAYBE IT'S HAPPENING. MAYBE I AM GOING DEAD INSIDE, TOO.
YOU KNOW, KNOWING YOU'RE IN THERE SOMEWHERE MAKES IT SOMEHOW MORE SATISFYING.
IT MIGHT SOUND A LITTLE FUNNY-- BUT I'VE NEVER FELT SO FREE.
HUMPH!
WHAT THE FUCK--?
I WISH I COULD SLEEP.
HERE YOU GO, HONEY. YOU MUST BE STARVING.
SLEEP FOREVER AND EVER.
HUH?-- A HOT DOG? WHAT'S THIS WHITE SHIT ALL OVER IT?
HEY-- AIN'T YOU THE FUCKIN' BITCH THAT--?
DROP THE HOT DOG, LADY!

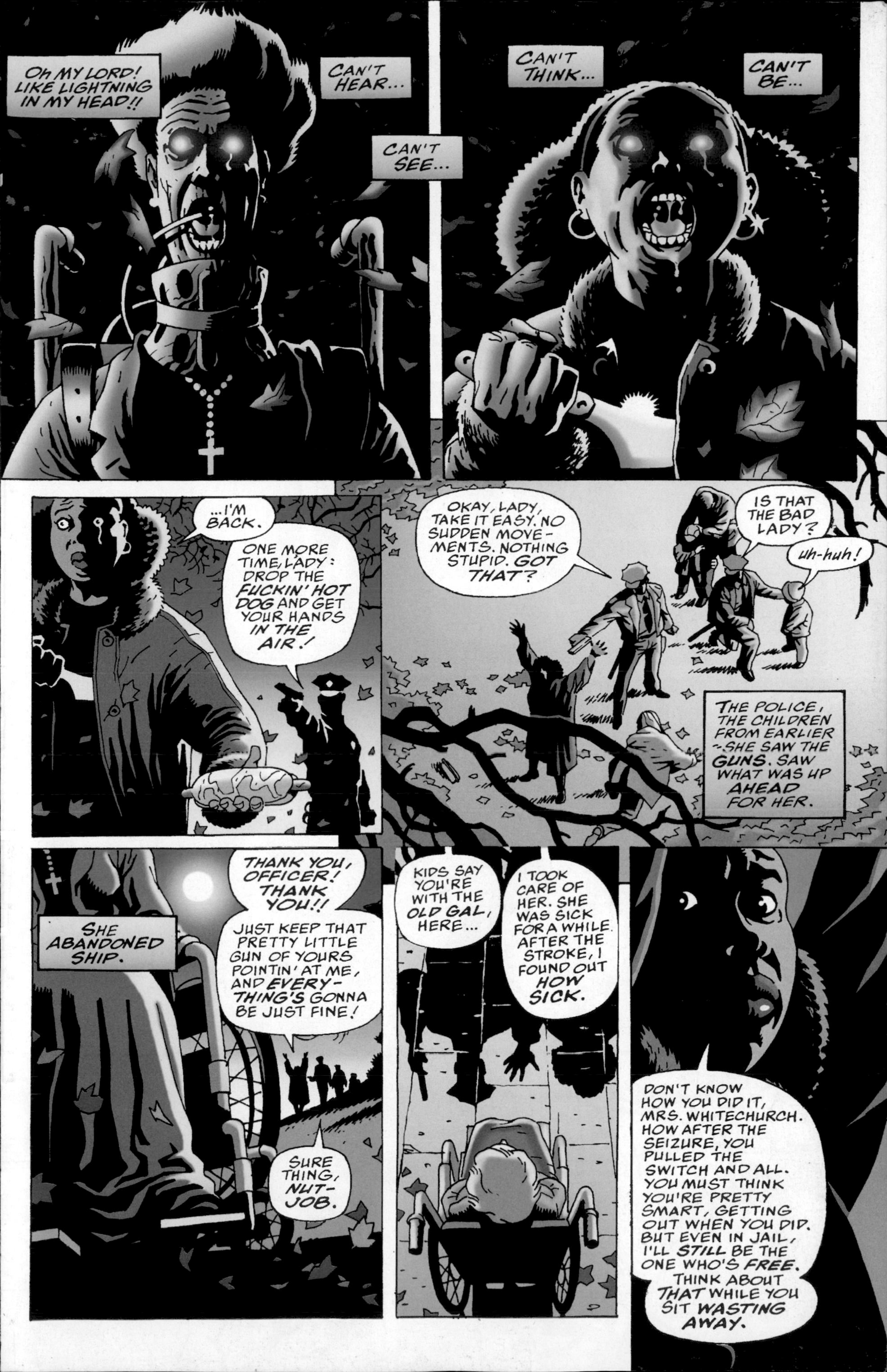
Oh MY LORD! LIKE LIGHTNING IN MY HEAD!!
CAN'T HEAR...
CAN'T SEE...
CAN'T THINK...
CAN'T BE...
...I'M BACK.
ONE MORE TIME, LADY: DROP THE FUCKIN' HOT DOG AND GET YOUR HANDS IN THE AIR!
OKAY, LADY, TAKE IT EASY. NO SUDDEN MOVE-MENTS. NOTHING STUPID. GOT THAT?
IS THAT THE BAD LADY?
uh-huh!
THE POLICE, THE CHILDREN FROM EARLIER -- SHE SAW THE GUNS. SAW WHAT WAS UP AHEAD FOR HER.
SHE ABANDONED SHIP.
THANK YOU, OFFICER! THANK YOU!!
JUST KEEP THAT PRETTY LITTLE GUN OF YOURS POINTIN' AT ME, AND EVERY-THING'S GONNA BE JUST FINE!
SURE THING, NUT-JOB.
KIDS SAY YOU'RE WITH THE OLD GAL, HERE...
I TOOK CARE OF HER. SHE WAS SICK FOR A WHILE. AFTER THE STROKE, I FOUND OUT HOW SICK.
DON'T KNOW HOW YOU DID IT, MRS. WHITECHURCH. HOW AFTER THE SEIZURE, YOU PULLED THE SWITCH AND ALL. YOU MUST THINK YOU'RE PRETTY SMART, GETTING OUT WHEN YOU DID. BUT EVEN IN JAIL, I'LL STILL BE THE ONE WHO'S FREE.
THINK ABOUT THAT WHILE YOU SIT WASTING AWAY.

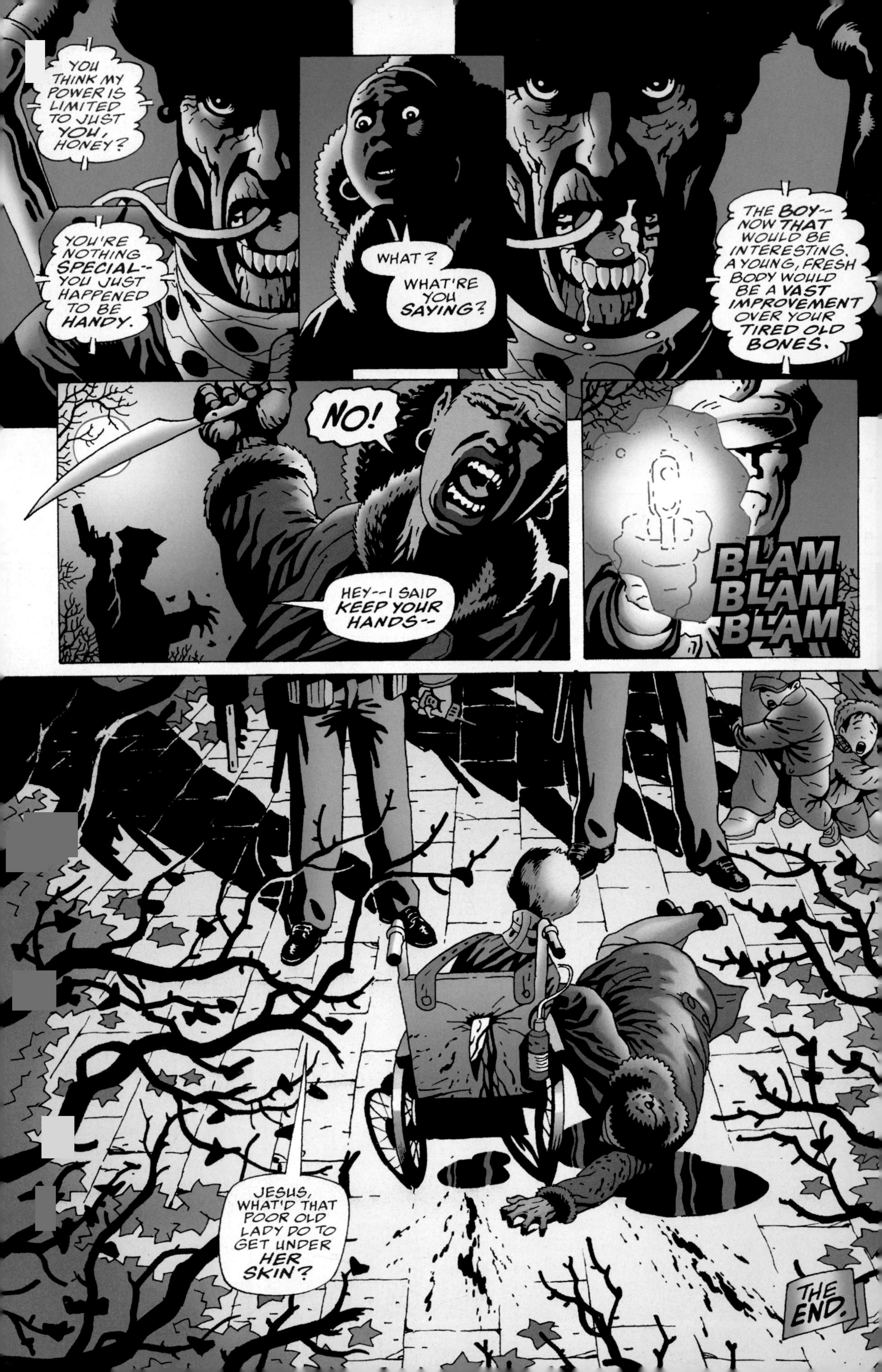
YOU THINK MY POWER IS LIMITED TO JUST YOU, HONEY?
YOU'RE NOTHING SPECIAL-- YOU JUST HAPPENED TO BE HANDY.
WHAT?
WHAT'RE YOU SAYING?
THE BOY-- NOW THAT WOULD BE INTERESTING. A YOUNG, FRESH BODY WOULD BE A VAST IMPROVEMENT OVER YOUR TIRED OLD BONES.
NO!
HEY--I SAID KEEP YOUR HANDS--
BLAM
BLAM
BLAM
JESUS, WHAT'D THAT POOR OLD LADY DO TO GET UNDER HER SKIN?
THE END.

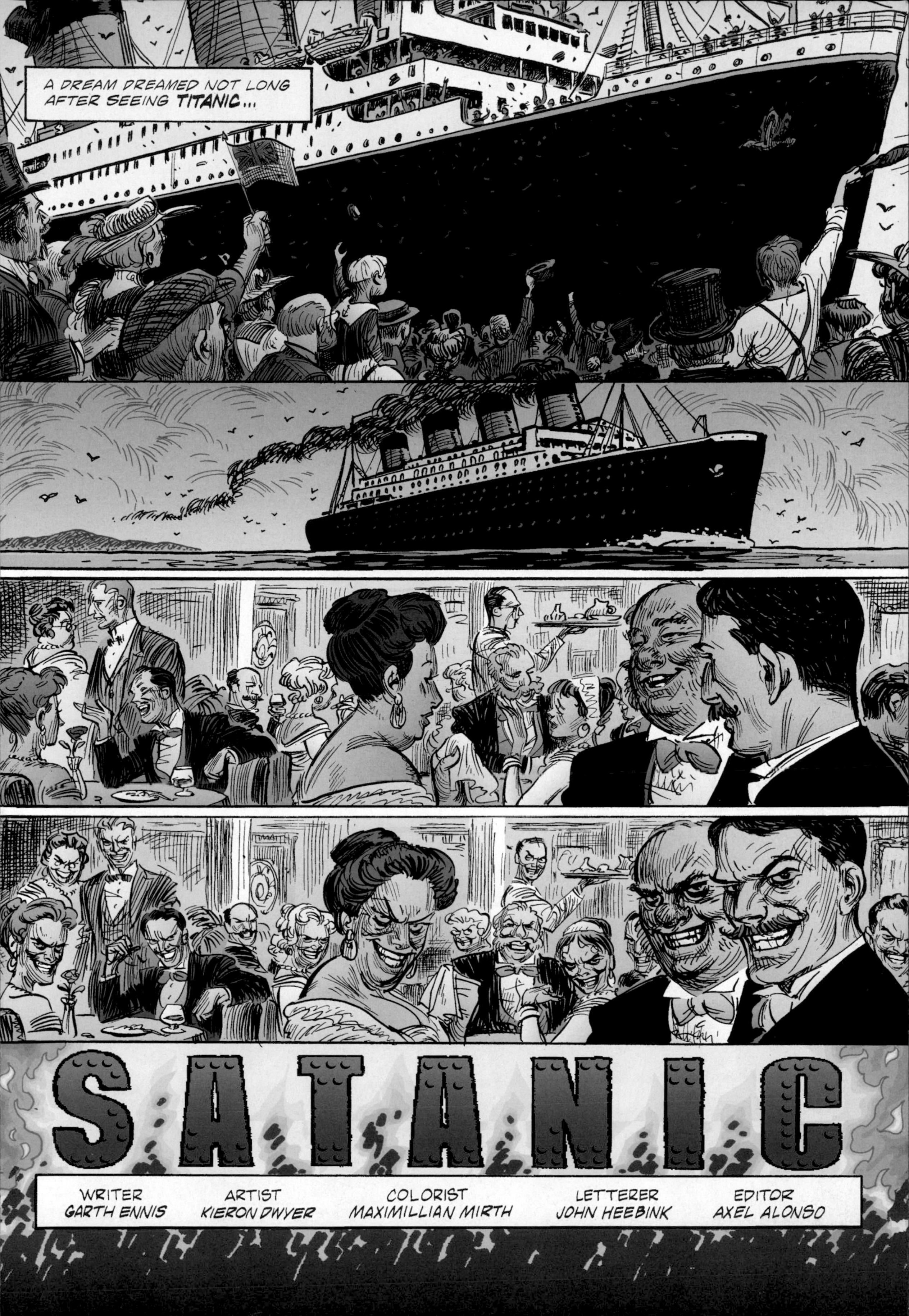
A DREAM DREAMED NOT LONG AFTER SEEING TITANIC...
SATANIC
WRITER GARTH ENNIS
ARTIST KIERON DWYER
COLORIST MAXIMILLIAN MIRTH
LETTERER JOHN HEEBINK
EDITOR AXEL ALONSO

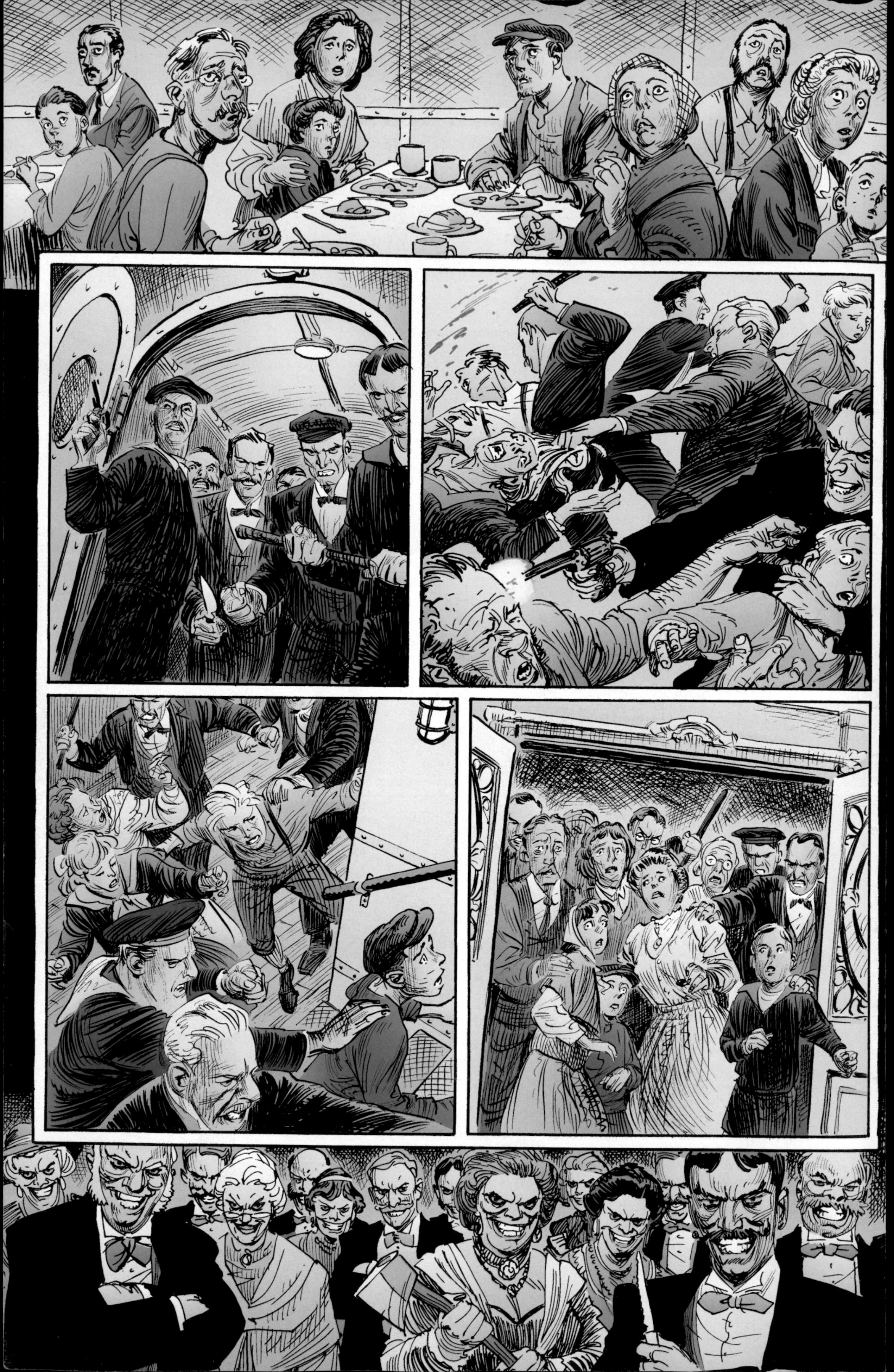

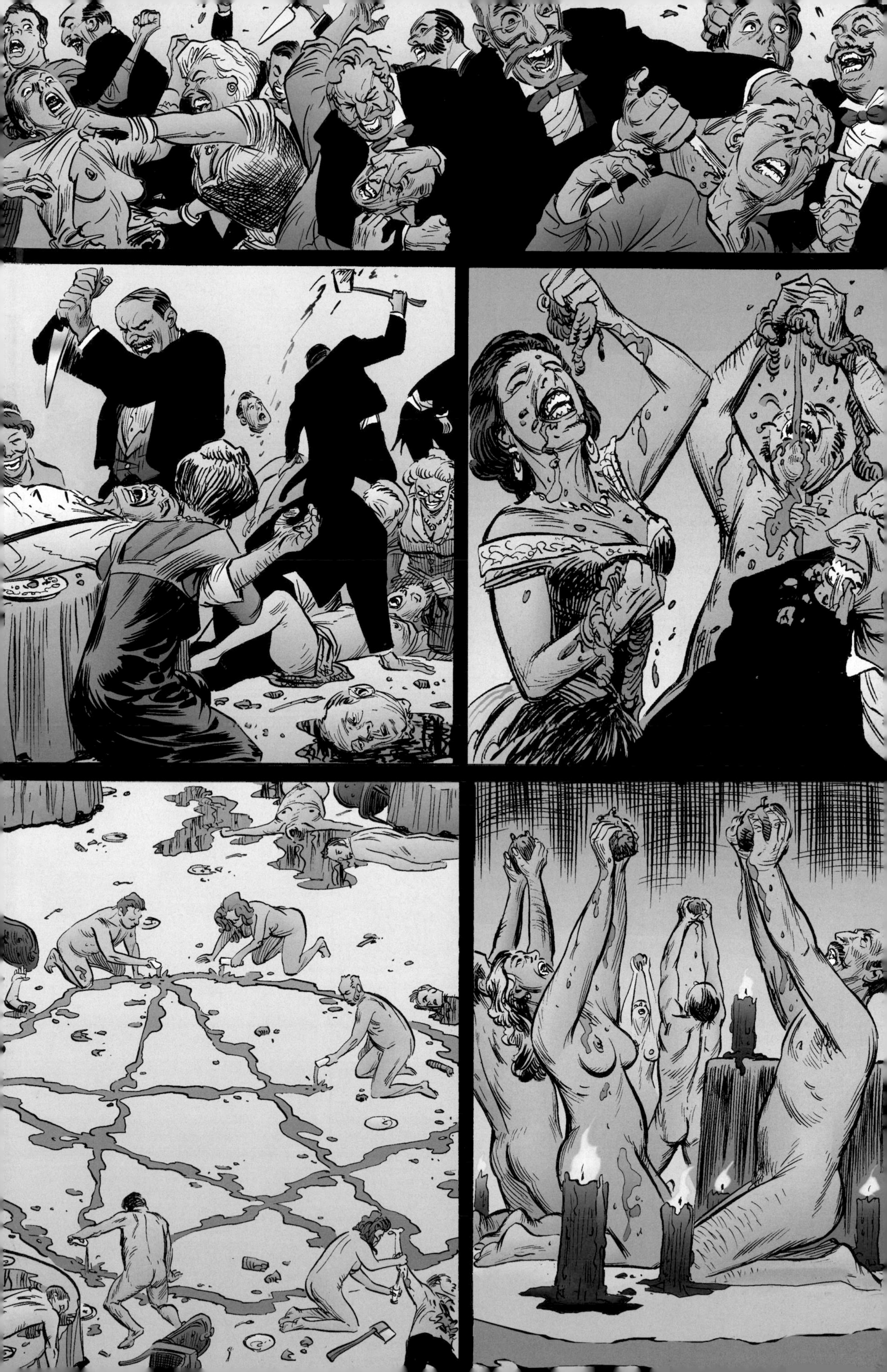

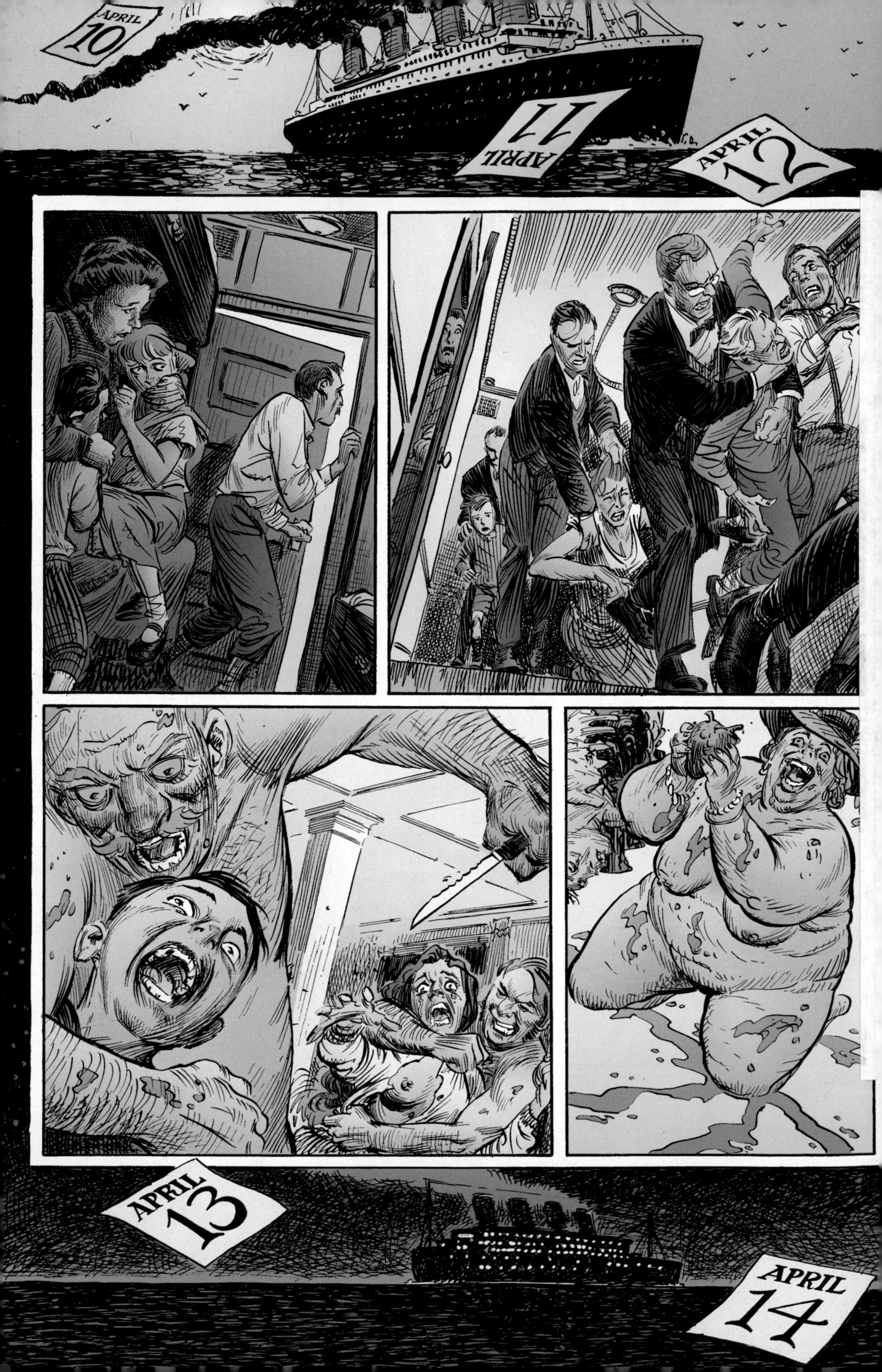
APRIL
10
APRIL
11
APRIL
12
APRIL
13
APRIL
14

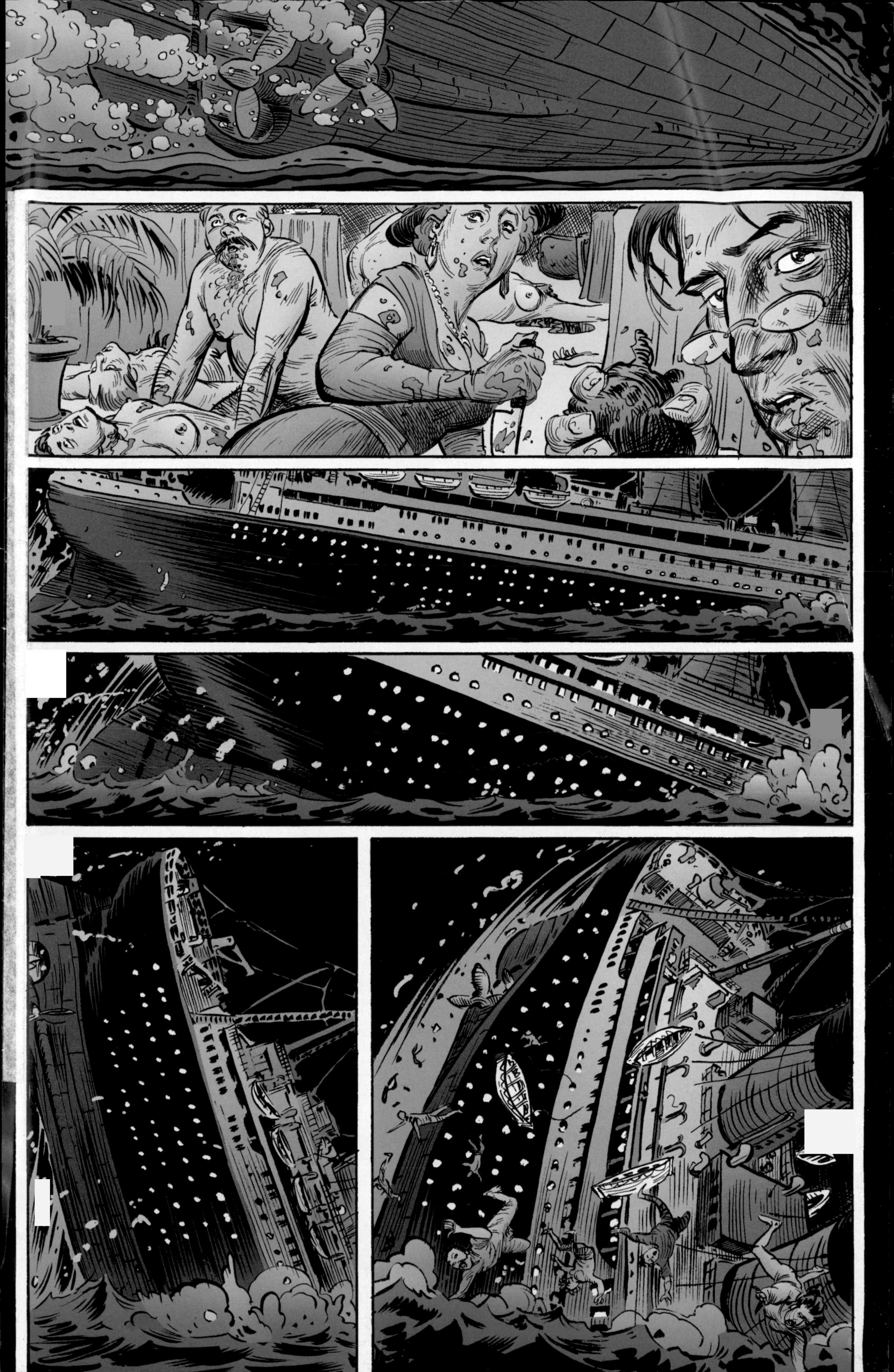

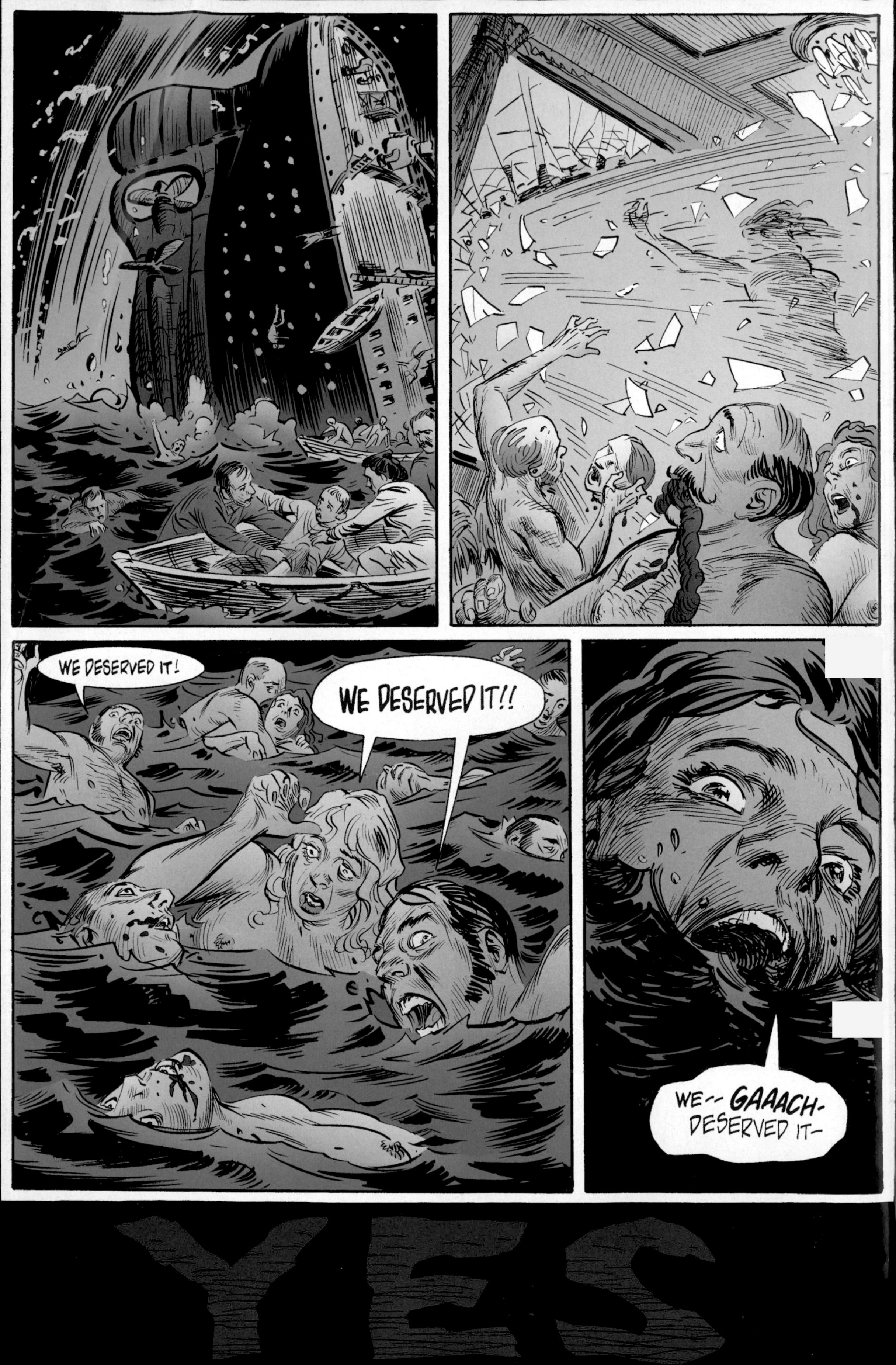
WE DESERVED IT!
WE DESERVED IT!!
WE-- GAAACH- DESERVED IT-
YES

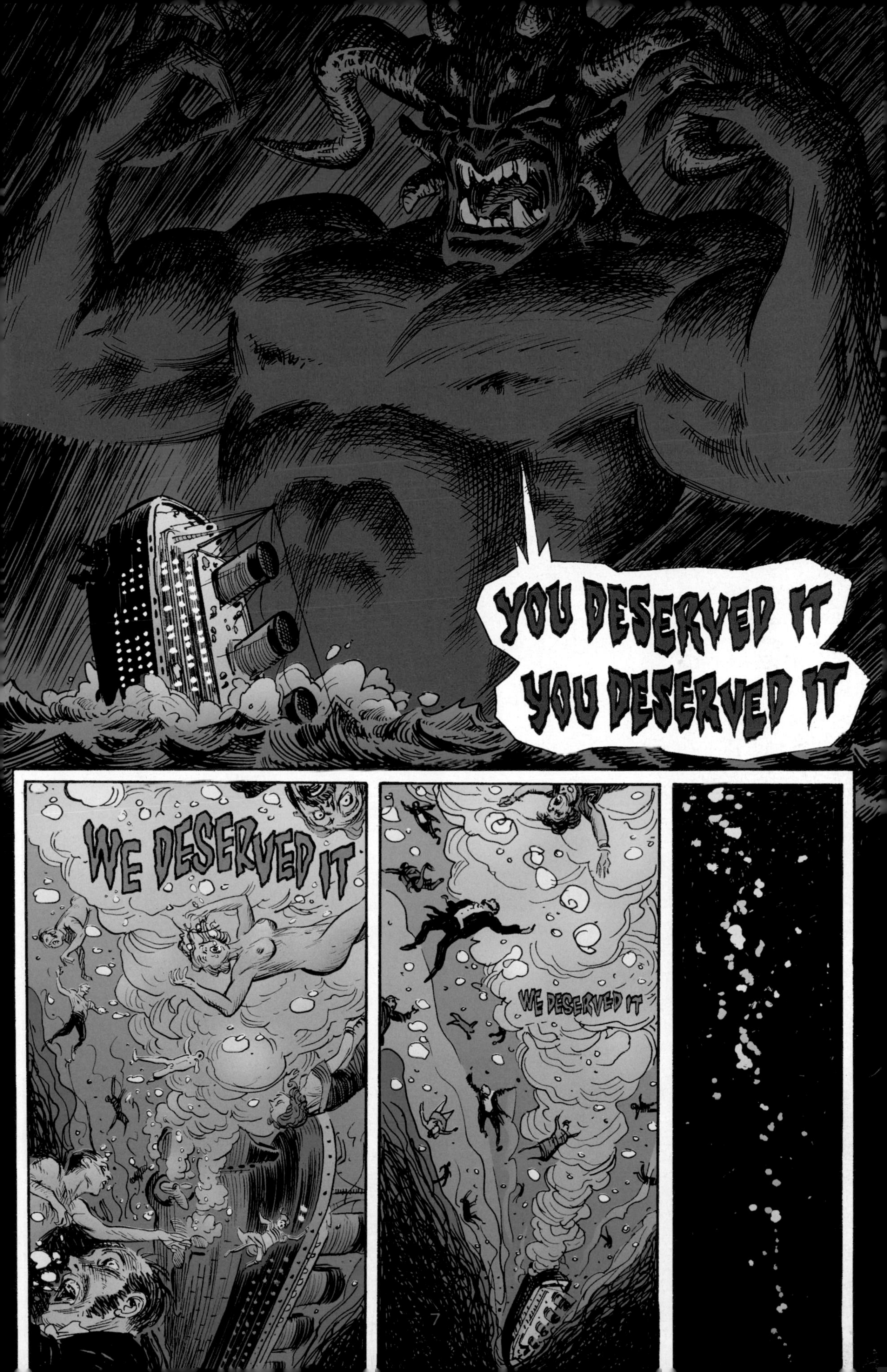
YOU DESERVED IT
YOU DESERVED IT
WE DESERVED IT
WE DESERVED IT

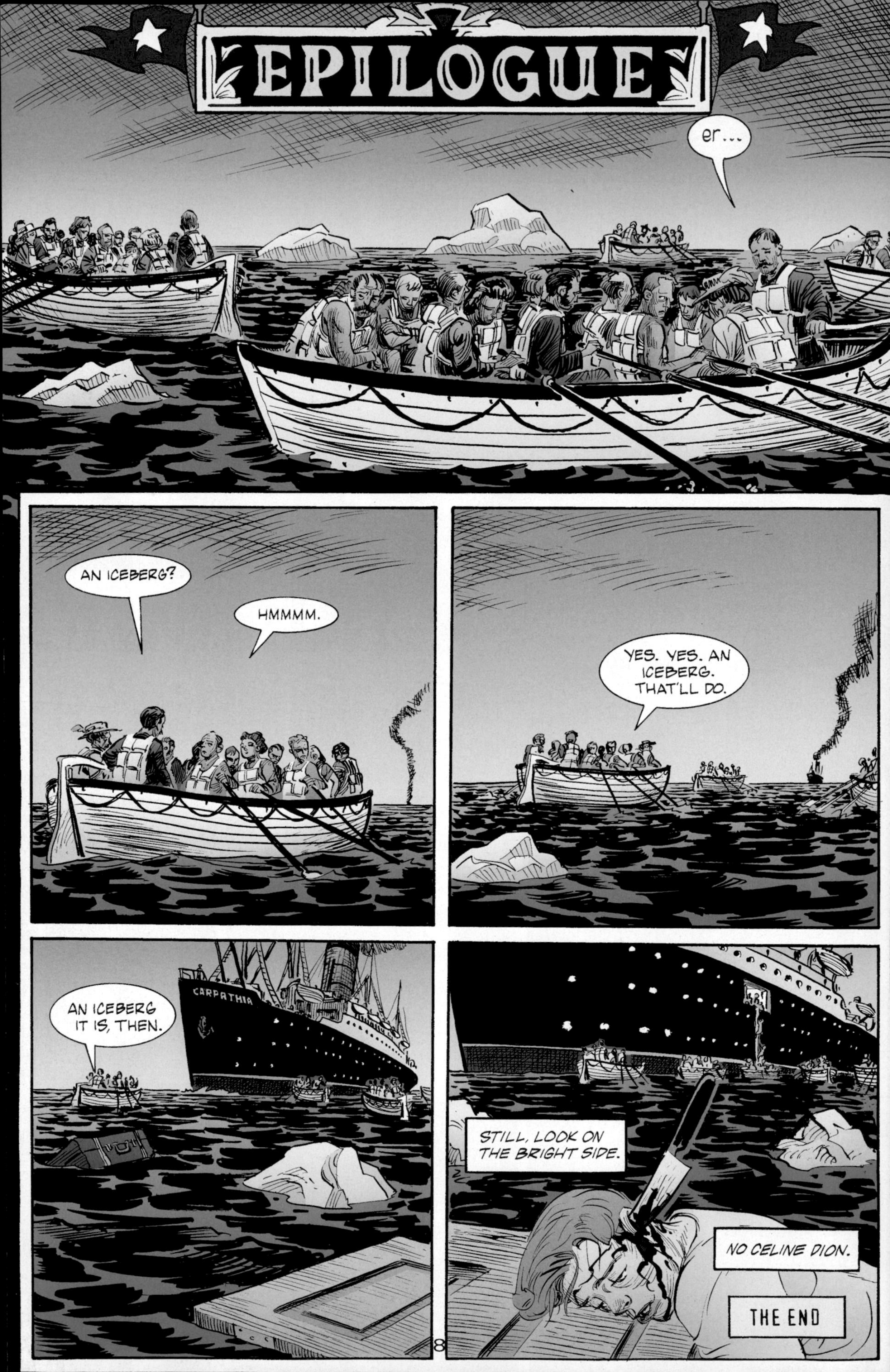
EPILOGUE
er...
AN ICEBERG?
HMMMM.
YES. YES. AN ICEBERG. THAT'LL DO.
AN ICEBERG IT IS, THEN.
CARPATHIA
STILL, LOOK ON THE BRIGHT SIDE.
NO CELINE DION.
THE END

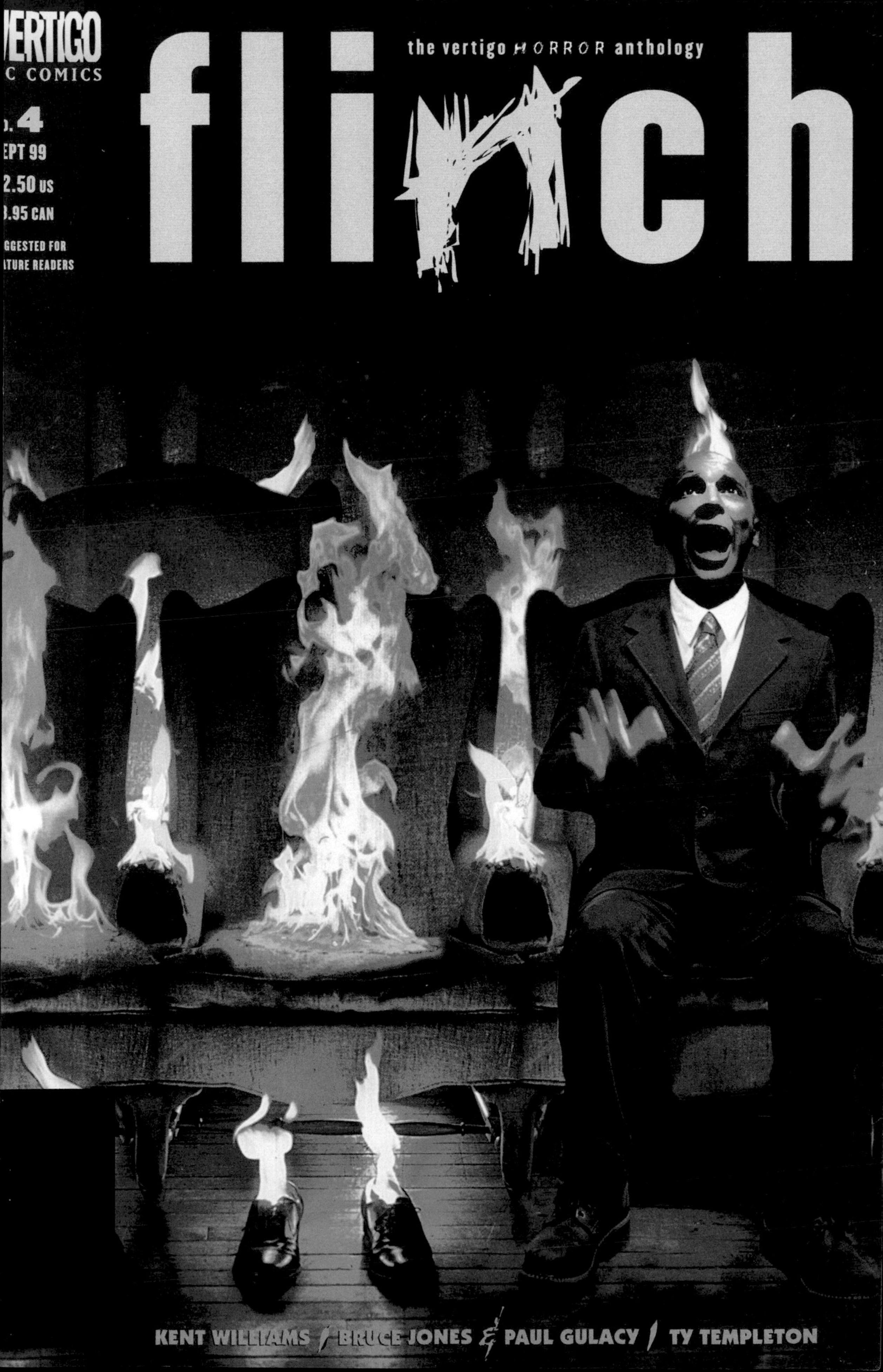

VERTIGO
DC COMICS
the vertigo HORROR anthology
flinch
NO. 4
SEPT 99
$2.50 US
$3.95 CAN
SUGGESTED FOR
MATURE READERS
KENT WILLIAMS / BRUCE JONES & PAUL GULACY / TY TEMPLETON

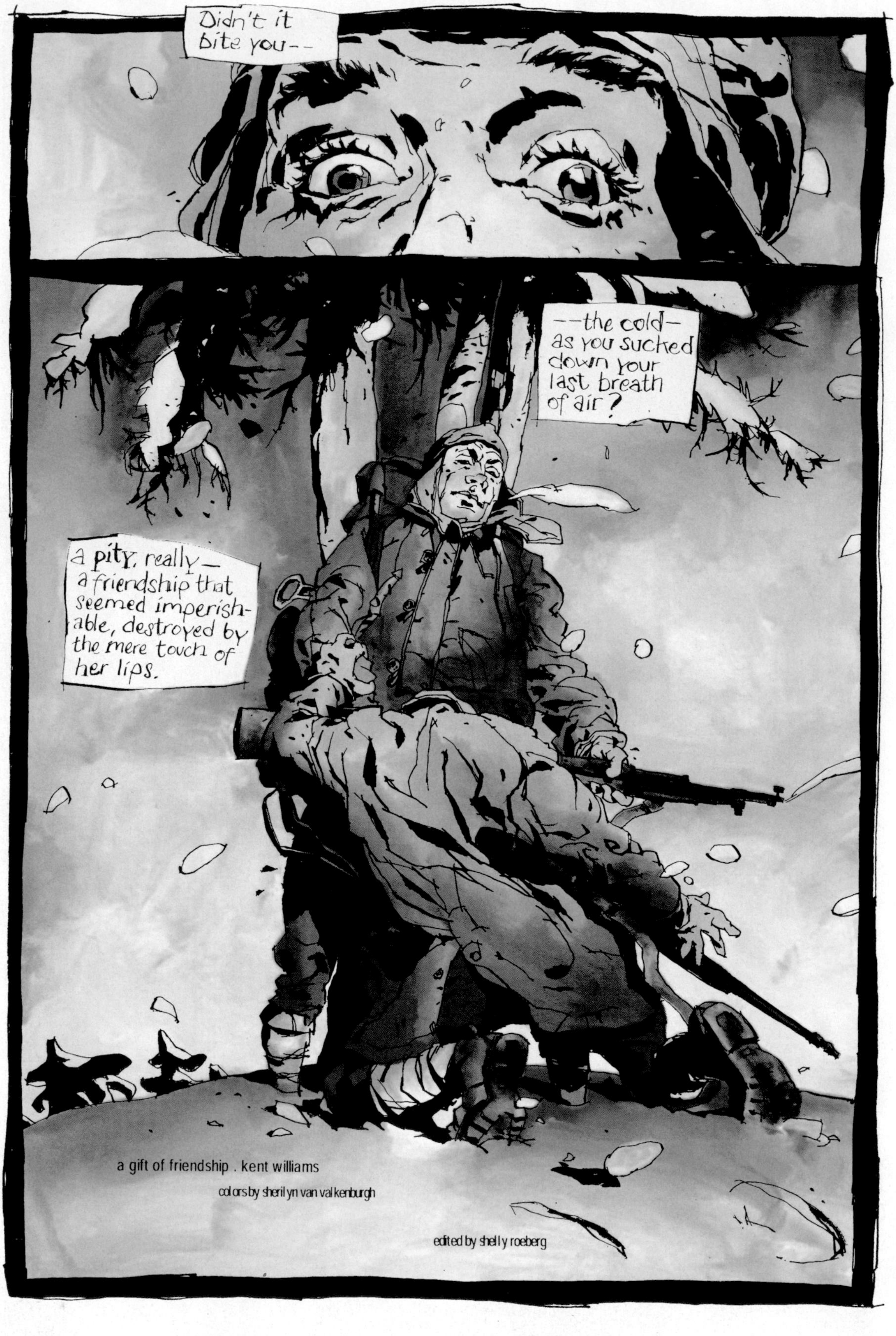
Didn't it bite you--
--the cold--as you sucked down your last breath of air?
a pity, really--a friendship that seemed imperishable, destroyed by the mere touch of her lips.
a gift of friendship . kent williams
colors by sherilyn van valkenburgh
edited by shelly roeberg

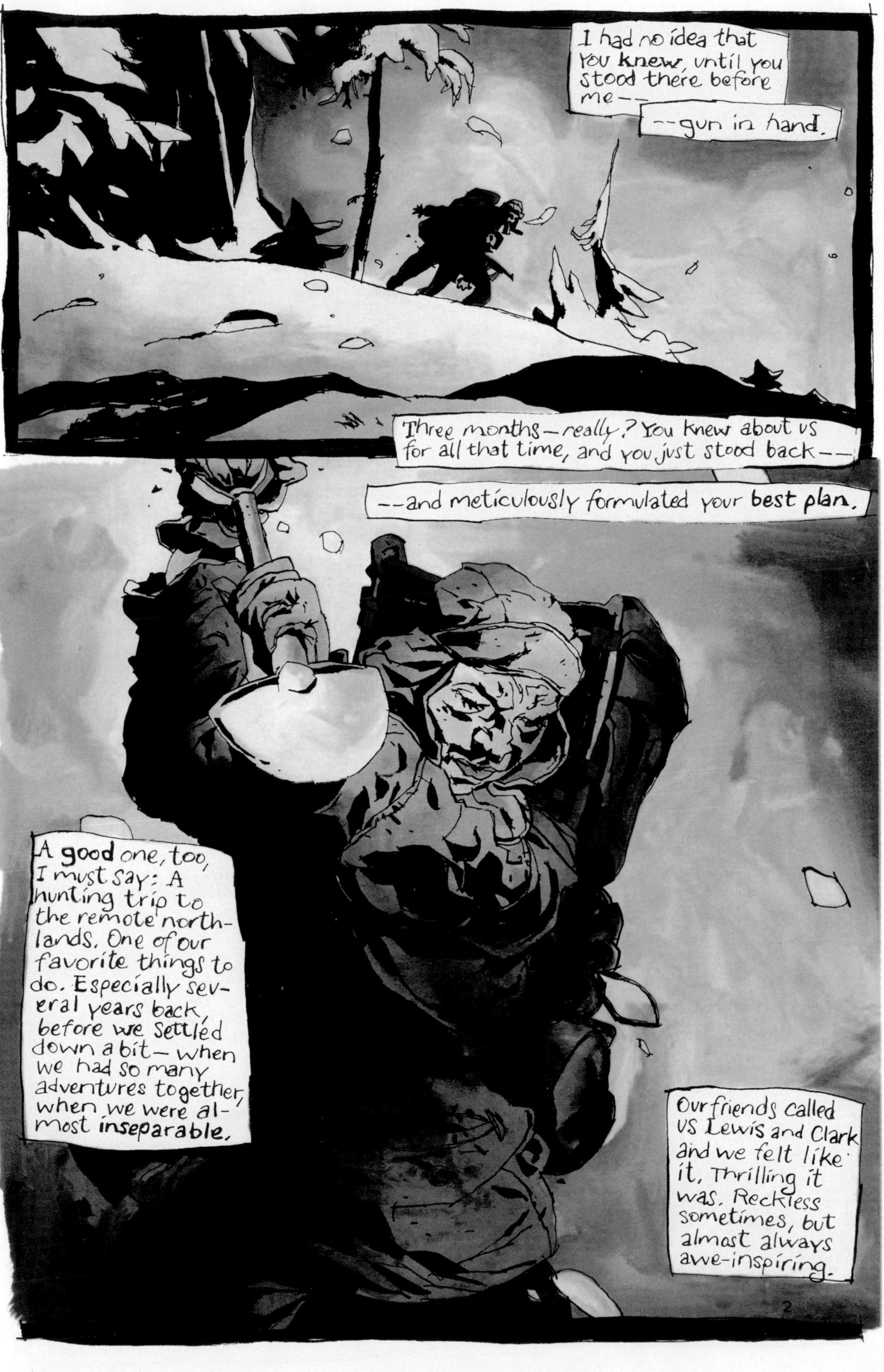
I had no idea that you knew, until you stood there before me--
--gun in hand.
Three months—really? You knew about us for all that time, and you just stood back--
--and meticulously formulated your best plan.
A good one, too, I must say: A hunting trip to the remote northlands. One of our favorite things to do. Especially several years back, before we settled down a bit—when we had so many adventures together, when we were almost inseparable.
Our friends called us Lewis and Clark and we felt like it. Thrilling it was. Reckless sometimes, but almost always awe-inspiring.
2

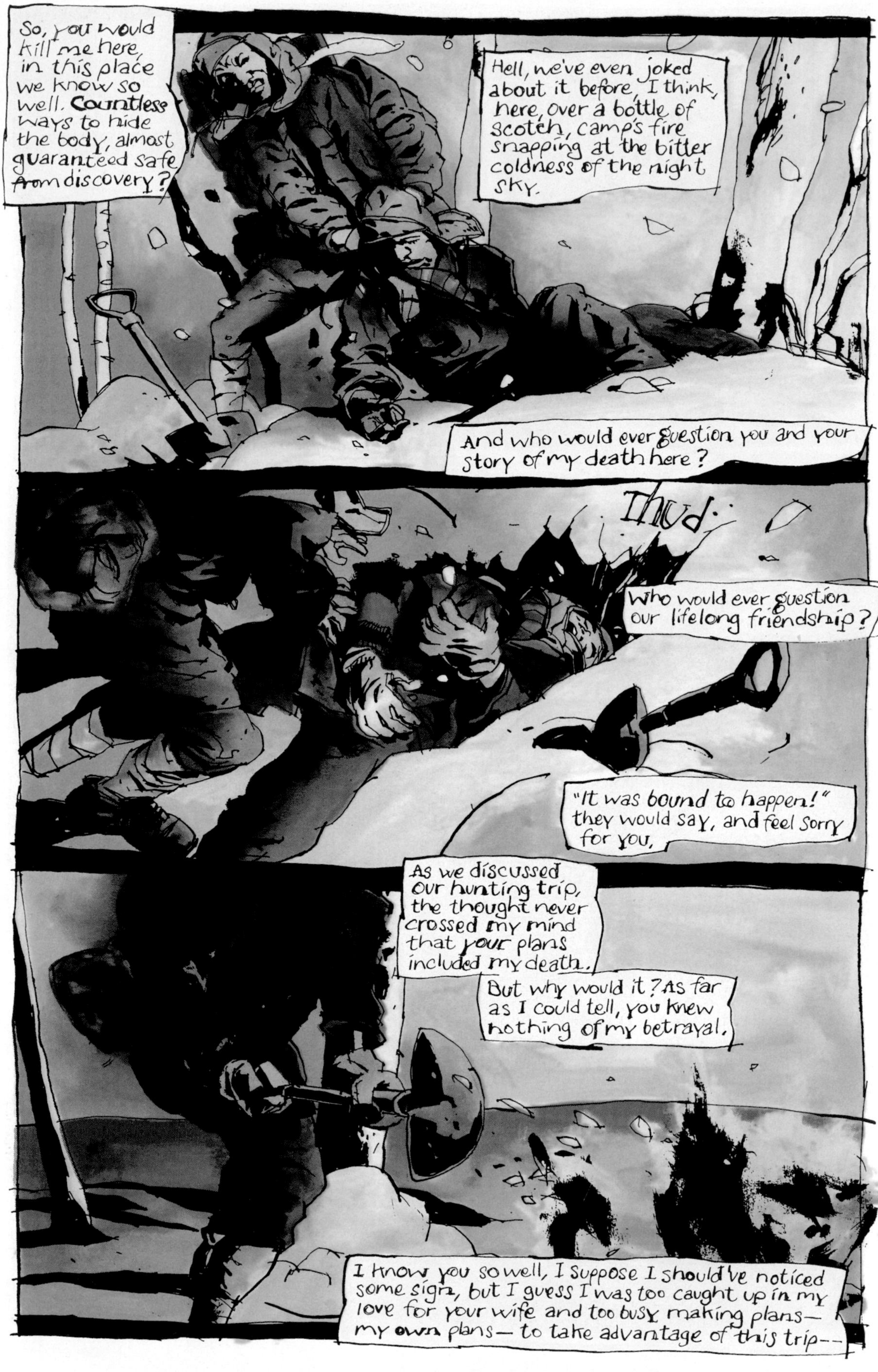
So, you would kill me here, in this place we know so well. Countless ways to hide the body, almost guaranteed safe from discovery?
Hell, we've even joked about it before, I think, here, over a bottle of scotch, camp's fire snapping at the bitter coldness of the night sky.
And who would ever question you and your story of my death here?
THUD
Who would ever question our lifelong friendship?
"It was bound to happen!" they would say, and feel sorry for you,
As we discussed our hunting trip, the thought never crossed my mind that your plans included my death.
But why would it? As far as I could tell, you knew nothing of my betrayal.
I know you so well, I suppose I should've noticed some sign, but I guess I was too caught up in my love for your wife and too busy making plans— my own plans— to take advantage of this trip--

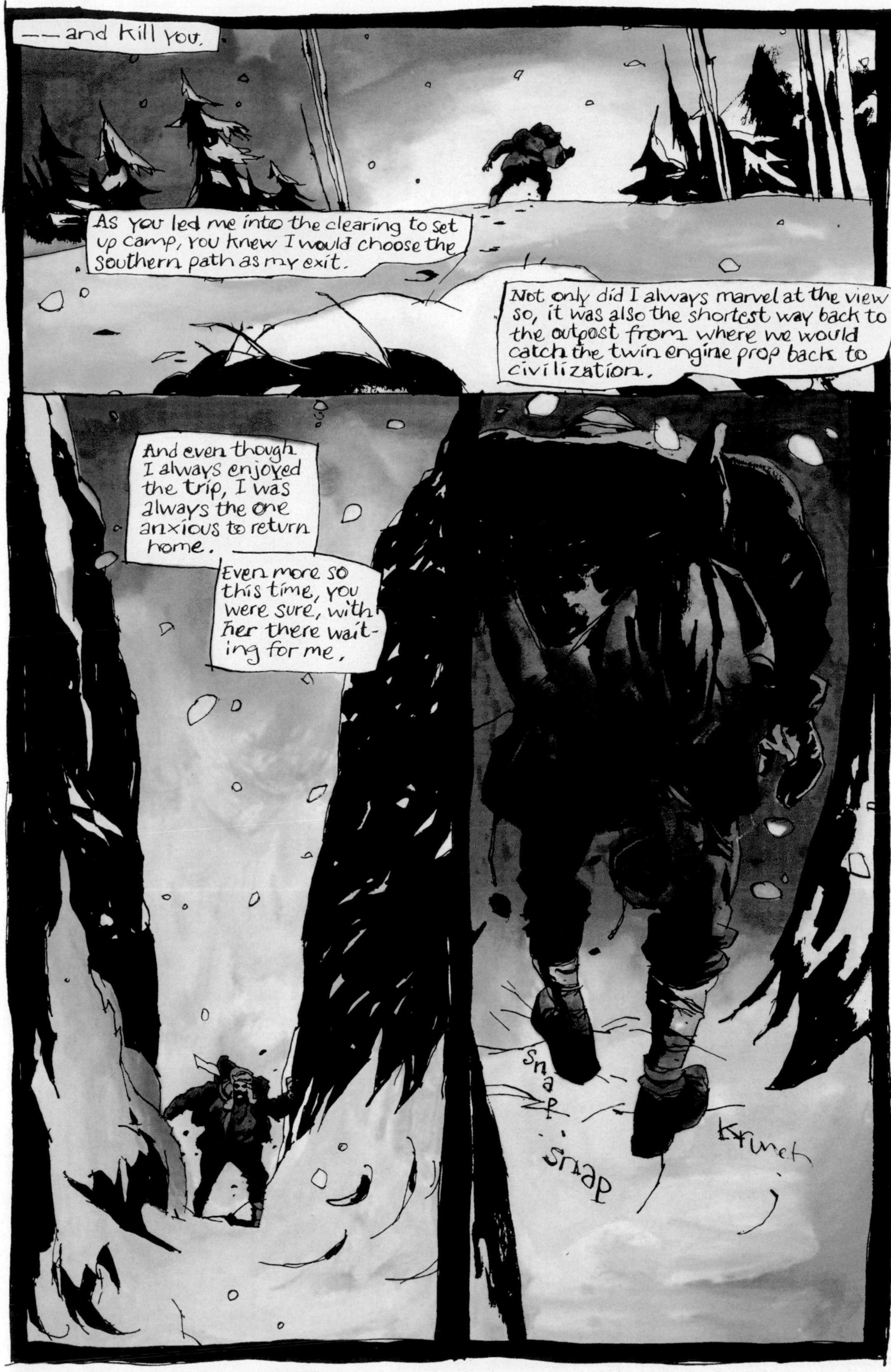
--and kill you.
As you led me into the clearing to set up camp, you knew I would choose the southern path as my exit.
Not only did I always marvel at the view so, it was also the shortest way back to the outpost from where we would catch the twin engine prop back to civilization.
And even though I always enjoyed the trip, I was always the one anxious to return home.
Even more so this time, you were sure, with her there waiting for me.
Snap
Snap
Krunch

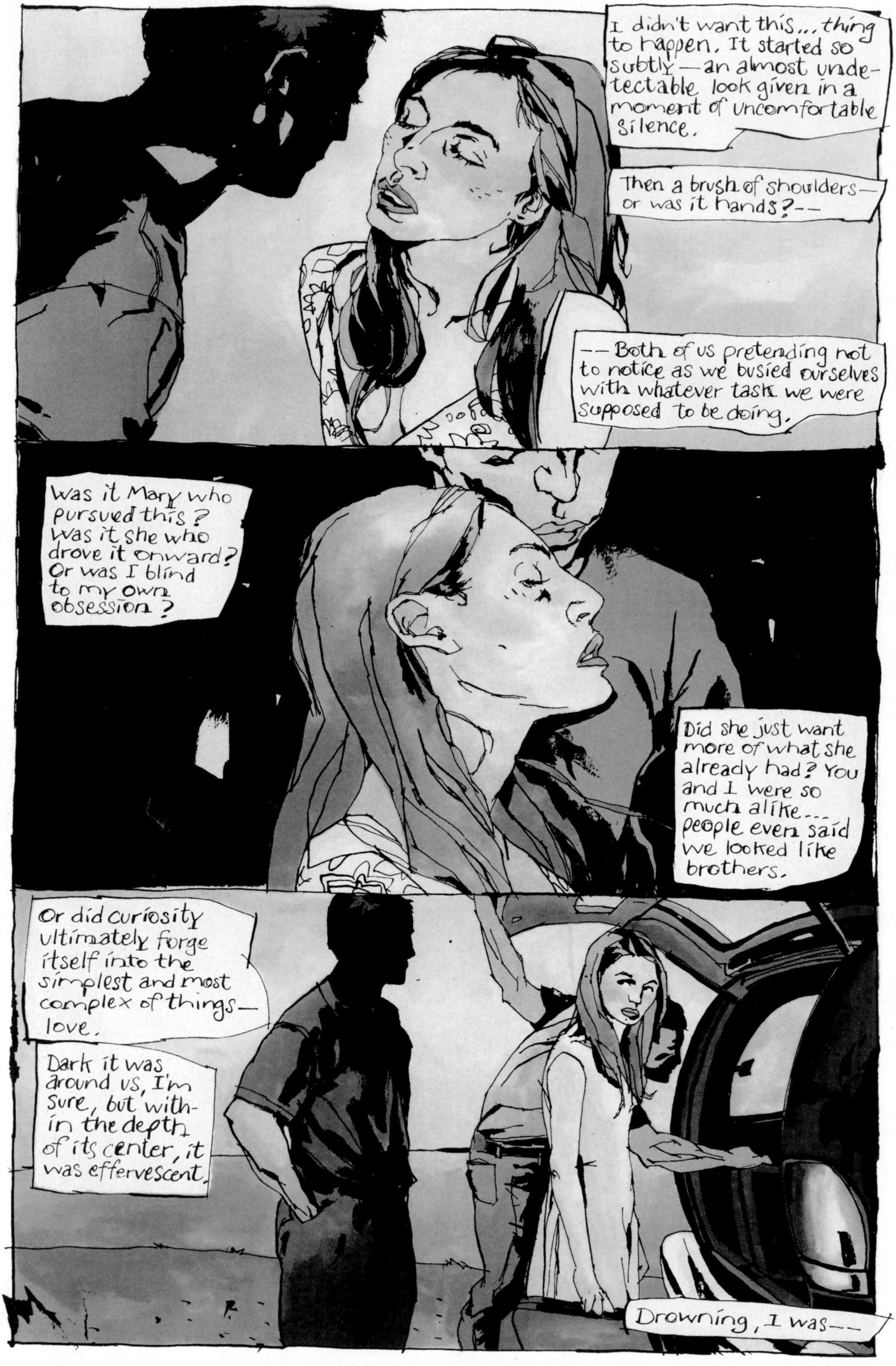
I didn't want this... thing to happen. It started so subtly — an almost undetectable look given in a moment of uncomfortable silence.
Then a brush of shoulders — or was it hands?--
-- Both of us pretending not to notice as we busied ourselves with whatever task we were supposed to be doing.
Was it Mary who pursued this? Was it she who drove it onward? Or was I blind to my own obsession?
Did she just want more of what she already had? You and I were so much alike... people even said we looked like brothers.
Or did curiosity ultimately forge itself into the simplest and most complex of things — love.
Dark it was around us, I'm sure, but within the depth of its center, it was effervescent.
Drowning, I was--

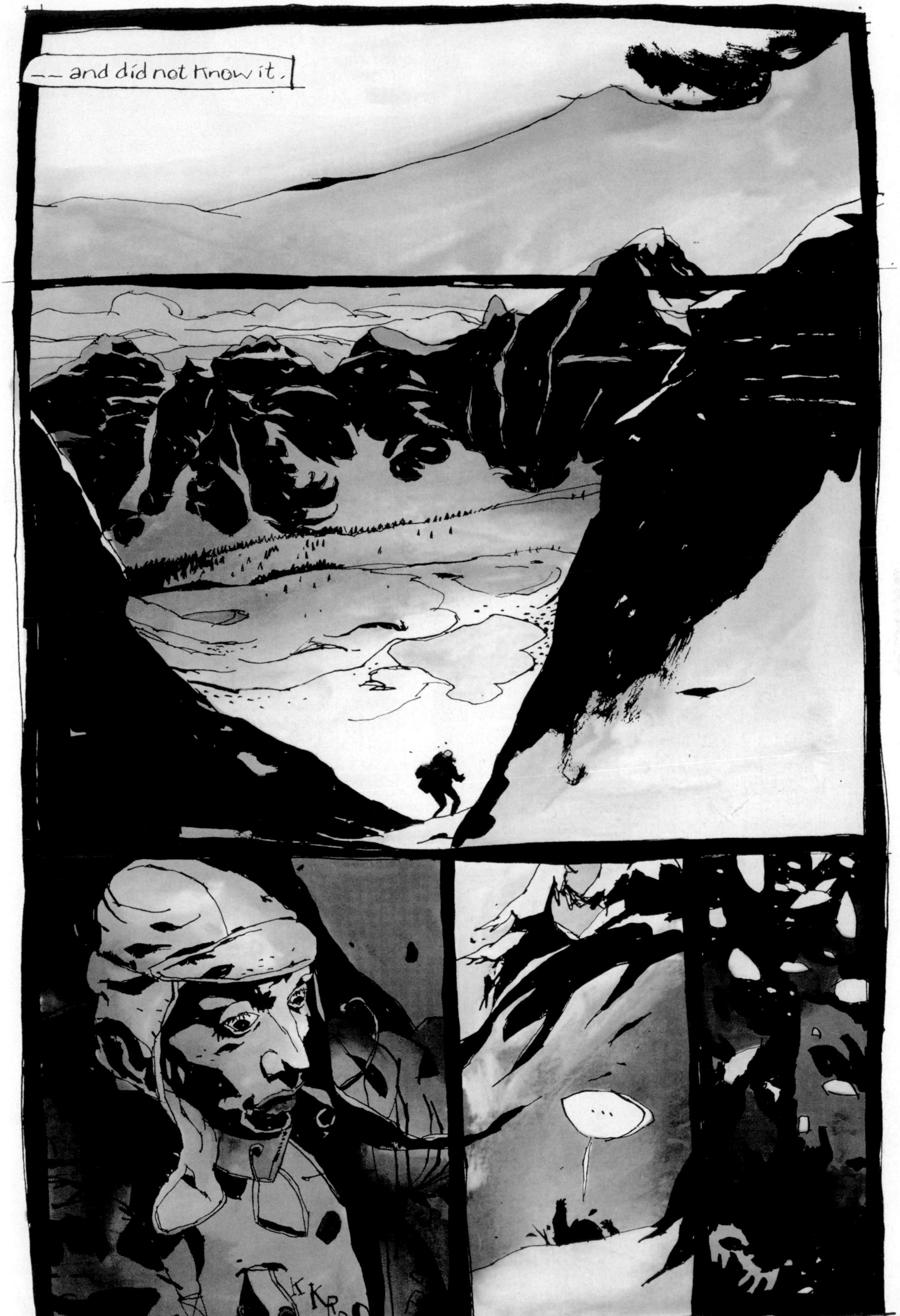
-- and did not know it.
...
KKRRRRR

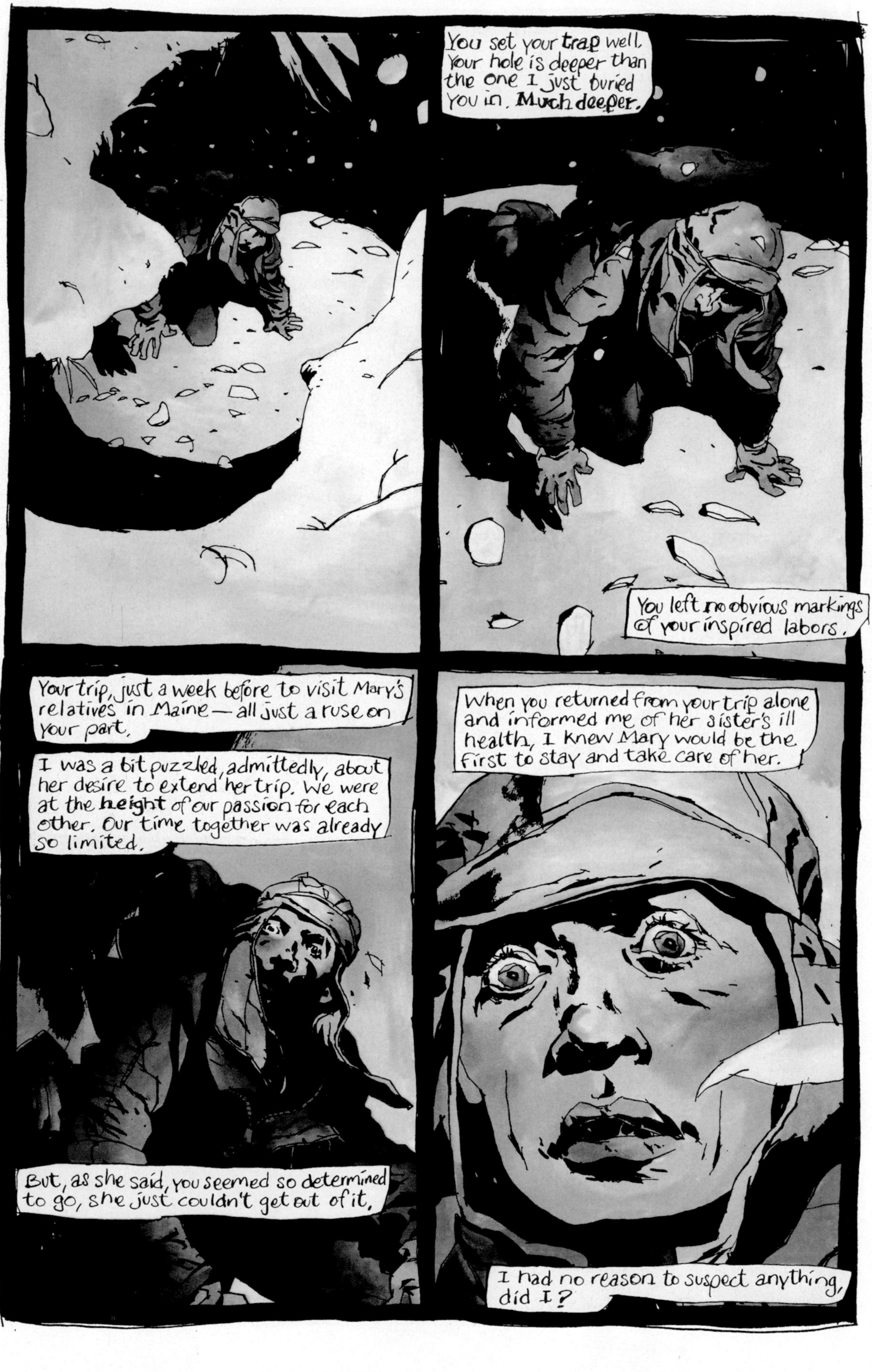
You set your trap well. Your hole is deeper than the one I just buried you in. Much deeper.
You left no obvious markings of your inspired labors.
Your trip, just a week before to visit Mary's relatives in Maine — all just a ruse on your part.
I was a bit puzzled, admittedly, about her desire to extend her trip. We were at the height of our passion for each other. Our time together was already so limited.
But, as she said, you seemed so determined to go, she just couldn't get out of it.
When you returned from your trip alone and informed me of her sister's ill health, I knew Mary would be the first to stay and take care of her.
I had no reason to suspect anything, did I?

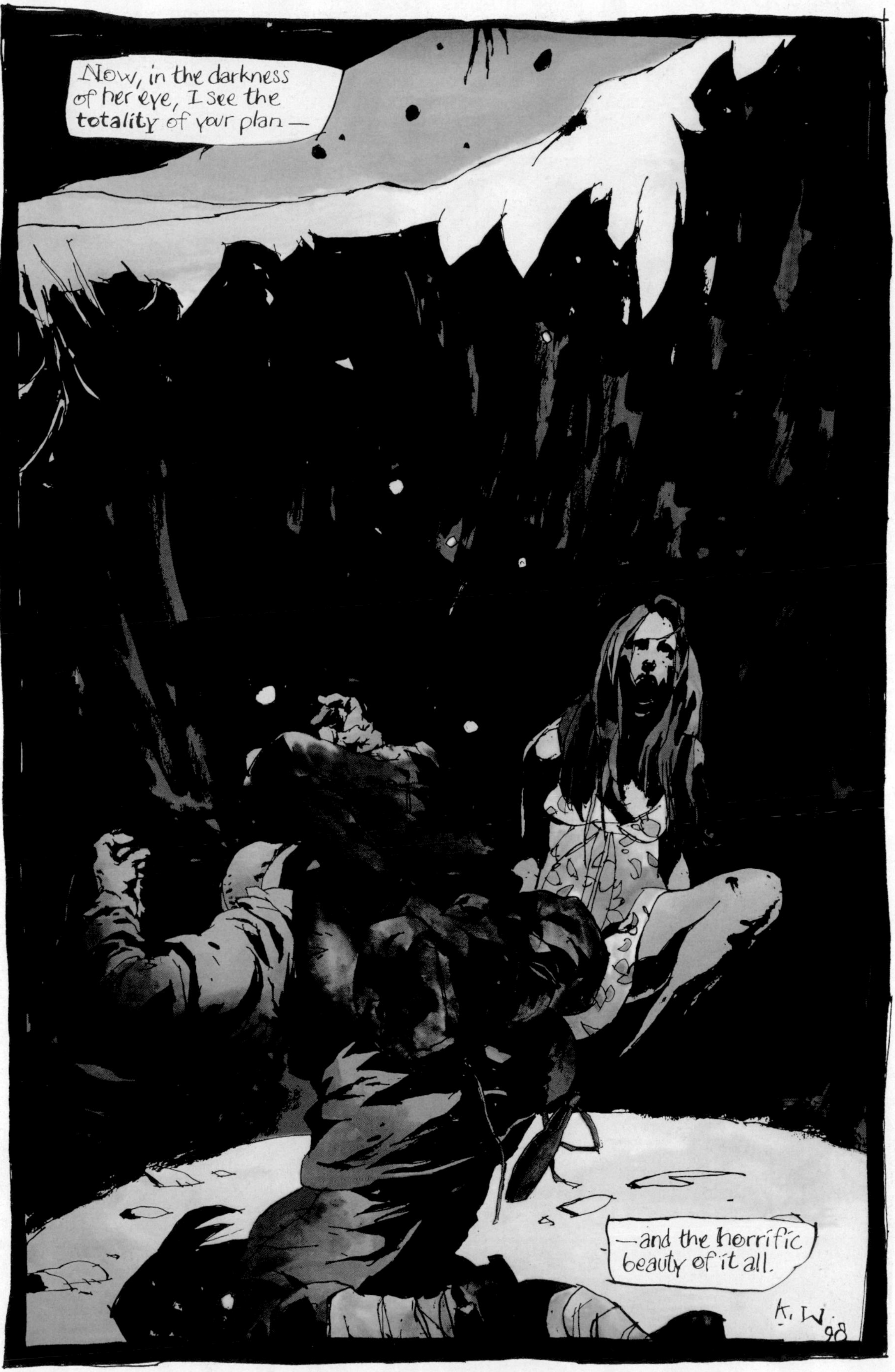
Now, in the darkness of her eye, I see the totality of your plan—
—and the horrific beauty of it all.
K.W. 98

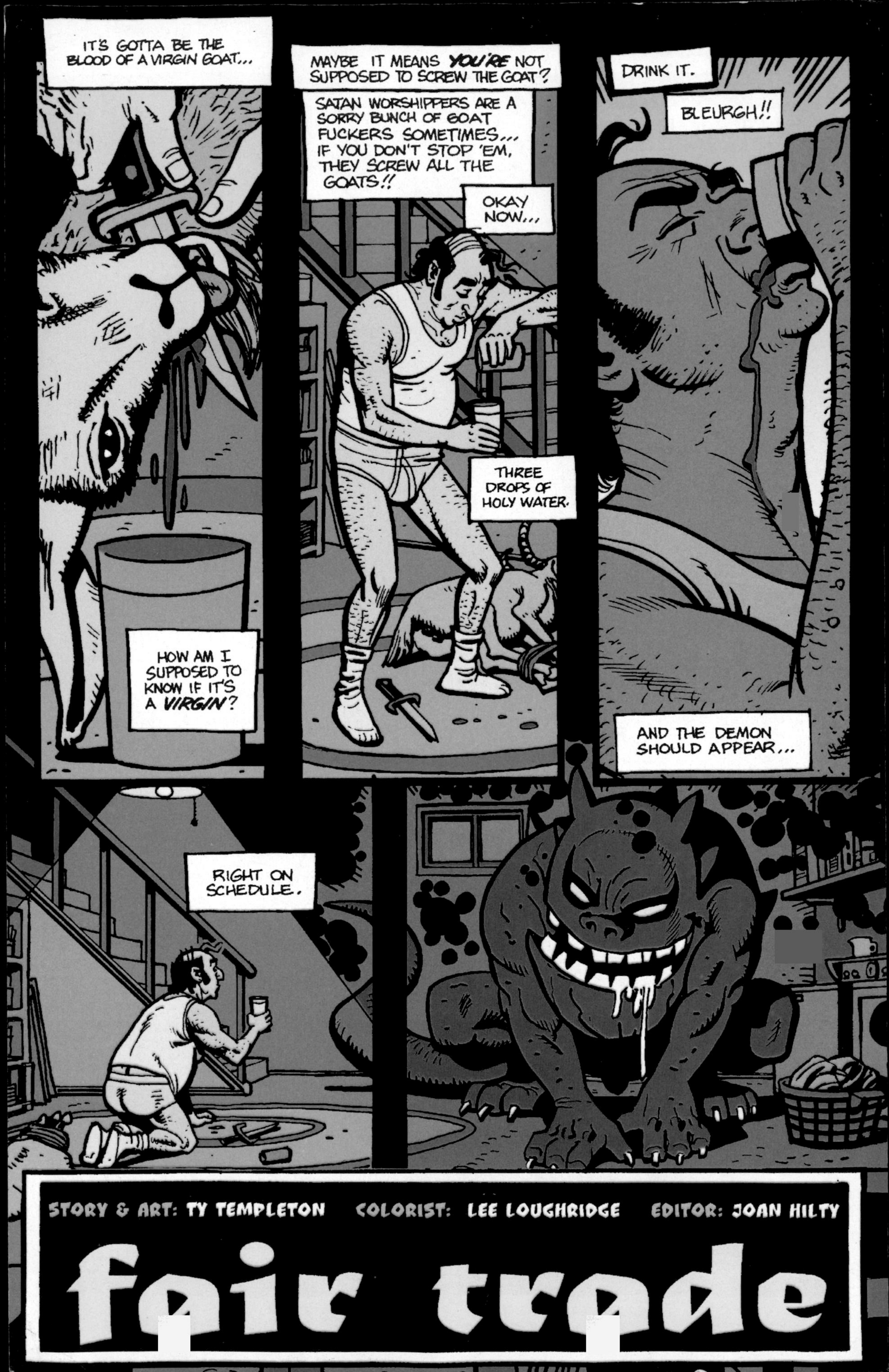

IT'S GOTTA BE THE BLOOD OF A VIRGIN GOAT...
HOW AM I SUPPOSED TO KNOW IF IT'S A VIRGIN?
MAYBE IT MEANS YOU'RE NOT SUPPOSED TO SCREW THE GOAT?
SATAN WORSHIPPERS ARE A SORRY BUNCH OF GOAT FUCKERS SOMETIMES... IF YOU DON'T STOP 'EM, THEY SCREW ALL THE GOATS!!
OKAY NOW...
THREE DROPS OF HOLY WATER.
DRINK IT.
BLEURGH!!
AND THE DEMON SHOULD APPEAR...
RIGHT ON SCHEDULE.
STORY & ART: TY TEMPLETON COLORIST: LEE LOUGHRIDGE EDITOR: JOAN HILTY
fair trade

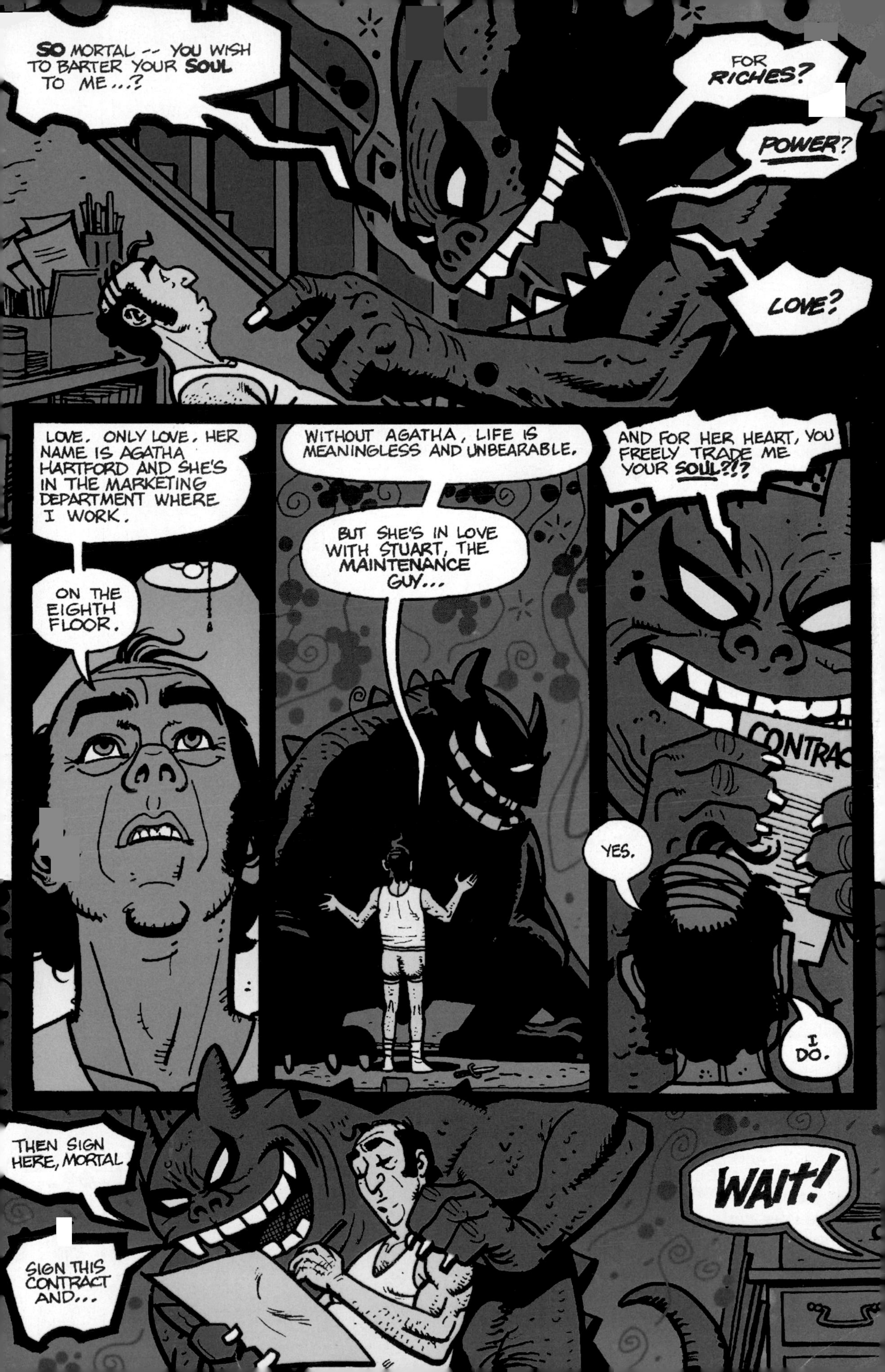
SO MORTAL -- YOU WISH TO BARTER YOUR SOUL TO ME...?
FOR RICHES?
POWER?
LOVE?
LOVE. ONLY LOVE. HER NAME IS AGATHA HARTFORD AND SHE'S IN THE MARKETING DEPARTMENT WHERE I WORK.
ON THE EIGHTH FLOOR.
WITHOUT AGATHA, LIFE IS MEANINGLESS AND UNBEARABLE.
BUT SHE'S IN LOVE WITH STUART, THE MAINTENANCE GUY...
AND FOR HER HEART, YOU FREELY TRADE ME YOUR SOUL?!?
YES.
I DO.
THEN SIGN HERE, MORTAL.
SIGN THIS CONTRACT AND...
WAIT!

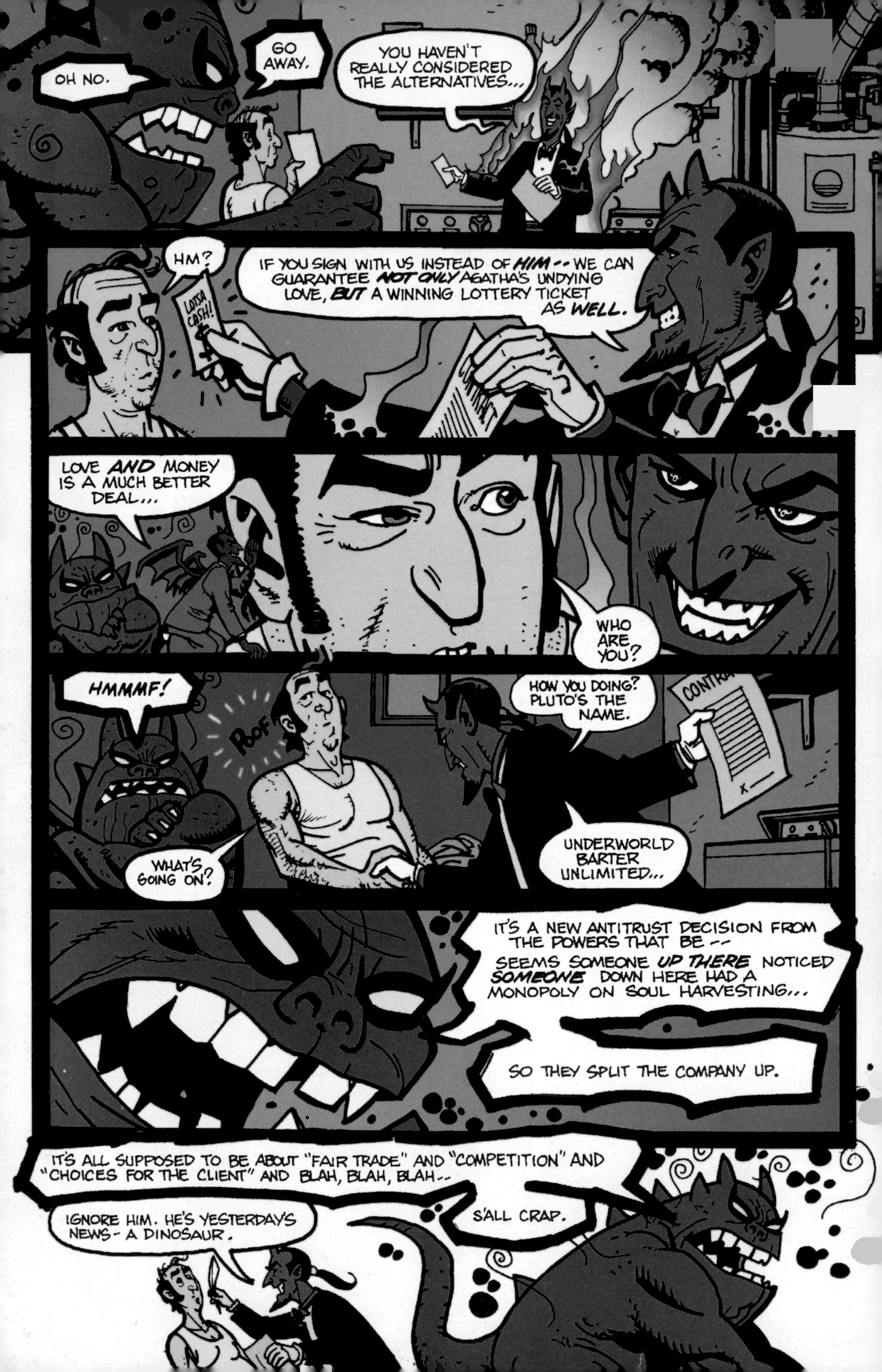
OH NO.
GO AWAY.
YOU HAVEN'T REALLY CONSIDERED THE ALTERNATIVES...
HM?
IF YOU SIGN WITH US INSTEAD OF *HIM* -- WE CAN GUARANTEE *NOT ONLY* AGATHA'S UNDYING LOVE, *BUT* A WINNING LOTTERY TICKET AS *WELL*.
LOTSA CASH!
LOVE *AND* MONEY IS A MUCH BETTER DEAL...
WHO ARE YOU?
HMMMF!
POOF
HOW YOU DOING? PLUTO'S THE NAME.
CONTRA
WHAT'S GOING ON?
UNDERWORLD BARTER UNLIMITED...
IT'S A NEW ANTITRUST DECISION FROM THE POWERS THAT BE -- SEEMS SOMEONE *UP THERE* NOTICED *SOMEONE* DOWN HERE HAD A MONOPOLY ON SOUL HARVESTING...
SO THEY SPLIT THE COMPANY UP.
IT'S ALL SUPPOSED TO BE ABOUT "FAIR TRADE" AND "COMPETITION" AND "CHOICES FOR THE CLIENT" AND BLAH, BLAH, BLAH--
S'ALL CRAP.
IGNORE HIM. HE'S YESTERDAY'S NEWS - A DINOSAUR.

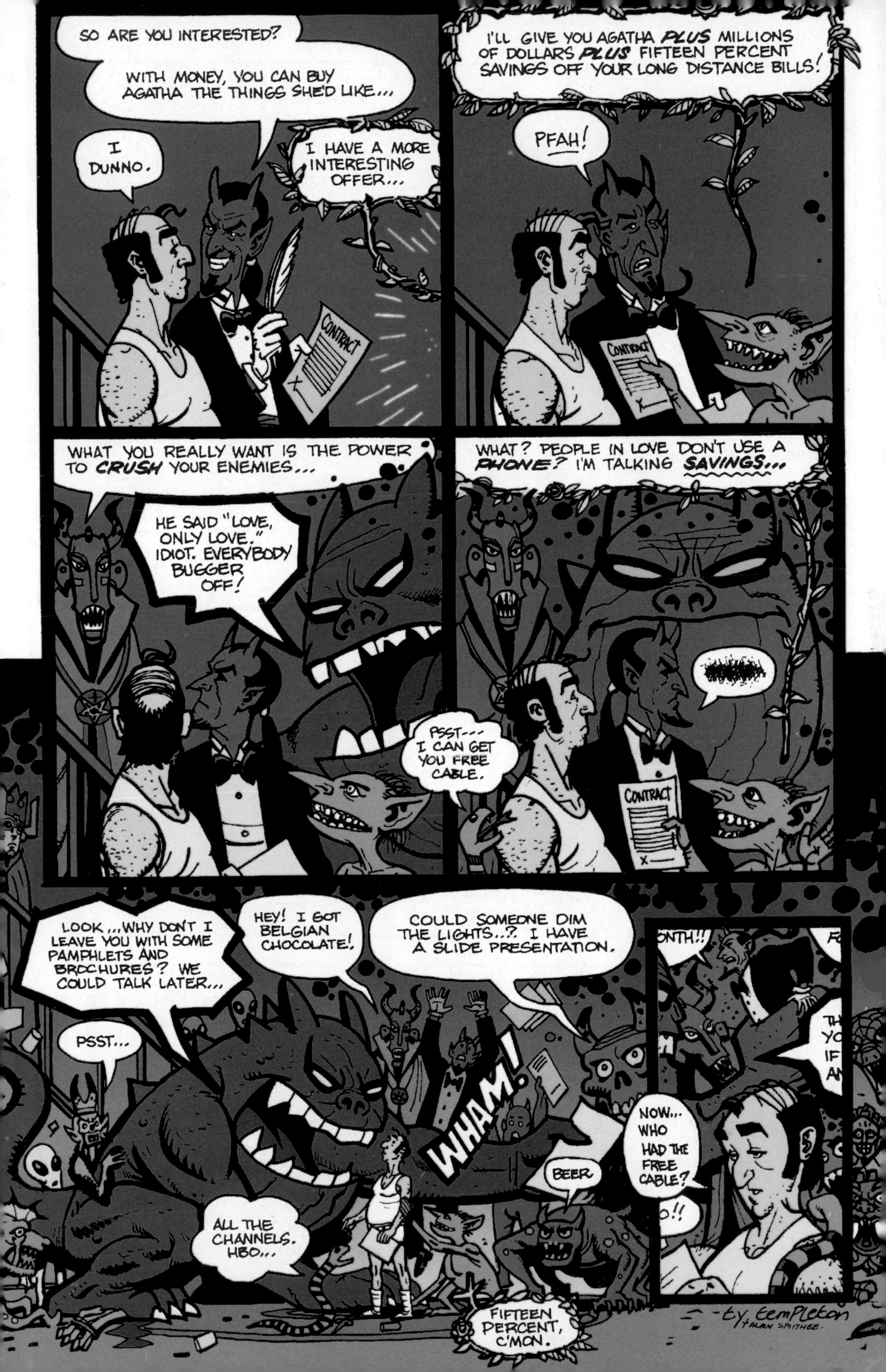

SO ARE YOU INTERESTED?
WITH MONEY, YOU CAN BUY AGATHA THE THINGS SHE'D LIKE...
I DUNNO.
I HAVE A MORE INTERESTING OFFER...
CONTRACT
I'LL GIVE YOU AGATHA PLUS MILLIONS OF DOLLARS PLUS FIFTEEN PERCENT SAVINGS OFF YOUR LONG DISTANCE BILLS!
PFAH!
CONTRACT
WHAT YOU REALLY WANT IS THE POWER TO CRUSH YOUR ENEMIES...
HE SAID "LOVE, ONLY LOVE." IDIOT. EVERYBODY BUGGER OFF!
PSST--- I CAN GET YOU FREE CABLE.
WHAT? PEOPLE IN LOVE DON'T USE A PHONE? I'M TALKING SAVINGS...
CONTRACT
LOOK...WHY DON'T I LEAVE YOU WITH SOME PAMPHLETS AND BROCHURES? WE COULD TALK LATER...
HEY! I GOT BELGIAN CHOCOLATE!
COULD SOMEONE DIM THE LIGHTS..? I HAVE A SLIDE PRESENTATION.
PSST...
WHAM!
ALL THE CHANNELS. HBO...
BEER
NOW... WHO HAD THE FREE CABLE?
FIFTEEN PERCENT, C'MON.
-by Templeton
+ALAN SMITHEE.

LIE PERFECTLY *STILL,* THAT'S THE *SECRET.*

DON'T MOVE...DON'T EVEN *BREATHE.*

WHAT'S *THAT--?!*

NOTHIN', *PRAYIN' MANTIS.* KEEP STILL...

WHAT WAS IT PROFESSOR TESSER USED TO TEACH BACK EAST? THE MALE MANTIS IS IRRESISTIBLY DRAWN TO THE *FEMALE...*HE *HEARS, SEES, THINKS* OF *NOTHING* BUT *HER.* HIS WHOLE *WORLD* BECOMES HIS *NEED* FOR HER.

YEAH... CONCENTRATE ON *THAT*...AND DON'T BREATHE...

IGNORE THE *SCREAMS*... THE *FOOTFALLS*...

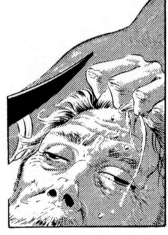

COMING CLOSER...

CLOSER...

# PLAYING DEAD

**Written by**
## BR JCE J NES

**Illustrated by**
## PAUL GULACY

**Lettered by**
## CLEM ROBINS

**Edited by**
## AXEL ALONSO

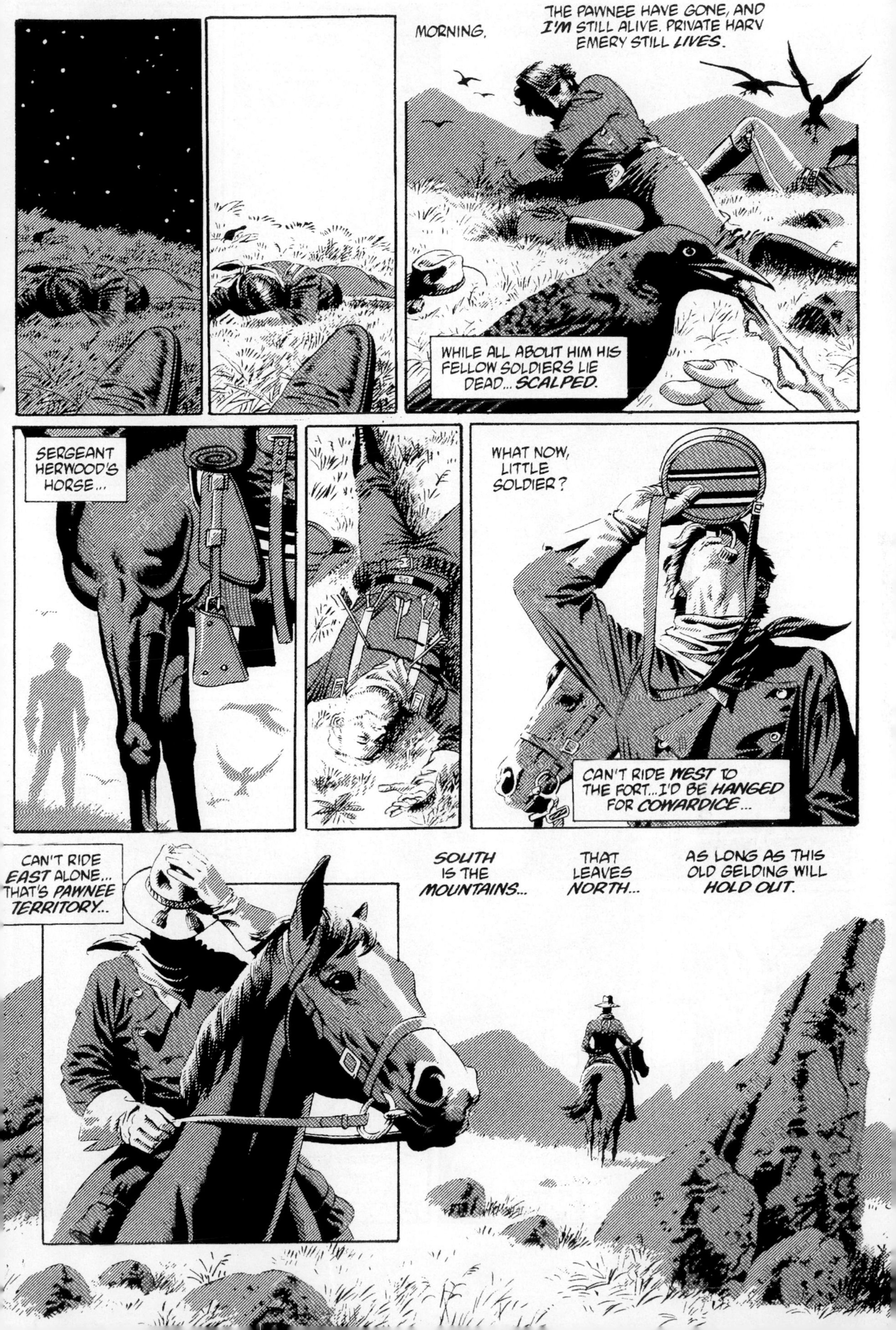
MORNING.
THE PAWNEE HAVE GONE, AND I'M STILL ALIVE. PRIVATE HARV EMERY STILL LIVES.
WHILE ALL ABOUT HIM HIS FELLOW SOLDIERS LIE DEAD... SCALPED.
SERGEANT HERWOOD'S HORSE...
WHAT NOW, LITTLE SOLDIER?
CAN'T RIDE WEST TO THE FORT... I'D BE HANGED FOR COWARDICE...
CAN'T RIDE EAST ALONE... THAT'S PAWNEE TERRITORY...
SOUTH IS THE MOUNTAINS...
THAT LEAVES NORTH...
AS LONG AS THIS OLD GELDING WILL HOLD OUT.

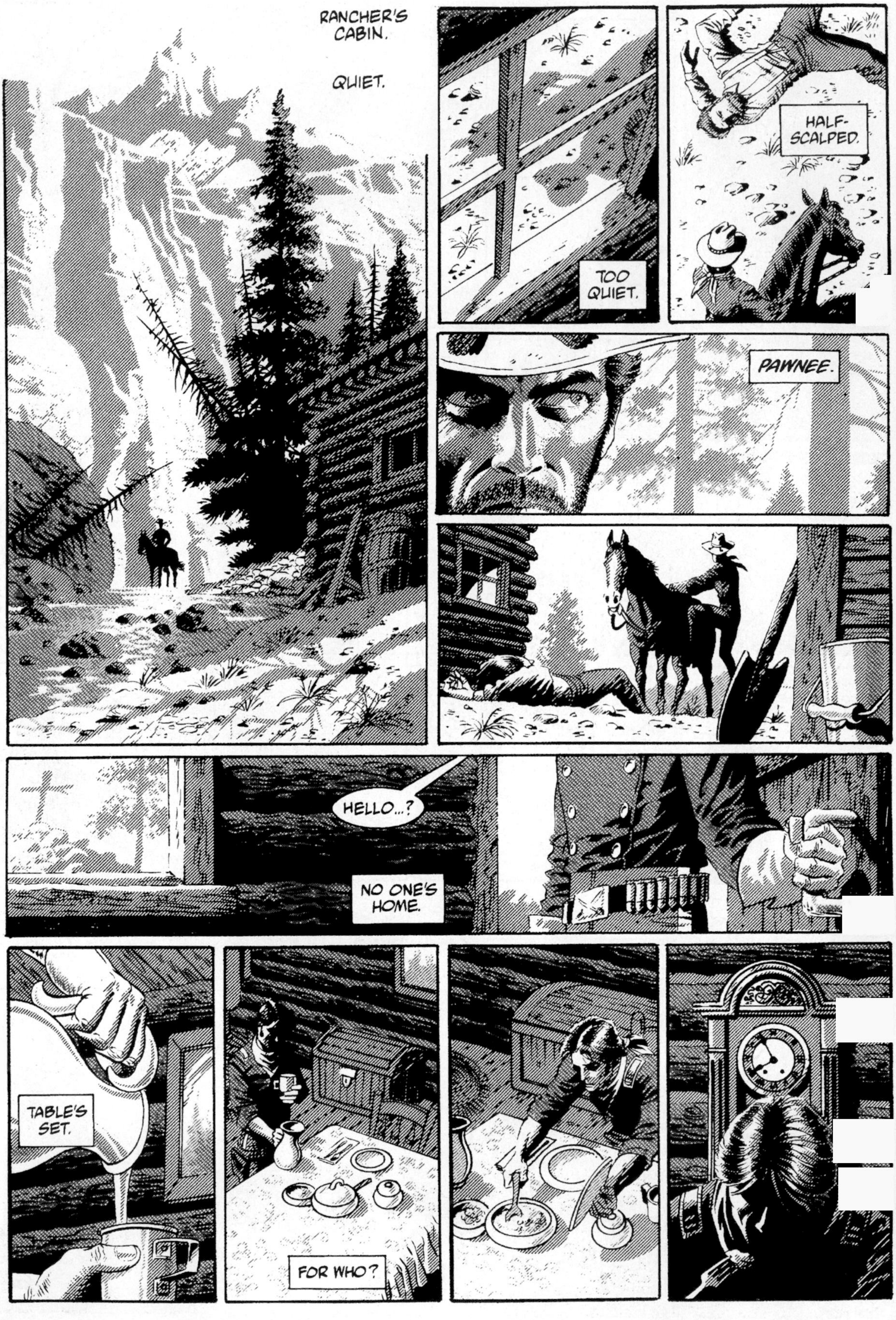
RANCHER'S CABIN.
QUIET.
TOO QUIET.
HALF-SCALPED.
PAWNEE.
HELLO...?
NO ONE'S HOME.
TABLE'S SET.
FOR WHO?

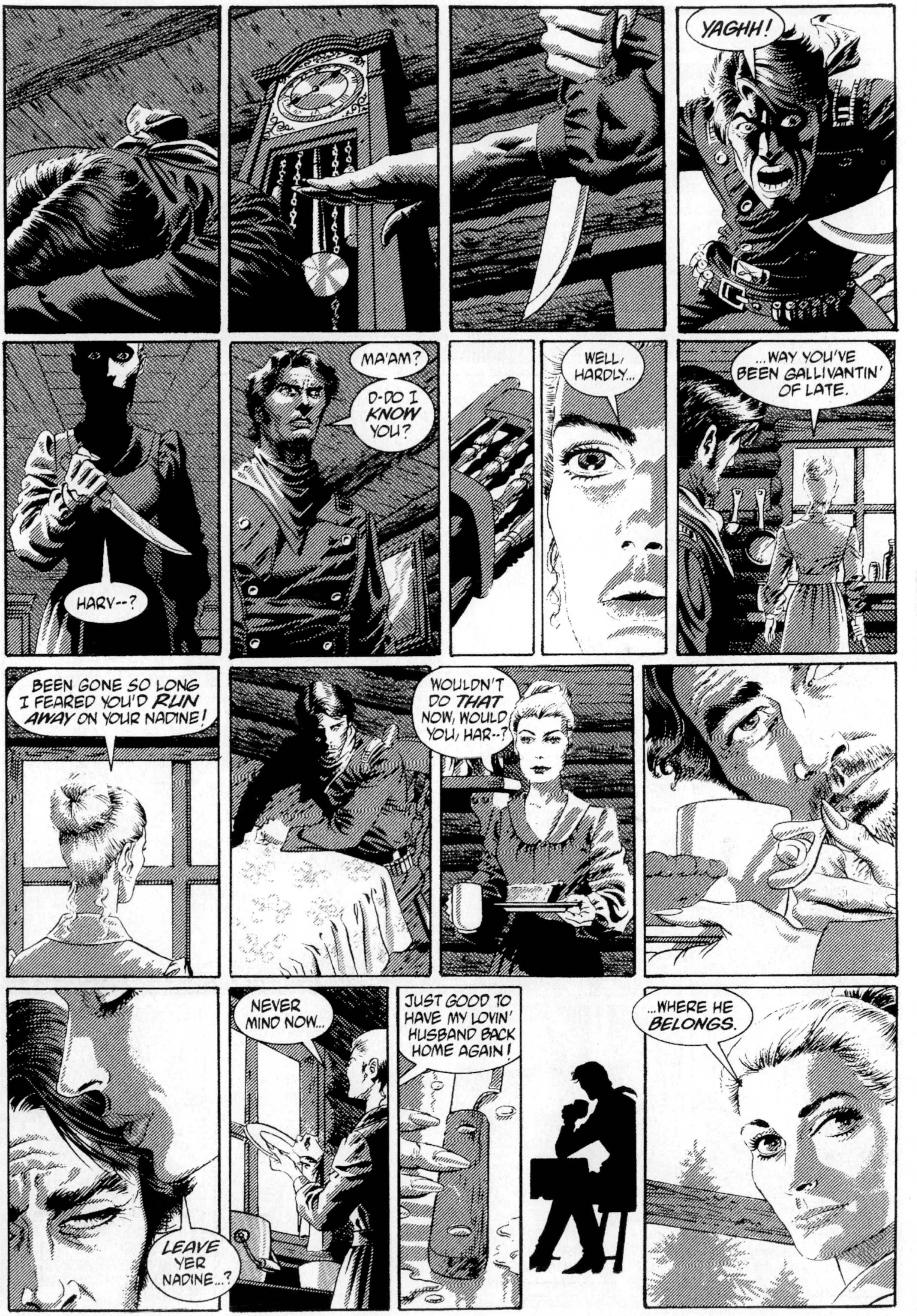
YAGHH!
HARV--?
MA'AM?
D-DO I KNOW YOU?
WELL, HARDLY...
...WAY YOU'VE BEEN GALLIVANTIN' OF LATE.
BEEN GONE SO LONG I FEARED YOU'D RUN AWAY ON YOUR NADINE!
WOULDN'T DO THAT NOW, WOULD YOU, HAR--?
LEAVE YER NADINE...?
NEVER MIND NOW...
JUST GOOD TO HAVE MY LOVIN' HUSBAND BACK HOME AGAIN!
...WHERE HE BELONGS.

POOR SOUL. MUSTA HID OUT WHEN THE PAWNEE ATTACKED.

NOW SHE'S *STILL HIDIN'*...GONE TO SOME *DARK PLACE* IN HER MIND...

SOME *SAFE PLACE* WHERE THE WORLD IS STILL RIGHT AND *I'M* HER *DEAD HUSBAND.*

"HARV HOLTEN." EVEN *LOOKS* LIKE ME, 'CEPT FER THE *BEARD.*

HARV HONEY? YOU COMIN' TO *BED,* DARLIN'?

LOVE ME, HONEY! LOVE YER *NADINE!*

MUST BE DREAMIN'... PAWNEE MUSTA SCALPED ME AN' SENT ME TO HEAVEN ...

NADINE?

IT'S OKAY, NADINE... YOU'RE SAFE WITH *HARV* NOW. YOU DON'T NEED THE *KNIFE.*

AWRIGHT... *KEEP IT,* THEN... IF IT MAKES YOU FEEL BETTER...

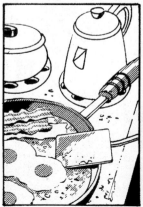

AWOL NOW FER SURE.

BUT S'POSE I WAS TO LET THIS HERE *BEARD* GROW...?

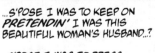

...S'POSE I WAS TO KEEP ON *PRETENDIN'* I WAS THIS BEAUTIFUL WOMAN'S HUSBAND...?

...S'POSE I WAS TO DRESS IN HIS *CLOTHES*... RUN HIS *RANCH*...?

...S'POSE IT WAS HARV *EMERY* THAT *DIED* ...AND HARV *HOLTEN* WENT RIGHT ON *LIVIN'*?

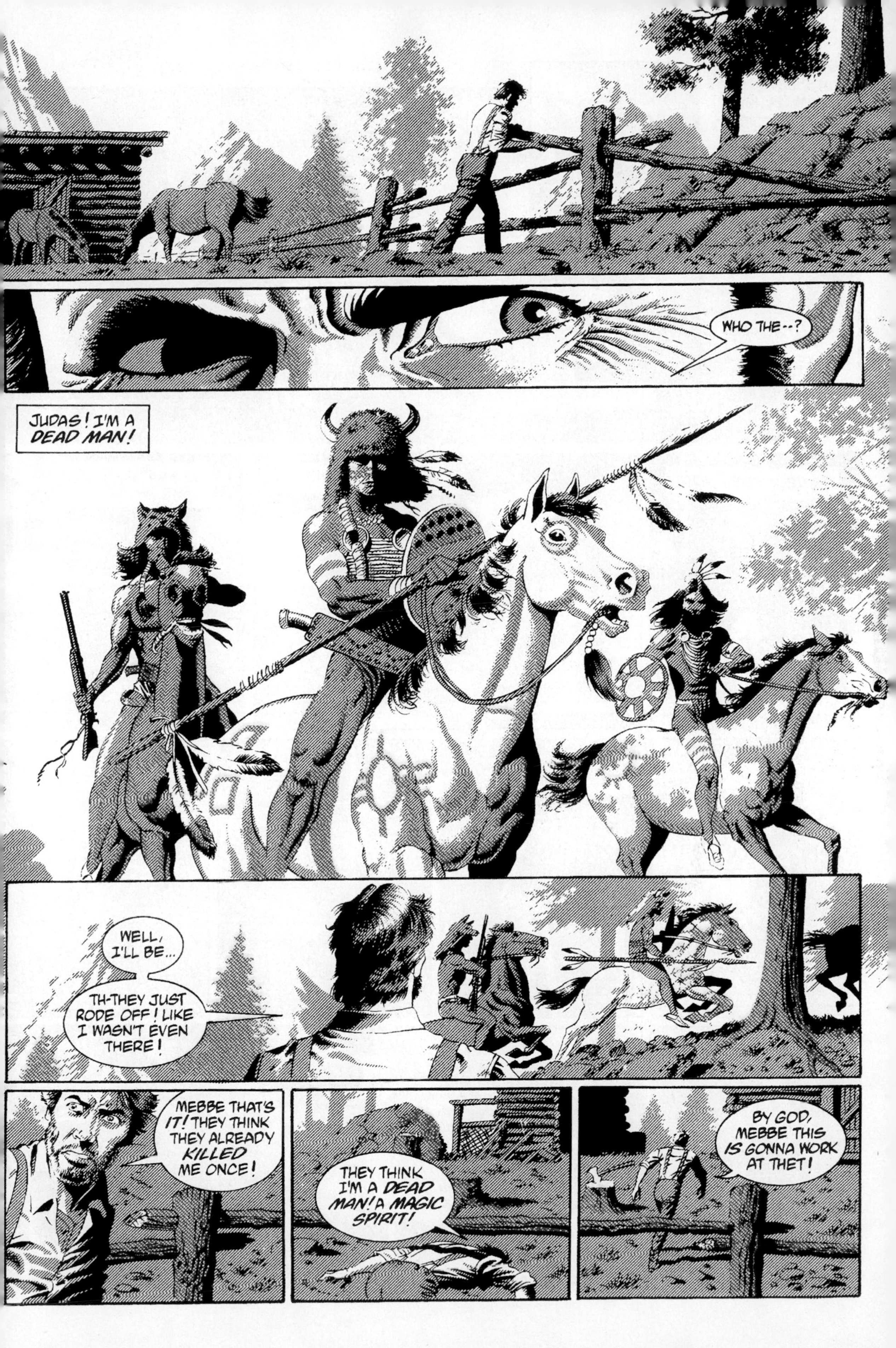
WHO THE--?
JUDAS! I'M A DEAD MAN!
WELL, I'LL BE...
TH-THEY JUST RODE OFF! LIKE I WASN'T EVEN THERE!
MEBBE THAT'S IT! THEY THINK THEY ALREADY KILLED ME ONCE!
THEY THINK I'M A DEAD MAN! A MAGIC SPIRIT!
BY GOD, MEBBE THIS IS GONNA WORK AT THET!

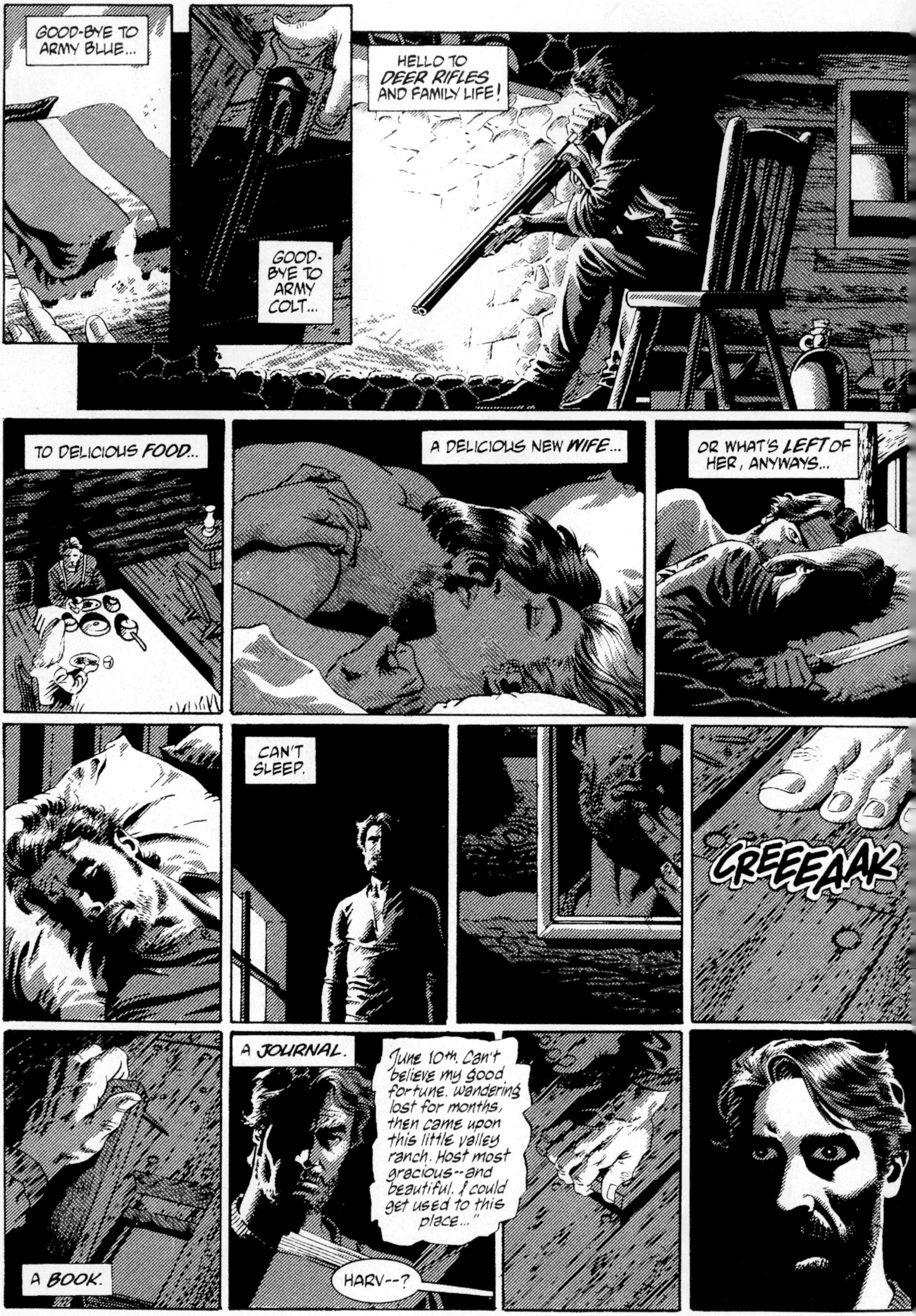

GOOD-BYE TO ARMY BLUE...
GOOD-BYE TO ARMY COLT...
HELLO TO DEER RIFLES AND FAMILY LIFE!
TO DELICIOUS FOOD..
A DELICIOUS NEW WIFE...
OR WHAT'S LEFT OF HER, ANYWAYS...
CAN'T SLEEP.
CREEEAAK
A BOOK.
A JOURNAL.
June 10th. Can't believe my good fortune. Wandering lost for months, then came upon this little valley ranch. Host most gracious--and beautiful. I could get used to this place..."
HARV--?

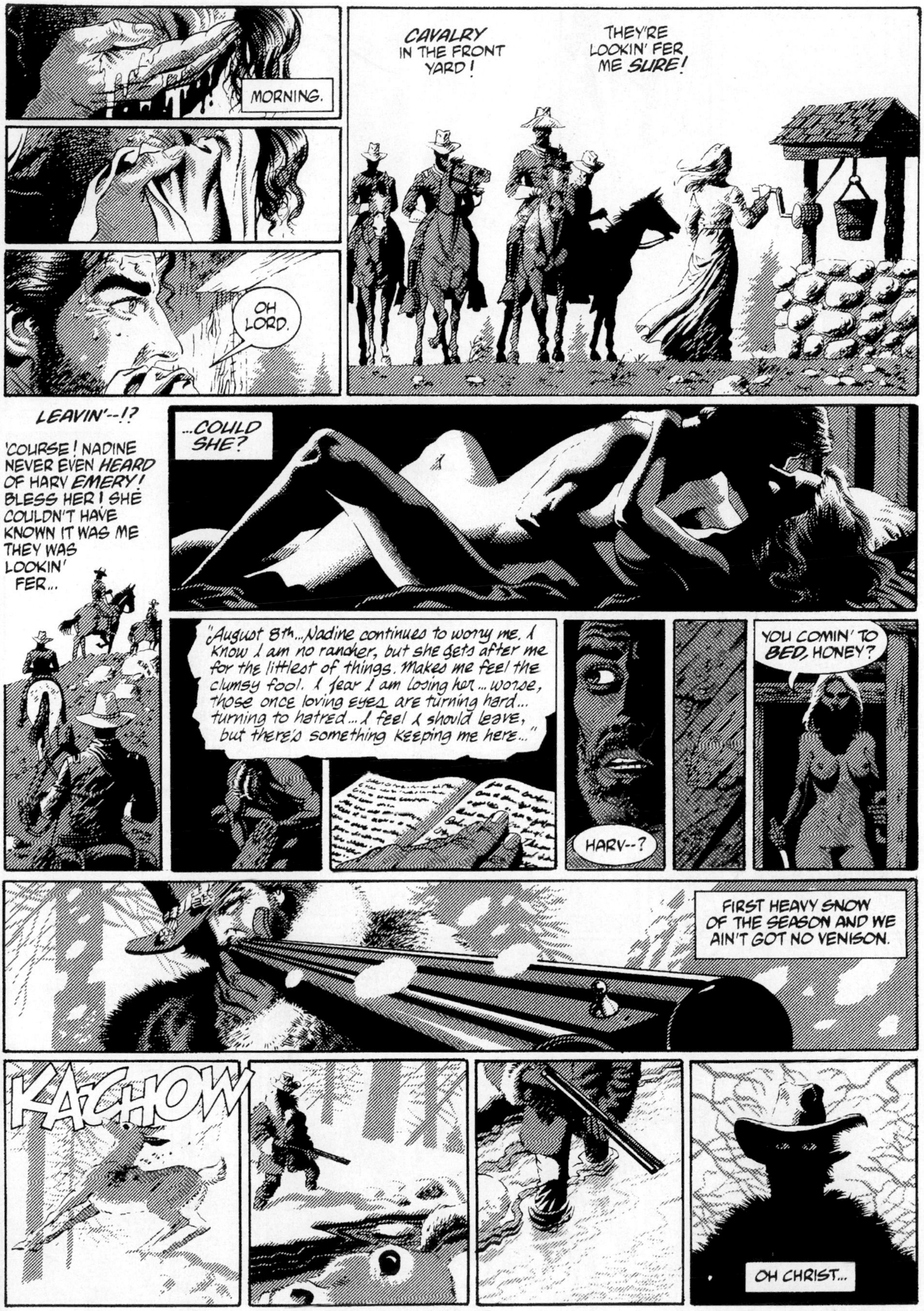
MORNING.
OH LORD.
CAVALRY IN THE FRONT YARD!
THEY'RE LOOKIN' FER ME SURE!
LEAVIN'--!?
'COURSE! NADINE NEVER EVEN HEARD OF HARV EMERY! BLESS HER! SHE COULDN'T HAVE KNOWN IT WAS ME THEY WAS LOOKIN' FER...
...COULD SHE?
"August 8th...Nadine continues to worry me. I know I am no rancher, but she gets after me for the littlest of things. Makes me feel the clumsy fool. I fear I am losing her...worse, those once loving eyes are turning hard... turning to hatred...I feel I should leave, but there's something keeping me here..."
HARV--?
YOU COMIN' TO BED, HONEY?
FIRST HEAVY SNOW OF THE SEASON AND WE AIN'T GOT NO VENISON.
KA-CHOW
OH CHRIST...

HE **KNOWS** I'M NO DEAD SPIRIT, YET HE LEFT ME BE...

...JEST LIKE THE **OTHERS.** WHY?

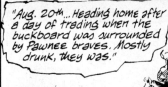
"Aug. 20th... Heading home after a day of trading when the buckboard was surrounded by Pawnee braves. Mostly drunk, they was."

"I gave them what little liquor I had in the wagon..."

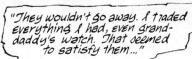
"They wouldn't go away. I traded everything I had, even granddaddy's watch. That seemed to satisfy them..."

"All but one..."

"He raised his war hatchet in trade, pointed to Nadine."

NO! NO TRADE FOR WOMAN!

"The big brave offered to fight for Nadine, hand to hand. I lowered my head in fear."

"The brave laughed. They all laughed. Then they took their turns with Nadine... made me watch."

"They vanished...but did something to Nadine... a light in her eyes... not gone... but **changed**... especially when she looked at me..."

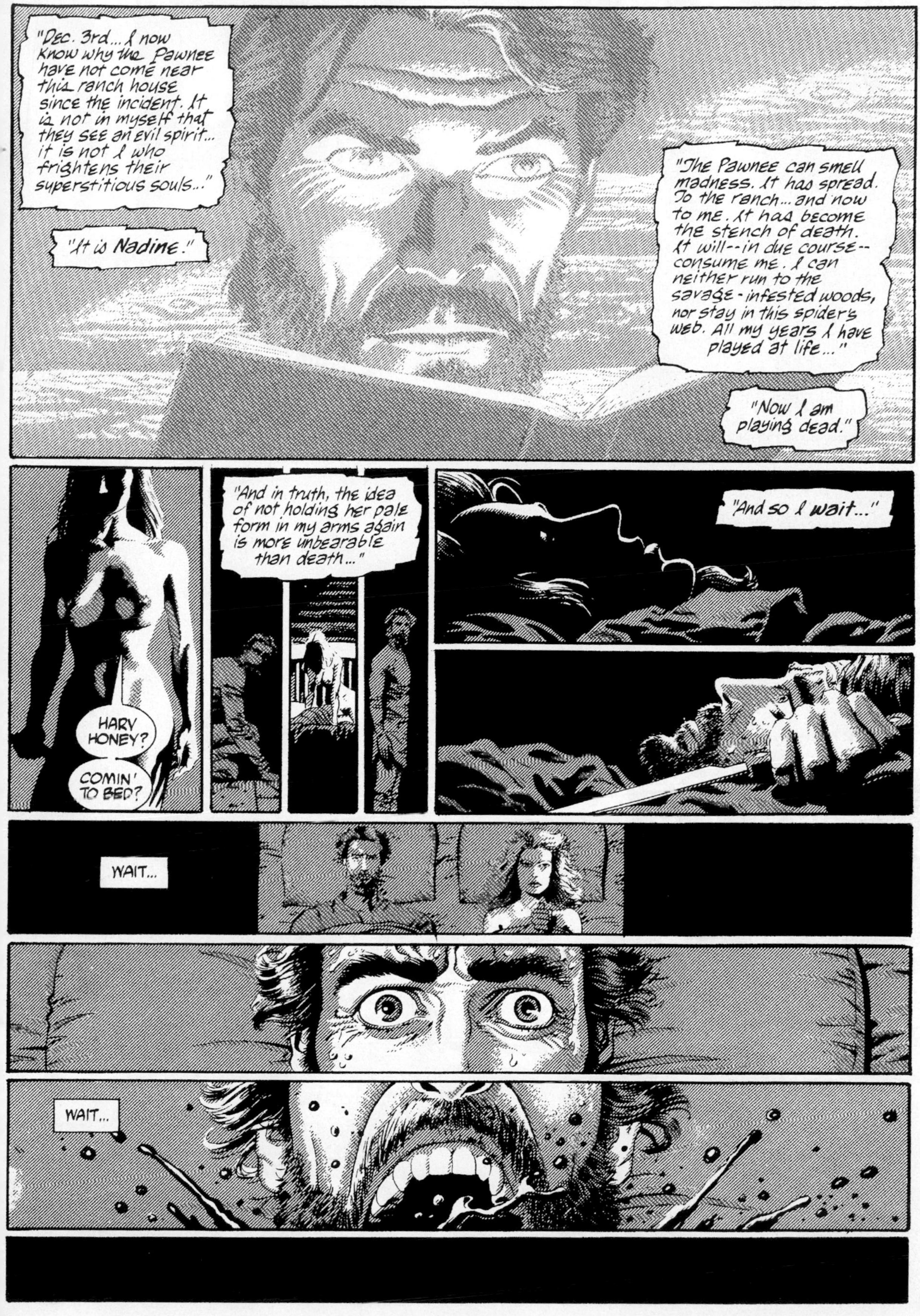
"Dec. 3rd... I now know why the Pawnee have not come near this ranch house since the incident. It is not in myself that they see an evil spirit... it is not I who frightens their superstitious souls..."
"It is Nadine."
"The Pawnee can smell madness. It has spread. To the ranch... and now to me. It has become the stench of death. It will--in due course--consume me. I can neither run to the savage-infested woods, nor stay in this spider's web. All my years I have played at life..."
"Now I am playing dead."
HARV HONEY?
COMIN' TO BED?
"And in truth, the idea of not holding her pale form in my arms again is more unbearable than death..."
"And so I wait..."
WAIT...
WAIT...

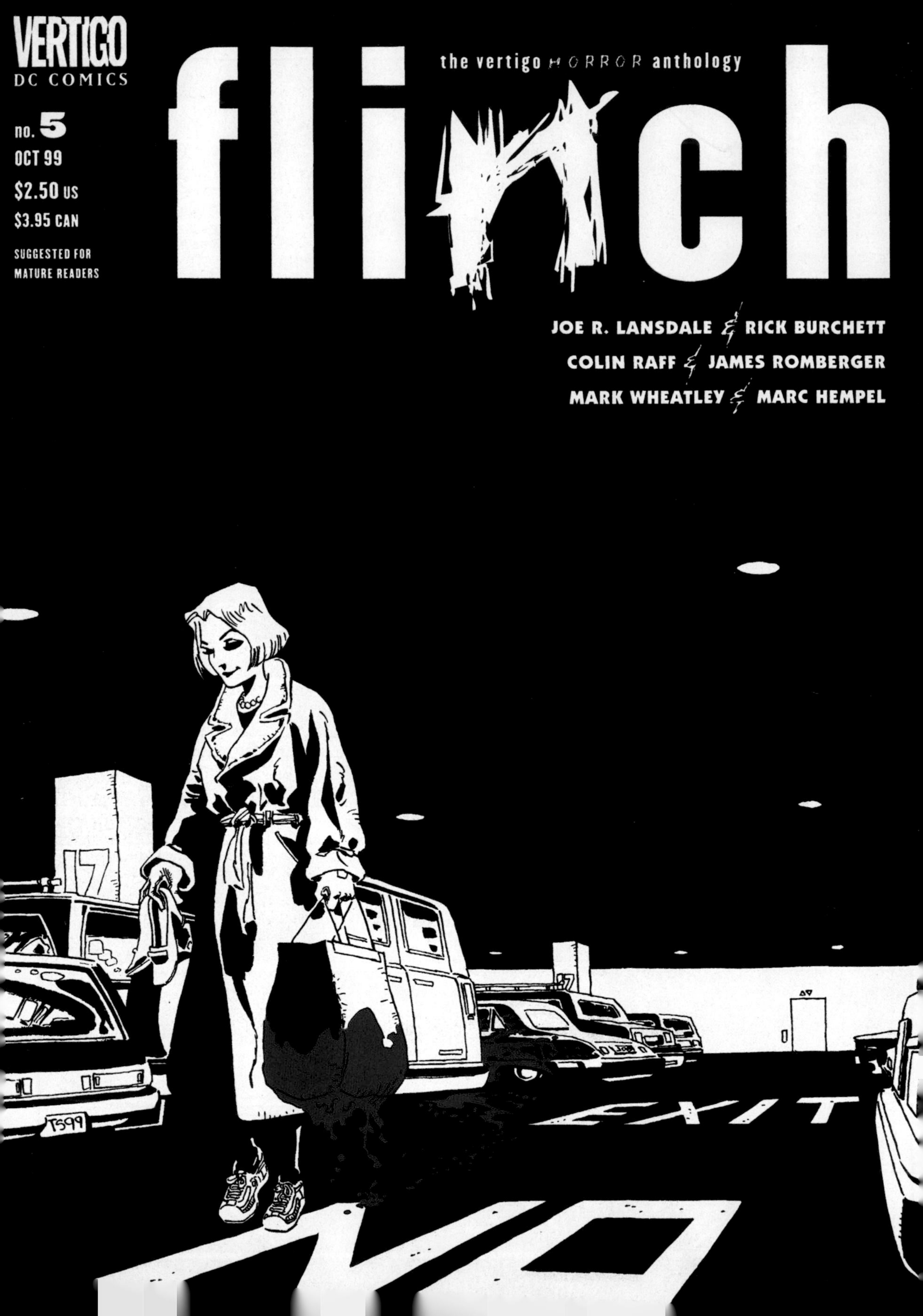

VERTIGO
DC COMICS
no. 5
OCT 99
$2.50 US
$3.95 CAN
SUGGESTED FOR MATURE READERS
the vertigo HORROR anthology
flinch
JOE R. LANSDALE & RICK BURCHETT
COLIN RAFF & JAMES ROMBERGER
MARK WHEATLEY & MARC HEMPEL
17
EXIT
TS99

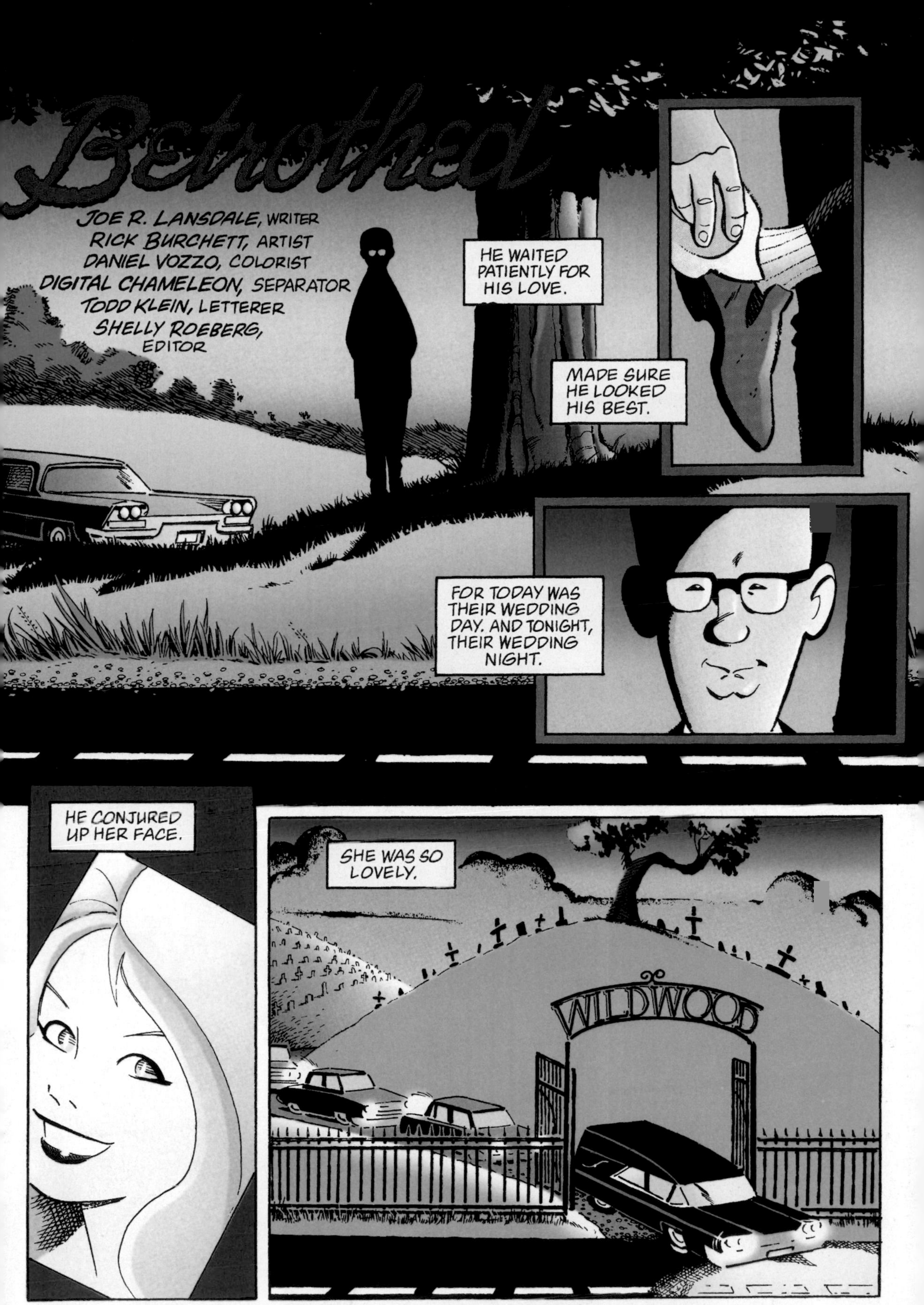
Betrothed
JOE R. LANSDALE, WRITER
RICK BURCHETT, ARTIST
DANIEL VOZZO, COLORIST
DIGITAL CHAMELEON, SEPARATOR
TODD KLEIN, LETTERER
SHELLY ROEBERG, EDITOR
HE WAITED PATIENTLY FOR HIS LOVE.
MADE SURE HE LOOKED HIS BEST.
FOR TODAY WAS THEIR WEDDING DAY. AND TONIGHT, THEIR WEDDING NIGHT.
HE CONJURED UP HER FACE.
SHE WAS SO LOVELY.
WILDWOOD

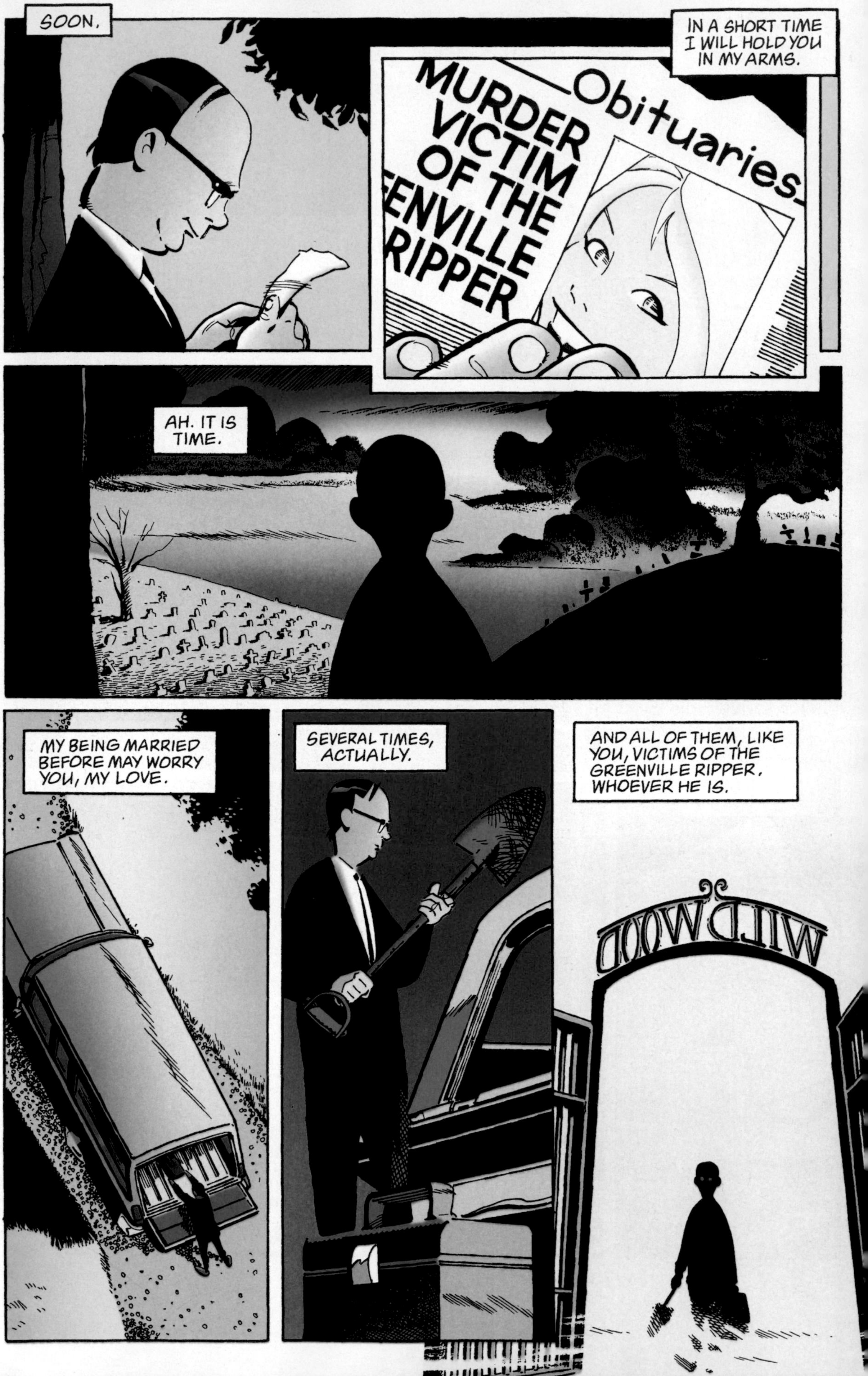
SOON.
IN A SHORT TIME I WILL HOLD YOU IN MY ARMS.
Obituaries
MURDER VICTIM OF THE ENVILLE RIPPER
AH. IT IS TIME.
MY BEING MARRIED BEFORE MAY WORRY YOU, MY LOVE.
SEVERAL TIMES, ACTUALLY.
AND ALL OF THEM, LIKE YOU, VICTIMS OF THE GREENVILLE RIPPER, WHOEVER HE IS.
WILDWOOD

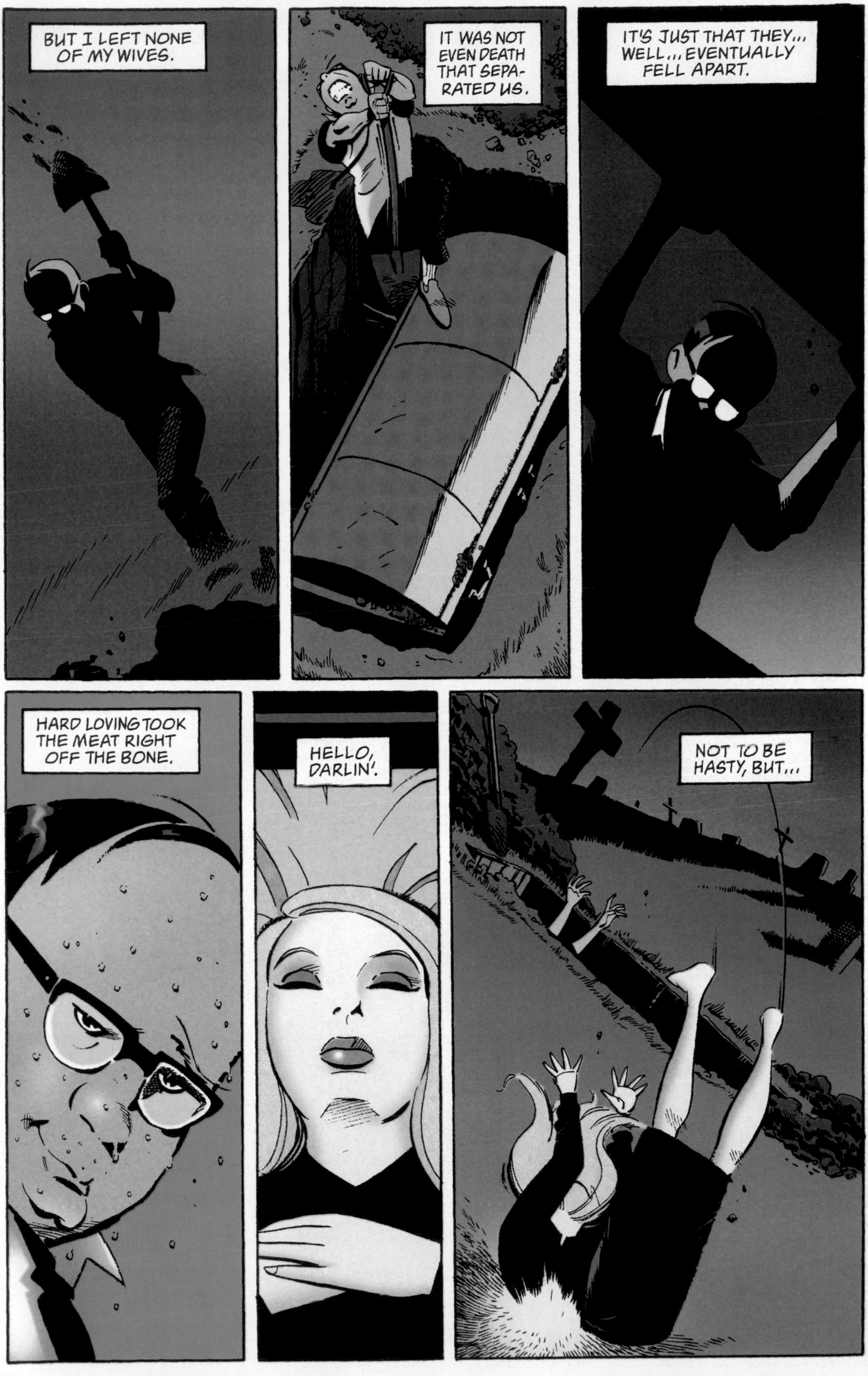
BUT I LEFT NONE OF MY WIVES.
IT WAS NOT EVEN DEATH THAT SEPARATED US.
IT'S JUST THAT THEY... WELL... EVENTUALLY FELL APART.
HARD LOVING TOOK THE MEAT RIGHT OFF THE BONE.
HELLO, DARLIN'.
NOT TO BE HASTY, BUT...

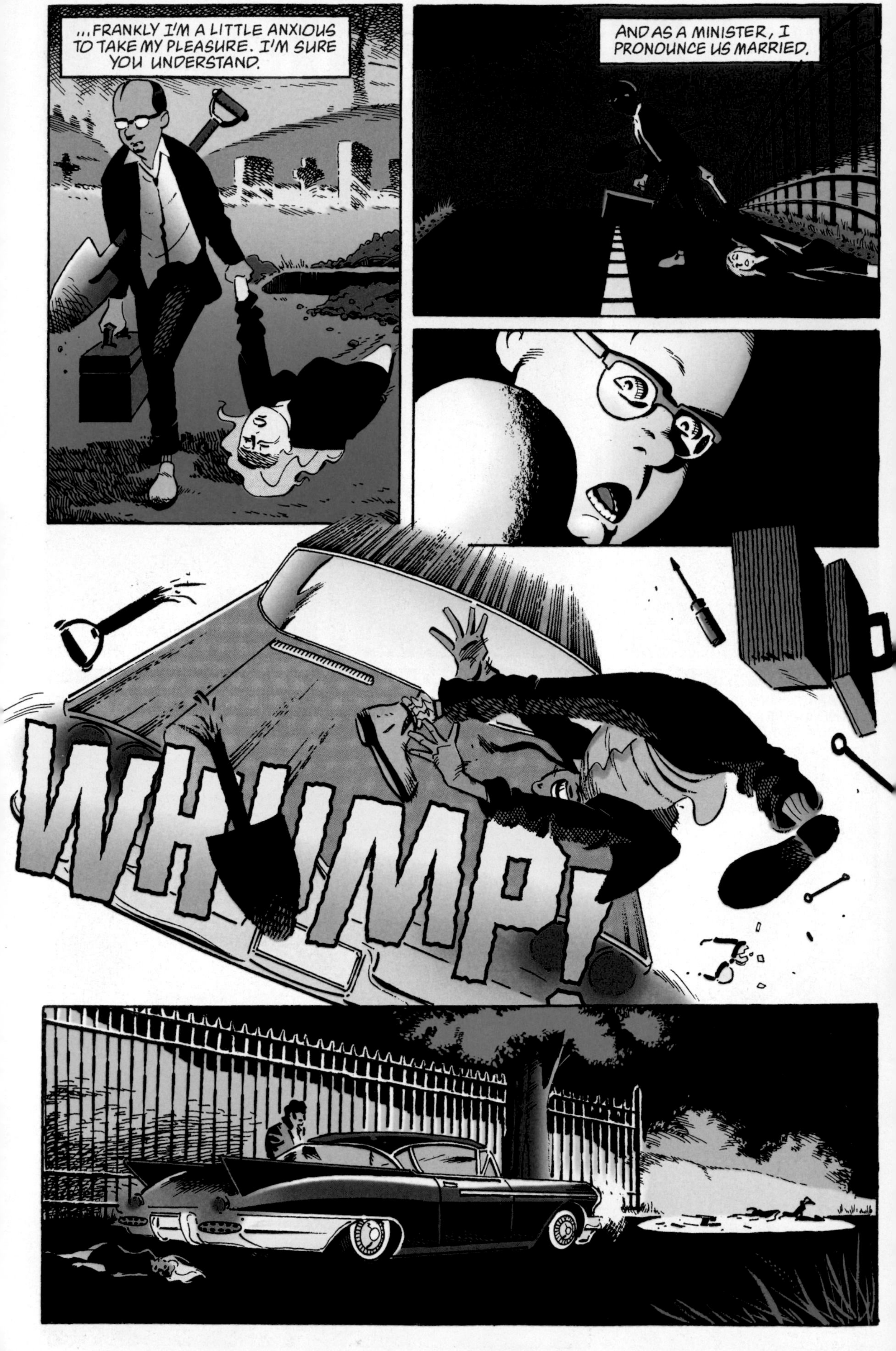
...FRANKLY I'M A LITTLE ANXIOUS TO TAKE MY PLEASURE. I'M SURE YOU UNDERSTAND.
AND AS A MINISTER, I PRONOUNCE US MARRIED.
WHUMP!

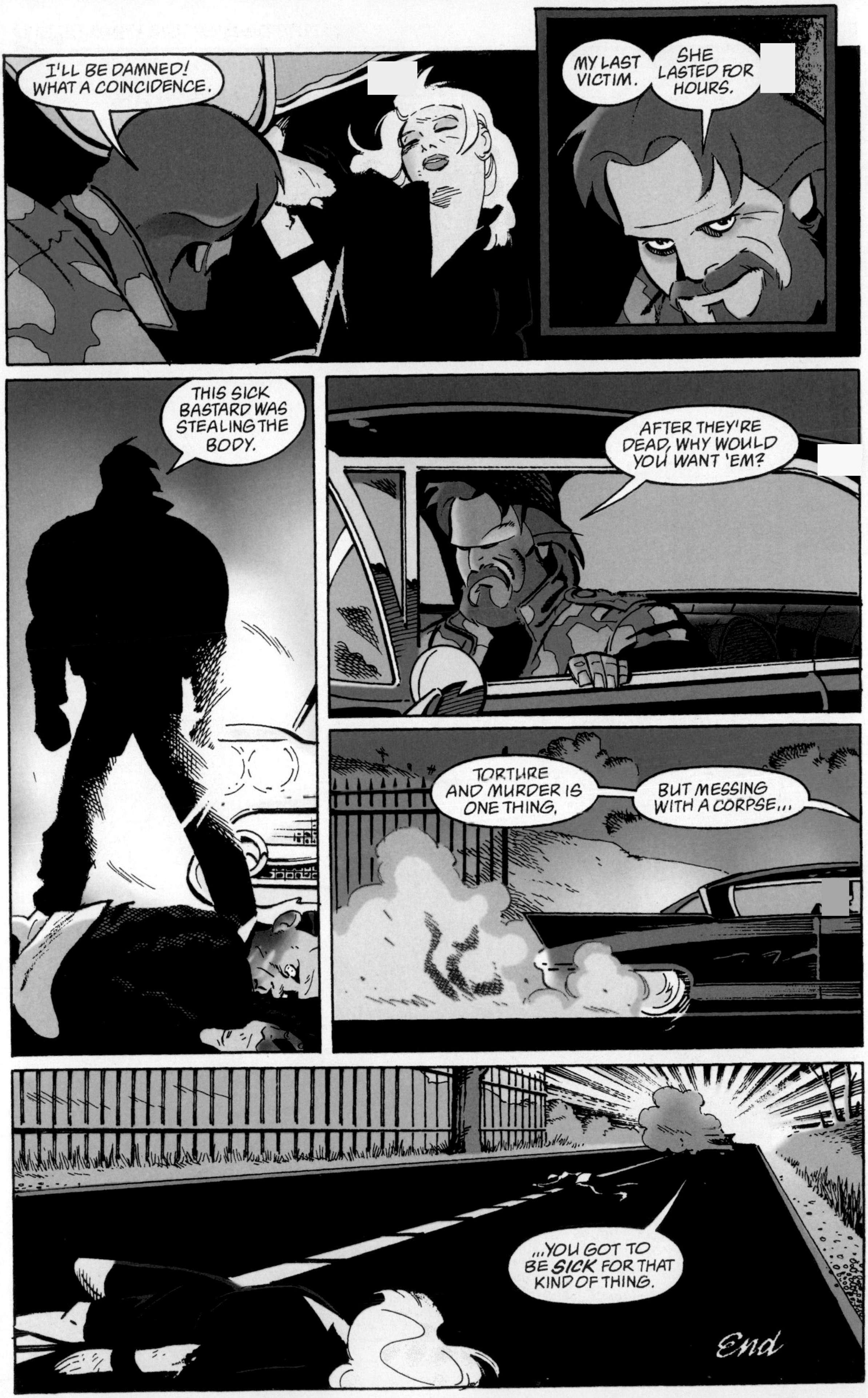
I'LL BE DAMNED! WHAT A COINCIDENCE.
MY LAST VICTIM.
SHE LASTED FOR HOURS.
THIS SICK BASTARD WAS STEALING THE BODY.
AFTER THEY'RE DEAD, WHY WOULD YOU WANT 'EM?
TORTURE AND MURDER IS ONE THING,
BUT MESSING WITH A CORPSE...
...YOU GOT TO BE SICK FOR THAT KIND OF THING.
End

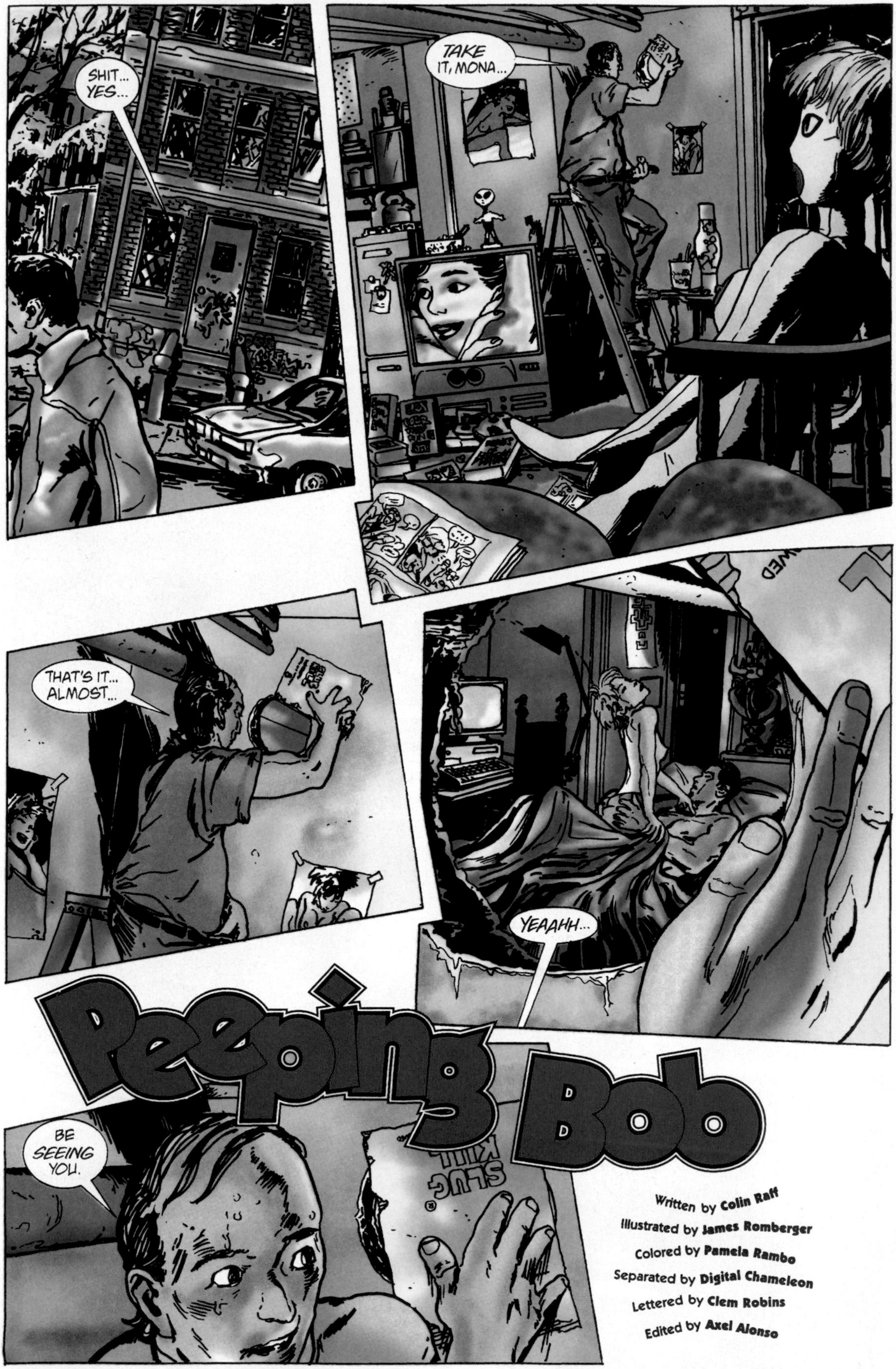
SHIT... YES...
TAKE IT, MONA...
THAT'S IT... ALMOST...
YEAAHH...
Peeping Bob
BE SEEING YOU.
Written by Colin Raff
Illustrated by James Romberger
Colored by Pamela Rambo
Separated by Digital Chameleon
Lettered by Clem Robins
Edited by Axel Alonso

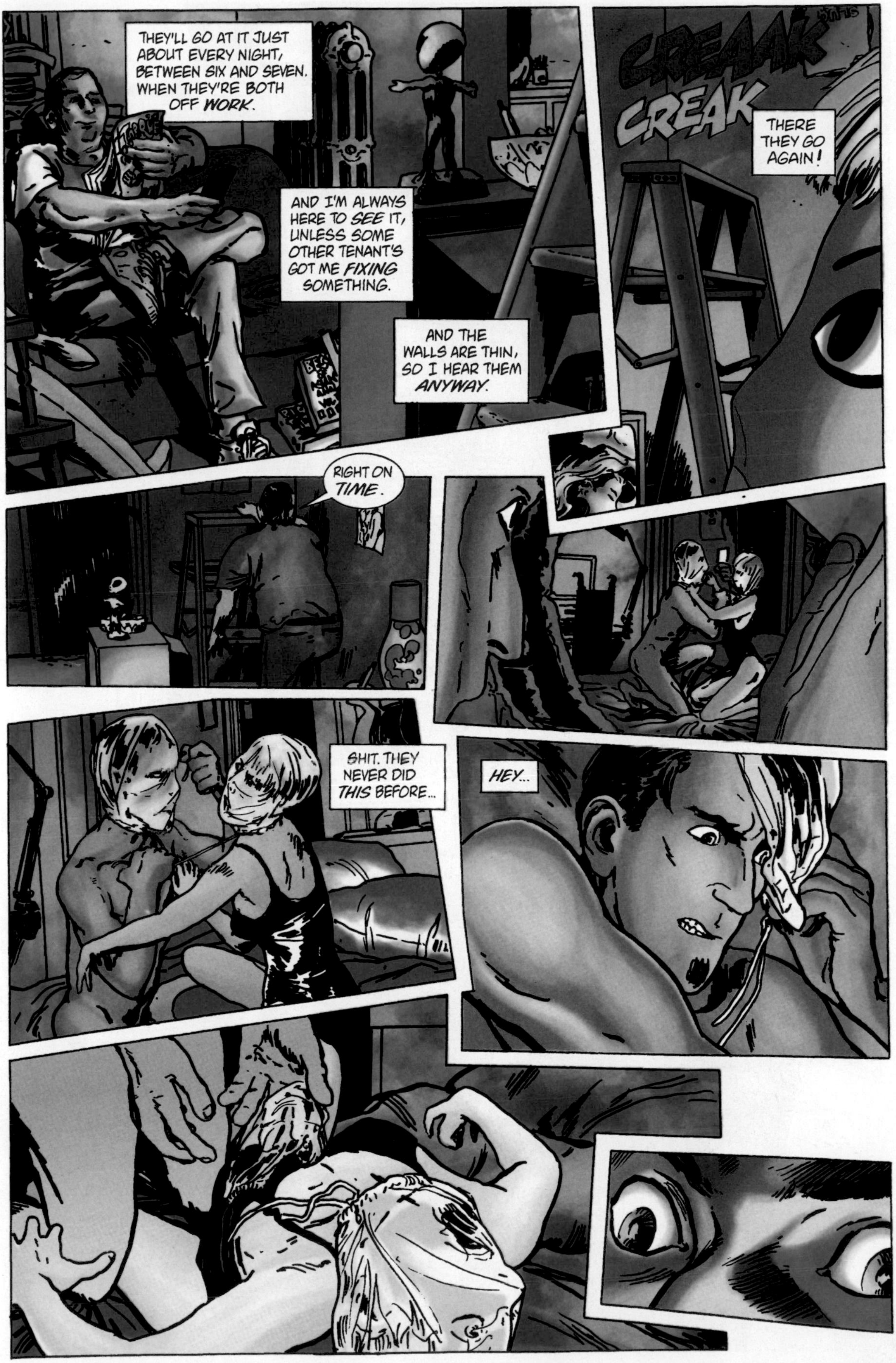
THEY'LL GO AT IT JUST ABOUT EVERY NIGHT, BETWEEN SIX AND SEVEN. WHEN THEY'RE BOTH OFF WORK.
AND I'M ALWAYS HERE TO SEE IT, UNLESS SOME OTHER TENANT'S GOT ME FIXING SOMETHING.
AND THE WALLS ARE THIN, SO I HEAR THEM ANYWAY.
CREAAK
CREAK
THERE THEY GO AGAIN!
RIGHT ON TIME.
SHIT. THEY NEVER DID THIS BEFORE...
HEY...

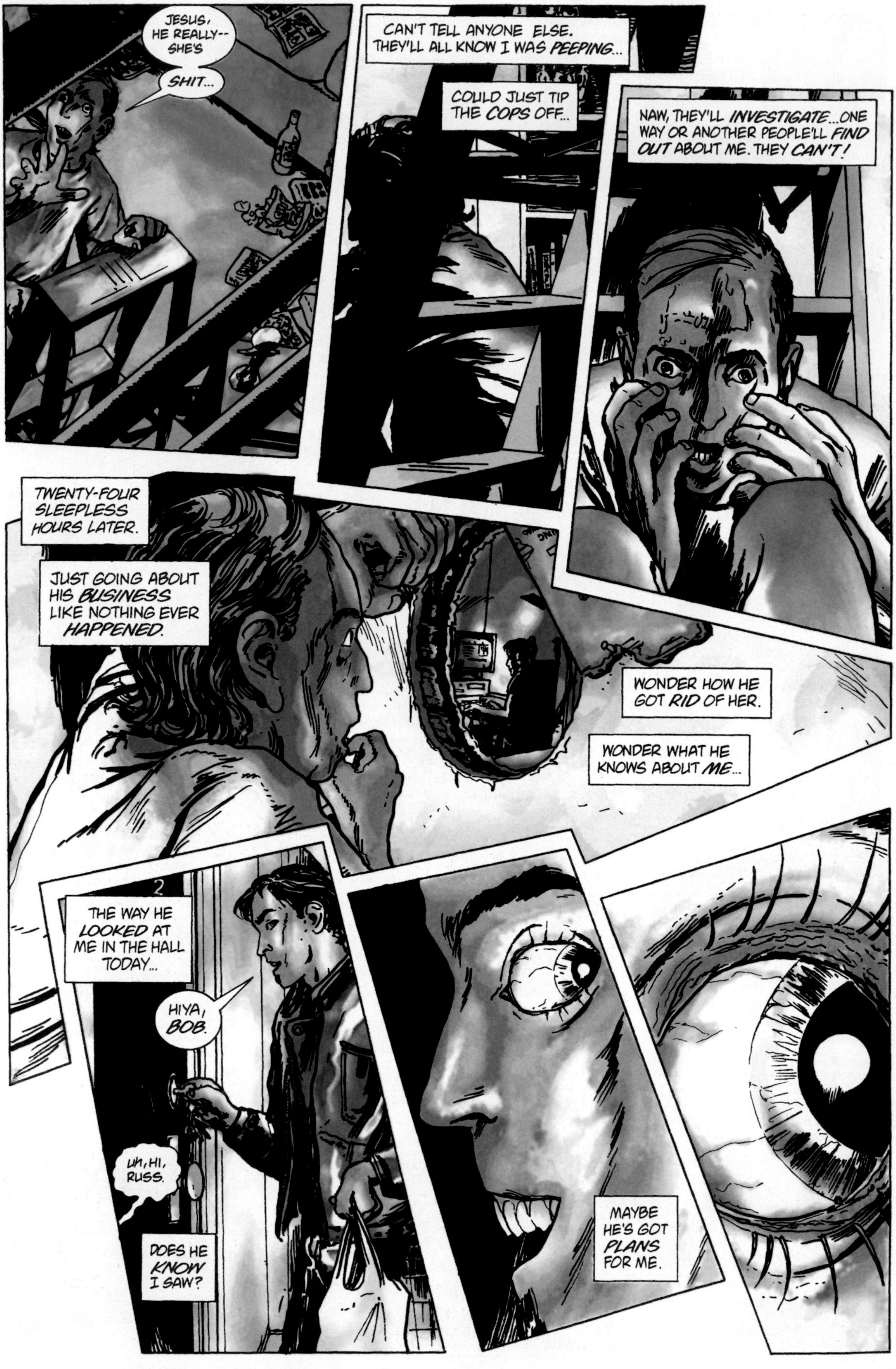
JESUS, HE REALLY-- SHE'S
SHIT...
CAN'T TELL ANYONE ELSE. THEY'LL ALL KNOW I WAS PEEPING...
COULD JUST TIP THE COPS OFF...
NAW, THEY'LL INVESTIGATE...ONE WAY OR ANOTHER PEOPLE'LL FIND OUT ABOUT ME. THEY CAN'T!
TWENTY-FOUR SLEEPLESS HOURS LATER.
JUST GOING ABOUT HIS BUSINESS LIKE NOTHING EVER HAPPENED.
WONDER HOW HE GOT RID OF HER.
WONDER WHAT HE KNOWS ABOUT ME...
THE WAY HE LOOKED AT ME IN THE HALL TODAY...
HIYA, BOB.
UH, HI, RUSS.
DOES HE KNOW I SAW?
MAYBE HE'S GOT PLANS FOR ME.

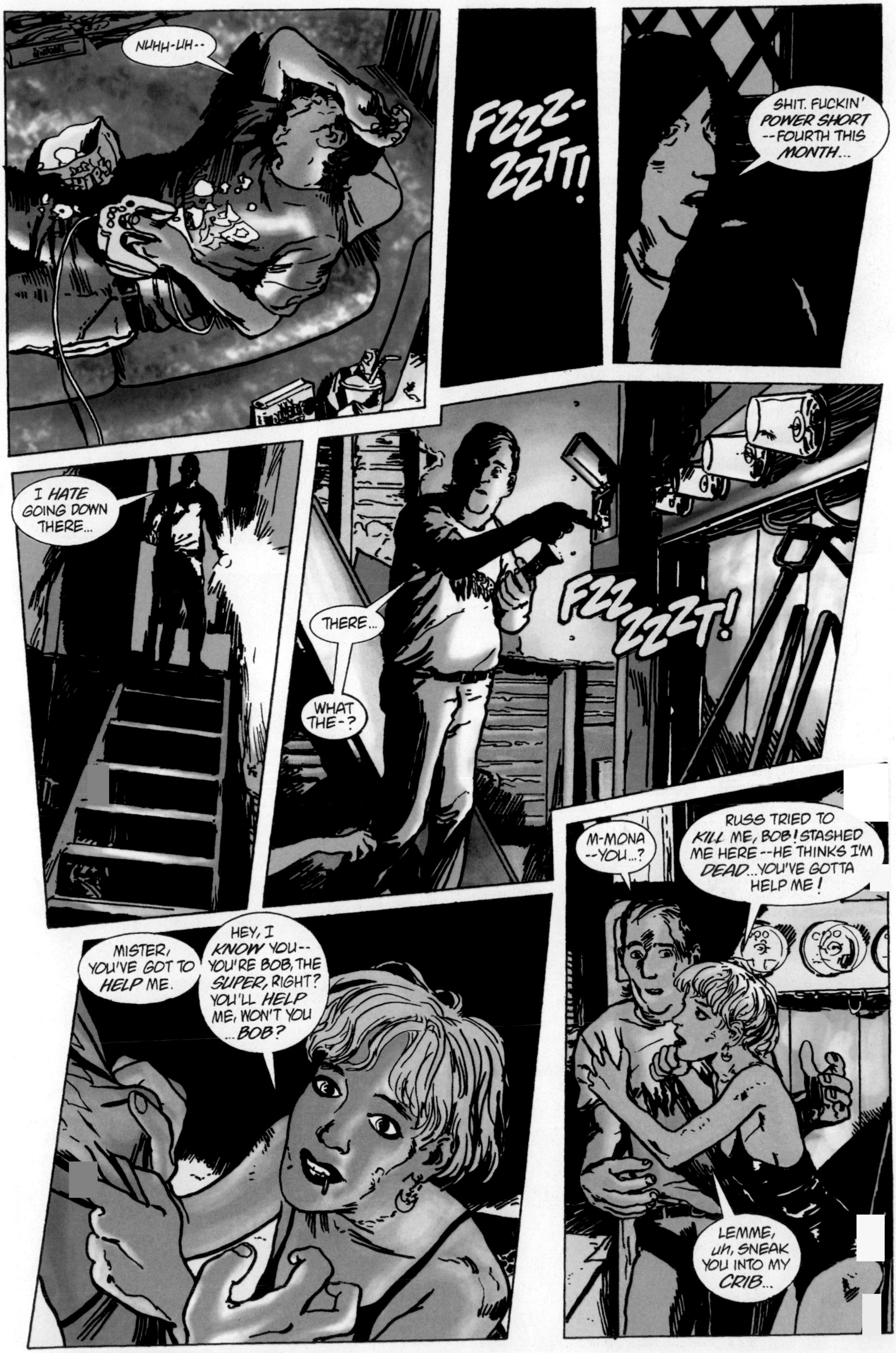
NUHH-UH--
FZZZ-ZZTT!
SHIT. FUCKIN' POWER SHORT --FOURTH THIS MONTH...
I HATE GOING DOWN THERE...
THERE...
WHAT THE-?
FZZZZZT!
M-MONA --YOU...?
RUSS TRIED TO KILL ME, BOB! STASHED ME HERE--HE THINKS I'M DEAD...YOU'VE GOTTA HELP ME!
MISTER, YOU'VE GOT TO HELP ME.
HEY, I KNOW YOU-- YOU'RE BOB, THE SUPER, RIGHT? YOU'LL HELP ME, WON'T YOU ...BOB?
LEMME, uh, SNEAK YOU INTO MY CRIB...

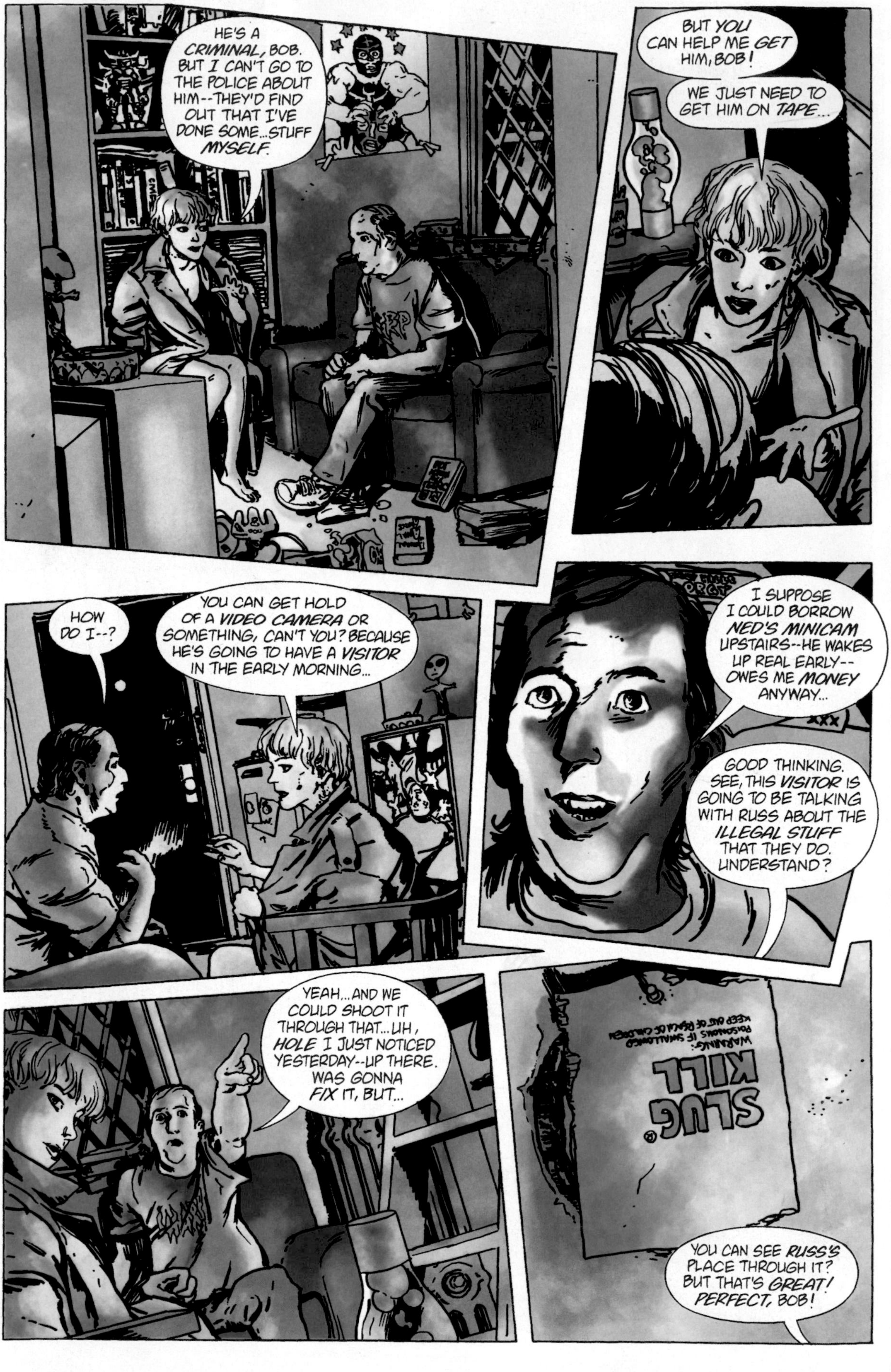
HE'S A CRIMINAL, BOB. BUT I CAN'T GO TO THE POLICE ABOUT HIM--THEY'D FIND OUT THAT I'VE DONE SOME...STUFF MYSELF.
BUT YOU CAN HELP ME GET HIM, BOB!
WE JUST NEED TO GET HIM ON TAPE...
HOW DO I--?
YOU CAN GET HOLD OF A VIDEO CAMERA OR SOMETHING, CAN'T YOU? BECAUSE HE'S GOING TO HAVE A VISITOR IN THE EARLY MORNING...
I SUPPOSE I COULD BORROW NED'S MINICAM UPSTAIRS--HE WAKES UP REAL EARLY--OWES ME MONEY ANYWAY...
GOOD THINKING. SEE, THIS VISITOR IS GOING TO BE TALKING WITH RUSS ABOUT THE ILLEGAL STUFF THAT THEY DO. UNDERSTAND?
YEAH...AND WE COULD SHOOT IT THROUGH THAT...UH, HOLE I JUST NOTICED YESTERDAY--UP THERE. WAS GONNA FIX IT, BUT...
YOU CAN SEE RUSS'S PLACE THROUGH IT? BUT THAT'S GREAT! PERFECT, BOB!

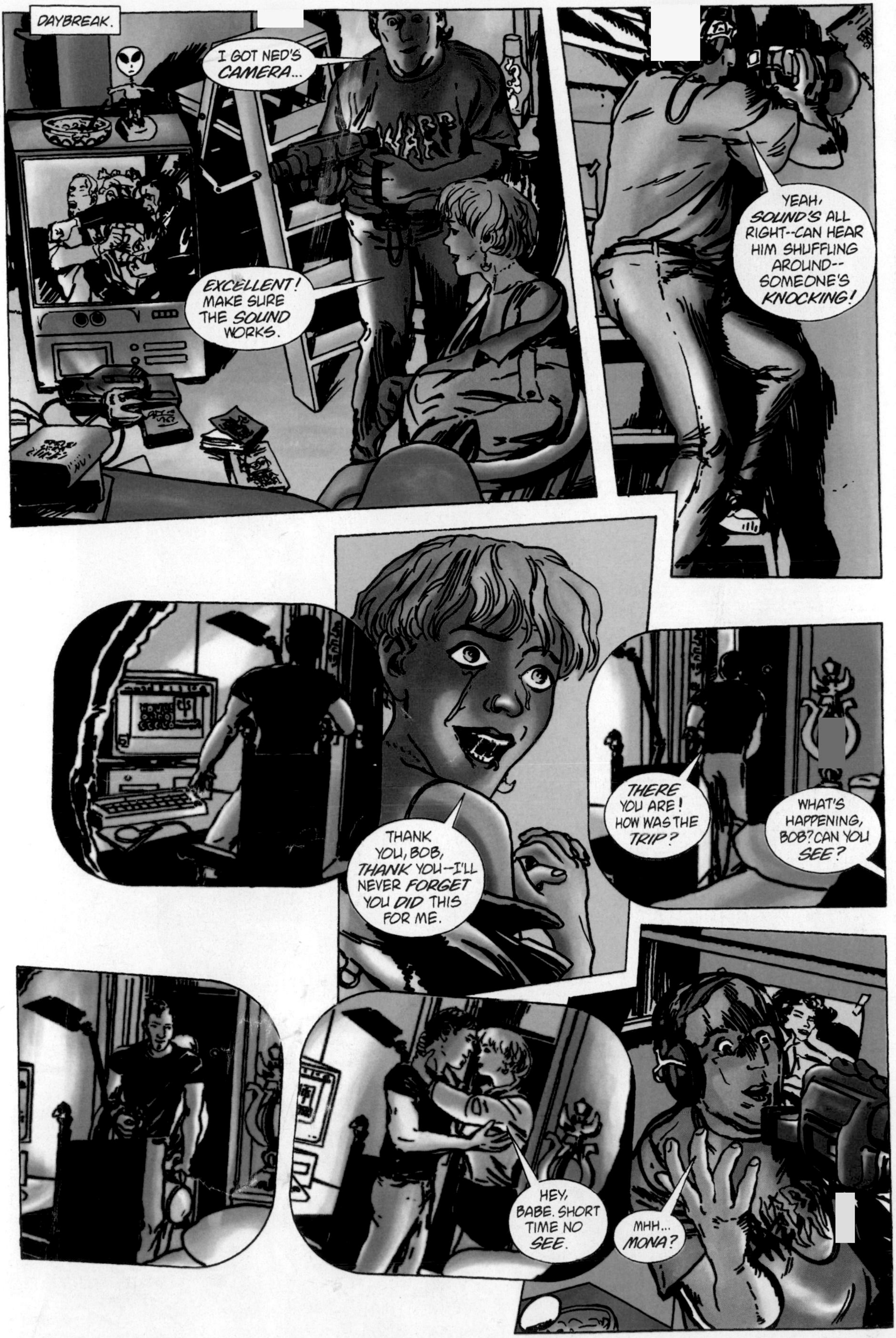
DAYBREAK.
I GOT NED'S CAMERA...
EXCELLENT! MAKE SURE THE SOUND WORKS.
YEAH, SOUND'S ALL RIGHT--CAN HEAR HIM SHUFFLING AROUND--SOMEONE'S KNOCKING!
THANK YOU, BOB, THANK YOU--I'LL NEVER FORGET YOU DID THIS FOR ME.
THERE YOU ARE! HOW WAS THE TRIP?
WHAT'S HAPPENING, BOB? CAN YOU SEE?
HEY, BABE. SHORT TIME NO SEE.
MHH... MONA?

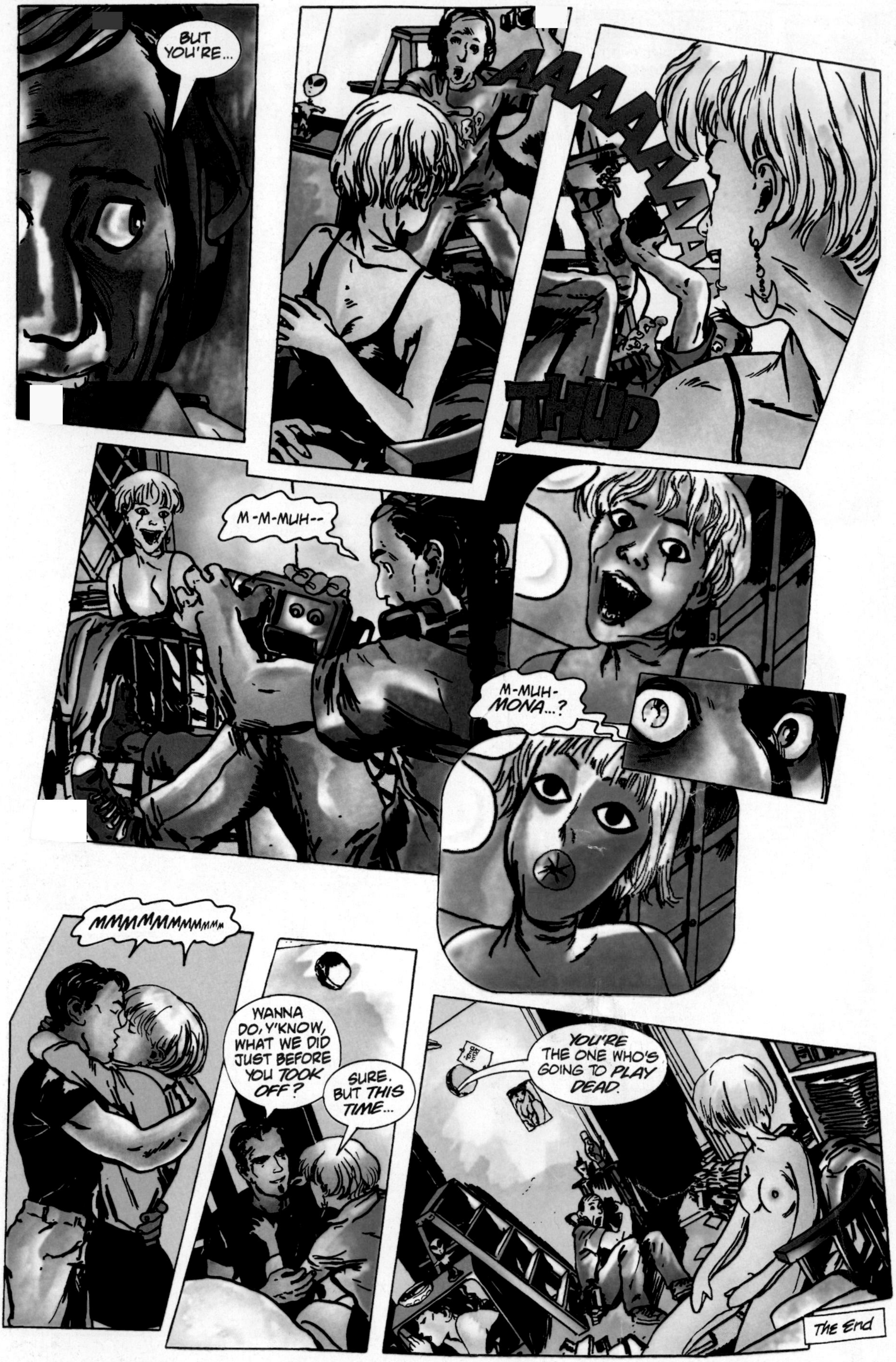
BUT YOU'RE...
AAAAAAAAA
THUD
M-M-MUH--
M-MUH-MONA...?
MMMMMMMMMMM
WANNA DO, Y'KNOW, WHAT WE DID JUST BEFORE YOU TOOK OFF?
SURE. BUT THIS TIME...
YOU'RE THE ONE WHO'S GOING TO PLAY DEAD.
The End

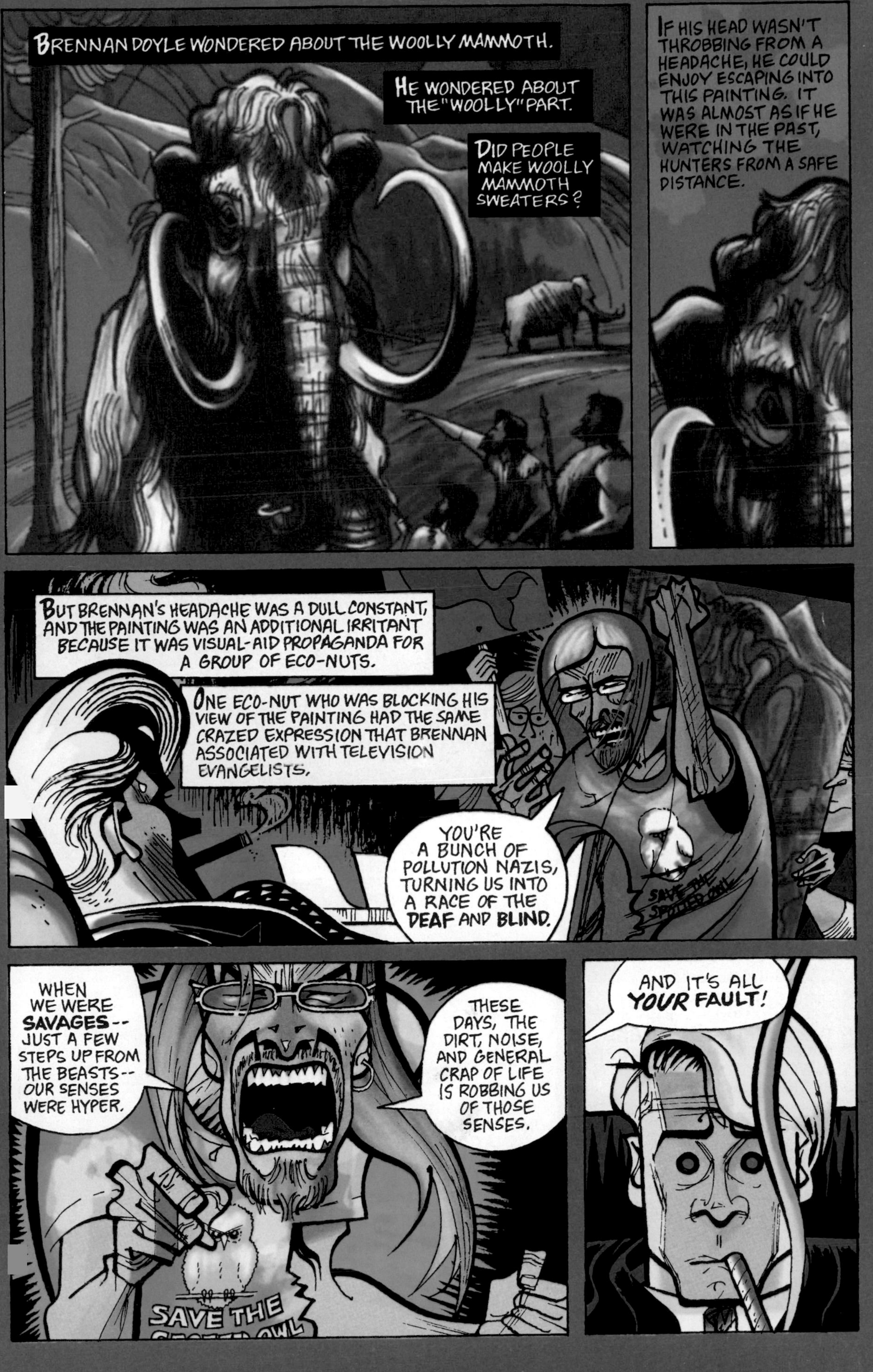
BRENNAN DOYLE WONDERED ABOUT THE WOOLLY MAMMOTH.
HE WONDERED ABOUT THE "WOOLLY" PART.
DID PEOPLE MAKE WOOLLY MAMMOTH SWEATERS?
IF HIS HEAD WASN'T THROBBING FROM A HEADACHE, HE COULD ENJOY ESCAPING INTO THIS PAINTING. IT WAS ALMOST AS IF HE WERE IN THE PAST, WATCHING THE HUNTERS FROM A SAFE DISTANCE.
BUT BRENNAN'S HEADACHE WAS A DULL CONSTANT, AND THE PAINTING WAS AN ADDITIONAL IRRITANT BECAUSE IT WAS VISUAL-AID PROPAGANDA FOR A GROUP OF ECO-NUTS.
ONE ECO-NUT WHO WAS BLOCKING HIS VIEW OF THE PAINTING HAD THE SAME CRAZED EXPRESSION THAT BRENNAN ASSOCIATED WITH TELEVISION EVANGELISTS.
YOU'RE A BUNCH OF POLLUTION NAZIS, TURNING US INTO A RACE OF THE **DEAF** AND **BLIND**.
WHEN WE WERE **SAVAGES**-- JUST A FEW STEPS UP FROM THE BEASTS-- OUR SENSES WERE HYPER.
THESE DAYS, THE DIRT, NOISE, AND GENERAL CRAP OF LIFE IS ROBBING US OF THOSE SENSES.
SAVE THE
AND IT'S ALL ***YOUR*** **FAULT**!

MR. WICKER, **CHEMNATION** ISN'T THE ONLY INDUSTRY OUT HERE. HOW COME YOU'RE LAYING IT ON US?

FUMES

MARK WHEATLEY • Writer
MARC HEMPEL • Artist
JOSÉ VILLARRUBIA • Colorist
DIGITAL CHAMELEON • Separator
JOAN HILTY • Editor

**LOOK** OUT THERE! HOW MANY SMOKE-STACKS CAN YOU COUNT?

TWO MILES OF THAT IS **CHEMNATION**. YOUR COMPANY MANUFACTURES EVERYTHING FROM ARTIFICIAL SWEETENERS TO REALLY NASTY PESTICIDES. CHEMNATION **STINKS**. THIS MANUFACTURING PLANT PRODUCES AN INCREDIBLE AMOUNT OF **SMELLY SMOKE, VAPORS** AND **FUMES**.

AND IT GETS **WORSE**.

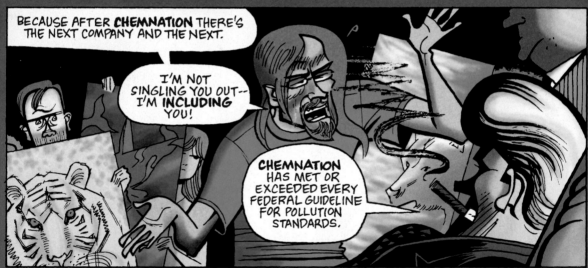

BECAUSE AFTER **CHEMNATION** THERE'S THE NEXT COMPANY AND THE NEXT.

I'M NOT SINGLING YOU OUT—I'M **INCLUDING** YOU!

**CHEMNATION** HAS MET OR EXCEEDED EVERY FEDERAL GUIDELINE FOR POLLUTION STANDARDS.

THE GUIDELINES! **HA!** YOUR **COMPANY**— AND ALL THOSE **OTHER** COMPANIES HAVE PAID FOR THE LOBBYISTS IN WASHINGTON THAT **WROTE** THOSE **GUIDELINES**.

**YEAH?**

AND WHAT ABOUT **CHEMNATION'S** DONATIONS TO YOUR SCREWY ECOLOGICAL GROUPS?

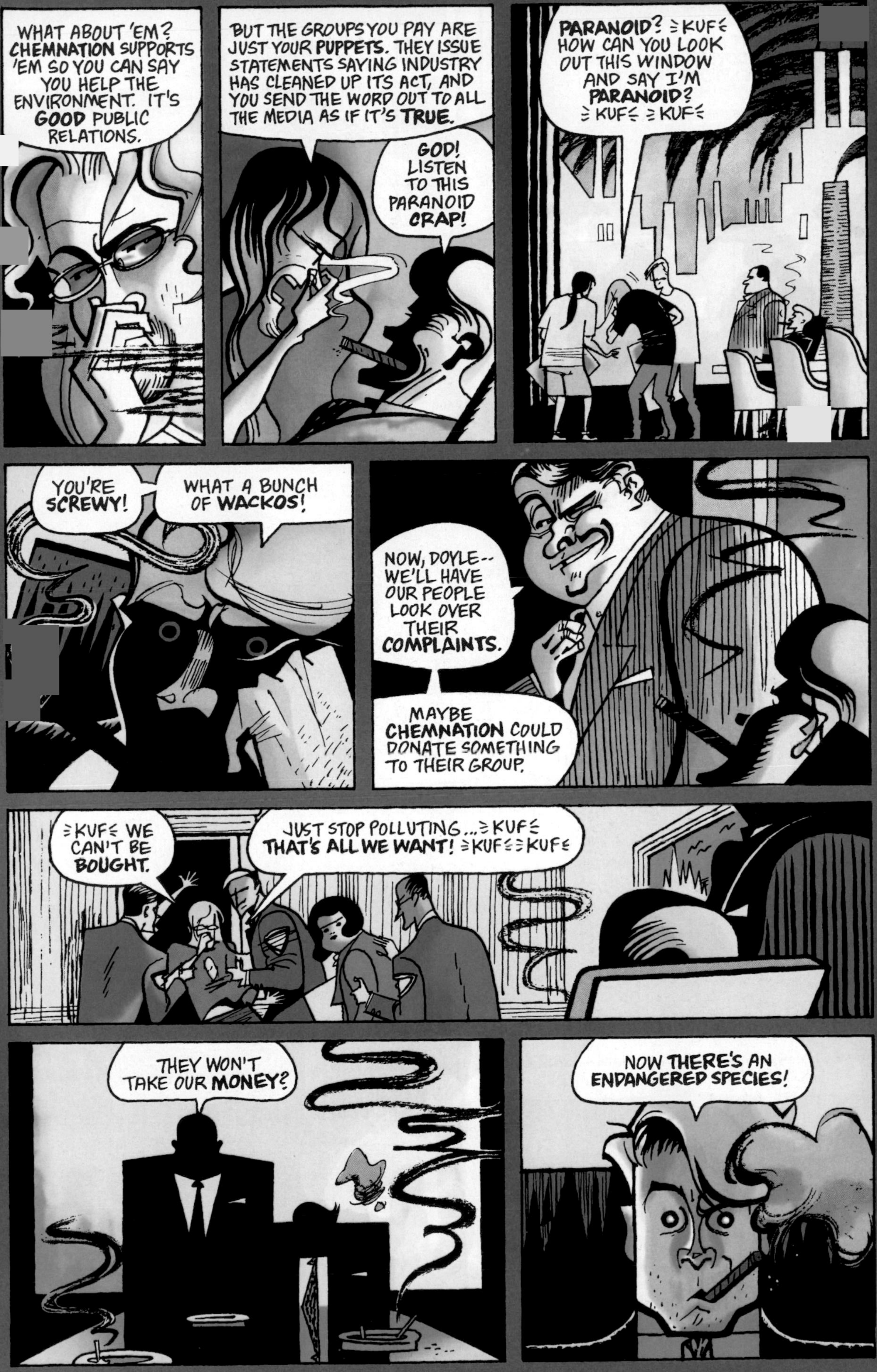
WHAT ABOUT 'EM? CHEMNATION SUPPORTS 'EM SO YOU CAN SAY YOU HELP THE ENVIRONMENT. IT'S GOOD PUBLIC RELATIONS.
BUT THE GROUPS YOU PAY ARE JUST YOUR PUPPETS. THEY ISSUE STATEMENTS SAYING INDUSTRY HAS CLEANED UP ITS ACT, AND YOU SEND THE WORD OUT TO ALL THE MEDIA AS IF IT'S TRUE.
GOD! LISTEN TO THIS PARANOID CRAP!
PARANOID? ≥KUF≤ HOW CAN YOU LOOK OUT THIS WINDOW AND SAY I'M PARANOID? ≥KUF≤ ≥KUF≤
YOU'RE SCREWY!
WHAT A BUNCH OF WACKOS!
NOW, DOYLE-- WE'LL HAVE OUR PEOPLE LOOK OVER THEIR COMPLAINTS.
MAYBE CHEMNATION COULD DONATE SOMETHING TO THEIR GROUP.
≥KUF≤ WE CAN'T BE BOUGHT.
JUST STOP POLLUTING... ≥KUF≤ THAT'S ALL WE WANT! ≥KUF≤ ≥KUF≤
THEY WON'T TAKE OUR MONEY?
NOW THERE'S AN ENDANGERED SPECIES!

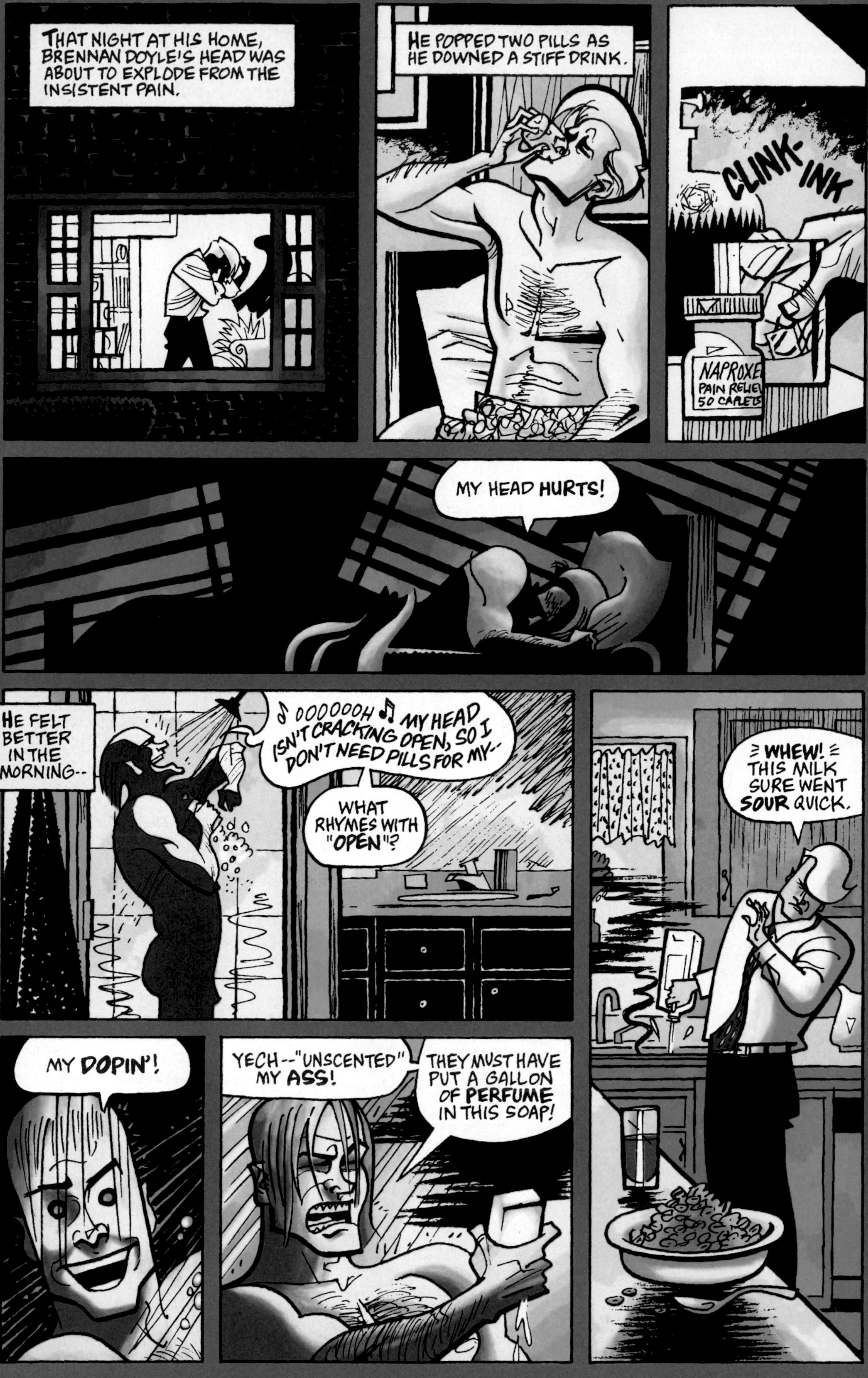
THAT NIGHT AT HIS HOME, BRENNAN DOYLE'S HEAD WAS ABOUT TO EXPLODE FROM THE INSISTENT PAIN.
HE POPPED TWO PILLS AS HE DOWNED A STIFF DRINK.
CLINK-INK
NAPROXE PAIN RELIEV 50 CAPLETS
MY HEAD HURTS!
HE FELT BETTER IN THE MORNING--
♪ OOOOOOH ♫ MY HEAD ISN'T CRACKING OPEN, SO I DON'T NEED PILLS FOR MY--
WHAT RHYMES WITH "OPEN"?
MY DOPIN'!
YECH--"UNSCENTED" MY ASS!
THEY MUST HAVE PUT A GALLON OF PERFUME IN THIS SOAP!
WHEW! THIS MILK SURE WENT SOUR QUICK.

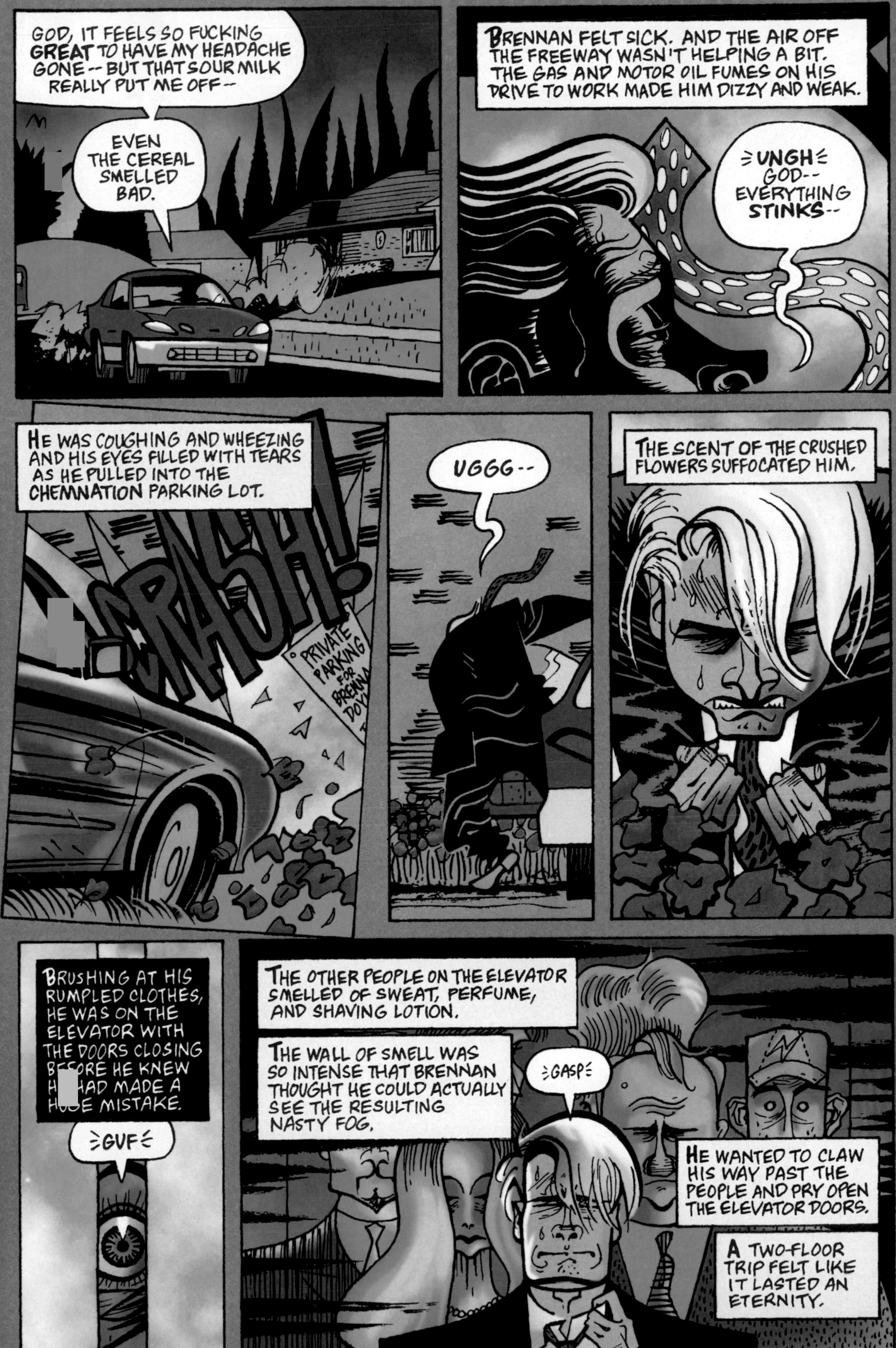
GOD, IT FEELS SO FUCKING GREAT TO HAVE MY HEADACHE GONE -- BUT THAT SOUR MILK REALLY PUT ME OFF --
EVEN THE CEREAL SMELLED BAD.
BRENNAN FELT SICK. AND THE AIR OFF THE FREEWAY WASN'T HELPING A BIT. THE GAS AND MOTOR OIL FUMES ON HIS DRIVE TO WORK MADE HIM DIZZY AND WEAK.
UNGH GOD-- EVERYTHING STINKS--
HE WAS COUGHING AND WHEEZING AND HIS EYES FILLED WITH TEARS AS HE PULLED INTO THE CHEMNATION PARKING LOT.
CRASH!
PRIVATE PARKING FOR
UGGG--
THE SCENT OF THE CRUSHED FLOWERS SUFFOCATED HIM.
BRUSHING AT HIS RUMPLED CLOTHES, HE WAS ON THE ELEVATOR WITH THE DOORS CLOSING BEFORE HE KNEW HE HAD MADE A HUGE MISTAKE.
GUF
THE OTHER PEOPLE ON THE ELEVATOR SMELLED OF SWEAT, PERFUME, AND SHAVING LOTION.
THE WALL OF SMELL WAS SO INTENSE THAT BRENNAN THOUGHT HE COULD ACTUALLY SEE THE RESULTING NASTY FOG.
GASP
HE WANTED TO CLAW HIS WAY PAST THE PEOPLE AND PRY OPEN THE ELEVATOR DOORS.
A TWO-FLOOR TRIP FELT LIKE IT LASTED AN ETERNITY.

IN HIS OFFICE, THE AROMAS WERE TOO MUCH.

FRESH FLOWERS. AN EXOTIC FISH TANK.

HE WRAPPED DUCT TAPE OVER HIS MOUTH AND NOSE.

THE DUCT TAPE DID IT.

THE SCENT OF THE ADHESIVE OVERWHELMED HIM.

THE GORGE SURGED INTO HIS THROAT.

BRENNAN PASSED OUT, GAGGING ON HIS OWN VOMIT, SURE HE WAS SINKING INTO DEATH.

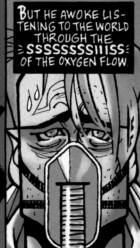

BUT HE AWOKE LISTENING TO THE WORLD THROUGH THE SSSSSSSSSIIISS OF THE OXYGEN FLOW.

DOCTOR-- WHAT HAPPENED TO HIM?

WELL, WE'RE GOING TO NEED TO RUN SOME TESTS.

BUT, CONSIDERING HOW YOU FOUND MR. DOYLE-- WITH HIS FACE DUCT-TAPED-- IT APPEARS HE HAS BECOME HYPER-SENSITIVE TO SMELLS.

YES! EVERYTHING SMELLS AWFUL!

BUT YOU'RE BETTER?

IT'S THIS CANNED AIR! IT SMELLS, TOO -- BUT WITH THE MASK ON, THE OTHER SMELLS ARE NOT SO BAD.

BUT YOU CAN STILL SMELL THIS ROOM?

YES, SOMETHING ROTTEN-- LIKE --

DOC, I CAN SMELL YOUR FOOT FUNGUS!

MY FOOT -- BUT HOW COULD YOU KNOW?

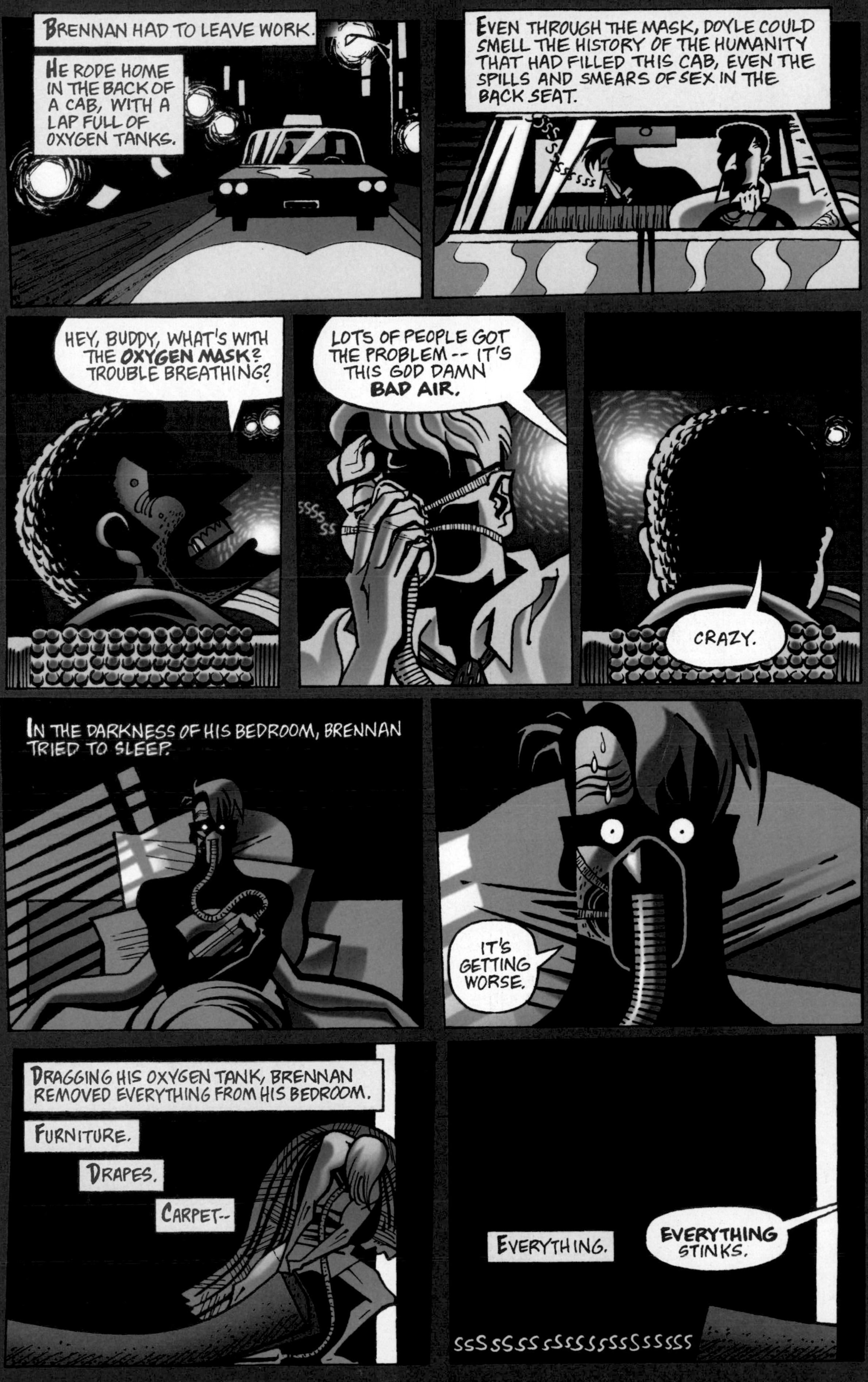
BRENNAN HAD TO LEAVE WORK.
HE RODE HOME IN THE BACK OF A CAB, WITH A LAP FULL OF OXYGEN TANKS.
EVEN THROUGH THE MASK, DOYLE COULD SMELL THE HISTORY OF THE HUMANITY THAT HAD FILLED THIS CAB, EVEN THE SPILLS AND SMEARS OF SEX IN THE BACK SEAT.
SSSSSSSSSS
HEY, BUDDY, WHAT'S WITH THE OXYGEN MASK? TROUBLE BREATHING?
LOTS OF PEOPLE GOT THE PROBLEM -- IT'S THIS GOD DAMN BAD AIR.
SSSSSS
CRAZY.
IN THE DARKNESS OF HIS BEDROOM, BRENNAN TRIED TO SLEEP.
IT'S GETTING WORSE.
DRAGGING HIS OXYGEN TANK, BRENNAN REMOVED EVERYTHING FROM HIS BEDROOM.
FURNITURE.
DRAPES.
CARPET--
EVERYTHING.
EVERYTHING STINKS.
SSSSSSSSSSSSSSSSSSSSSS

HE CLEANED AND SCRUBBED FOR HOURS BUT THE SMELL OF THE DETERGENT WAS TOO MUCH.

HE USED JUST WATER -- BUT SOON THE SMELL OF HIS OWN SWEAT BEGAN TO IRRITATE HIM.

≋UGH!≋

HE SHOWERED. IT DIDN'T HELP.

≋SNF≋ ≋SNF≋ WHAT THE HELL IS THAT AWFUL SMELL?

≋UGH≋ IT'S ME, MY HAIR, THE ROTTING SMELL OF LIFELESS HAIR.

HE SHAVED HIS BODY, BUT THE SMELL PERSISTED.

HIS FINGERNAILS AND TOENAILS WERE THE NEW SOURCE OF STENCH.

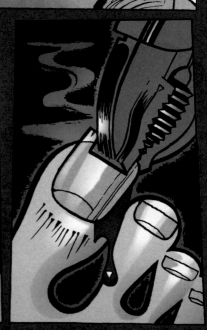

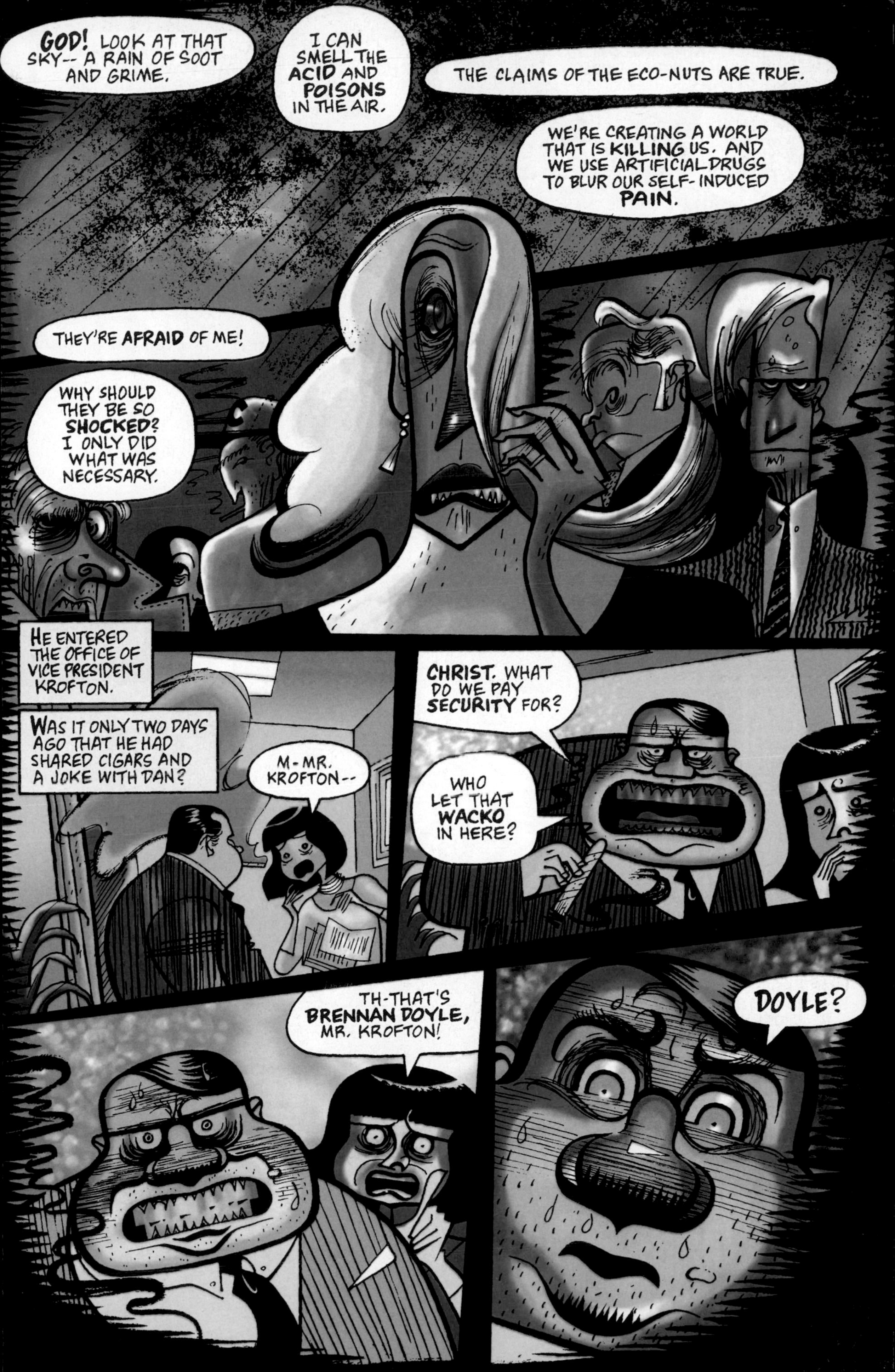
GOD! LOOK AT THAT SKY-- A RAIN OF SOOT AND GRIME.
I CAN SMELL THE ACID AND POISONS IN THE AIR.
THE CLAIMS OF THE ECO-NUTS ARE TRUE.
WE'RE CREATING A WORLD THAT IS KILLING US. AND WE USE ARTIFICIAL DRUGS TO BLUR OUR SELF-INDUCED PAIN.
THEY'RE AFRAID OF ME!
WHY SHOULD THEY BE SO SHOCKED? I ONLY DID WHAT WAS NECESSARY.
HE ENTERED THE OFFICE OF VICE PRESIDENT KROFTON.
WAS IT ONLY TWO DAYS AGO THAT HE HAD SHARED CIGARS AND A JOKE WITH DAN?
M-MR. KROFTON--
CHRIST. WHAT DO WE PAY SECURITY FOR?
WHO LET THAT WACKO IN HERE?
TH-THAT'S BRENNAN DOYLE, MR. KROFTON!
DOYLE?

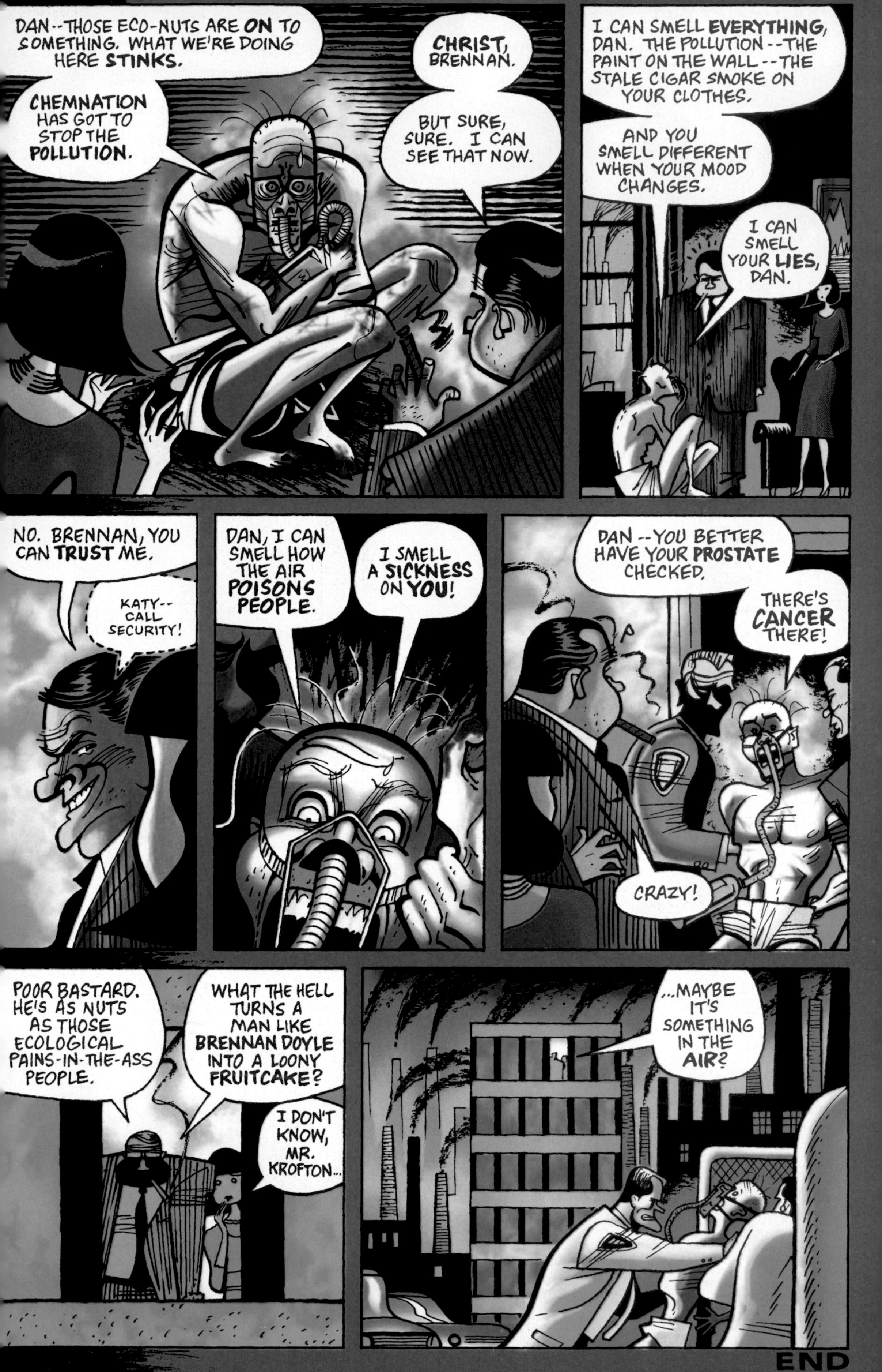
DAN--THOSE ECO-NUTS ARE **ON** TO SOMETHING. WHAT WE'RE DOING HERE **STINKS**.
**CHEMNATION** HAS GOT TO STOP THE **POLLUTION**.
**CHRIST,** BRENNAN.
BUT SURE, SURE. I CAN SEE THAT NOW.
I CAN SMELL **EVERYTHING**, DAN. THE POLLUTION--THE PAINT ON THE WALL--THE STALE CIGAR SMOKE ON YOUR CLOTHES.
AND YOU SMELL DIFFERENT WHEN YOUR MOOD CHANGES.
I CAN SMELL YOUR **LIES**, DAN.
NO. BRENNAN, YOU CAN **TRUST** ME.
KATY--CALL SECURITY!
DAN, I CAN SMELL HOW THE AIR **POISONS PEOPLE**.
I SMELL A **SICKNESS** ON **YOU**!
DAN--YOU BETTER HAVE YOUR **PROSTATE** CHECKED.
THERE'S **CANCER** THERE!
CRAZY!
POOR BASTARD. HE'S AS NUTS AS THOSE ECOLOGICAL PAINS-IN-THE-ASS PEOPLE.
WHAT THE HELL TURNS A MAN LIKE **BRENNAN DOYLE** INTO A LOONY **FRUITCAKE**?
I DON'T KNOW, MR. KROFTON...
...MAYBE IT'S SOMETHING IN THE **AIR**?
END

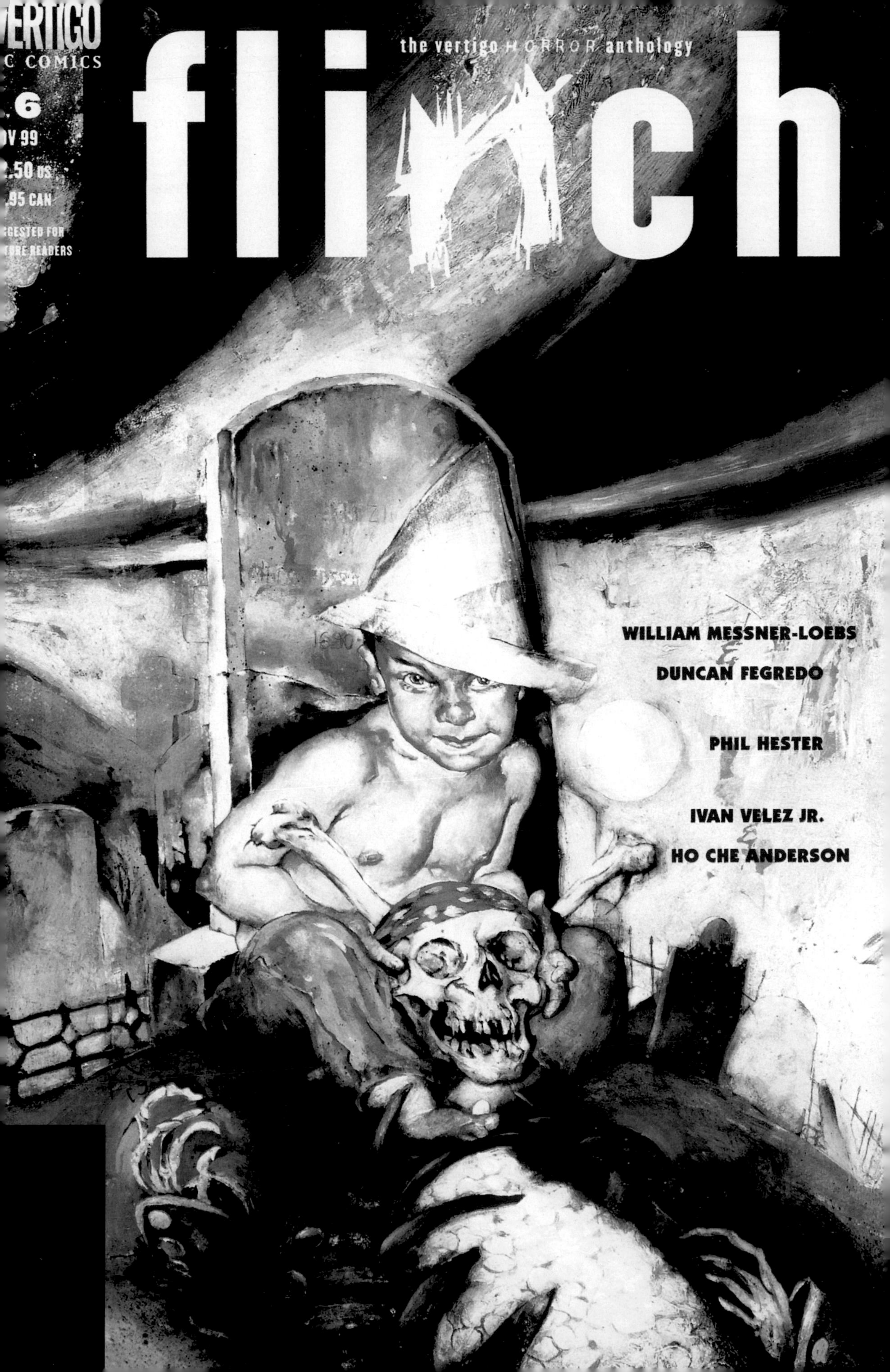

ERTIGO
C COMICS
6
V 99
.50 US
.95 CAN
GESTED FOR
URE READERS
fli ch
the vertigo HORROR anthology
WILLIAM MESSNER-LOEBS
&
DUNCAN FEGREDO
PHIL HESTER
IVAN VELEZ JR.
&
HO CHE ANDERSON

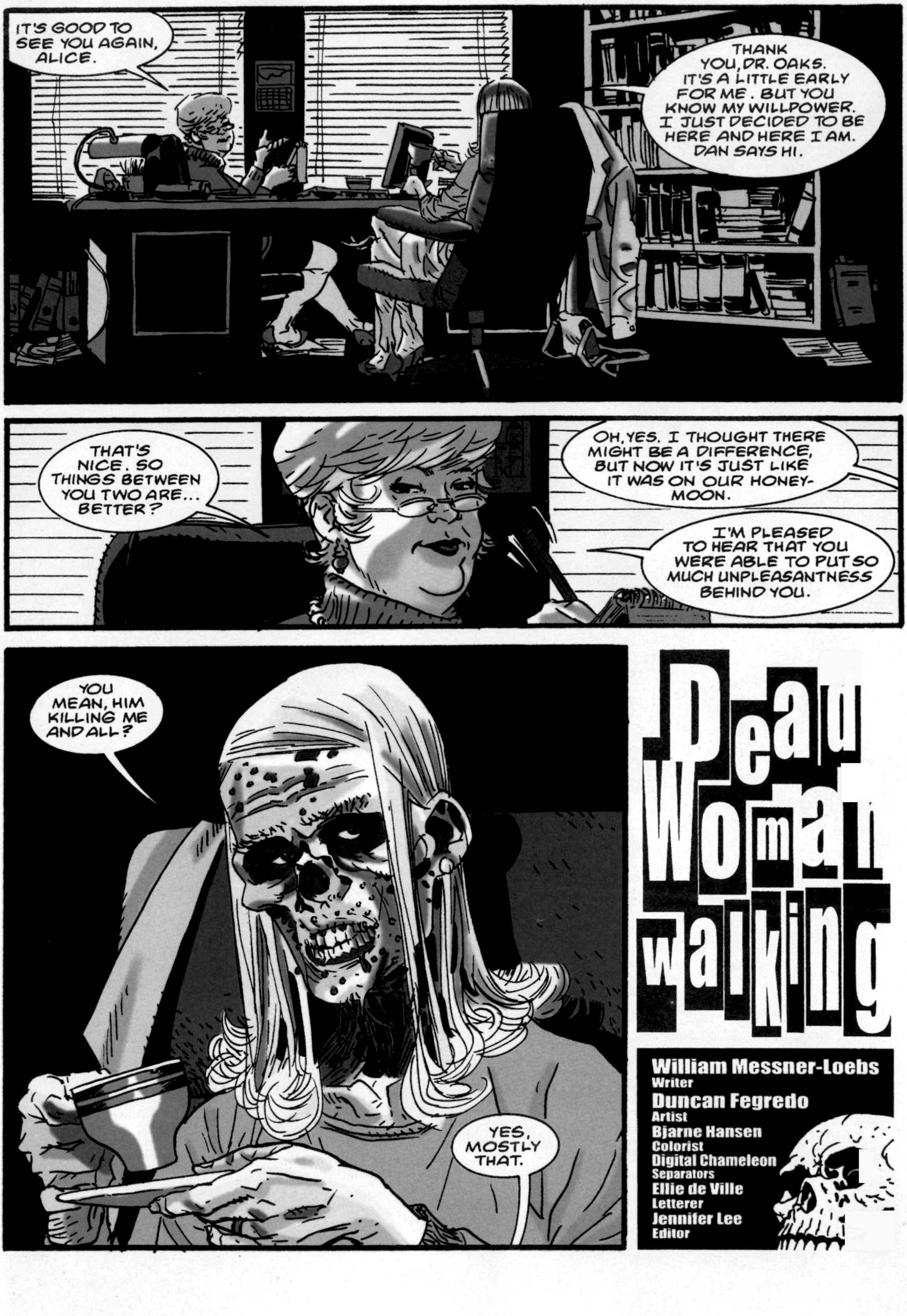
IT'S GOOD TO SEE YOU AGAIN, ALICE.
THANK YOU, DR. OAKS. IT'S A LITTLE EARLY FOR ME. BUT YOU KNOW MY WILLPOWER. I JUST DECIDED TO BE HERE AND HERE I AM. DAN SAYS HI.
THAT'S NICE. SO THINGS BETWEEN YOU TWO ARE... BETTER?
OH, YES. I THOUGHT THERE MIGHT BE A DIFFERENCE, BUT NOW IT'S JUST LIKE IT WAS ON OUR HONEY-MOON.
I'M PLEASED TO HEAR THAT YOU WERE ABLE TO PUT SO MUCH UNPLEASANTNESS BEHIND YOU.
YOU MEAN, HIM KILLING ME AND ALL?
YES, MOSTLY THAT.
Dead Woman walking
William Messner-Loebs
Writer
Duncan Fegredo
Artist
Bjarne Hansen
Colorist
Digital Chameleon
Separators
Ellie de Ville
Letterer
Jennifer Lee
Editor

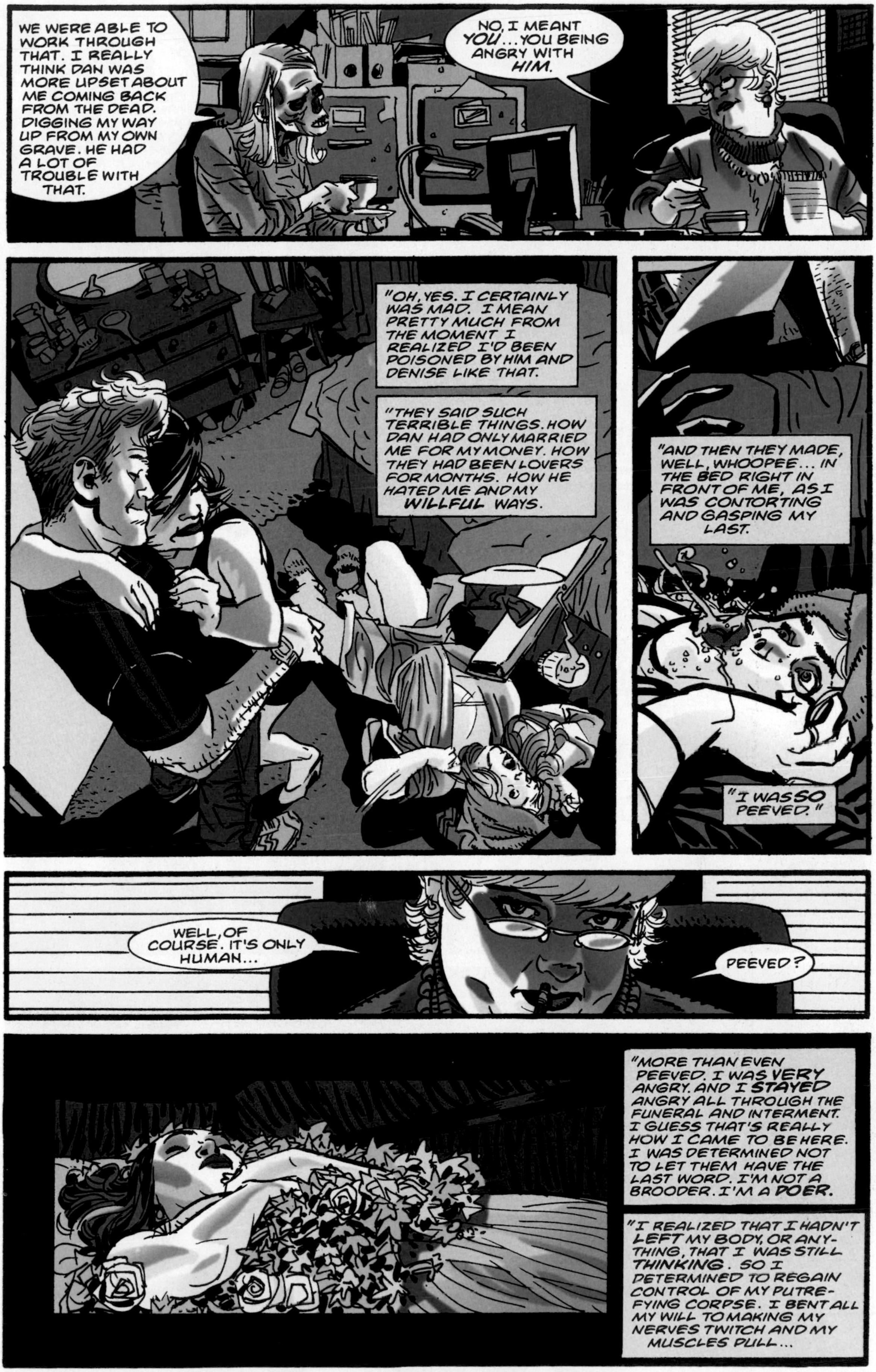
WE WERE ABLE TO WORK THROUGH THAT. I REALLY THINK DAN WAS MORE UPSET ABOUT ME COMING BACK FROM THE DEAD. DIGGING MY WAY UP FROM MY OWN GRAVE. HE HAD A LOT OF TROUBLE WITH THAT.
NO, I MEANT YOU... YOU BEING ANGRY WITH HIM.
"OH, YES. I CERTAINLY WAS MAD. I MEAN PRETTY MUCH FROM THE MOMENT I REALIZED I'D BEEN POISONED BY HIM AND DENISE LIKE THAT.
"THEY SAID SUCH TERRIBLE THINGS. HOW DAN HAD ONLY MARRIED ME FOR MY MONEY. HOW THEY HAD BEEN LOVERS FOR MONTHS. HOW HE HATED ME AND MY WILLFUL WAYS.
"AND THEN THEY MADE, WELL, WHOOPEE... IN THE BED RIGHT IN FRONT OF ME, AS I WAS CONTORTING AND GASPING MY LAST.
"I WAS SO PEEVED."
WELL, OF COURSE. IT'S ONLY HUMAN...
PEEVED?
"MORE THAN EVEN PEEVED. I WAS VERY ANGRY. AND I STAYED ANGRY ALL THROUGH THE FUNERAL AND INTERMENT. I GUESS THAT'S REALLY HOW I CAME TO BE HERE. I WAS DETERMINED NOT TO LET THEM HAVE THE LAST WORD. I'M NOT A BROODER. I'M A DOER.
"I REALIZED THAT I HADN'T LEFT MY BODY, OR ANYTHING, THAT I WAS STILL THINKING. SO I DETERMINED TO REGAIN CONTROL OF MY PUTREFYING CORPSE. I BENT ALL MY WILL TO MAKING MY NERVES TWITCH AND MY MUSCLES PULL...

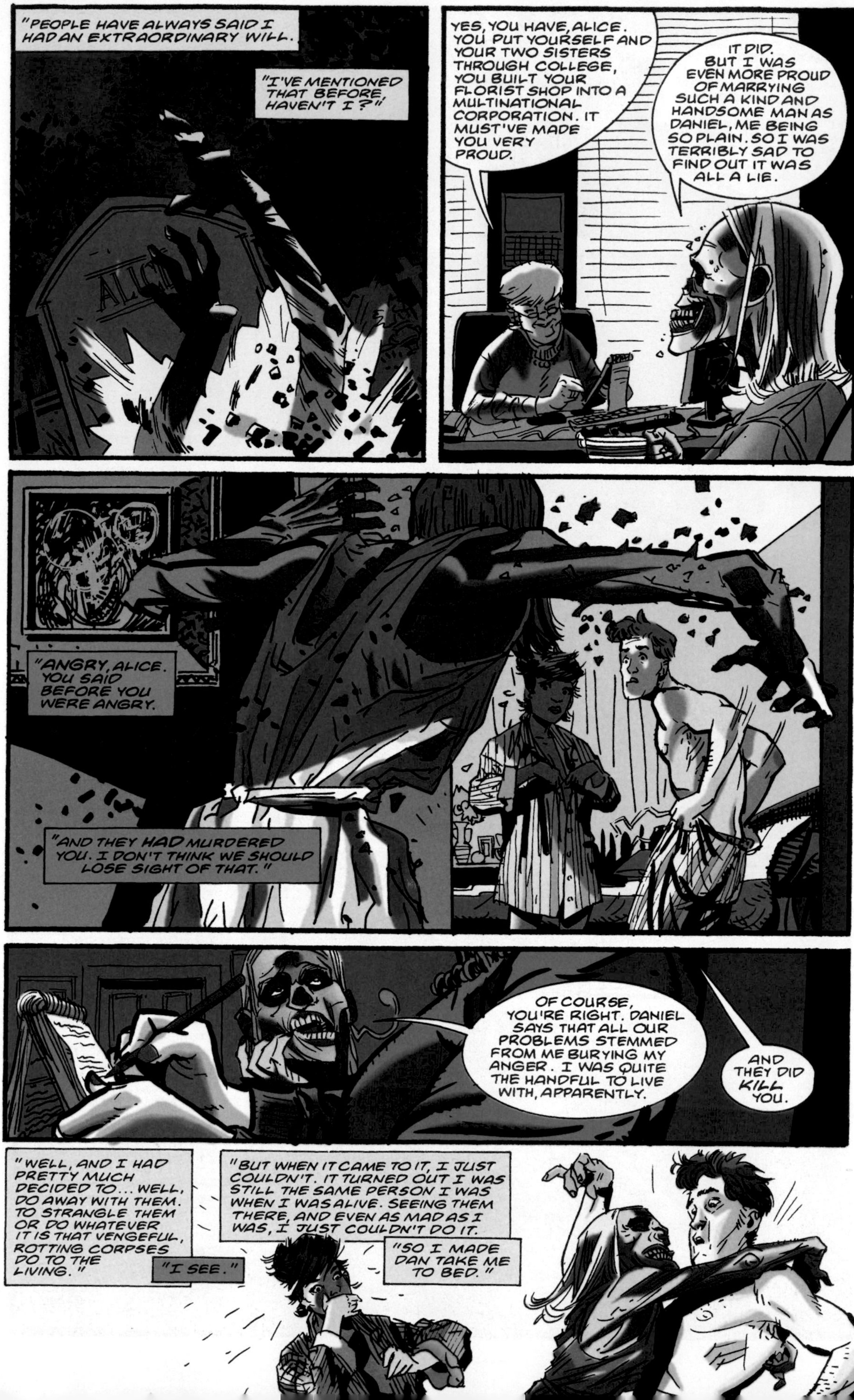
"PEOPLE HAVE ALWAYS SAID I HAD AN EXTRAORDINARY WILL.
"I'VE MENTIONED THAT BEFORE, HAVEN'T I?"
ALICE
YES, YOU HAVE, ALICE. YOU PUT YOURSELF AND YOUR TWO SISTERS THROUGH COLLEGE, YOU BUILT YOUR FLORIST SHOP INTO A MULTINATIONAL CORPORATION. IT MUST'VE MADE YOU VERY PROUD.
IT DID. BUT I WAS EVEN MORE PROUD OF MARRYING SUCH A KIND AND HANDSOME MAN AS DANIEL, ME BEING SO PLAIN. SO I WAS TERRIBLY SAD TO FIND OUT IT WAS ALL A LIE.
"ANGRY, ALICE. YOU SAID BEFORE YOU WERE ANGRY.
"AND THEY HAD MURDERED YOU. I DON'T THINK WE SHOULD LOSE SIGHT OF THAT."
OF COURSE, YOU'RE RIGHT. DANIEL SAYS THAT ALL OUR PROBLEMS STEMMED FROM ME BURYING MY ANGER. I WAS QUITE THE HANDFUL TO LIVE WITH, APPARENTLY.
AND THEY DID KILL YOU.
"WELL, AND I HAD PRETTY MUCH DECIDED TO... WELL, DO AWAY WITH THEM. TO STRANGLE THEM OR DO WHATEVER IT IS THAT VENGEFUL, ROTTING CORPSES DO TO THE LIVING."
"I SEE."
"BUT WHEN IT CAME TO IT, I JUST COULDN'T. IT TURNED OUT I WAS STILL THE SAME PERSON I WAS WHEN I WAS ALIVE. SEEING THEM THERE, AND EVEN AS MAD AS I WAS, I JUST COULDN'T DO IT.
"SO I MADE DAN TAKE ME TO BED."

WHY, EXACTLY?

I'M NOT SURE. TIT FOR TAT, PERHAPS. AND MAYBE I THOUGHT IT WOULD DRIVE HIM INSANE. OR DRIVE DENISE INSANE. SOMETHING. THEY WERE BOTH KIND OF IN SHOCK FROM SEEING ME, AND... SMELLING ME.

I'M SURE THEY WERE JUST TOTALLY OVER-WHELMED BY SOME-THING SO... ODD.

TO TELL THE TRUTH, I WAS PRETTY EMOTIONAL MYSELF.

SO DAN TORE OFF MY RAGS AND WENT TO IT. I WAS SURPRISED AT HIS... INTENSITY. I GUESS IF YOU'RE GOING TO MAKE LOVE TO THE REANIMATED CORPSE OF YOUR MURDERED WIFE... WELL, YOU MIGHT AS WELL BE ENTHUSIASTIC.

"HE WAS NOT JUST IN ME, HE WAS IN ME, IF YOU GET MY DRIFT. HE WAS UP TO HIS ELBOWS. HE WAS TEARING ME TO PIECES."

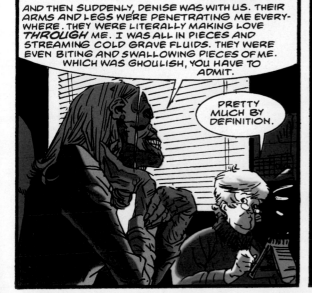

AND THEN SUDDENLY, DENISE WAS WITH US. THEIR ARMS AND LEGS WERE PENETRATING ME EVERY-WHERE. THEY WERE LITERALLY MAKING LOVE THROUGH ME. I WAS ALL IN PIECES AND STREAMING COLD GRAVE FLUIDS. THEY WERE EVEN BITING AND SWALLOWING PIECES OF ME. WHICH WAS GHOULISH, YOU HAVE TO ADMIT.

PRETTY MUCH BY DEFINITION.

I'VE ALWAYS BEEN A SHY PERSON AND NEVER EXPECTED ANYTHING LIKE THIS TO HAPPEN. I CERTAINLY DIDN'T EXPECT TO ENJOY IT, BUT I DID.

I ALSO DIDN'T EXPECT TO BE BACK IN ONE PIECE AT THE END OF IT, BUT THAT HAPPENED, TOO. MY BITS AND BLOBS KIND OF CRAWLED TOGETHER, EVEN OOZING BACK OUT OF THEM.

AND THEN WHAT HAPPENED?

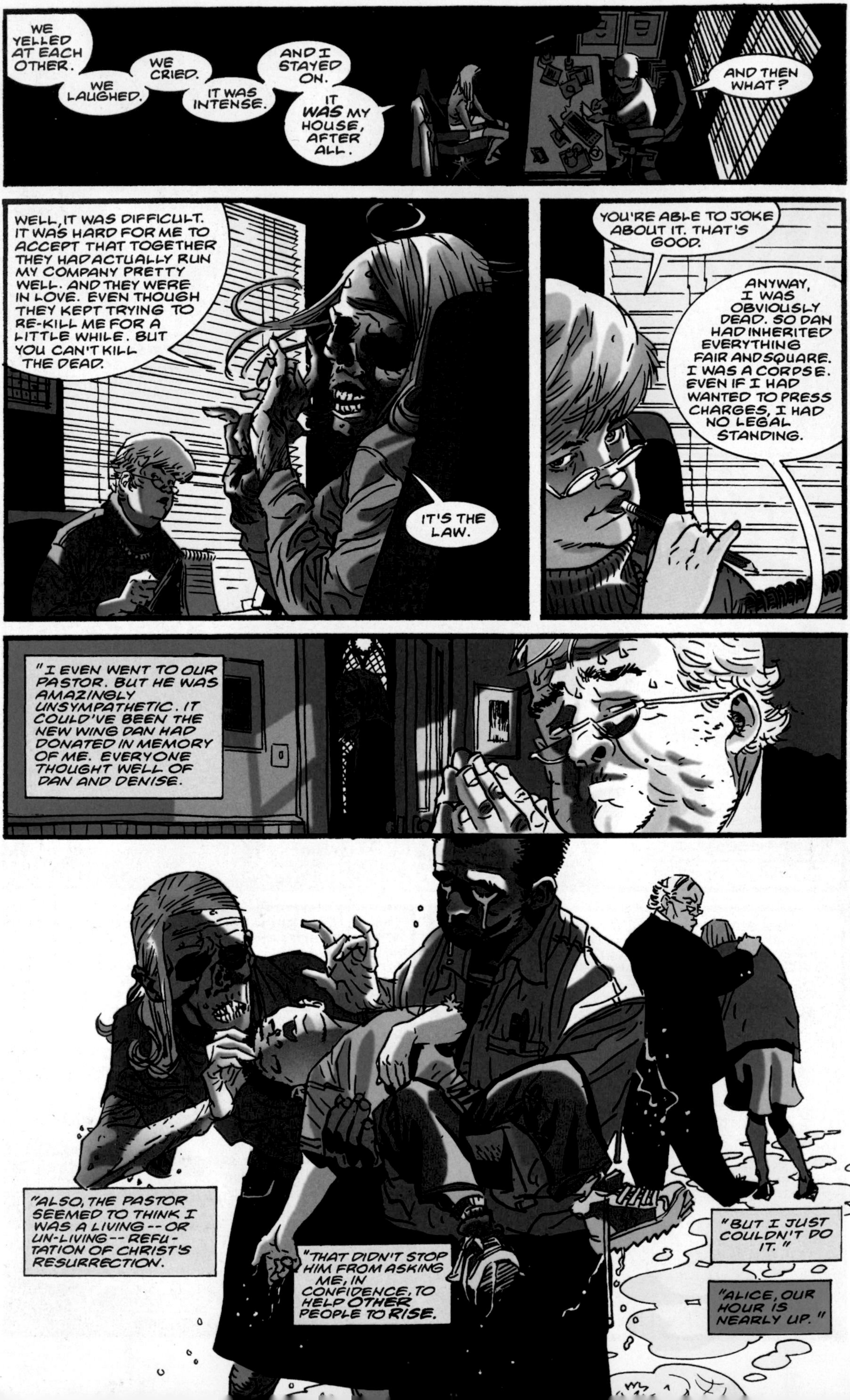
WE YELLED AT EACH OTHER.
WE LAUGHED.
WE CRIED.
IT WAS INTENSE.
AND I STAYED ON.
IT WAS MY HOUSE, AFTER ALL.
AND THEN WHAT?
WELL, IT WAS DIFFICULT. IT WAS HARD FOR ME TO ACCEPT THAT TOGETHER THEY HAD ACTUALLY RUN MY COMPANY PRETTY WELL. AND THEY WERE IN LOVE. EVEN THOUGH THEY KEPT TRYING TO RE-KILL ME FOR A LITTLE WHILE. BUT YOU CAN'T KILL THE DEAD.
IT'S THE LAW.
YOU'RE ABLE TO JOKE ABOUT IT. THAT'S GOOD.
ANYWAY, I WAS OBVIOUSLY DEAD. SO DAN HAD INHERITED EVERYTHING FAIR AND SQUARE. I WAS A CORPSE. EVEN IF I HAD WANTED TO PRESS CHARGES, I HAD NO LEGAL STANDING.
"I EVEN WENT TO OUR PASTOR. BUT HE WAS AMAZINGLY UNSYMPATHETIC. IT COULD'VE BEEN THE NEW WING DAN HAD DONATED IN MEMORY OF ME. EVERYONE THOUGHT WELL OF DAN AND DENISE.
"ALSO, THE PASTOR SEEMED TO THINK I WAS A LIVING -- OR UN-LIVING -- REFU-TATION OF CHRIST'S RESURRECTION.
"THAT DIDN'T STOP HIM FROM ASKING ME, IN CONFIDENCE, TO HELP OTHER PEOPLE TO RISE.
"BUT I JUST COULDN'T DO IT."
"ALICE, OUR HOUR IS NEARLY UP."

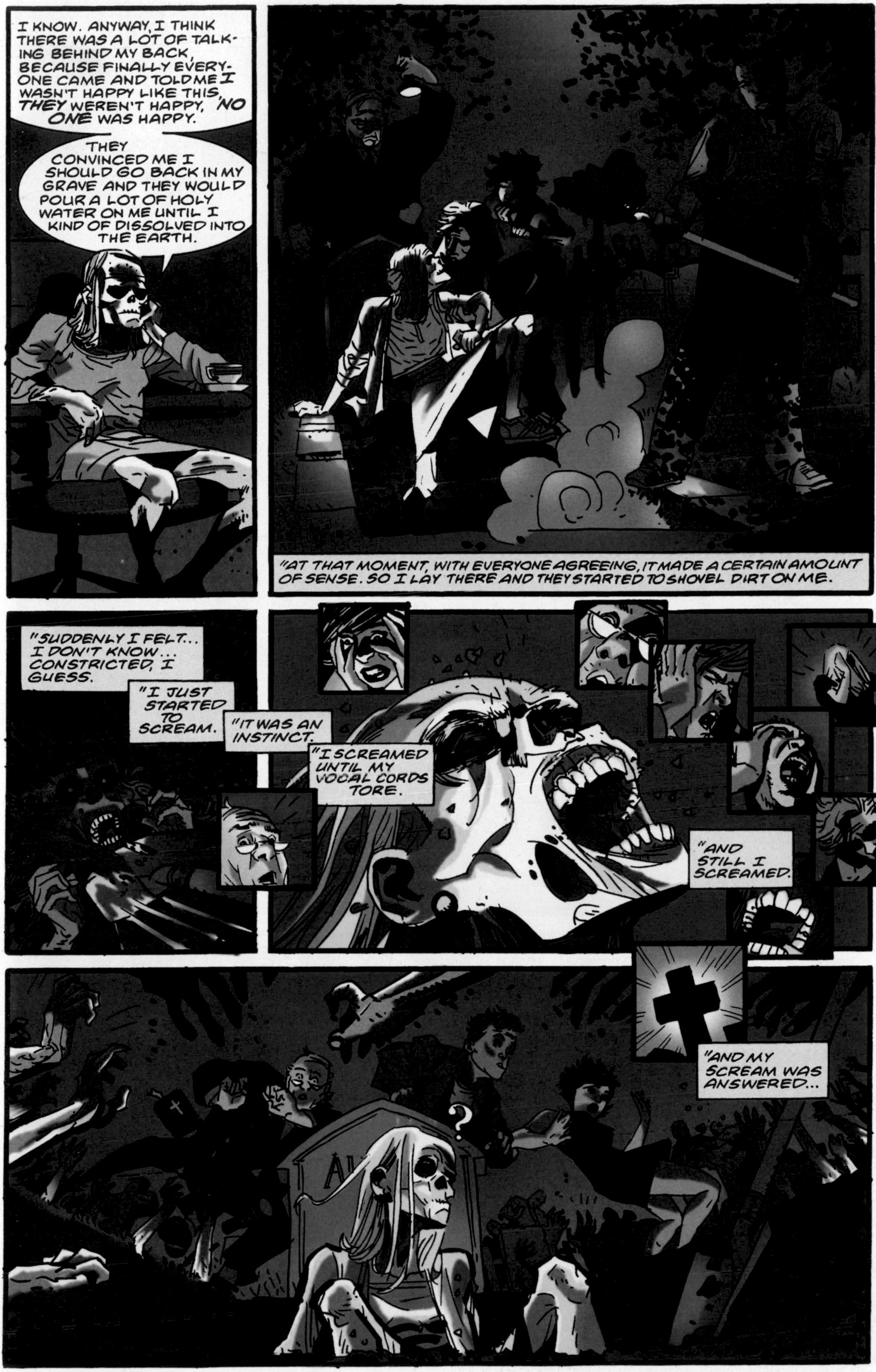

I KNOW. ANYWAY, I THINK THERE WAS A LOT OF TALKING BEHIND MY BACK, BECAUSE FINALLY EVERYONE CAME AND TOLD ME I WASN'T HAPPY LIKE THIS, THEY WEREN'T HAPPY, NO ONE WAS HAPPY.
THEY CONVINCED ME I SHOULD GO BACK IN MY GRAVE AND THEY WOULD POUR A LOT OF HOLY WATER ON ME UNTIL I KIND OF DISSOLVED INTO THE EARTH.
"AT THAT MOMENT, WITH EVERYONE AGREEING, IT MADE A CERTAIN AMOUNT OF SENSE. SO I LAY THERE AND THEY STARTED TO SHOVEL DIRT ON ME.
"SUDDENLY I FELT... I DON'T KNOW... CONSTRICTED, I GUESS.
"I JUST STARTED TO SCREAM.
"IT WAS AN INSTINCT.
"I SCREAMED UNTIL MY VOCAL CORDS TORE.
"AND STILL I SCREAMED.
"AND MY SCREAM WAS ANSWERED...
?

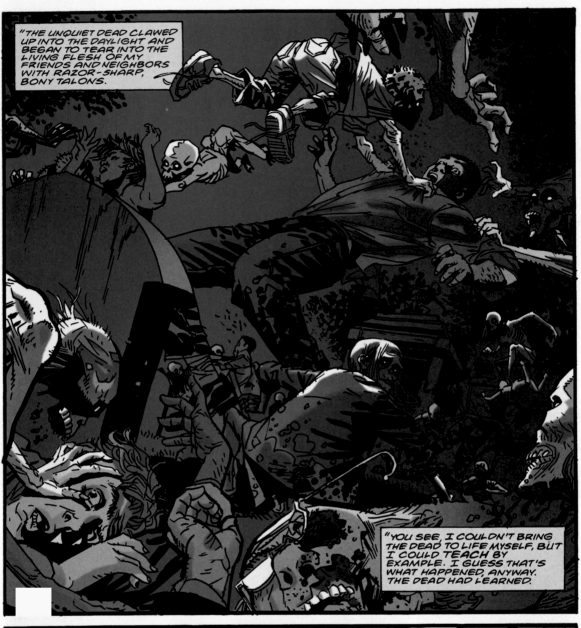

"THE UNQUIET DEAD CLAWED UP INTO THE DAYLIGHT AND BEGAN TO TEAR INTO THE LIVING FLESH OF MY FRIENDS AND NEIGHBORS WITH RAZOR-SHARP, BONY TALONS.

"YOU SEE, I COULDN'T BRING THE DEAD TO LIFE MYSELF, BUT I COULD TEACH BY EXAMPLE. I GUESS THAT'S WHAT HAPPENED, ANYWAY. THE DEAD HAD LEARNED.

"THEN EVEN THOSE NEWLY DEAD RETURNED TO LIFE, INCLUDING DAN AND DENISE AND THE MINISTER.

"SURPRISED ME."

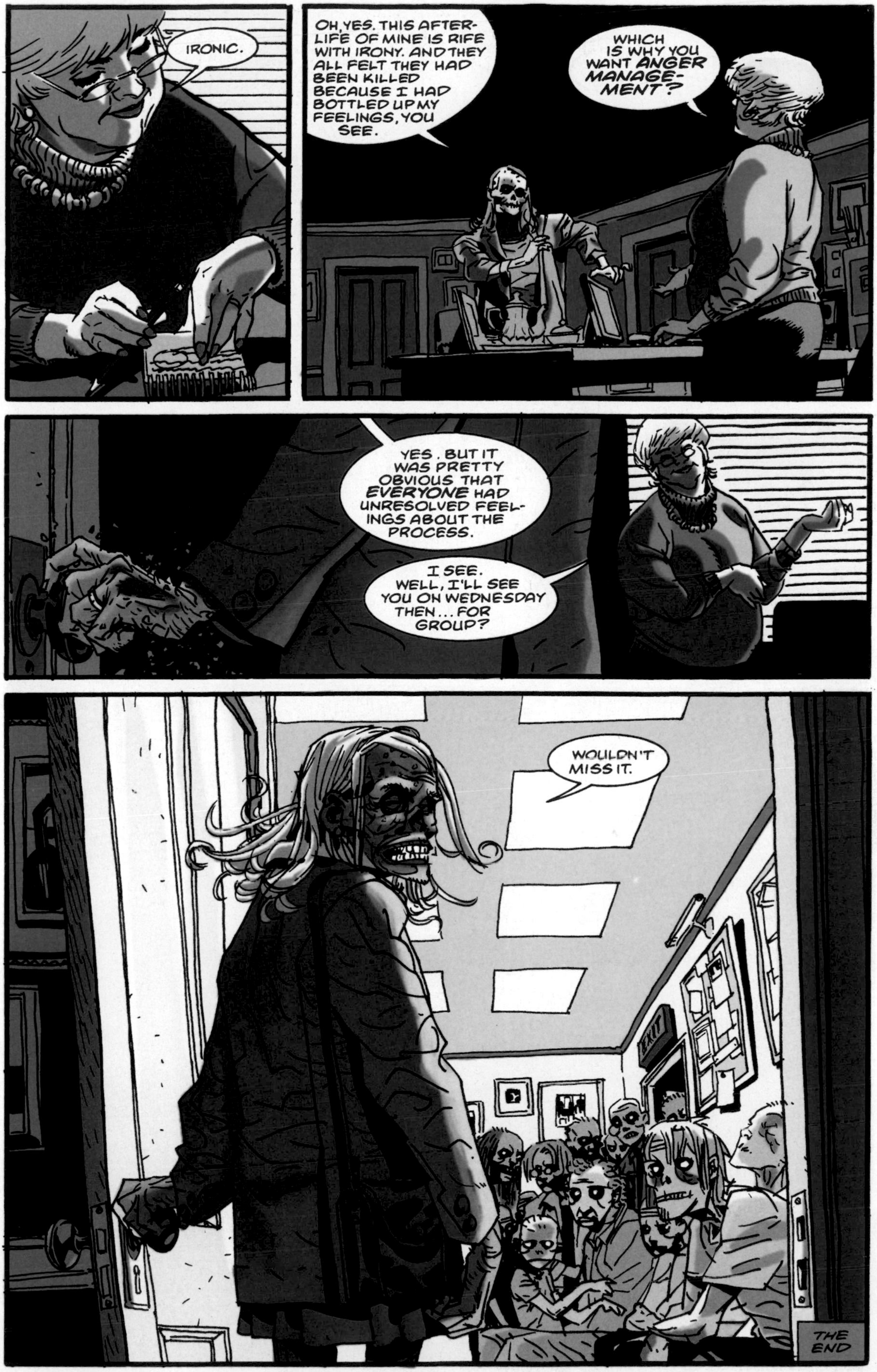
IRONIC.
OH, YES. THIS AFTER-LIFE OF MINE IS RIFE WITH IRONY. AND THEY ALL FELT THEY HAD BEEN KILLED BECAUSE I HAD BOTTLED UP MY FEELINGS, YOU SEE.
WHICH IS WHY YOU WANT ANGER MANAGEMENT?
YES. BUT IT WAS PRETTY OBVIOUS THAT EVERYONE HAD UNRESOLVED FEELINGS ABOUT THE PROCESS.
I SEE. WELL, I'LL SEE YOU ON WEDNESDAY THEN... FOR GROUP?
WOULDN'T MISS IT.
EXIT
THE END

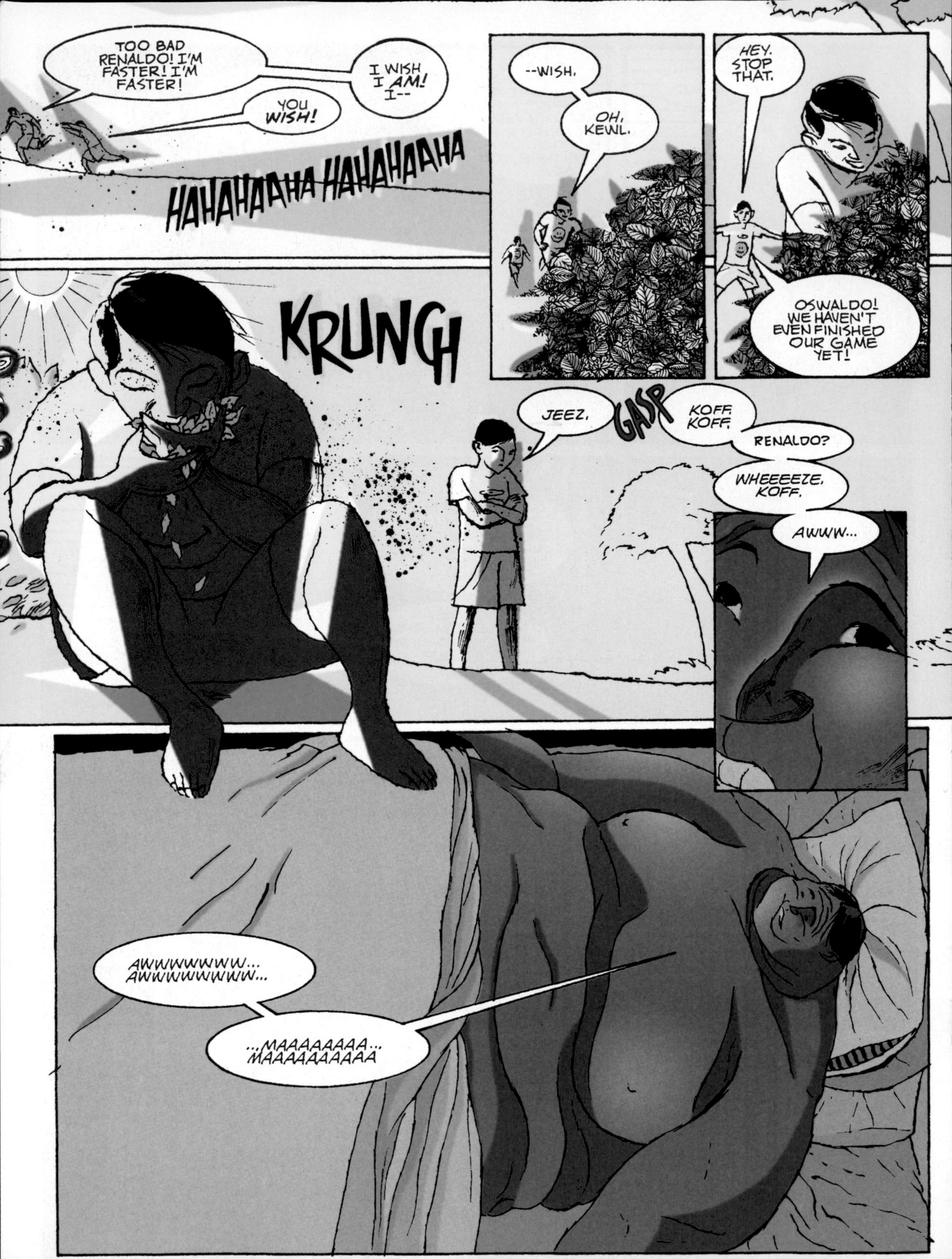
TOO BAD RENALDO! I'M FASTER! I'M FASTER!
YOU WISH!
I WISH I AM! I--
HAHAHAAHA HAHAHAAHA
--WISH.
OH, KEWL.
HEY. STOP THAT.
OSWALDO! WE HAVEN'T EVEN FINISHED OUR GAME YET!
KRUNCH
JEEZ.
GASP
KOFF. KOFF.
RENALDO?
WHEEEEZE. KOFF.
AWWW...
AWWWWWWWW... AWWWWWWWWW...
...MAAAAAAAAA... MAAAAAAAAAAA

# EL OGRO

IVAN VELEZ, JR. WRITER
HO CHE ANDERSON ARTIST
NOELLE GIDDINGS COLORIST
DIGITAL CHAMELEON SEPARATOR
JOHN WORKMAN LETTERER
JOAN HILTY EDITOR

SUNDAY.

ROSARIO AND VICTOR.

MAAAA...

MAA

MMAAAAAA

FUNNY HOW HE NEVER CALLS FOR PA.

YES. A HOOT.

MMMMM

YAWWWWN. YES, BABY. I'M COMING.

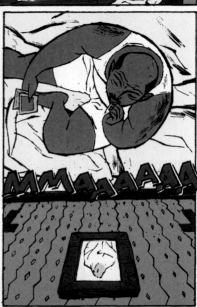

MMMAAAAAA

MAAAA-

UMMM, SAND-WICHES.

VICTOR, I CAN'T LIFT THE BUCKET BY MY-SELF.

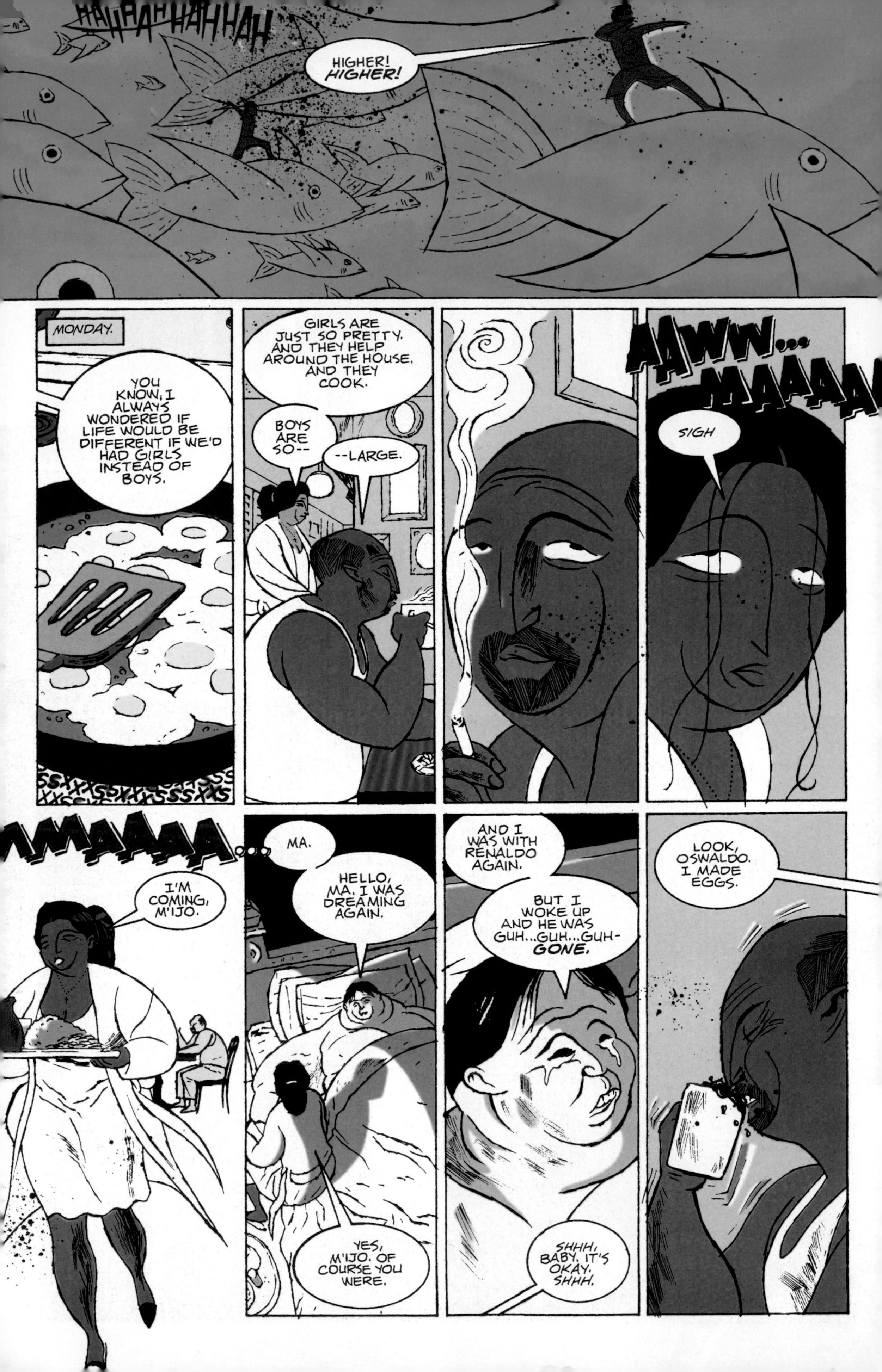
HAHAHAH HAHHAH
HIGHER! HIGHER!
MONDAY.
YOU KNOW, I ALWAYS WONDERED IF LIFE WOULD BE DIFFERENT IF WE'D HAD GIRLS INSTEAD OF BOYS.
GIRLS ARE JUST SO PRETTY. AND THEY HELP AROUND THE HOUSE. AND THEY COOK.
BOYS ARE SO--
--LARGE.
AAWW... MAAAA
SIGH
MMAAAAA...
I'M COMING, M'IJO.
MA.
HELLO, MA. I WAS DREAMING AGAIN.
YES, M'IJO. OF COURSE YOU WERE.
AND I WAS WITH RENALDO AGAIN.
BUT I WOKE UP AND HE WAS GUH...GUH...GUH-GONE.
SHHH, BABY. IT'S OKAY. SHHH.
LOOK, OSWALDO. I MADE EGGS.

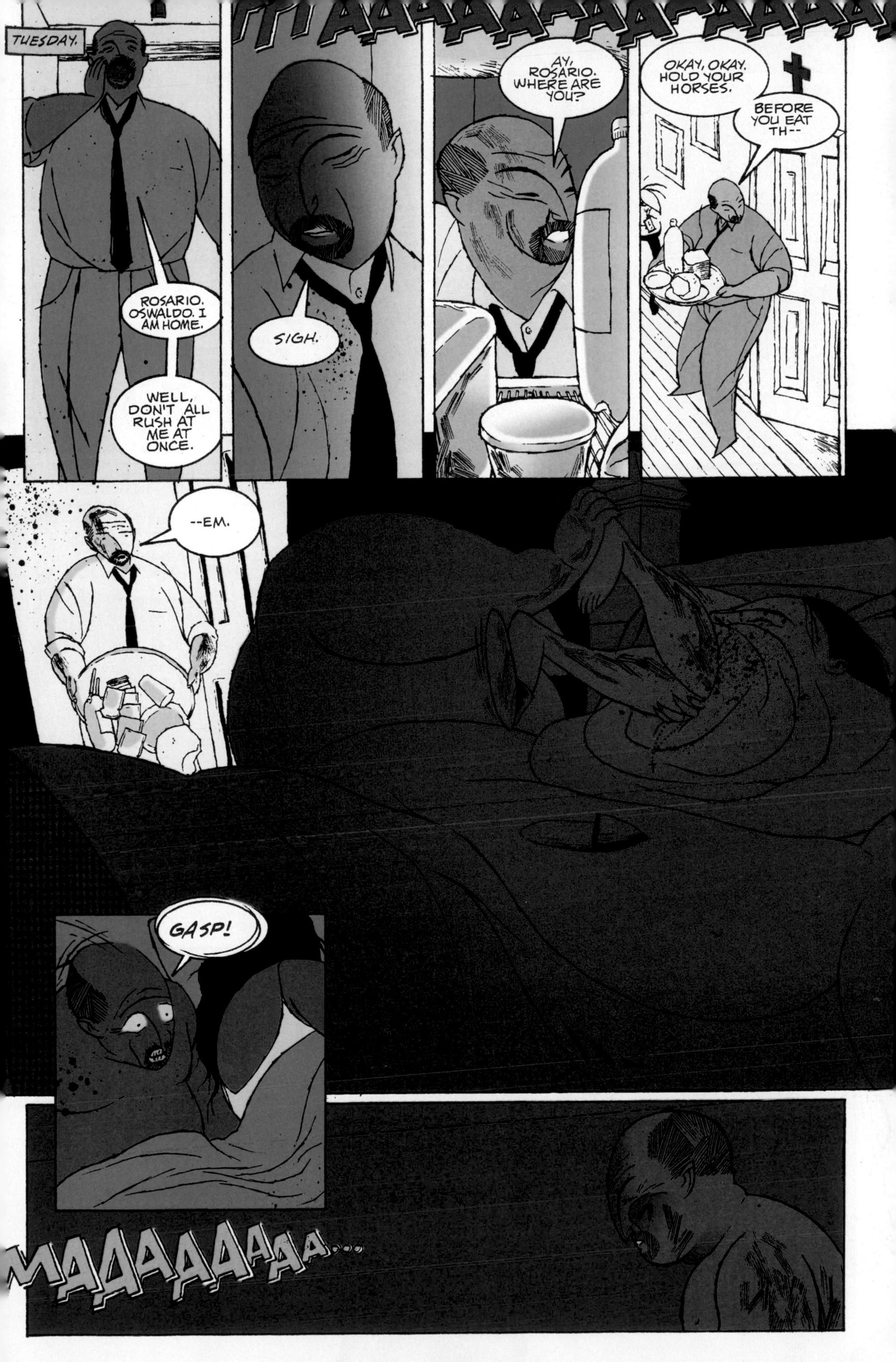
TUESDAY.
ROSARIO. OSWALDO. I AM HOME.
WELL, DON'T ALL RUSH AT ME AT ONCE.
SIGH.
AY, ROSARIO. WHERE ARE YOU?
OKAY, OKAY. HOLD YOUR HORSES.
BEFORE YOU EAT TH--
--EM.
GASP!
MAAAAAAAA...

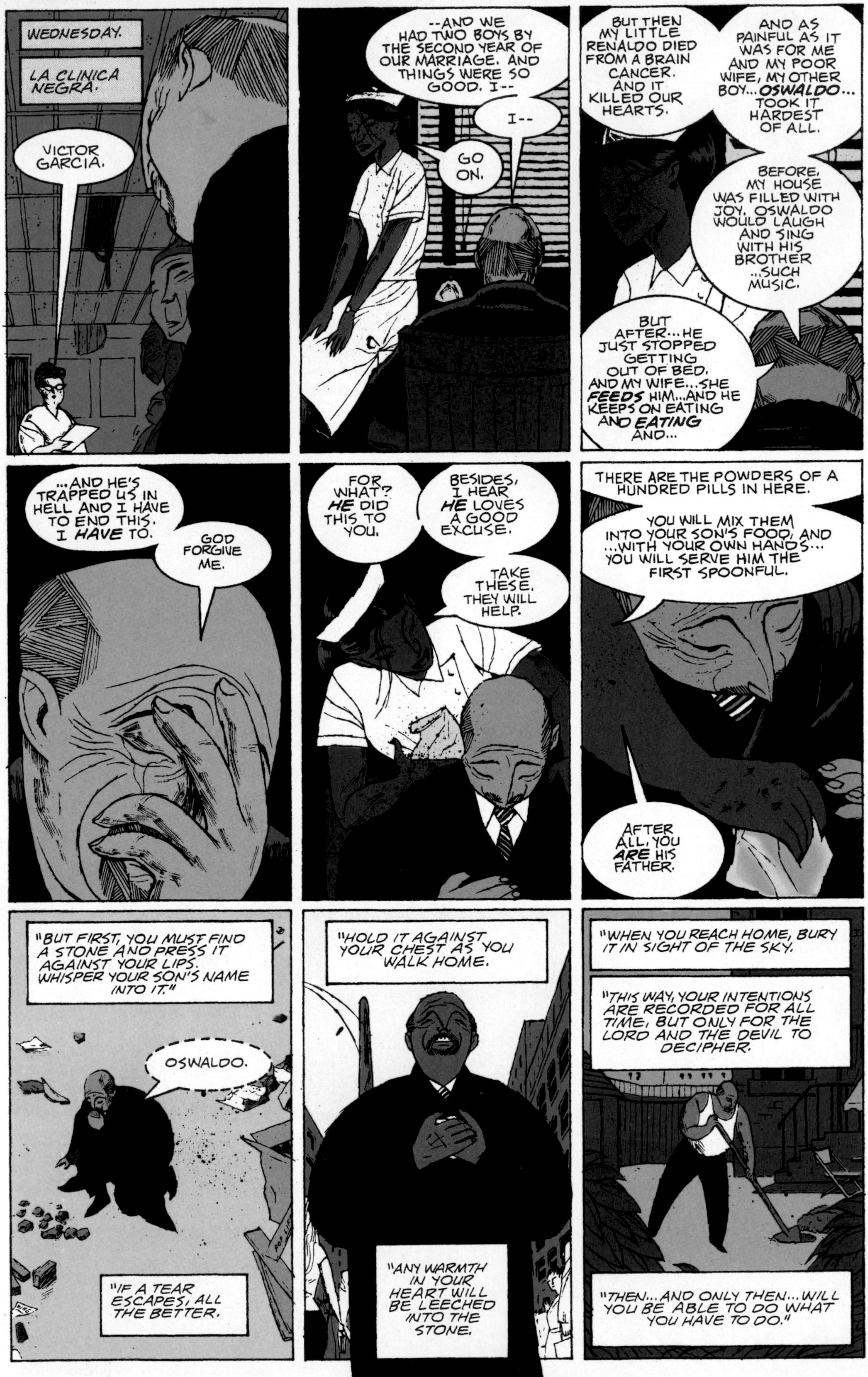
WEDNESDAY.
LA CLINICA NEGRA.
VICTOR GARCIA.
--AND WE HAD TWO BOYS BY THE SECOND YEAR OF OUR MARRIAGE. AND THINGS WERE SO GOOD. I--
I--
GO ON.
BUT THEN MY LITTLE RENALDO DIED FROM A BRAIN CANCER. AND IT KILLED OUR HEARTS.
AND AS PAINFUL AS IT WAS FOR ME AND MY POOR WIFE, MY OTHER BOY... OSWALDO... TOOK IT HARDEST OF ALL.
BEFORE, MY HOUSE WAS FILLED WITH JOY. OSWALDO WOULD LAUGH AND SING WITH HIS BROTHER ...SUCH MUSIC.
BUT AFTER... HE JUST STOPPED GETTING OUT OF BED. AND MY WIFE... SHE FEEDS HIM... AND HE KEEPS ON EATING AND EATING AND...
...AND HE'S TRAPPED US IN HELL AND I HAVE TO END THIS. I HAVE TO.
GOD FORGIVE ME.
FOR WHAT? HE DID THIS TO YOU.
BESIDES, I HEAR HE LOVES A GOOD EXCUSE.
TAKE THESE. THEY WILL HELP.
THERE ARE THE POWDERS OF A HUNDRED PILLS IN HERE.
YOU WILL MIX THEM INTO YOUR SON'S FOOD, AND ...WITH YOUR OWN HANDS... YOU WILL SERVE HIM THE FIRST SPOONFUL.
AFTER ALL, YOU ARE HIS FATHER.
"BUT FIRST, YOU MUST FIND A STONE AND PRESS IT AGAINST YOUR LIPS. WHISPER YOUR SON'S NAME INTO IT."
OSWALDO.
"IF A TEAR ESCAPES, ALL THE BETTER.
"HOLD IT AGAINST YOUR CHEST AS YOU WALK HOME.
"ANY WARMTH IN YOUR HEART WILL BE LEECHED INTO THE STONE.
"WHEN YOU REACH HOME, BURY IT IN SIGHT OF THE SKY.
"THIS WAY, YOUR INTENTIONS ARE RECORDED FOR ALL TIME, BUT ONLY FOR THE LORD AND THE DEVIL TO DECIPHER.
"THEN... AND ONLY THEN... WILL YOU BE ABLE TO DO WHAT YOU HAVE TO DO."

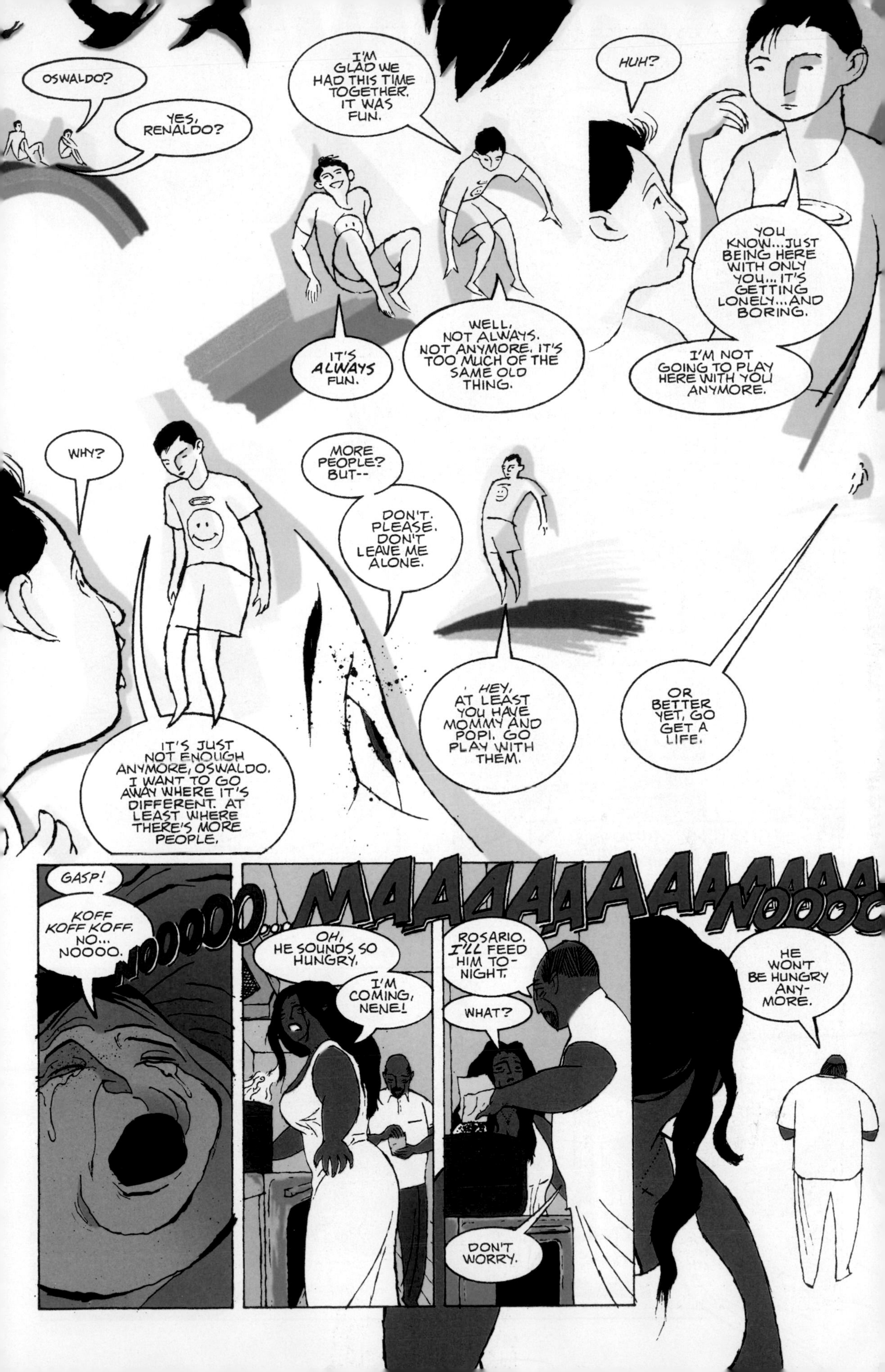
OSWALDO?
YES, RENALDO?
I'M GLAD WE HAD THIS TIME TOGETHER. IT WAS FUN.
IT'S ALWAYS FUN.
WELL, NOT ALWAYS. NOT ANYMORE. IT'S TOO MUCH OF THE SAME OLD THING.
HUH?
YOU KNOW...JUST BEING HERE WITH ONLY YOU... IT'S GETTING LONELY...AND BORING.
I'M NOT GOING TO PLAY HERE WITH YOU ANYMORE.
WHY?
IT'S JUST NOT ENOUGH ANYMORE, OSWALDO. I WANT TO GO AWAY WHERE IT'S DIFFERENT. AT LEAST WHERE THERE'S MORE PEOPLE.
MORE PEOPLE? BUT--
DON'T. PLEASE. DON'T LEAVE ME ALONE.
HEY, AT LEAST YOU HAVE MOMMY AND POPI. GO PLAY WITH THEM.
OR BETTER YET, GO GET A LIFE.
GASP!
KOFF KOFF KOFF. NO... NOOOO.
NOOOOOO...MAAAAAAAAAAA
NOOOO
OH, HE SOUNDS SO HUNGRY.
I'M COMING, NENE!
ROSARIO. I'LL FEED HIM TO-NIGHT.
WHAT?
DON'T WORRY.
HE WON'T BE HUNGRY ANY-MORE.

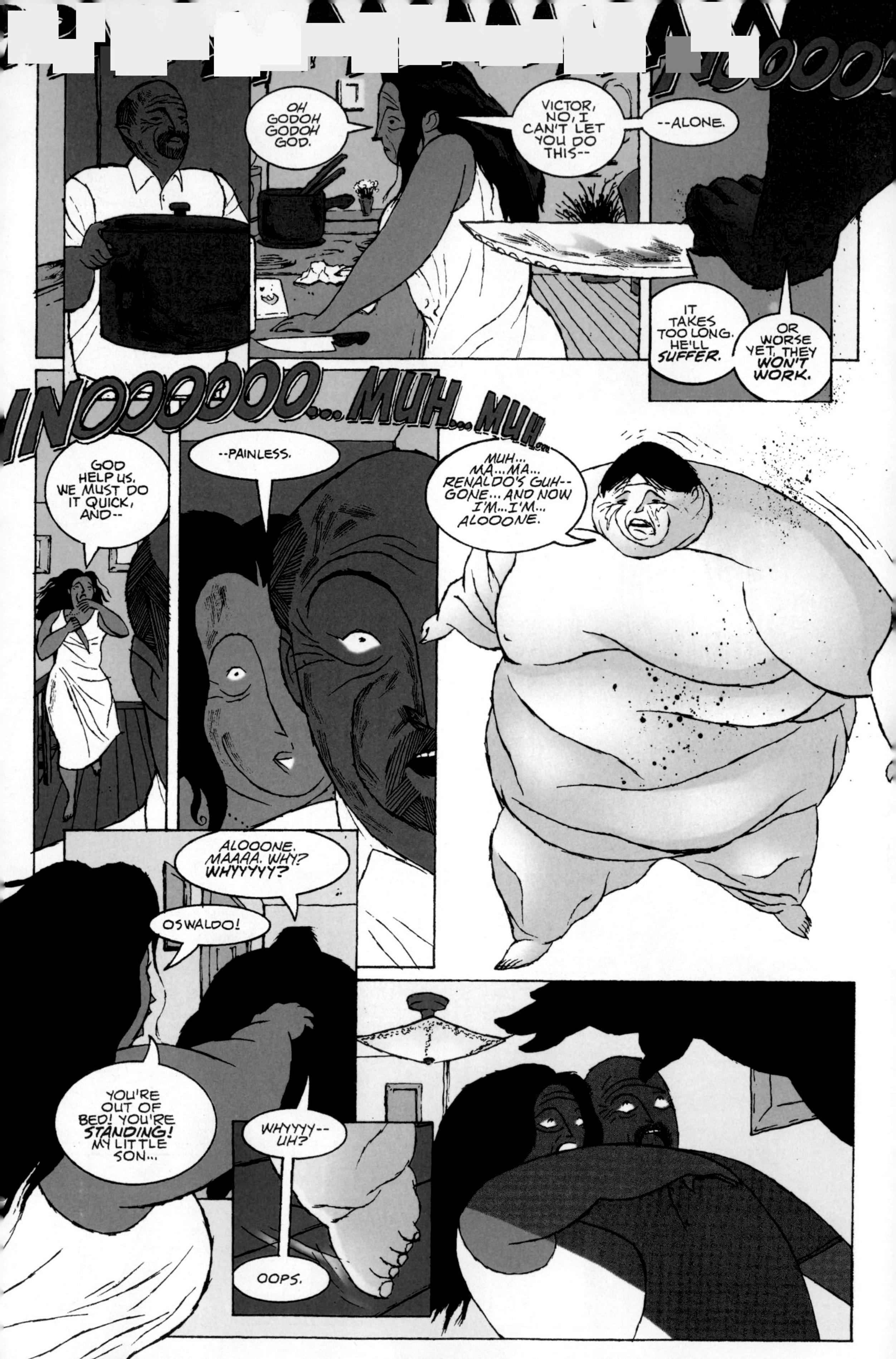
OH GODOH GODOH GOD.
VICTOR, NO, I CAN'T LET YOU DO THIS--
--ALONE.
IT TAKES TOO LONG. HE'LL *SUFFER.*
OR WORSE YET, THEY *WON'T WORK.*
NOOOOOOO...MUH...MUH...
GOD HELP US. WE MUST DO IT QUICK, AND--
--PAINLESS.
MUH... MA...MA... RENALDO'S GUH--GONE... AND NOW I'M...I'M... ALOOONE.
ALOOONE. MAAAA. WHY? *WHYYYYY?*
OSWALDO!
YOU'RE OUT OF BED! YOU'RE *STANDING!* MY LITTLE SON...
WHYYYY-- UH?
OOPS.

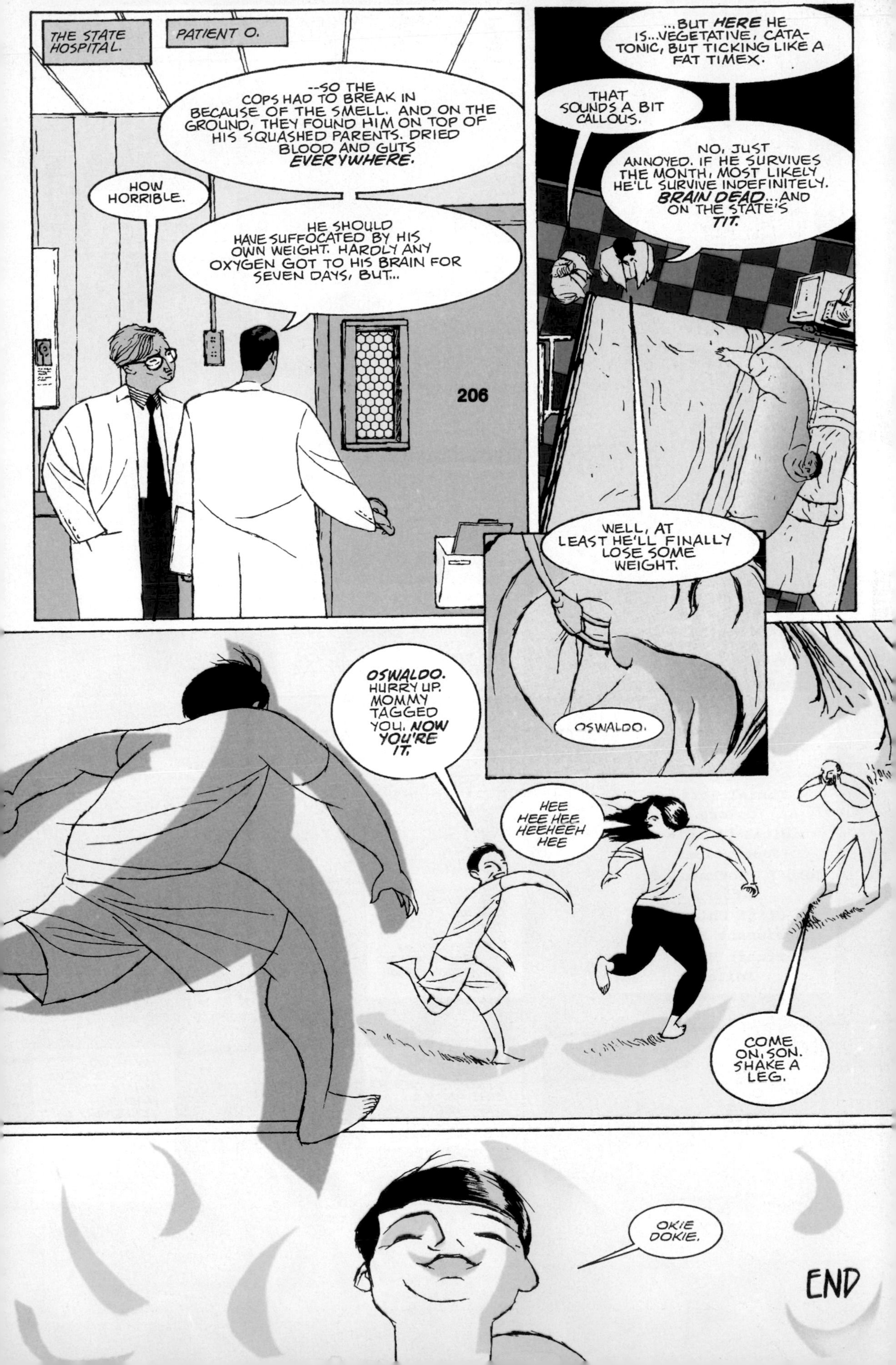
THE STATE HOSPITAL.
PATIENT O.
--SO THE COPS HAD TO BREAK IN BECAUSE OF THE SMELL. AND ON THE GROUND, THEY FOUND HIM ON TOP OF HIS SQUASHED PARENTS. DRIED BLOOD AND GUTS EVERYWHERE.
HOW HORRIBLE.
HE SHOULD HAVE SUFFOCATED BY HIS OWN WEIGHT. HARDLY ANY OXYGEN GOT TO HIS BRAIN FOR SEVEN DAYS, BUT...
206
...BUT HERE HE IS...VEGETATIVE, CATATONIC, BUT TICKING LIKE A FAT TIMEX.
THAT SOUNDS A BIT CALLOUS.
NO, JUST ANNOYED. IF HE SURVIVES THE MONTH, MOST LIKELY HE'LL SURVIVE INDEFINITELY. BRAIN DEAD...AND ON THE STATE'S TIT.
WELL, AT LEAST HE'LL FINALLY LOSE SOME WEIGHT.
OSWALDO.
OSWALDO. HURRY UP. MOMMY TAGGED YOU. NOW YOU'RE IT.
HEE HEE HEE HEEHEEH HEE
COME ON, SON. SHAKE A LEG.
OKIE DOKIE.
END

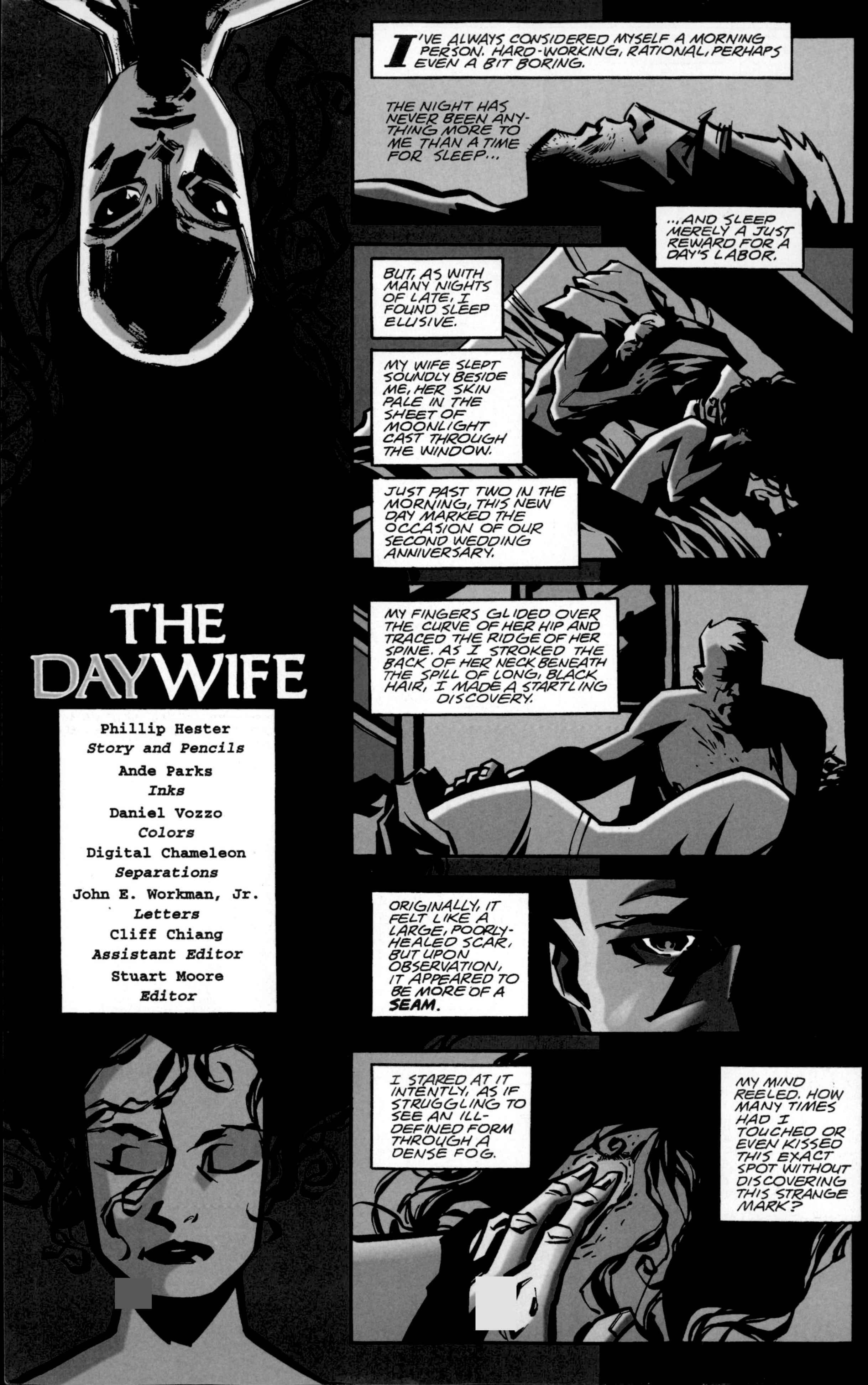
THE DAYWIFE
Phillip Hester
Story and Pencils
Ande Parks
Inks
Daniel Vozzo
Colors
Digital Chameleon
Separations
John E. Workman, Jr.
Letters
Cliff Chiang
Assistant Editor
Stuart Moore
Editor
I'VE ALWAYS CONSIDERED MYSELF A MORNING PERSON. HARD-WORKING, RATIONAL, PERHAPS EVEN A BIT BORING.
THE NIGHT HAS NEVER BEEN ANYTHING MORE TO ME THAN A TIME FOR SLEEP...
...AND SLEEP MERELY A JUST REWARD FOR A DAY'S LABOR.
BUT, AS WITH MANY NIGHTS OF LATE, I FOUND SLEEP ELUSIVE.
MY WIFE SLEPT SOUNDLY BESIDE ME, HER SKIN PALE IN THE SHEET OF MOONLIGHT CAST THROUGH THE WINDOW.
JUST PAST TWO IN THE MORNING, THIS NEW DAY MARKED THE OCCASION OF OUR SECOND WEDDING ANNIVERSARY.
MY FINGERS GLIDED OVER THE CURVE OF HER HIP AND TRACED THE RIDGE OF HER SPINE. AS I STROKED THE BACK OF HER NECK BENEATH THE SPILL OF LONG, BLACK HAIR, I MADE A STARTLING DISCOVERY.
ORIGINALLY, IT FELT LIKE A LARGE, POORLY-HEALED SCAR, BUT UPON OBSERVATION, IT APPEARED TO BE MORE OF A SEAM.
I STARED AT IT INTENTLY, AS IF STRUGGLING TO SEE AN ILL-DEFINED FORM THROUGH A DENSE FOG.
MY MIND REELED. HOW MANY TIMES HAD I TOUCHED OR EVEN KISSED THIS EXACT SPOT WITHOUT DISCOVERING THIS STRANGE MARK?

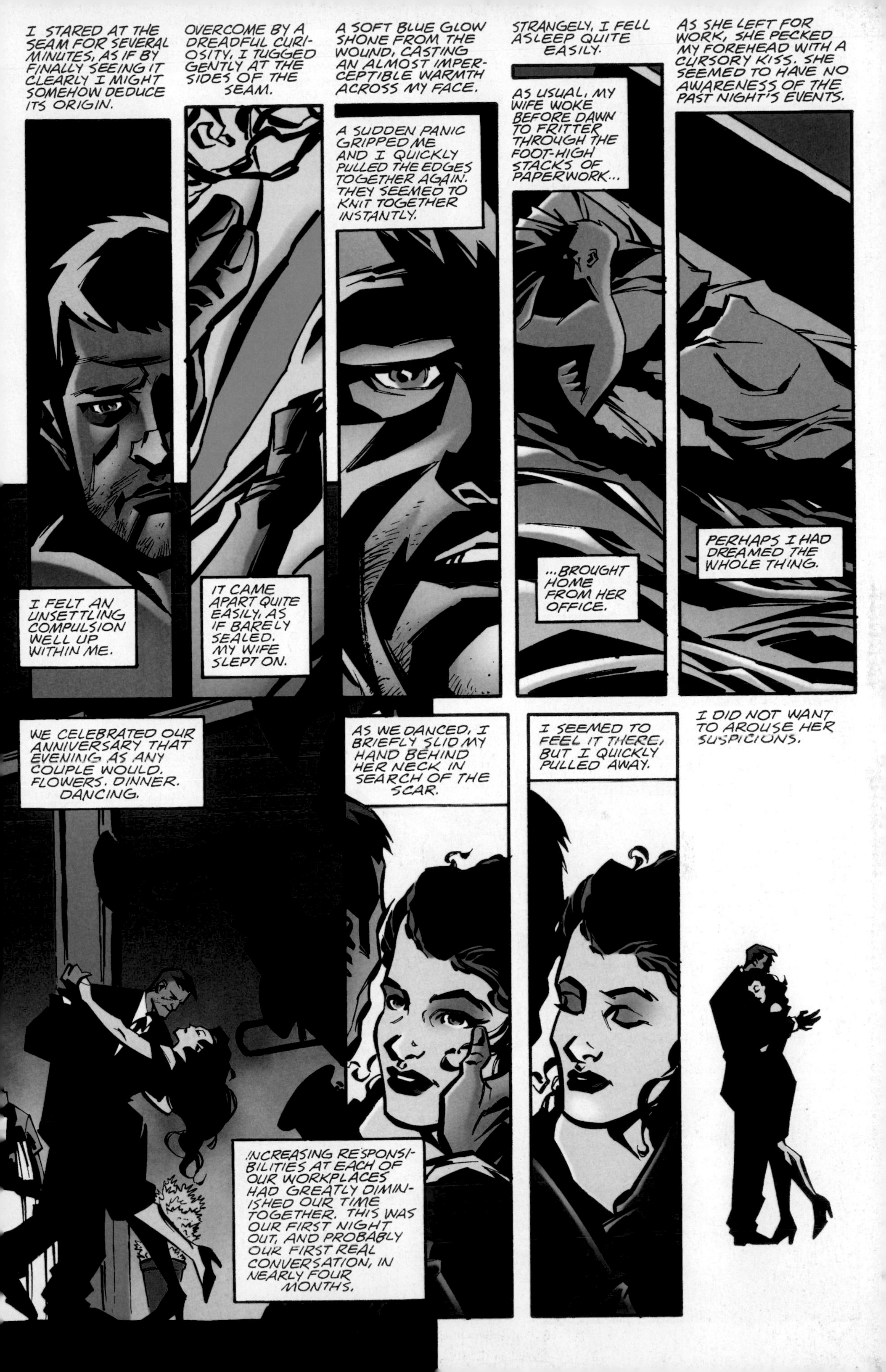
I STARED AT THE SEAM FOR SEVERAL MINUTES, AS IF BY FINALLY SEEING IT CLEARLY I MIGHT SOMEHOW DEDUCE ITS ORIGIN.
I FELT AN UNSETTLING COMPULSION WELL UP WITHIN ME.
OVERCOME BY A DREADFUL CURIOSITY, I TUGGED GENTLY AT THE SIDES OF THE SEAM.
IT CAME APART QUITE EASILY, AS IF BARELY SEALED. MY WIFE SLEPT ON.
A SOFT BLUE GLOW SHONE FROM THE WOUND, CASTING AN ALMOST IMPERCEPTIBLE WARMTH ACROSS MY FACE.
A SUDDEN PANIC GRIPPED ME AND I QUICKLY PULLED THE EDGES TOGETHER AGAIN. THEY SEEMED TO KNIT TOGETHER INSTANTLY.
STRANGELY, I FELL ASLEEP QUITE EASILY.
AS USUAL, MY WIFE WOKE BEFORE DAWN TO FRITTER THROUGH THE FOOT-HIGH STACKS OF PAPERWORK...
...BROUGHT HOME FROM HER OFFICE.
AS SHE LEFT FOR WORK, SHE PECKED MY FOREHEAD WITH A CURSORY KISS. SHE SEEMED TO HAVE NO AWARENESS OF THE PAST NIGHT'S EVENTS.
PERHAPS I HAD DREAMED THE WHOLE THING.
WE CELEBRATED OUR ANNIVERSARY THAT EVENING AS ANY COUPLE WOULD. FLOWERS. DINNER. DANCING.
INCREASING RESPONSIBILITIES AT EACH OF OUR WORKPLACES HAD GREATLY DIMINISHED OUR TIME TOGETHER. THIS WAS OUR FIRST NIGHT OUT, AND PROBABLY OUR FIRST REAL CONVERSATION, IN NEARLY FOUR MONTHS.
AS WE DANCED, I BRIEFLY SLID MY HAND BEHIND HER NECK IN SEARCH OF THE SCAR.
I SEEMED TO FEEL IT THERE, BUT I QUICKLY PULLED AWAY.
I DID NOT WANT TO AROUSE HER SUSPICIONS.

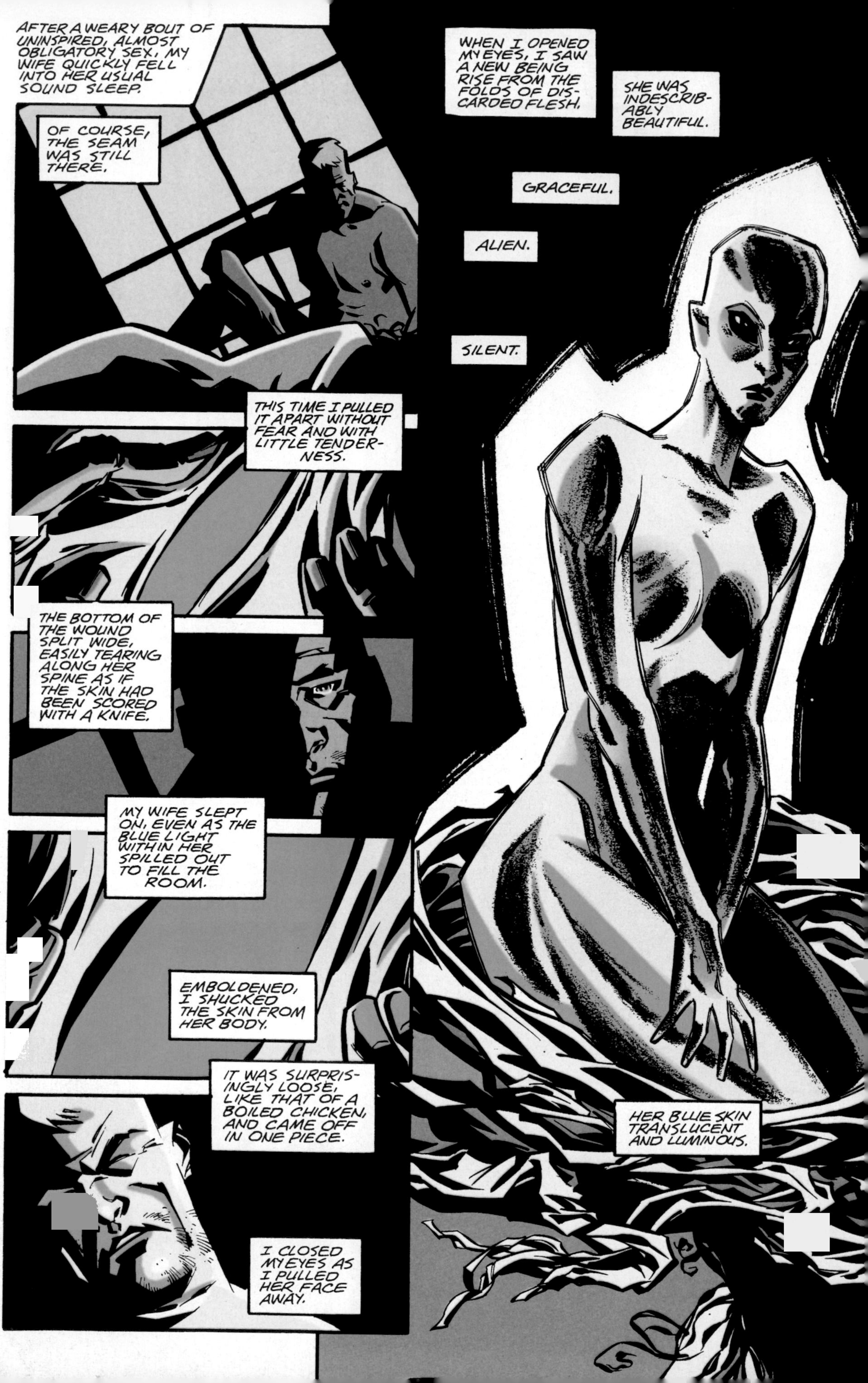
AFTER A WEARY BOUT OF UNINSPIRED, ALMOST OBLIGATORY SEX, MY WIFE QUICKLY FELL INTO HER USUAL SOUND SLEEP.
OF COURSE, THE SEAM WAS STILL THERE.
THIS TIME I PULLED IT APART WITHOUT FEAR AND WITH LITTLE TENDERNESS.
THE BOTTOM OF THE WOUND SPLIT WIDE, EASILY TEARING ALONG HER SPINE AS IF THE SKIN HAD BEEN SCORED WITH A KNIFE.
MY WIFE SLEPT ON, EVEN AS THE BLUE LIGHT WITHIN HER SPILLED OUT TO FILL THE ROOM.
EMBOLDENED, I SHUCKED THE SKIN FROM HER BODY.
IT WAS SURPRISINGLY LOOSE, LIKE THAT OF A BOILED CHICKEN, AND CAME OFF IN ONE PIECE.
I CLOSED MY EYES AS I PULLED HER FACE AWAY.
WHEN I OPENED MY EYES, I SAW A NEW BEING RISE FROM THE FOLDS OF DISCARDED FLESH.
SHE WAS INDESCRIBABLY BEAUTIFUL.
GRACEFUL.
ALIEN.
SILENT.
HER BLUE SKIN TRANSLUCENT AND LUMINOUS.

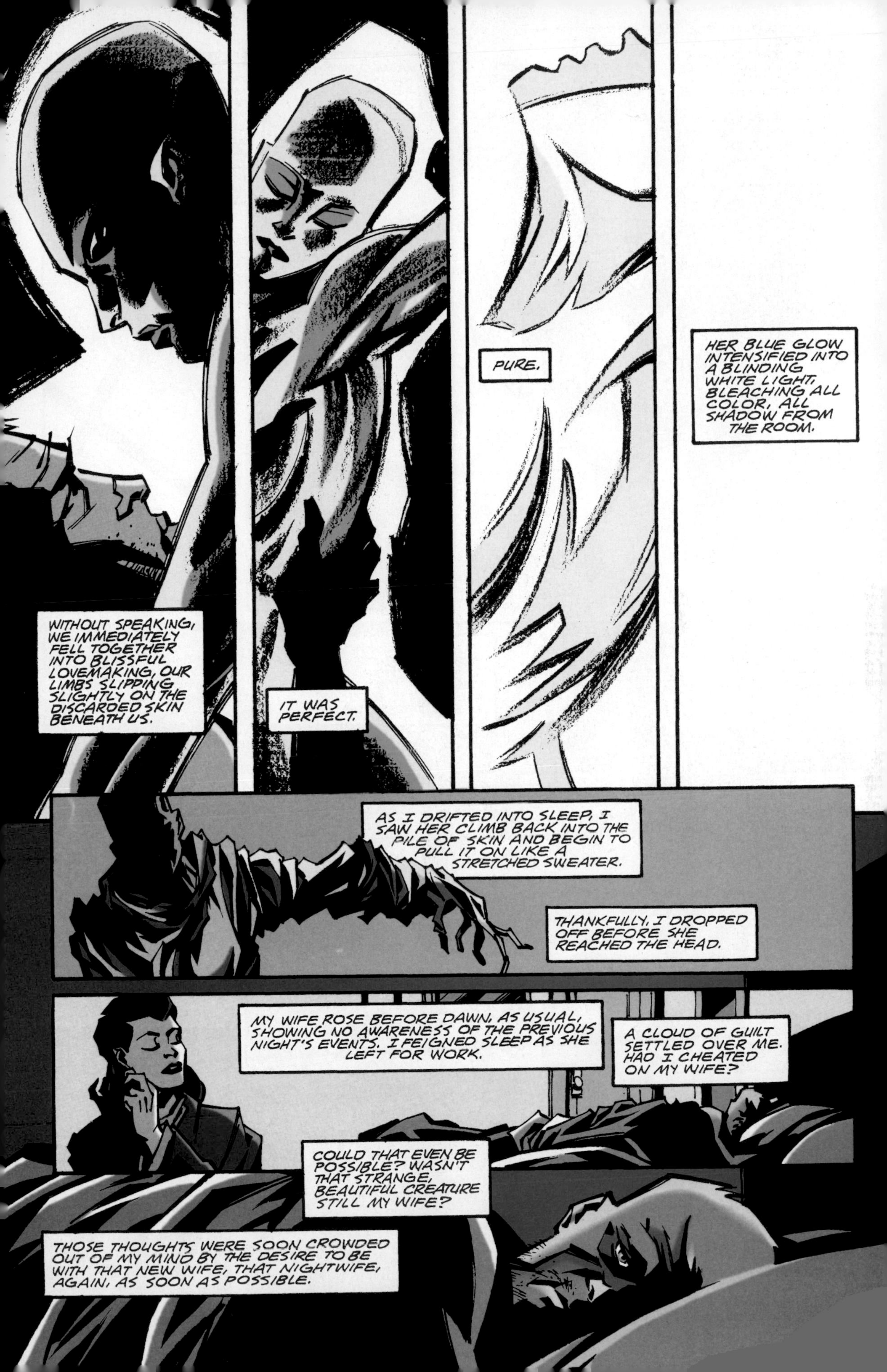
WITHOUT SPEAKING, WE IMMEDIATELY FELL TOGETHER INTO BLISSFUL LOVEMAKING, OUR LIMBS SLIPPING SLIGHTLY ON THE DISCARDED SKIN BENEATH US.
IT WAS PERFECT.
PURE.
HER BLUE GLOW INTENSIFIED INTO A BLINDING WHITE LIGHT, BLEACHING ALL COLOR, ALL SHADOW FROM THE ROOM.
AS I DRIFTED INTO SLEEP, I SAW HER CLIMB BACK INTO THE PILE OF SKIN AND BEGIN TO PULL IT ON LIKE A STRETCHED SWEATER.
THANKFULLY, I DROPPED OFF BEFORE SHE REACHED THE HEAD.
MY WIFE ROSE BEFORE DAWN, AS USUAL, SHOWING NO AWARENESS OF THE PREVIOUS NIGHT'S EVENTS. I FEIGNED SLEEP AS SHE LEFT FOR WORK.
A CLOUD OF GUILT SETTLED OVER ME. HAD I CHEATED ON MY WIFE?
COULD THAT EVEN BE POSSIBLE? WASN'T THAT STRANGE, BEAUTIFUL CREATURE STILL MY WIFE?
THOSE THOUGHTS WERE SOON CROWDED OUT OF MY MIND BY THE DESIRE TO BE WITH THAT NEW WIFE, THAT NIGHTWIFE, AGAIN, AS SOON AS POSSIBLE.

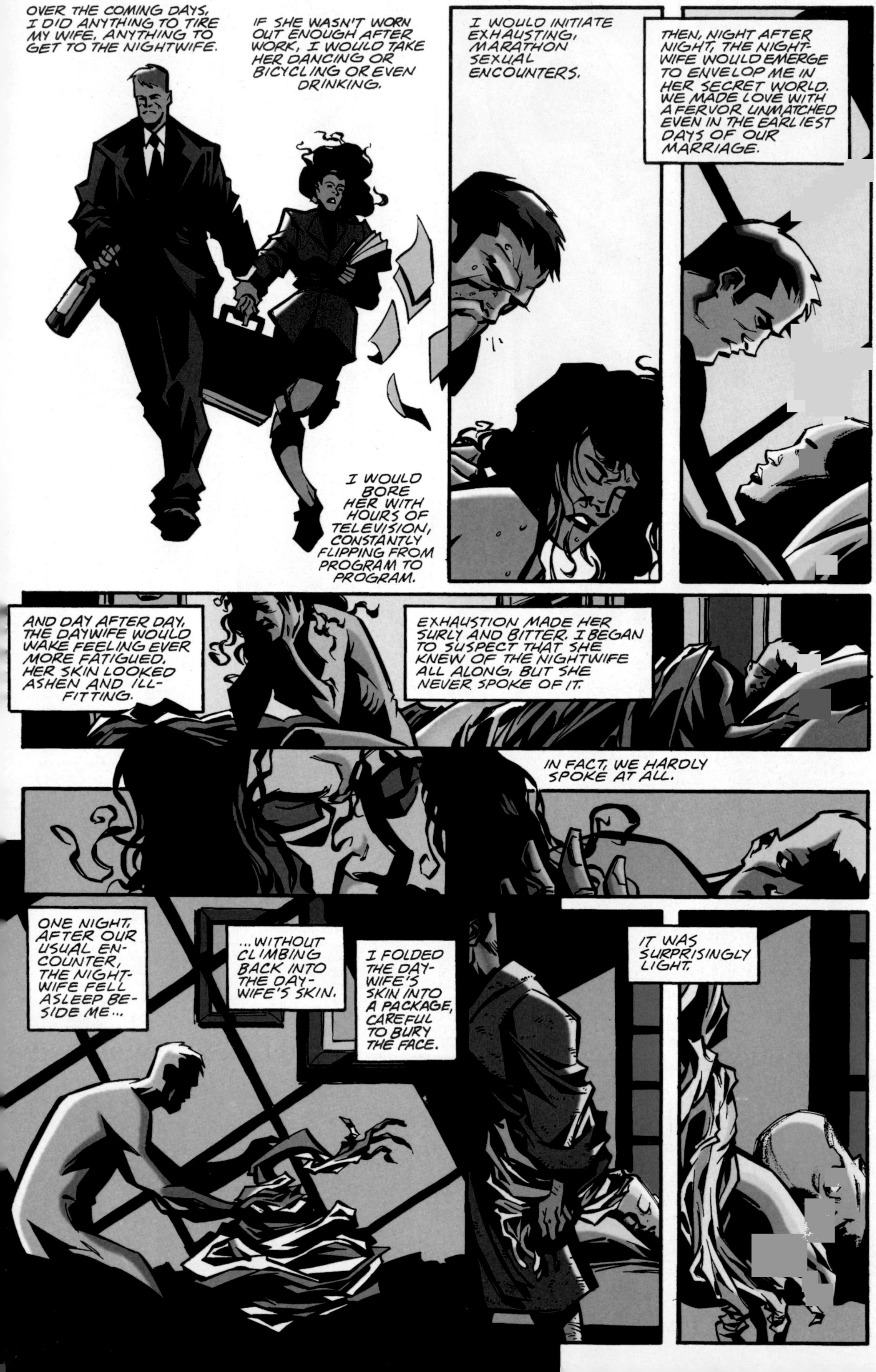
OVER THE COMING DAYS, I DID ANYTHING TO TIRE MY WIFE, ANYTHING TO GET TO THE NIGHTWIFE.
IF SHE WASN'T WORN OUT ENOUGH AFTER WORK, I WOULD TAKE HER DANCING OR BICYCLING OR EVEN DRINKING.
I WOULD BORE HER WITH HOURS OF TELEVISION, CONSTANTLY FLIPPING FROM PROGRAM TO PROGRAM.
I WOULD INITIATE EXHAUSTING, MARATHON SEXUAL ENCOUNTERS.
THEN, NIGHT AFTER NIGHT, THE NIGHT-WIFE WOULD EMERGE TO ENVELOP ME IN HER SECRET WORLD. WE MADE LOVE WITH A FERVOR UNMATCHED EVEN IN THE EARLIEST DAYS OF OUR MARRIAGE.
AND DAY AFTER DAY, THE DAYWIFE WOULD WAKE FEELING EVER MORE FATIGUED. HER SKIN LOOKED ASHEN AND ILL-FITTING.
EXHAUSTION MADE HER SURLY AND BITTER. I BEGAN TO SUSPECT THAT SHE KNEW OF THE NIGHTWIFE ALL ALONG, BUT SHE NEVER SPOKE OF IT.
IN FACT, WE HARDLY SPOKE AT ALL.
ONE NIGHT, AFTER OUR USUAL EN-COUNTER, THE NIGHT-WIFE FELL ASLEEP BE-SIDE ME...
...WITHOUT CLIMBING BACK INTO THE DAY-WIFE'S SKIN.
I FOLDED THE DAY-WIFE'S SKIN INTO A PACKAGE, CAREFUL TO BURY THE FACE.
IT WAS SURPRISINGLY LIGHT.

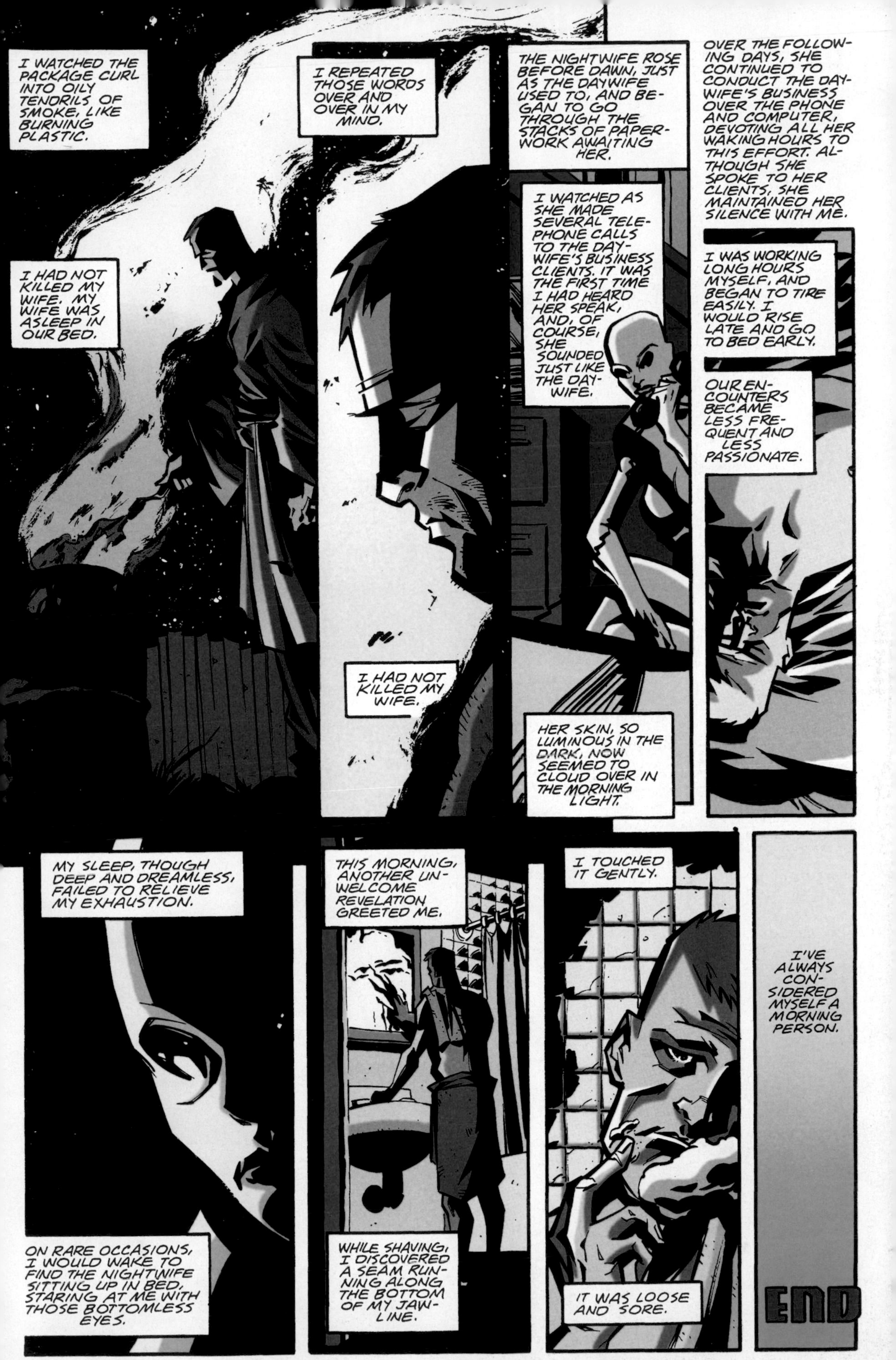
I WATCHED THE PACKAGE CURL INTO OILY TENDRILS OF SMOKE, LIKE BURNING PLASTIC.
I HAD NOT KILLED MY WIFE. MY WIFE WAS ASLEEP IN OUR BED.
I REPEATED THOSE WORDS OVER AND OVER IN MY MIND.
I HAD NOT KILLED MY WIFE.
THE NIGHTWIFE ROSE BEFORE DAWN, JUST AS THE DAYWIFE USED TO, AND BEGAN TO GO THROUGH THE STACKS OF PAPERWORK AWAITING HER.
I WATCHED AS SHE MADE SEVERAL TELEPHONE CALLS TO THE DAYWIFE'S BUSINESS CLIENTS. IT WAS THE FIRST TIME I HAD HEARD HER SPEAK, AND, OF COURSE, SHE SOUNDED JUST LIKE THE DAYWIFE.
HER SKIN, SO LUMINOUS IN THE DARK, NOW SEEMED TO CLOUD OVER IN THE MORNING LIGHT.
OVER THE FOLLOWING DAYS, SHE CONTINUED TO CONDUCT THE DAYWIFE'S BUSINESS OVER THE PHONE AND COMPUTER, DEVOTING ALL HER WAKING HOURS TO THIS EFFORT. ALTHOUGH SHE SPOKE TO HER CLIENTS, SHE MAINTAINED HER SILENCE WITH ME.
I WAS WORKING LONG HOURS MYSELF, AND BEGAN TO TIRE EASILY. I WOULD RISE LATE AND GO TO BED EARLY.
OUR ENCOUNTERS BECAME LESS FREQUENT AND LESS PASSIONATE.
MY SLEEP, THOUGH DEEP AND DREAMLESS, FAILED TO RELIEVE MY EXHAUSTION.
ON RARE OCCASIONS, I WOULD WAKE TO FIND THE NIGHTWIFE SITTING UP IN BED, STARING AT ME WITH THOSE BOTTOMLESS EYES.
THIS MORNING, ANOTHER UNWELCOME REVELATION GREETED ME.
WHILE SHAVING, I DISCOVERED A SEAM RUNNING ALONG THE BOTTOM OF MY JAWLINE.
I TOUCHED IT GENTLY.
IT WAS LOOSE AND SORE.
I'VE ALWAYS CONSIDERED MYSELF A MORNING PERSON.
END

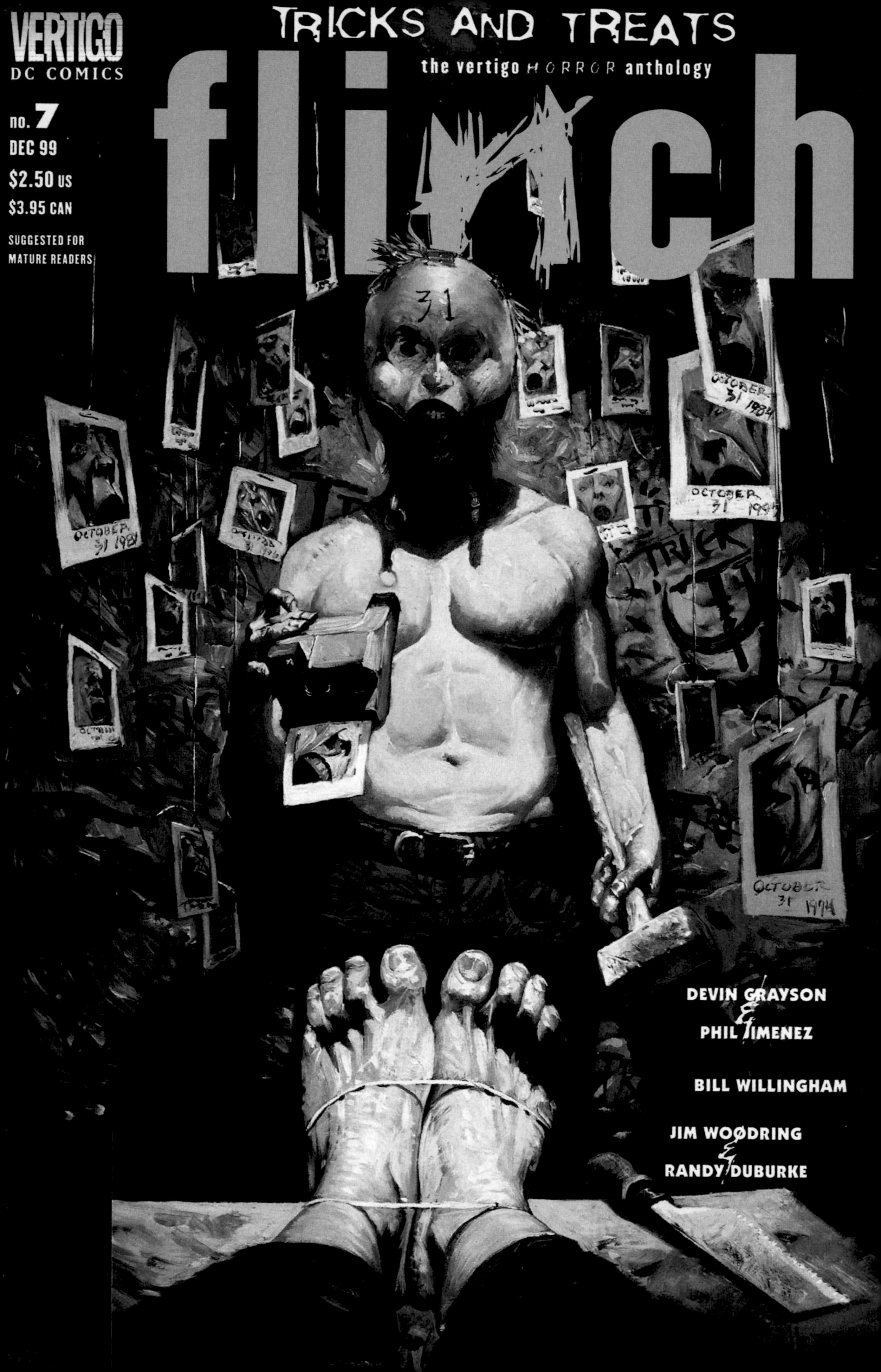
VERTIGO
DC COMICS
TRICKS AND TREATS
the vertigo HORROR anthology
flinch
no. 7
DEC 99
$2.50 US
$3.95 CAN
SUGGESTED FOR
MATURE READERS
31
OCTOBER 31 1984
OCTOBER 31 1994
OCTOBER 31 1974
TRICK
DEVIN GRAYSON
&
PHIL JIMENEZ
BILL WILLINGHAM
JIM WOODRING
&
RANDY DUBURKE

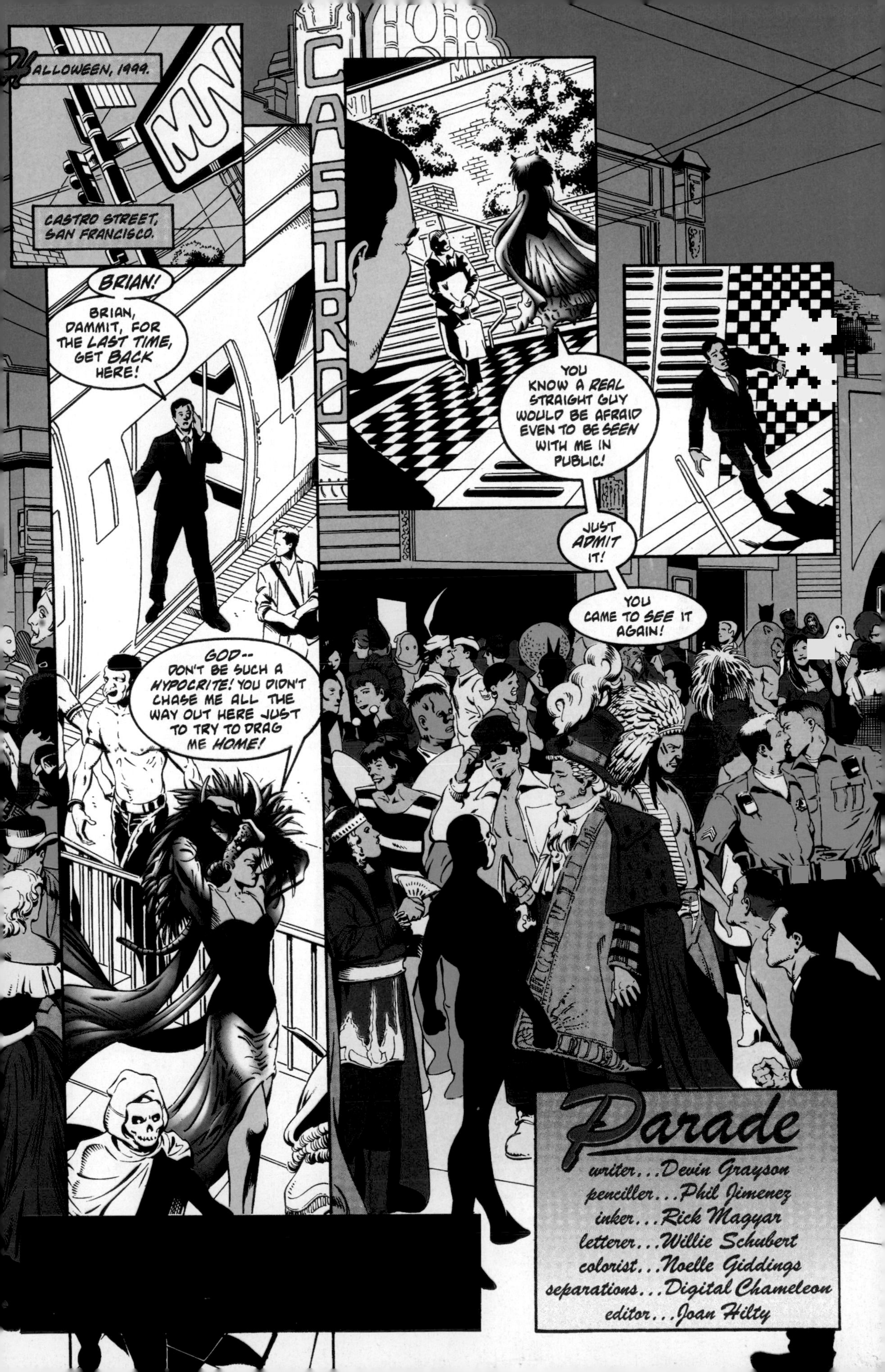
HALLOWEEN, 1999.
MUNI
CASTRO STREET, SAN FRANCISCO.
CASTRO
BRIAN!
BRIAN, DAMMIT, FOR THE LAST TIME, GET BACK HERE!
YOU KNOW A REAL STRAIGHT GUY WOULD BE AFRAID EVEN TO BE SEEN WITH ME IN PUBLIC!
JUST ADMIT IT!
YOU CAME TO SEE IT AGAIN!
GOD-- DON'T BE SUCH A HYPOCRITE! YOU DIDN'T CHASE ME ALL THE WAY OUT HERE JUST TO TRY TO DRAG ME HOME!
Parade
writer...Devin Grayson
penciller...Phil Jimenez
inker...Rick Magyar
letterer...Willie Schubert
colorist...Noelle Giddings
separations...Digital Chameleon
editor...Joan Hilty

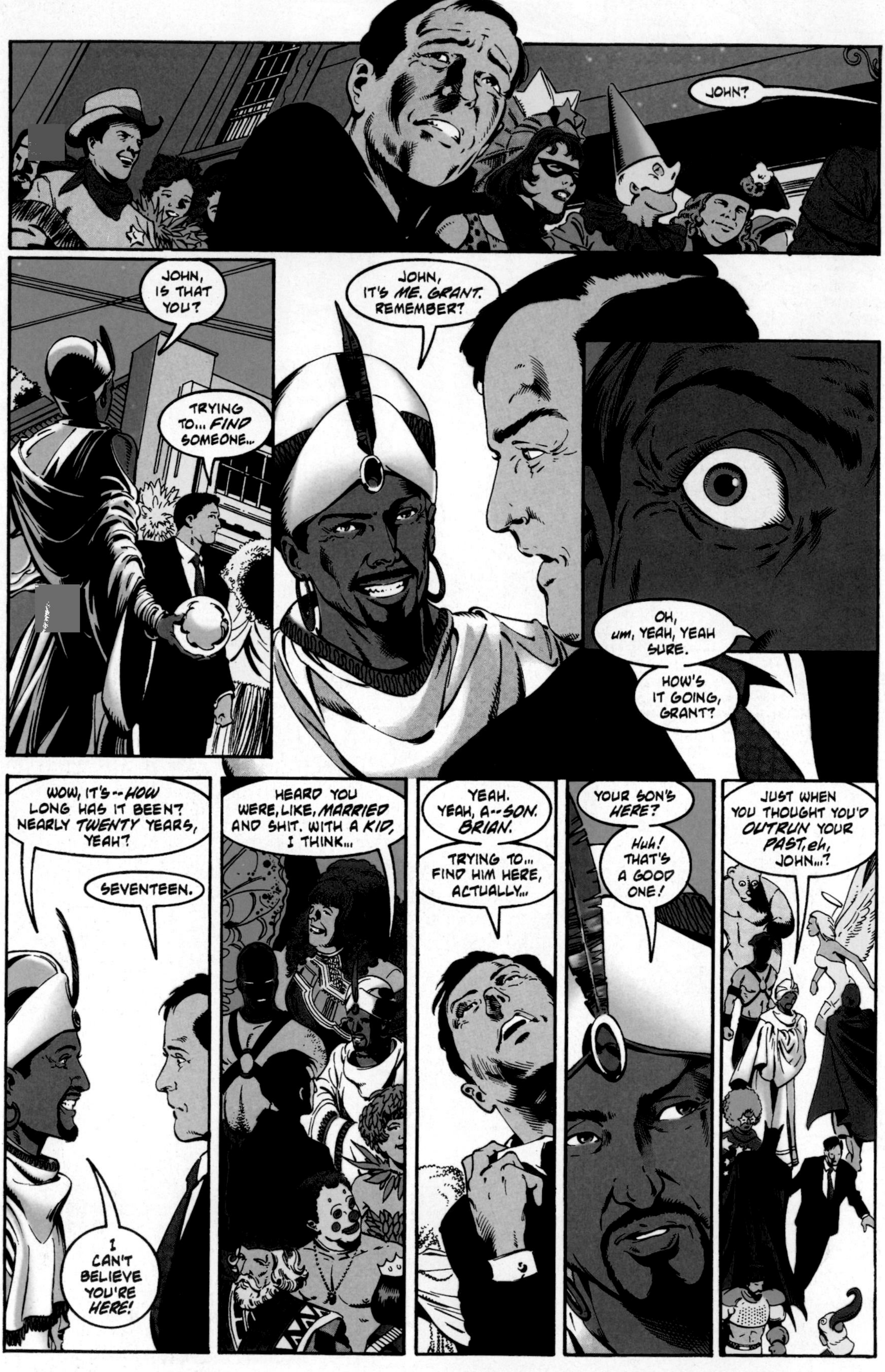

JOHN?
JOHN, IS THAT YOU?
TRYING TO... FIND SOMEONE...
JOHN, IT'S ME. GRANT. REMEMBER?
OH, um, YEAH, YEAH SURE.
HOW'S IT GOING, GRANT?
WOW, IT'S--HOW LONG HAS IT BEEN? NEARLY TWENTY YEARS, YEAH?
SEVENTEEN.
I CAN'T BELIEVE YOU'RE HERE!
HEARD YOU WERE, LIKE, MARRIED AND SHIT. WITH A KID, I THINK...
YEAH. YEAH, A--SON. BRIAN.
TRYING TO... FIND HIM HERE, ACTUALLY...
YOUR SON'S HERE?
Huh! THAT'S A GOOD ONE!
JUST WHEN YOU THOUGHT YOU'D OUTRUN YOUR PAST, eh, JOHN...?

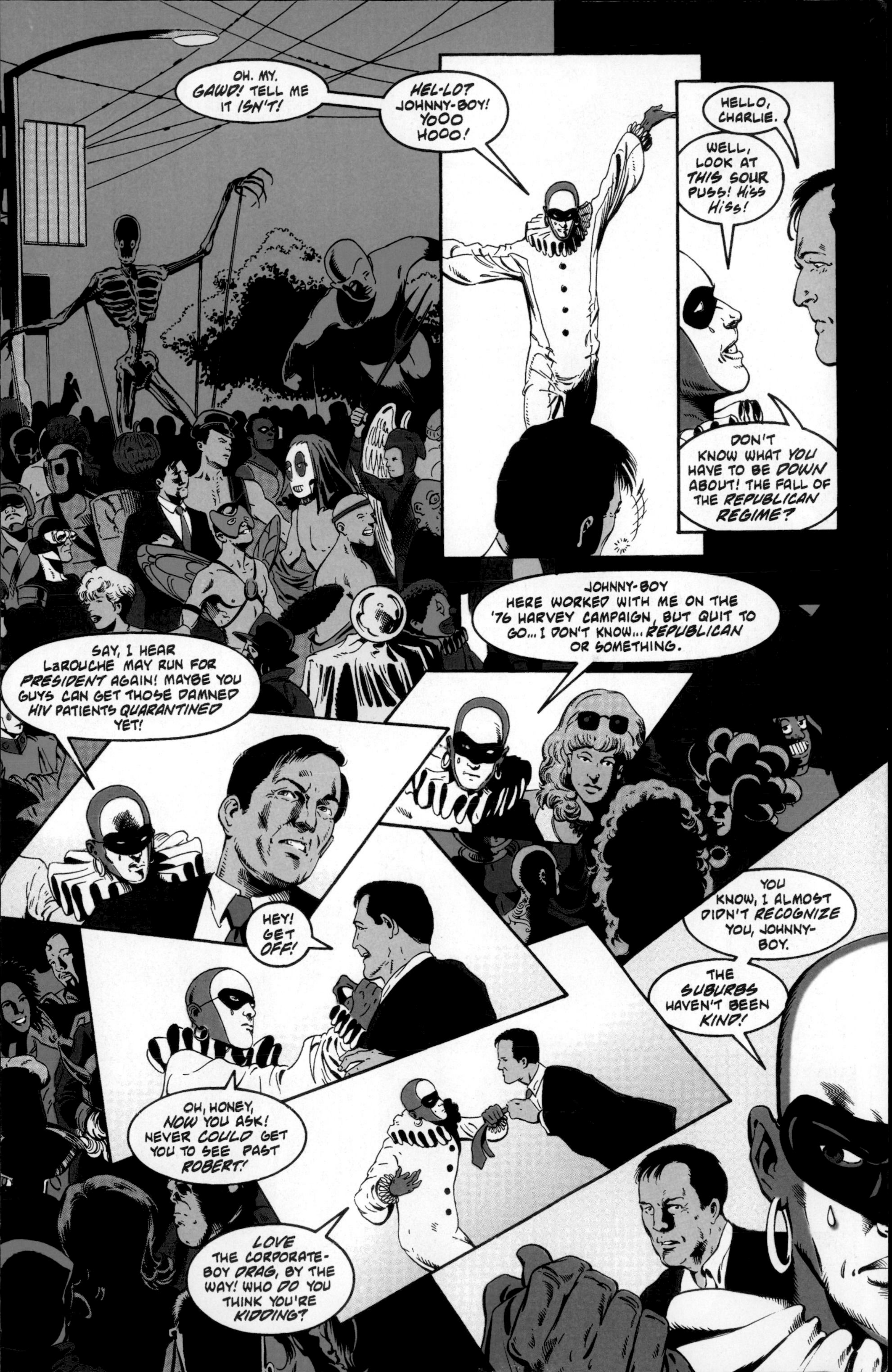
OH. MY. GAWD! TELL ME IT ISN'T!
HEL-LO? JOHNNY-BOY! YOOO HOOO!
HELLO, CHARLIE.
WELL, LOOK AT THIS SOUR PUSS! Hiss Hiss!
DON'T KNOW WHAT YOU HAVE TO BE DOWN ABOUT! THE FALL OF THE REPUBLICAN REGIME?
JOHNNY-BOY HERE WORKED WITH ME ON THE '76 HARVEY CAMPAIGN, BUT QUIT TO GO... I DON'T KNOW... REPUBLICAN OR SOMETHING.
SAY, I HEAR LaROUCHE MAY RUN FOR PRESIDENT AGAIN! MAYBE YOU GUYS CAN GET THOSE DAMNED HIV PATIENTS QUARANTINED YET!
YOU KNOW, I ALMOST DIDN'T RECOGNIZE YOU, JOHNNY-BOY.
THE SUBURBS HAVEN'T BEEN KIND!
HEY! GET OFF!
OH, HONEY, NOW YOU ASK! NEVER COULD GET YOU TO SEE PAST ROBERT!
LOVE THE CORPORATE-BOY DRAG, BY THE WAY! WHO DO YOU THINK YOU'RE KIDDING?

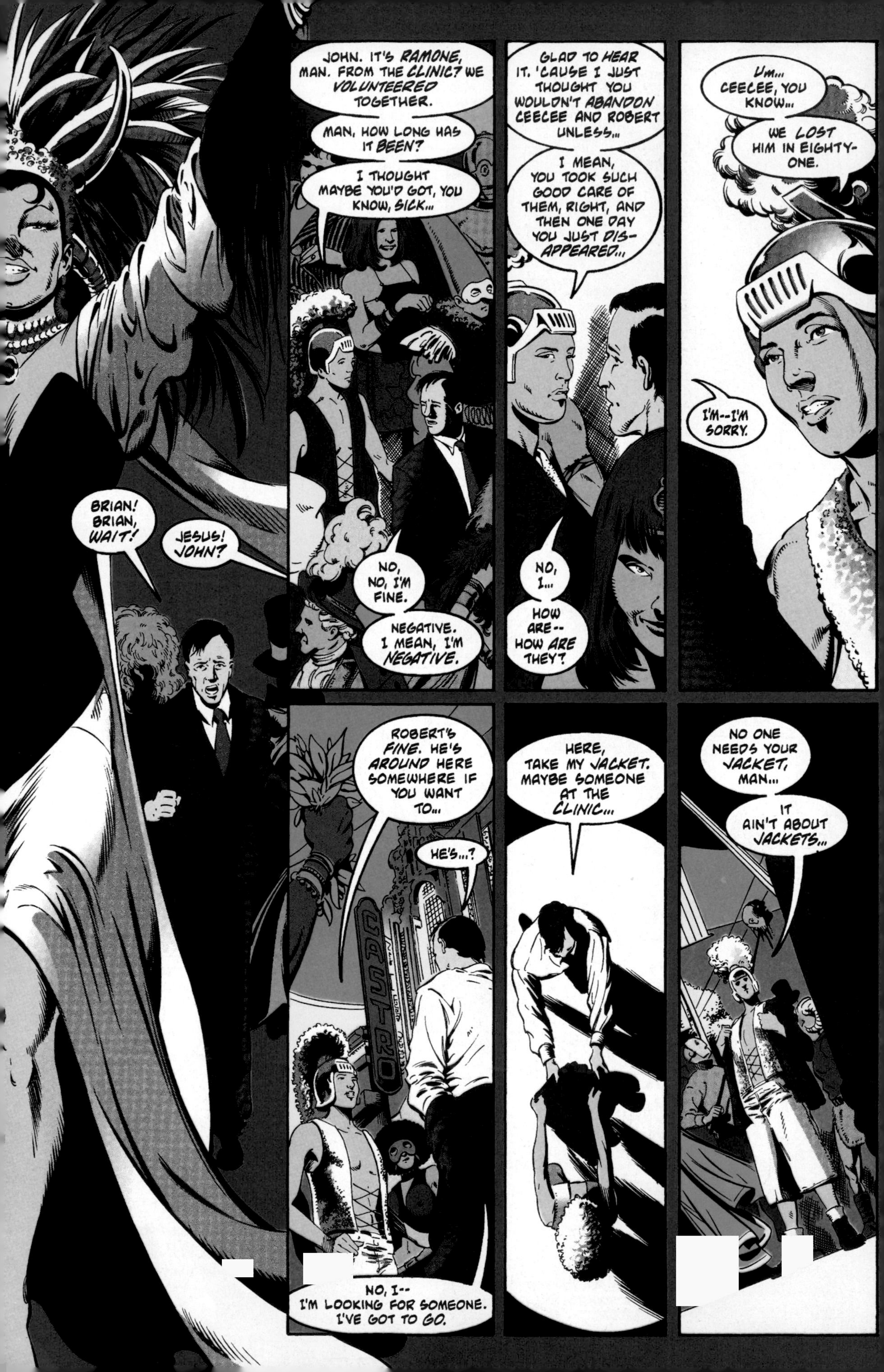

BRIAN! BRIAN, WAIT!
JESUS! JOHN?
JOHN. IT'S RAMONE, MAN. FROM THE CLINIC? WE VOLUNTEERED TOGETHER.
MAN, HOW LONG HAS IT BEEN?
I THOUGHT MAYBE YOU'D GOT, YOU KNOW, SICK...
NO, NO, I'M FINE.
NEGATIVE. I MEAN, I'M NEGATIVE.
GLAD TO HEAR IT. 'CAUSE I JUST THOUGHT YOU WOULDN'T ABANDON CEECEE AND ROBERT UNLESS...
I MEAN, YOU TOOK SUCH GOOD CARE OF THEM, RIGHT, AND THEN ONE DAY YOU JUST DIS-APPEARED...
NO, I...
HOW ARE-- HOW ARE THEY?
UM... CEECEE, YOU KNOW...
WE LOST HIM IN EIGHTY-ONE.
I'M--I'M SORRY.
ROBERT'S FINE. HE'S AROUND HERE SOMEWHERE IF YOU WANT TO...
HE'S...?
CASTRO
NO, I-- I'M LOOKING FOR SOMEONE. I'VE GOT TO GO.
HERE, TAKE MY JACKET. MAYBE SOMEONE AT THE CLINIC...
NO ONE NEEDS YOUR JACKET, MAN...
IT AIN'T ABOUT JACKETS...

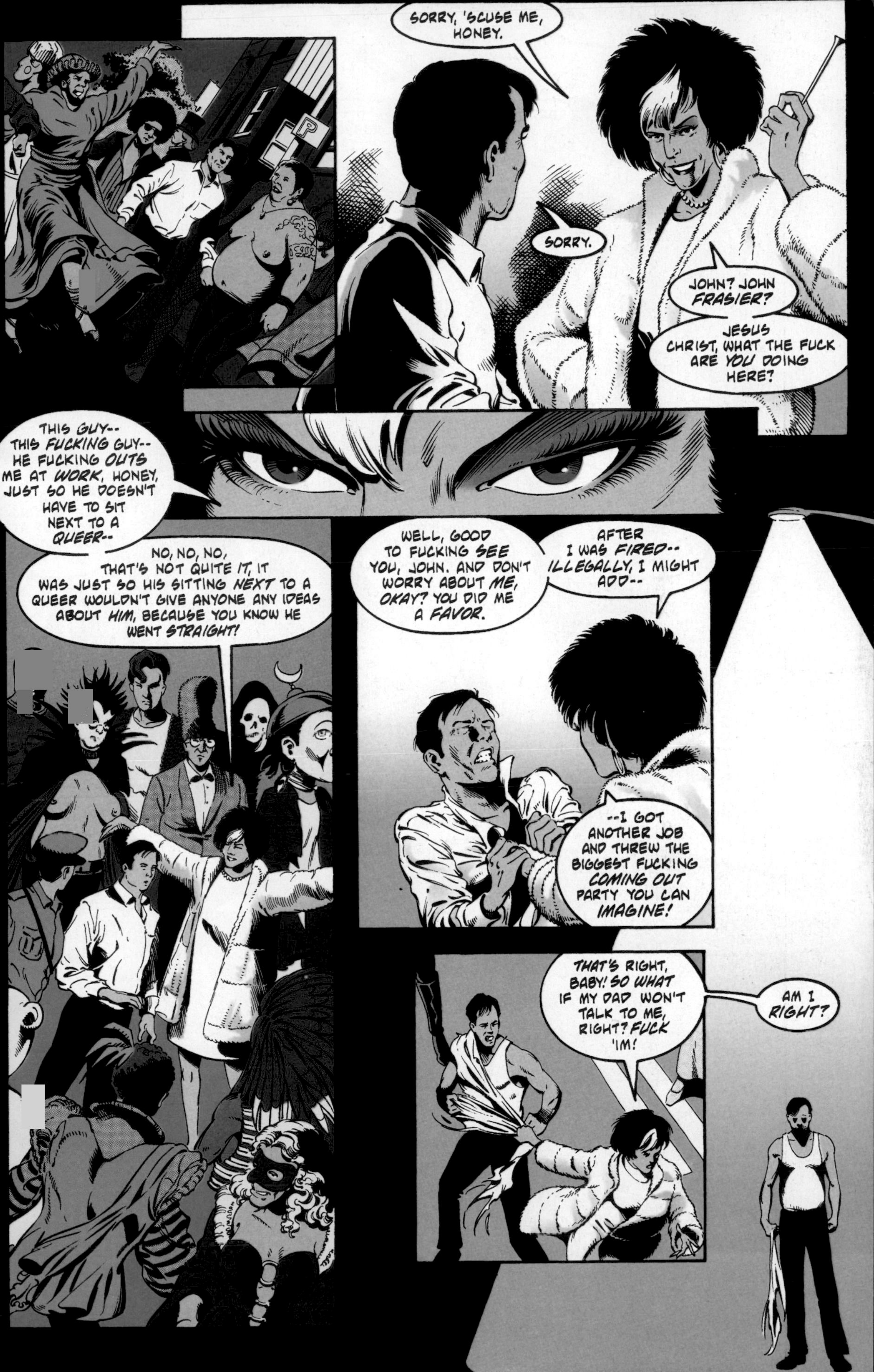
SORRY, 'SCUSE ME, HONEY.
SORRY.
JOHN? JOHN FRASIER?
JESUS CHRIST, WHAT THE FUCK ARE YOU DOING HERE?
THIS GUY-- THIS FUCKING GUY-- HE FUCKING OUTS ME AT WORK, HONEY, JUST SO HE DOESN'T HAVE TO SIT NEXT TO A QUEER--
NO, NO, NO, THAT'S NOT QUITE IT, IT WAS JUST SO HIS SITTING NEXT TO A QUEER WOULDN'T GIVE ANYONE ANY IDEAS ABOUT HIM, BECAUSE YOU KNOW HE WENT STRAIGHT!
WELL, GOOD TO FUCKING SEE YOU, JOHN. AND DON'T WORRY ABOUT ME, OKAY? YOU DID ME A FAVOR.
AFTER I WAS FIRED-- ILLEGALLY, I MIGHT ADD--
--I GOT ANOTHER JOB AND THREW THE BIGGEST FUCKING COMING OUT PARTY YOU CAN IMAGINE!
THAT'S RIGHT, BABY! SO WHAT IF MY DAD WON'T TALK TO ME, RIGHT? FUCK 'IM!
AM I RIGHT?

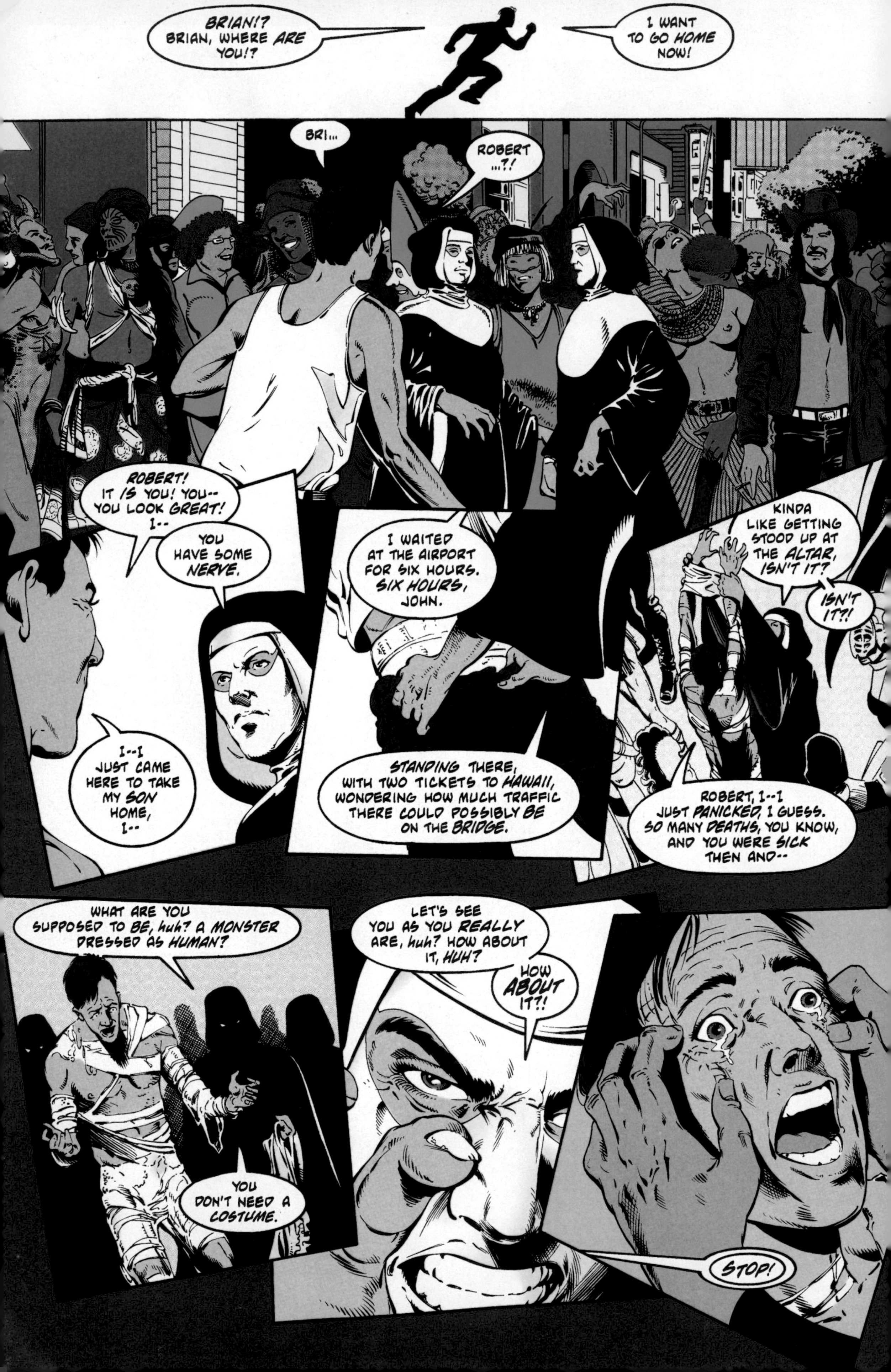
BRIAN!? BRIAN, WHERE ARE YOU!?
I WANT TO GO HOME NOW!
BRI...
ROBERT ...?!
ROBERT! IT IS YOU! YOU-- YOU LOOK GREAT! I--
YOU HAVE SOME NERVE.
I--I JUST CAME HERE TO TAKE MY SON HOME, I--
I WAITED AT THE AIRPORT FOR SIX HOURS. SIX HOURS, JOHN.
STANDING THERE, WITH TWO TICKETS TO HAWAII, WONDERING HOW MUCH TRAFFIC THERE COULD POSSIBLY BE ON THE BRIDGE.
KINDA LIKE GETTING STOOD UP AT THE ALTAR, ISN'T IT?
ISN'T IT?!
ROBERT, I--I JUST PANICKED, I GUESS. SO MANY DEATHS, YOU KNOW, AND YOU WERE SICK THEN AND--
WHAT ARE YOU SUPPOSED TO BE, huh? A MONSTER DRESSED AS HUMAN?
YOU DON'T NEED A COSTUME.
LET'S SEE YOU AS YOU REALLY ARE, huh? HOW ABOUT IT, HUH?
HOW ABOUT IT?!
STOP!

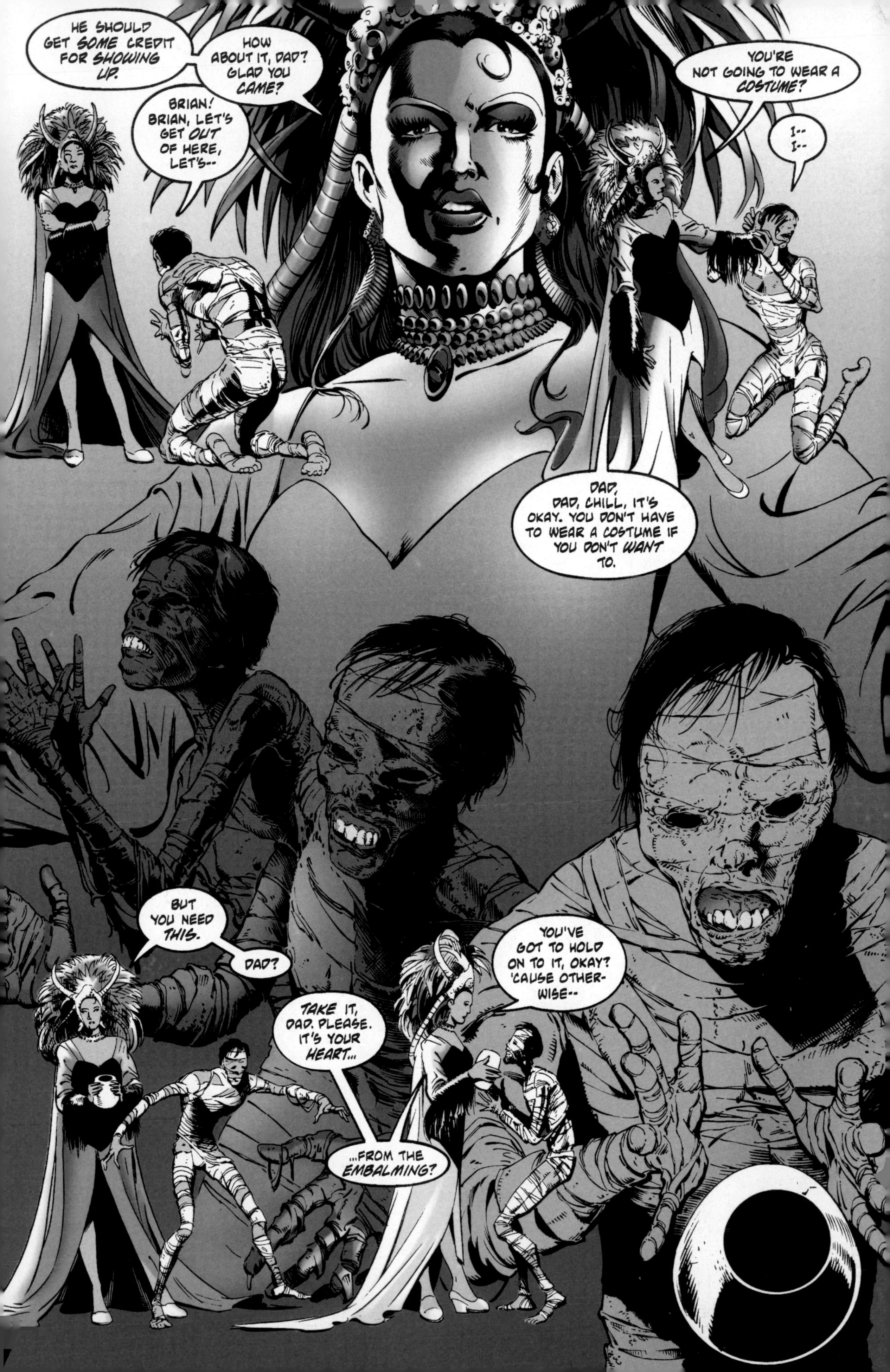
HE SHOULD GET SOME CREDIT FOR SHOWING UP.
HOW ABOUT IT, DAD? GLAD YOU CAME?
BRIAN! BRIAN, LET'S GET OUT OF HERE, LET'S--
YOU'RE NOT GOING TO WEAR A COSTUME?
I-- I--
DAD, DAD, CHILL, IT'S OKAY. YOU DON'T HAVE TO WEAR A COSTUME IF YOU DON'T WANT TO.
BUT YOU NEED THIS.
DAD?
TAKE IT, DAD. PLEASE. IT'S YOUR HEART...
...FROM THE EMBALMING?
YOU'VE GOT TO HOLD ON TO IT, OKAY? 'CAUSE OTHER-WISE--

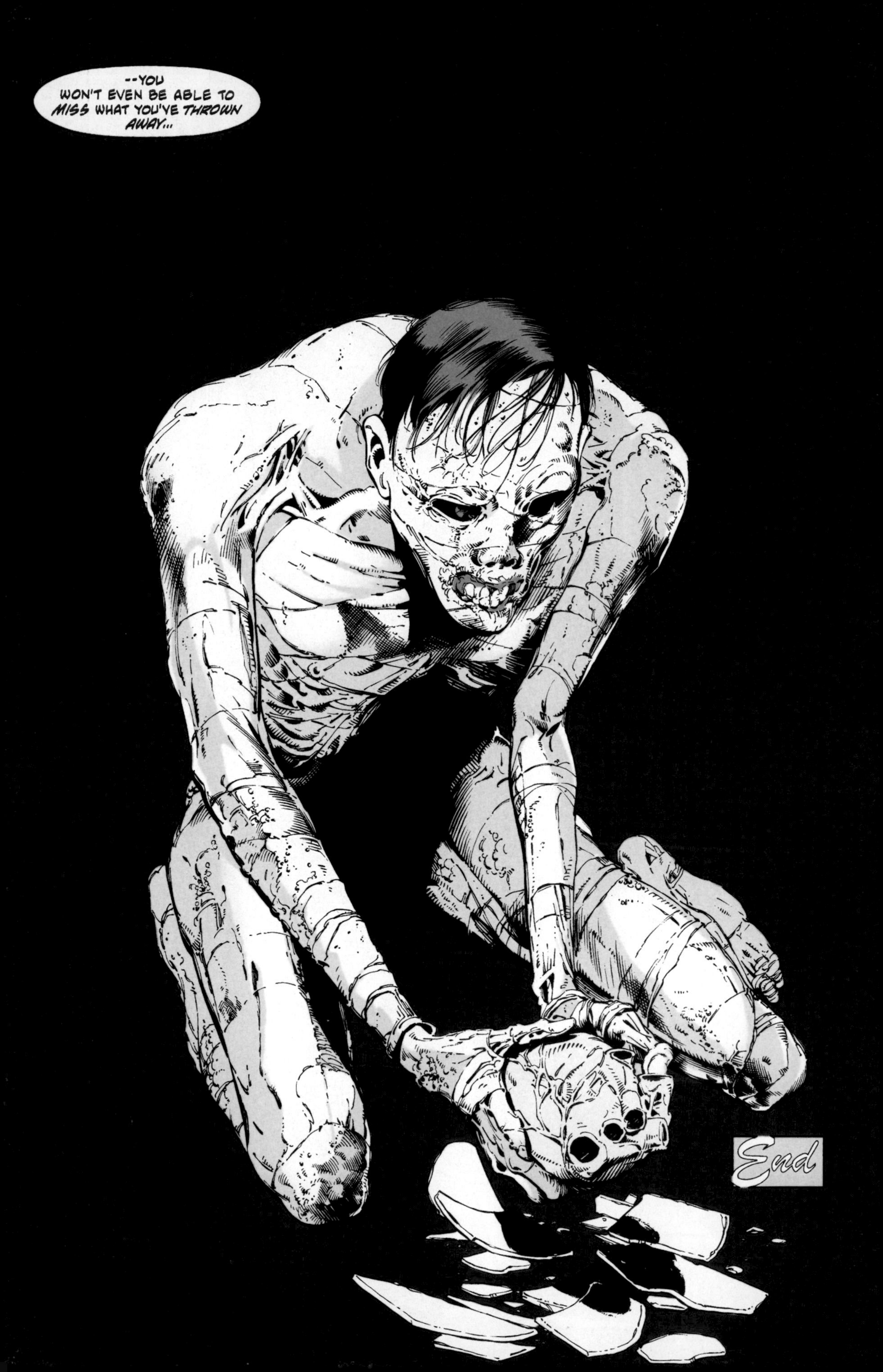
--YOU WON'T EVEN BE ABLE TO MISS WHAT YOU'VE THROWN AWAY...
End

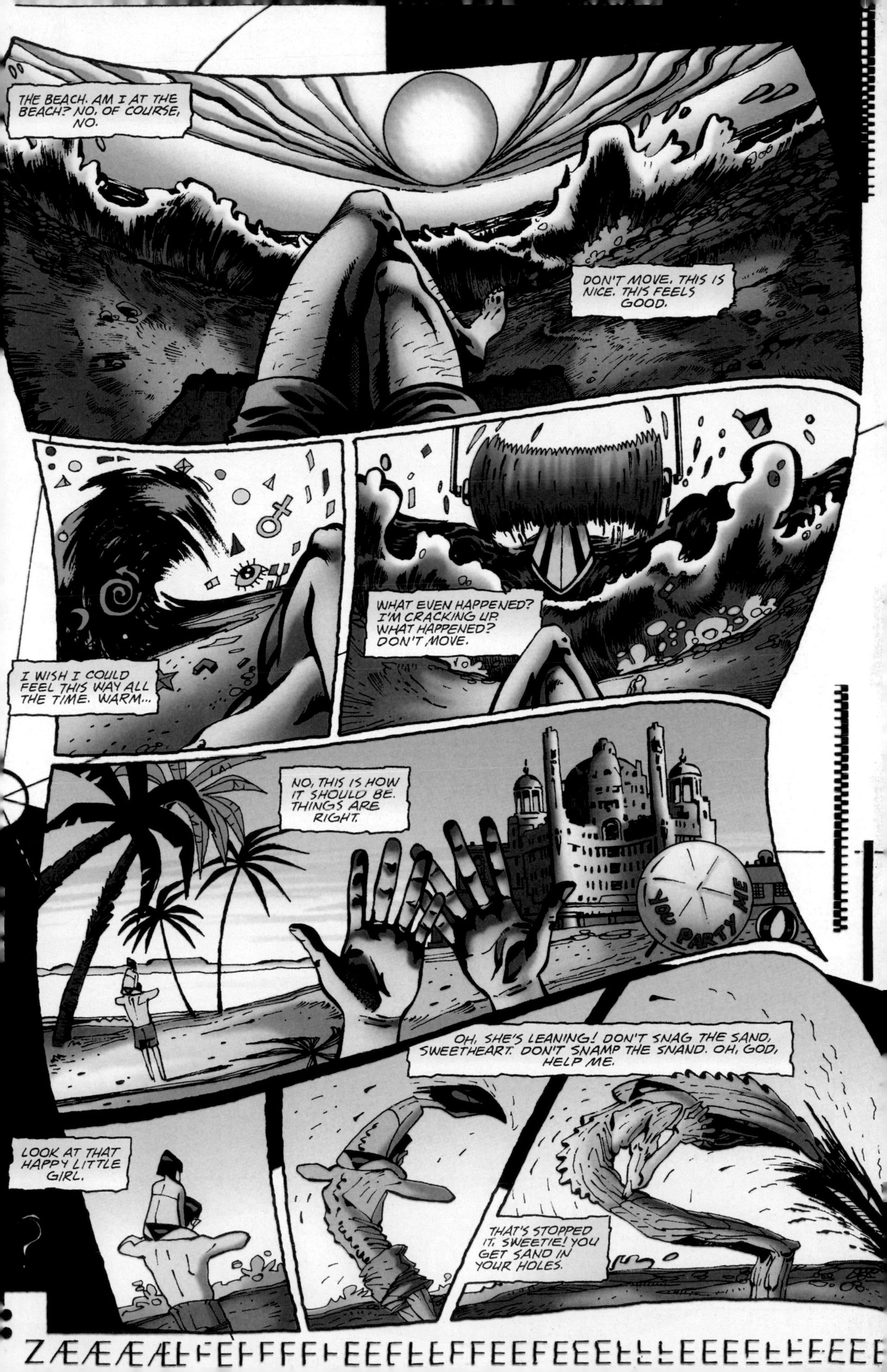
THE BEACH. AM I AT THE BEACH? NO. OF COURSE, NO.
DON'T MOVE. THIS IS NICE. THIS FEELS GOOD.
I WISH I COULD FEEL THIS WAY ALL THE TIME. WARM...
WHAT EVEN HAPPENED? I'M CRACKING UP. WHAT HAPPENED? DON'T MOVE.
NO, THIS IS HOW IT SHOULD BE. THINGS ARE RIGHT.
YOU PARTY ME
OH, SHE'S LEANING! DON'T SNAG THE SAND, SWEETHEART. DON'T SNAMP THE SNAND. OH, GOD, HELP ME.
LOOK AT THAT HAPPY LITTLE GIRL.
THAT'S STOPPED IT, SWEETIE! YOU GET SAND IN YOUR HOLES.
ZÆÆÆÆŁFEFFFFFEEFŁŁFFEEFEEEŁŁŁEEEEŁŁFEEE

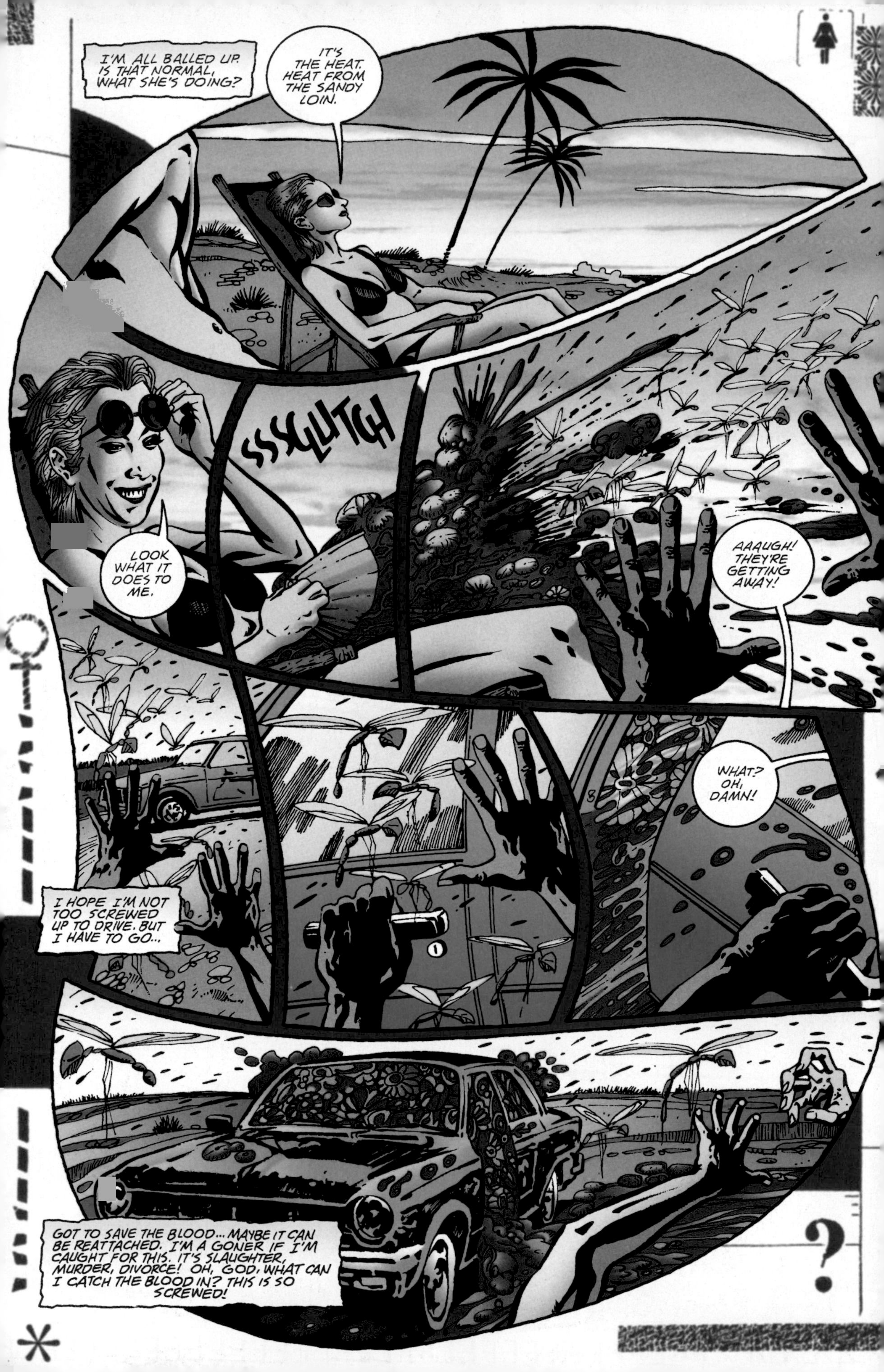
I'M ALL BALLED UP. IS THAT NORMAL, WHAT SHE'S DOING?
IT'S THE HEAT. HEAT FROM THE SANDY LOIN.
SSSGLUTCH
LOOK WHAT IT DOES TO ME.
AAAUGH! THEY'RE GETTING AWAY!
WHAT? OH, DAMN!
I HOPE I'M NOT TOO SCREWED UP TO DRIVE. BUT I HAVE TO GO...
GOT TO SAVE THE BLOOD... MAYBE IT CAN BE REATTACHED. I'M A GONER IF I'M CAUGHT FOR THIS. IT'S SLAUGHTER, MURDER, DIVORCE! OH, GOD, WHAT CAN I CATCH THE BLOOD IN? THIS IS SO SCREWED!

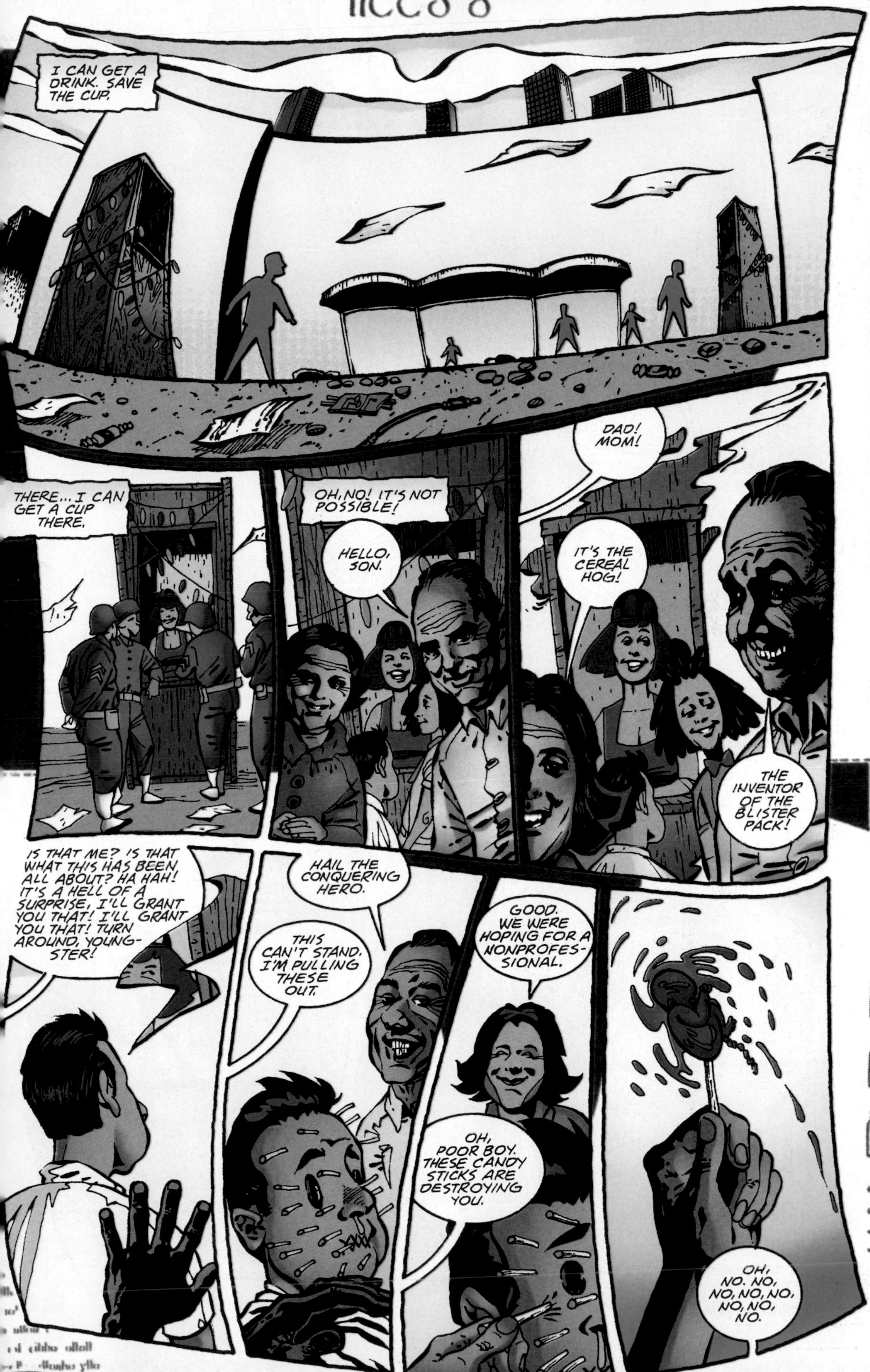
I CAN GET A DRINK. SAVE THE CUP.
THERE... I CAN GET A CUP THERE.
OH, NO! IT'S NOT POSSIBLE!
HELLO, SON.
DAD! MOM!
IT'S THE CEREAL HOG!
THE INVENTOR OF THE BLISTER PACK!
IS THAT ME? IS THAT WHAT THIS HAS BEEN ALL ABOUT? HA HAH! IT'S A HELL OF A SURPRISE, I'LL GRANT YOU THAT! I'LL GRANT YOU THAT! TURN AROUND, YOUNGSTER!
HAIL THE CONQUERING HERO.
THIS CAN'T STAND. I'M PULLING THESE OUT.
GOOD. WE WERE HOPING FOR A NONPROFESSIONAL.
OH, POOR BOY. THESE CANDY STICKS ARE DESTROYING YOU.
OH, NO. NO, NO, NO, NO, NO, NO, NO.

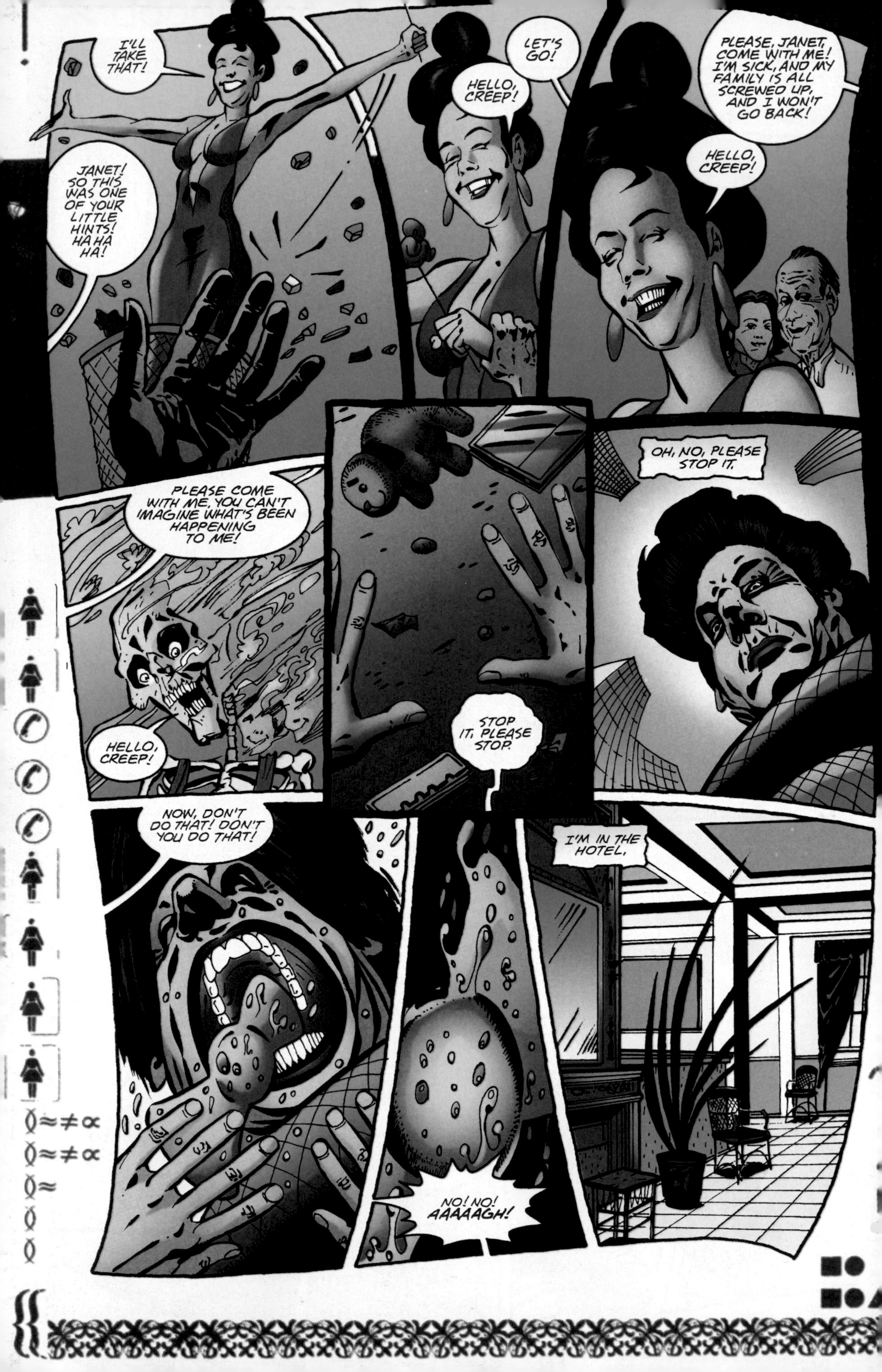
I'LL TAKE THAT!
JANET! SO THIS WAS ONE OF YOUR LITTLE HINTS! HA HA HA!
LET'S GO!
HELLO, CREEP!
PLEASE, JANET, COME WITH ME! I'M SICK, AND MY FAMILY IS ALL SCREWED UP, AND I WON'T GO BACK!
HELLO, CREEP!
PLEASE COME WITH ME, YOU CAN'T IMAGINE WHAT'S BEEN HAPPENING TO ME!
HELLO, CREEP!
STOP IT, PLEASE STOP.
OH, NO, PLEASE STOP IT.
NOW, DON'T DO THAT! DON'T YOU DO THAT!
NO! NO! AAAAAGH!
I'M IN THE HOTEL.

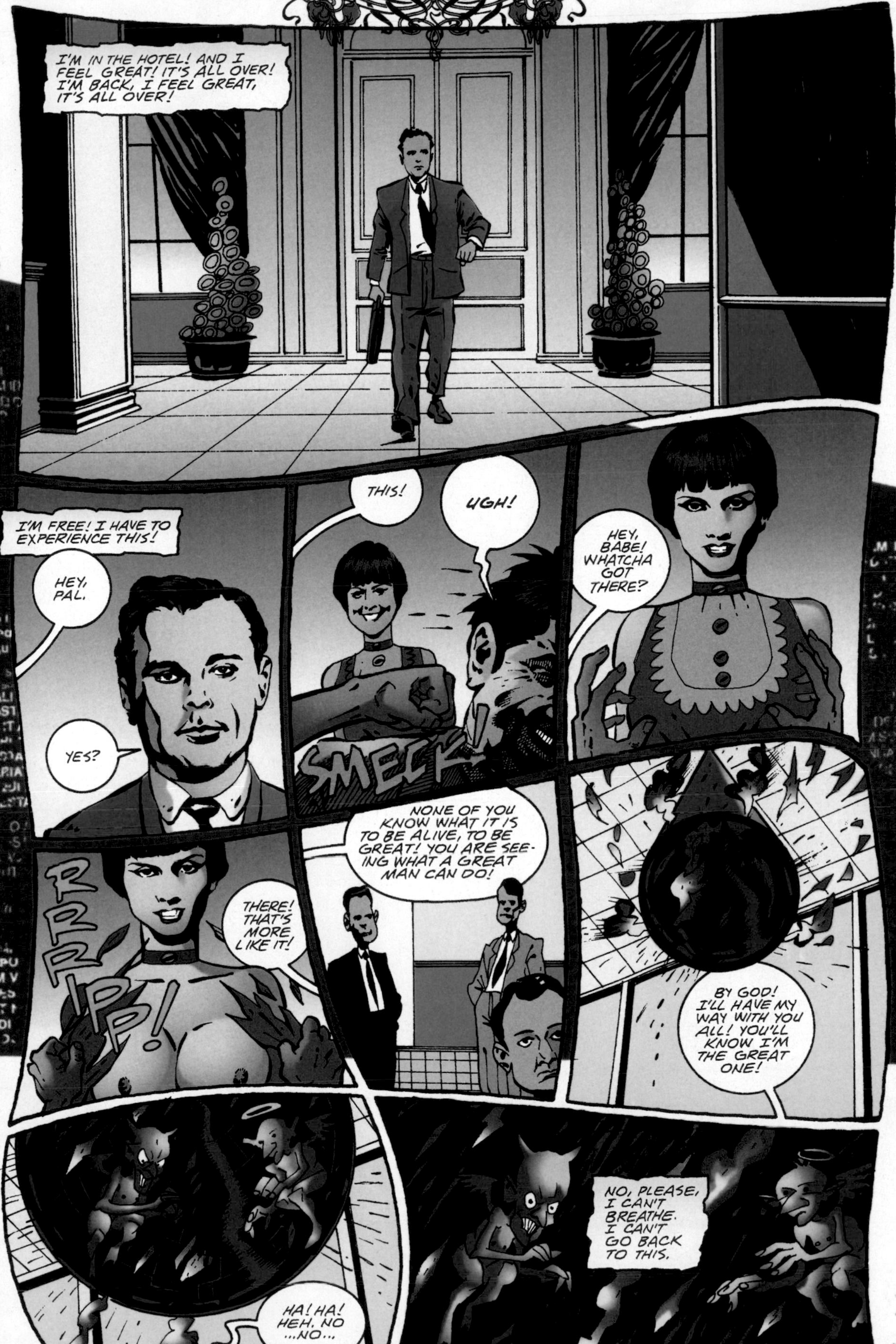
I'M IN THE HOTEL! AND I FEEL GREAT! IT'S ALL OVER! I'M BACK, I FEEL GREAT, IT'S ALL OVER!
I'M FREE! I HAVE TO EXPERIENCE THIS!
HEY, PAL.
YES?
THIS!
UGH!
SMECK!
HEY, BABE! WHATCHA GOT THERE?
RRRIPP!
THERE! THAT'S MORE LIKE IT!
NONE OF YOU KNOW WHAT IT IS TO BE ALIVE, TO BE GREAT! YOU ARE SEEING WHAT A GREAT MAN CAN DO!
BY GOD! I'LL HAVE MY WAY WITH YOU ALL! YOU'LL KNOW I'M THE GREAT ONE!
HA! HA! HEH. NO ...NO...
NO, PLEASE, I CAN'T BREATHE. I CAN'T GO BACK TO THIS.

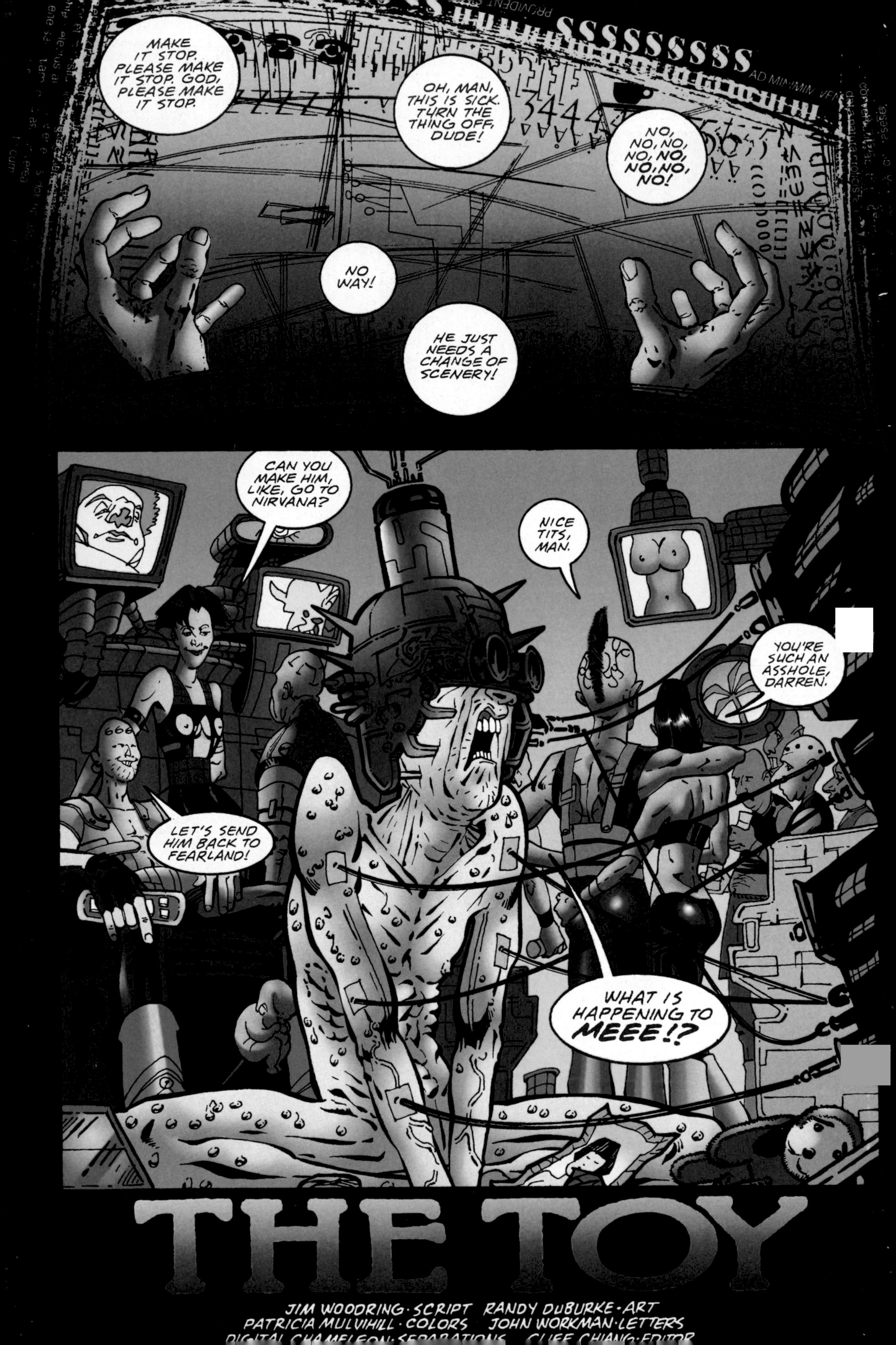
MAKE IT STOP. PLEASE MAKE IT STOP. GOD, PLEASE MAKE IT STOP.
OH, MAN, THIS IS SICK. TURN THE THING OFF, DUDE!
NO, NO, NO, NO, NO, NO, NO, NO!
NO WAY!
HE JUST NEEDS A CHANGE OF SCENERY!
CAN YOU MAKE HIM, LIKE, GO TO NIRVANA?
NICE TITS, MAN.
YOU'RE SUCH AN ASSHOLE, DARREN.
LET'S SEND HIM BACK TO FEARLAND!
WHAT IS HAPPENING TO MEEE!?

# THE TOY

JIM WOODRING · SCRIPT RANDY DUBURKE · ART
PATRICIA MULVIHILL · COLORS JOHN WORKMAN · LETTERS
DIGITAL CHAMELEON · SEPARATIONS CLIFF CHIANG · EDITOR

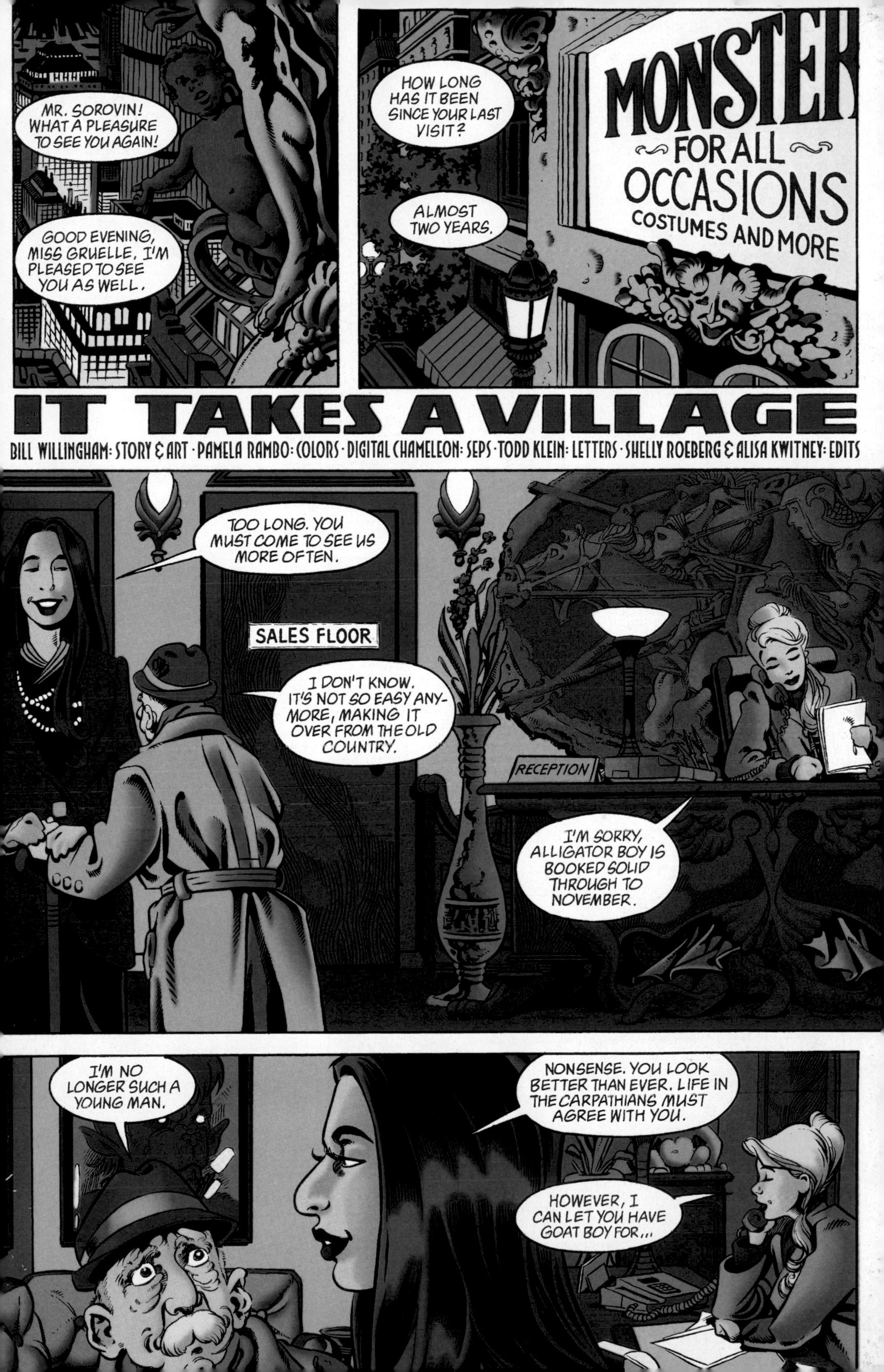
MR. SOROVIN! WHAT A PLEASURE TO SEE YOU AGAIN!
GOOD EVENING, MISS GRUELLE. I'M PLEASED TO SEE YOU AS WELL.
HOW LONG HAS IT BEEN SINCE YOUR LAST VISIT?
ALMOST TWO YEARS.
MONSTER FOR ALL OCCASIONS COSTUMES AND MORE
IT TAKES A VILLAGE
BILL WILLINGHAM: STORY & ART · PAMELA RAMBO: COLORS · DIGITAL CHAMELEON: SEPS · TODD KLEIN: LETTERS · SHELLY ROEBERG & ALISA KWITNEY: EDITS
TOO LONG. YOU MUST COME TO SEE US MORE OFTEN.
SALES FLOOR
I DON'T KNOW. IT'S NOT SO EASY ANYMORE, MAKING IT OVER FROM THE OLD COUNTRY.
RECEPTION
I'M SORRY, ALLIGATOR BOY IS BOOKED SOLID THROUGH TO NOVEMBER.
I'M NO LONGER SUCH A YOUNG MAN.
NONSENSE. YOU LOOK BETTER THAN EVER. LIFE IN THE CARPATHIANS MUST AGREE WITH YOU.
HOWEVER, I CAN LET YOU HAVE GOAT BOY FOR...

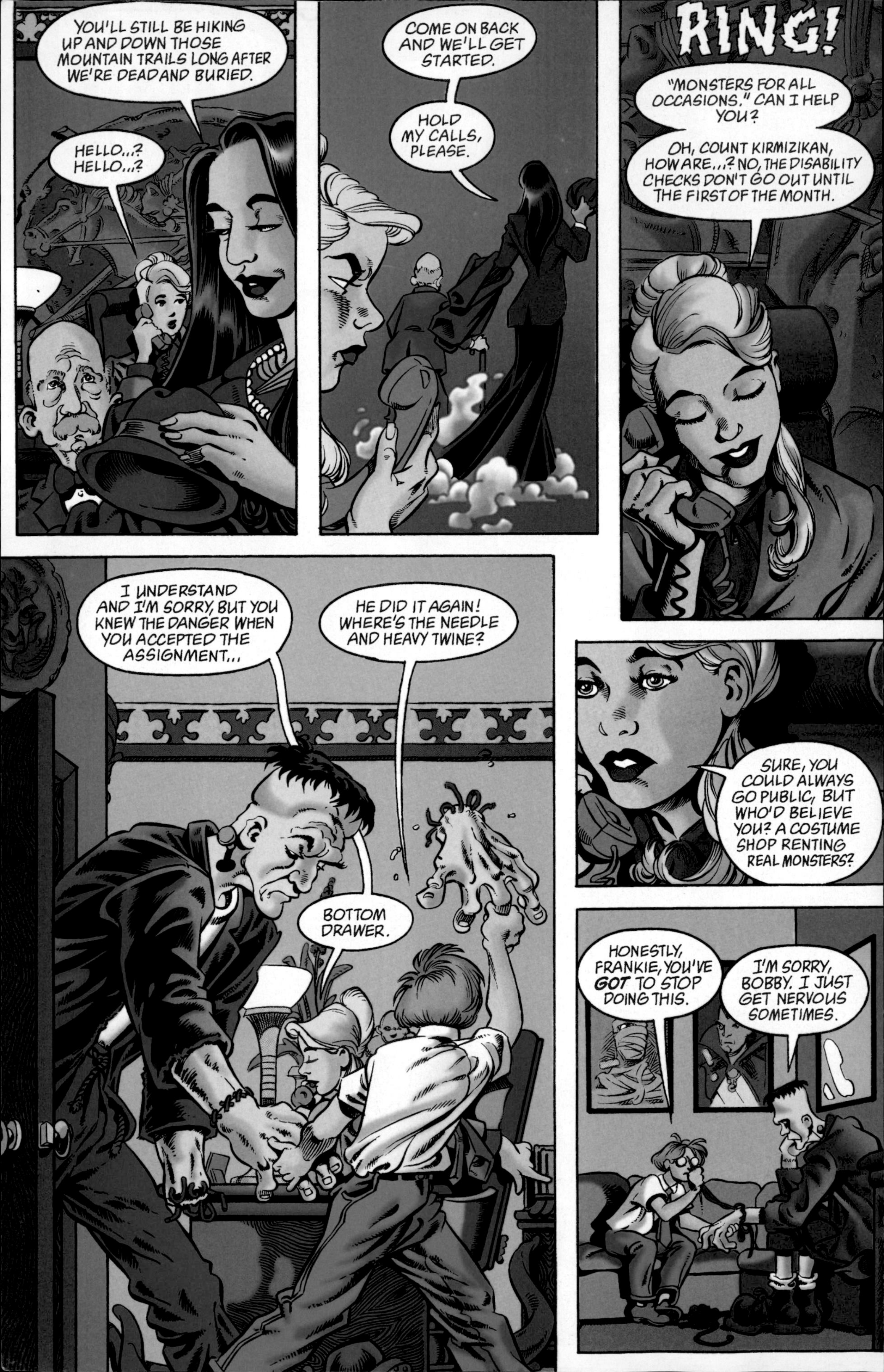
YOU'LL STILL BE HIKING UP AND DOWN THOSE MOUNTAIN TRAILS LONG AFTER WE'RE DEAD AND BURIED.
HELLO...? HELLO...?
COME ON BACK AND WE'LL GET STARTED.
HOLD MY CALLS, PLEASE.
RING!
"MONSTERS FOR ALL OCCASIONS." CAN I HELP YOU?
OH, COUNT KIRMIZIKAN, HOW ARE...? NO, THE DISABILITY CHECKS DON'T GO OUT UNTIL THE FIRST OF THE MONTH.
I UNDERSTAND AND I'M SORRY, BUT YOU KNEW THE DANGER WHEN YOU ACCEPTED THE ASSIGNMENT...
HE DID IT AGAIN! WHERE'S THE NEEDLE AND HEAVY TWINE?
BOTTOM DRAWER.
SURE, YOU COULD ALWAYS GO PUBLIC, BUT WHO'D BELIEVE YOU? A COSTUME SHOP RENTING REAL MONSTERS?
HONESTLY, FRANKIE, YOU'VE GOT TO STOP DOING THIS.
I'M SORRY, BOBBY. I JUST GET NERVOUS SOMETIMES.

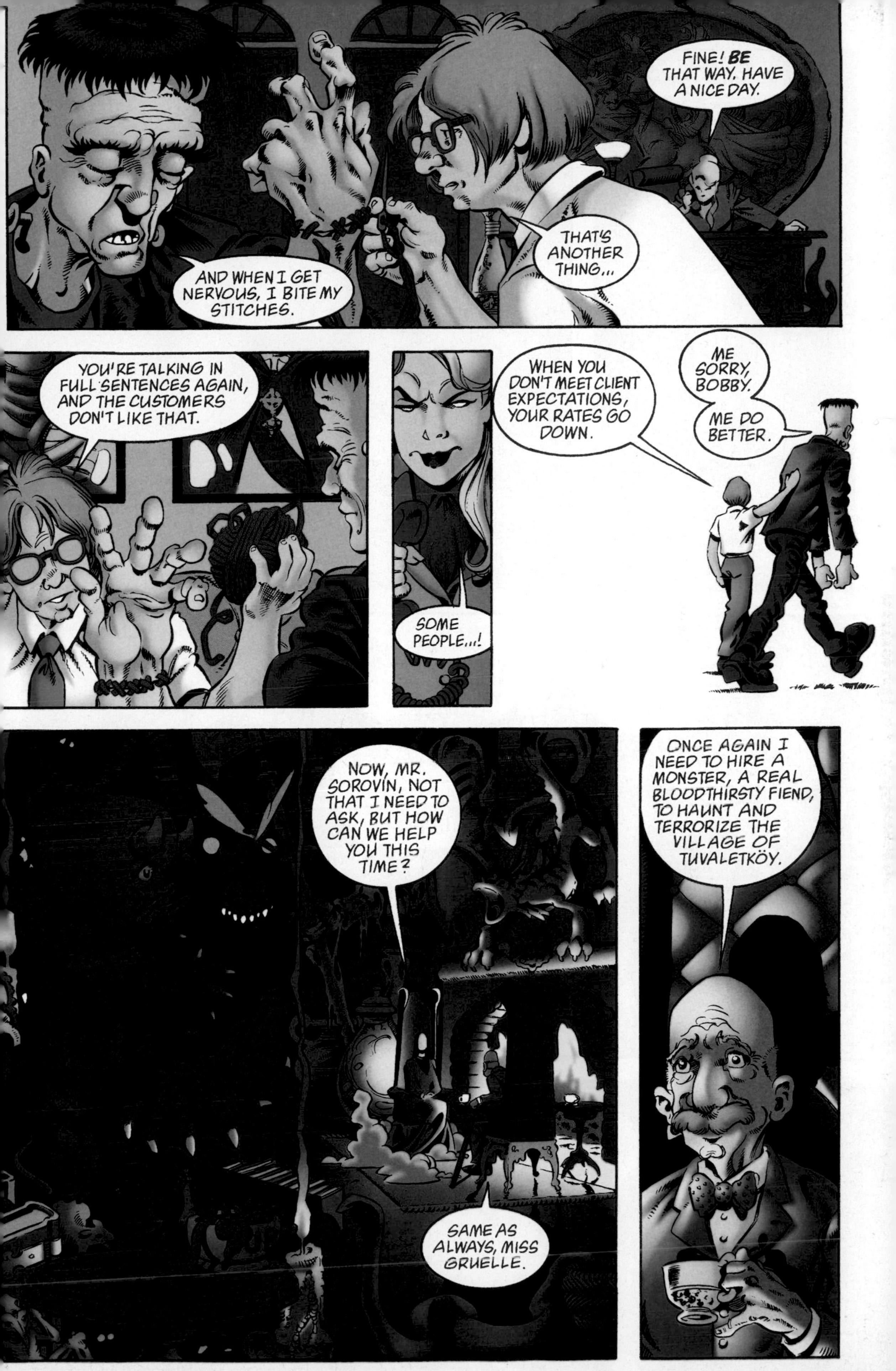
FINE! BE THAT WAY. HAVE A NICE DAY.
AND WHEN I GET NERVOUS, I BITE MY STITCHES.
THAT'S ANOTHER THING...
YOU'RE TALKING IN FULL SENTENCES AGAIN, AND THE CUSTOMERS DON'T LIKE THAT.
SOME PEOPLE...!
WHEN YOU DON'T MEET CLIENT EXPECTATIONS, YOUR RATES GO DOWN.
ME SORRY, BOBBY.
ME DO BETTER.
NOW, MR. SOROVIN, NOT THAT I NEED TO ASK, BUT HOW CAN WE HELP YOU THIS TIME?
SAME AS ALWAYS, MISS GRUELLE.
ONCE AGAIN I NEED TO HIRE A MONSTER, A REAL BLOODTHIRSTY FIEND, TO HAUNT AND TERRORIZE THE VILLAGE OF TUVALETKÖY.

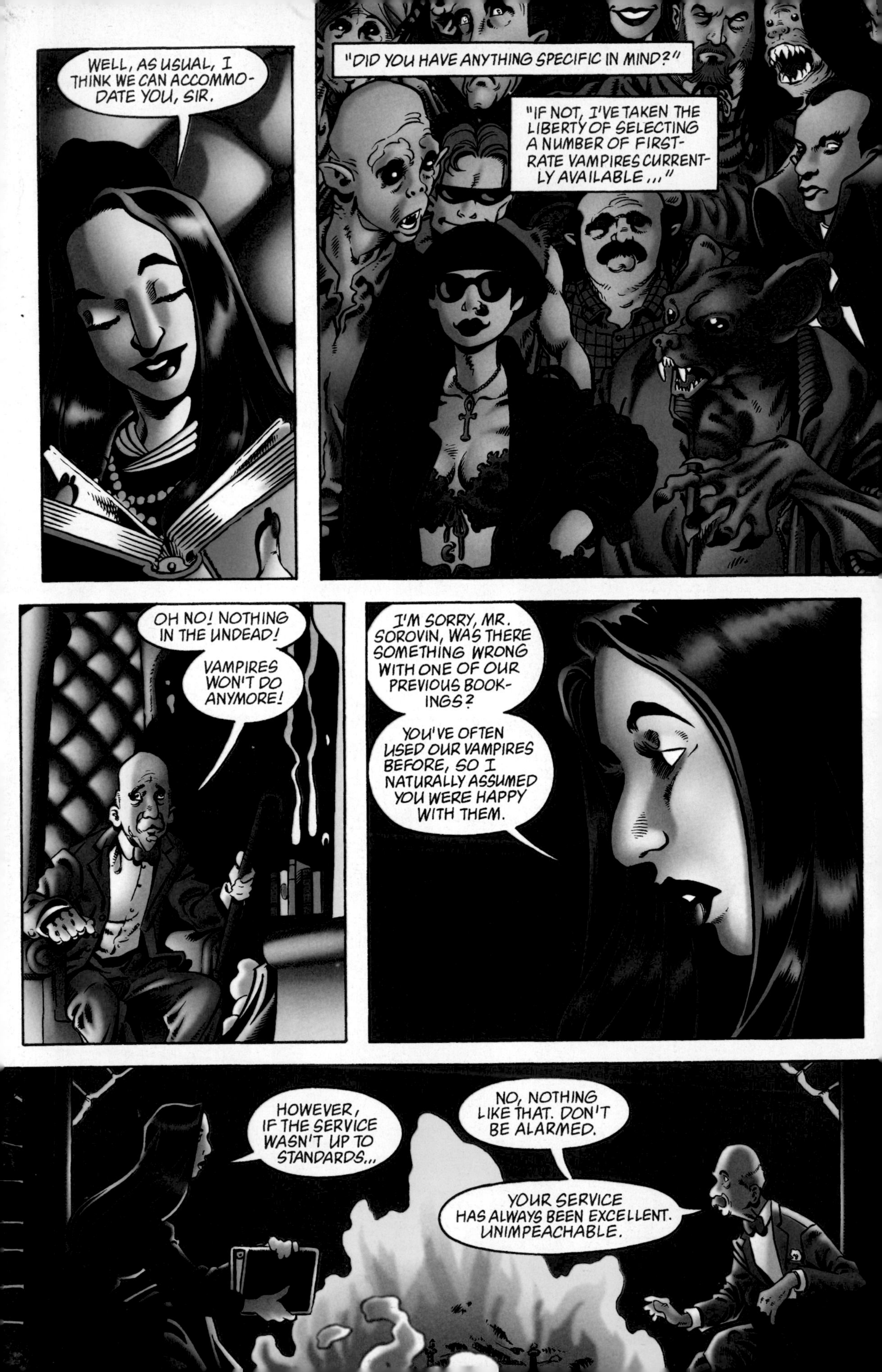
WELL, AS USUAL, I THINK WE CAN ACCOMMODATE YOU, SIR.
"DID YOU HAVE ANYTHING SPECIFIC IN MIND?"
"IF NOT, I'VE TAKEN THE LIBERTY OF SELECTING A NUMBER OF FIRST-RATE VAMPIRES CURRENTLY AVAILABLE..."
OH NO! NOTHING IN THE UNDEAD!
VAMPIRES WON'T DO ANYMORE!
I'M SORRY, MR. SOROVIN, WAS THERE SOMETHING WRONG WITH ONE OF OUR PREVIOUS BOOKINGS?
YOU'VE OFTEN USED OUR VAMPIRES BEFORE, SO I NATURALLY ASSUMED YOU WERE HAPPY WITH THEM.
HOWEVER, IF THE SERVICE WASN'T UP TO STANDARDS...
NO, NOTHING LIKE THAT. DON'T BE ALARMED.
YOUR SERVICE HAS ALWAYS BEEN EXCELLENT. UNIMPEACHABLE.

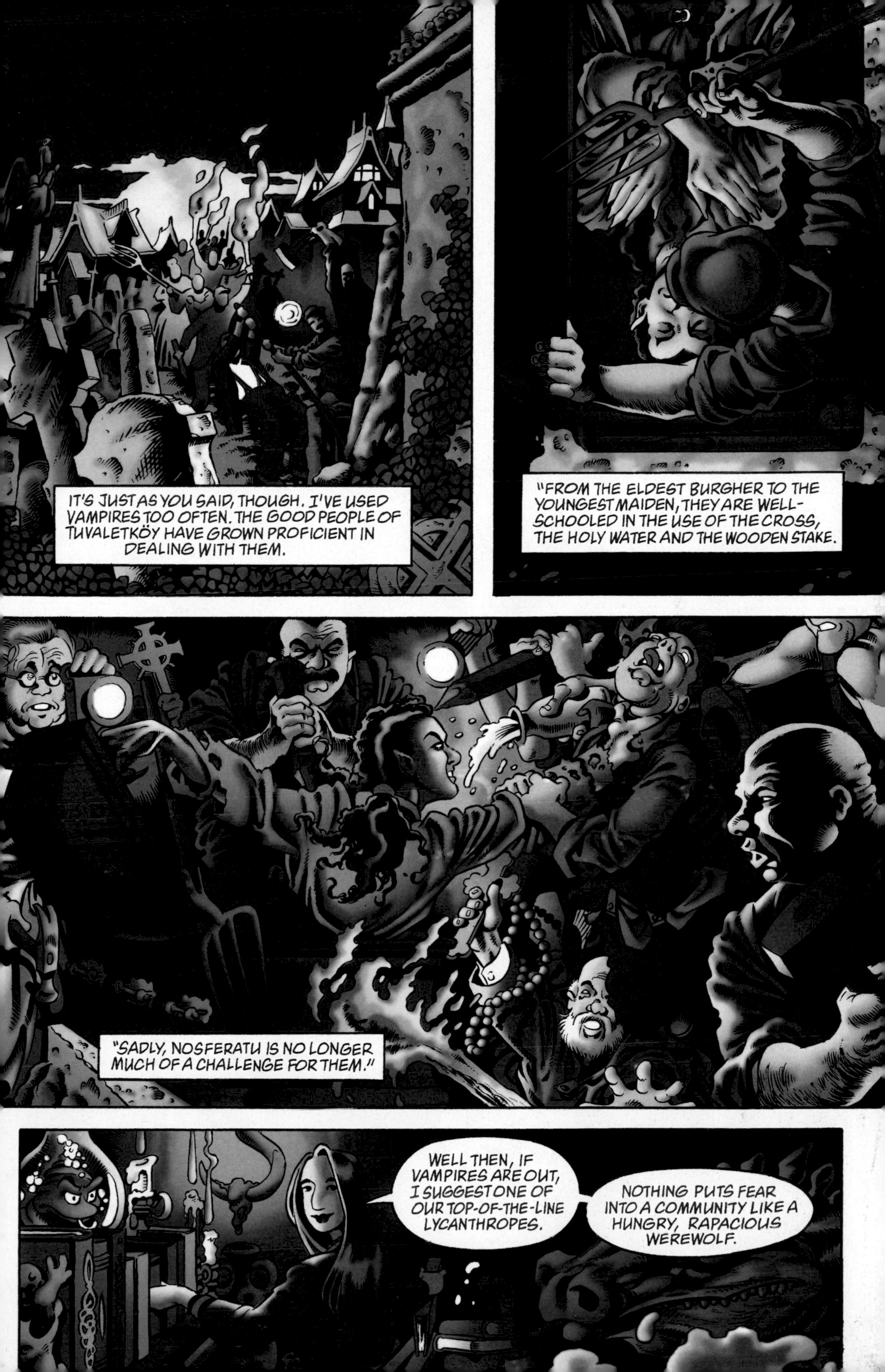
IT'S JUST AS YOU SAID, THOUGH. I'VE USED VAMPIRES TOO OFTEN. THE GOOD PEOPLE OF TUVALETKÖY HAVE GROWN PROFICIENT IN DEALING WITH THEM.
"FROM THE ELDEST BURGHER TO THE YOUNGEST MAIDEN, THEY ARE WELL-SCHOOLED IN THE USE OF THE CROSS, THE HOLY WATER AND THE WOODEN STAKE.
"SADLY, NOSFERATU IS NO LONGER MUCH OF A CHALLENGE FOR THEM."
WELL THEN, IF VAMPIRES ARE OUT, I SUGGEST ONE OF OUR TOP-OF-THE-LINE LYCANTHROPES.
NOTHING PUTS FEAR INTO A COMMUNITY LIKE A HUNGRY, RAPACIOUS WEREWOLF.

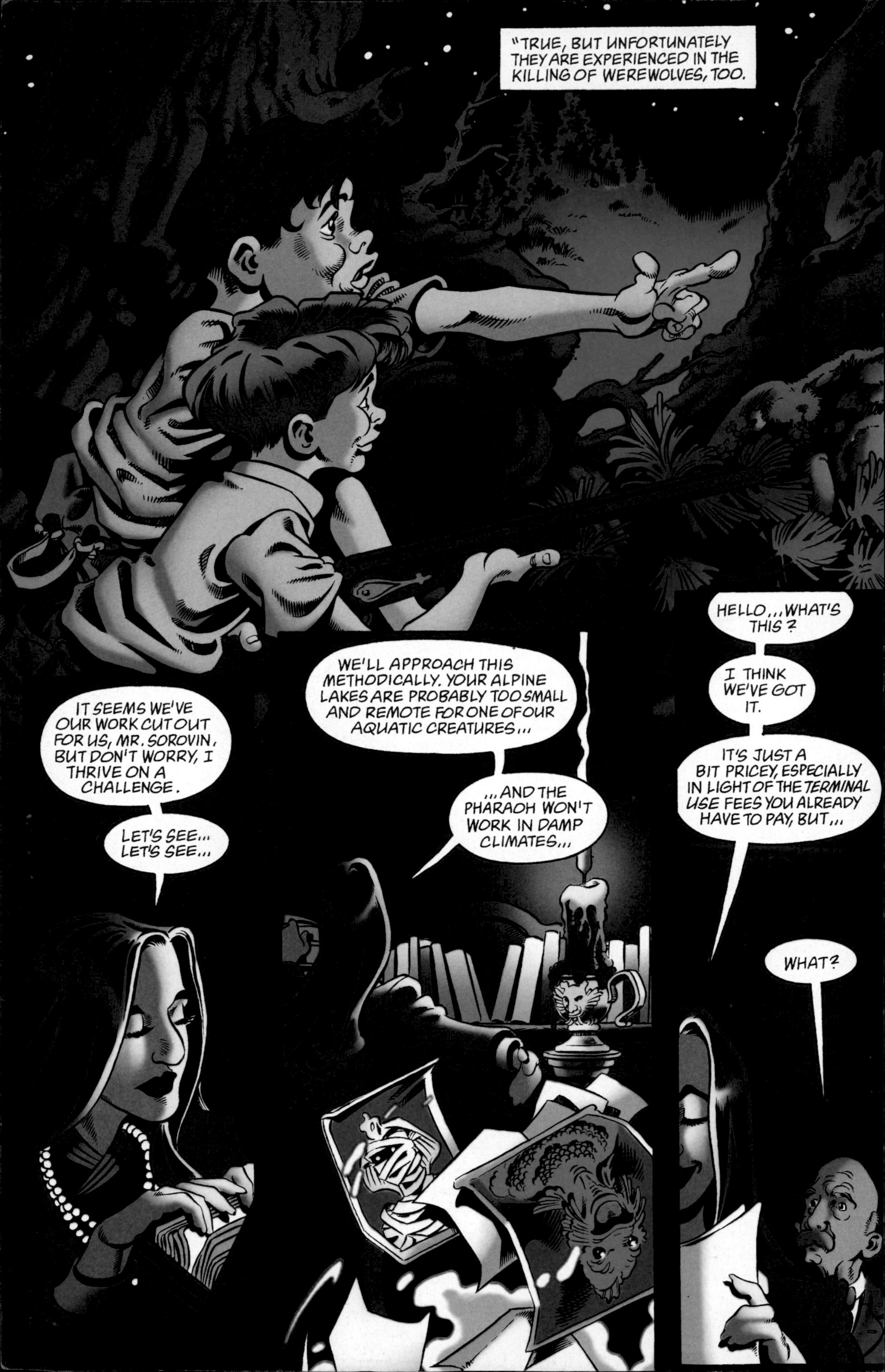
"TRUE, BUT UNFORTUNATELY THEY ARE EXPERIENCED IN THE KILLING OF WEREWOLVES, TOO.
IT SEEMS WE'VE OUR WORK CUT OUT FOR US, MR. SOROVIN, BUT DON'T WORRY, I THRIVE ON A CHALLENGE.
LET'S SEE... LET'S SEE...
WE'LL APPROACH THIS METHODICALLY. YOUR ALPINE LAKES ARE PROBABLY TOO SMALL AND REMOTE FOR ONE OF OUR AQUATIC CREATURES...
...AND THE PHARAOH WON'T WORK IN DAMP CLIMATES...
HELLO... WHAT'S THIS?
I THINK WE'VE GOT IT.
IT'S JUST A BIT PRICEY, ESPECIALLY IN LIGHT OF THE *TERMINAL USE* FEES YOU ALREADY HAVE TO PAY, BUT...
WHAT?

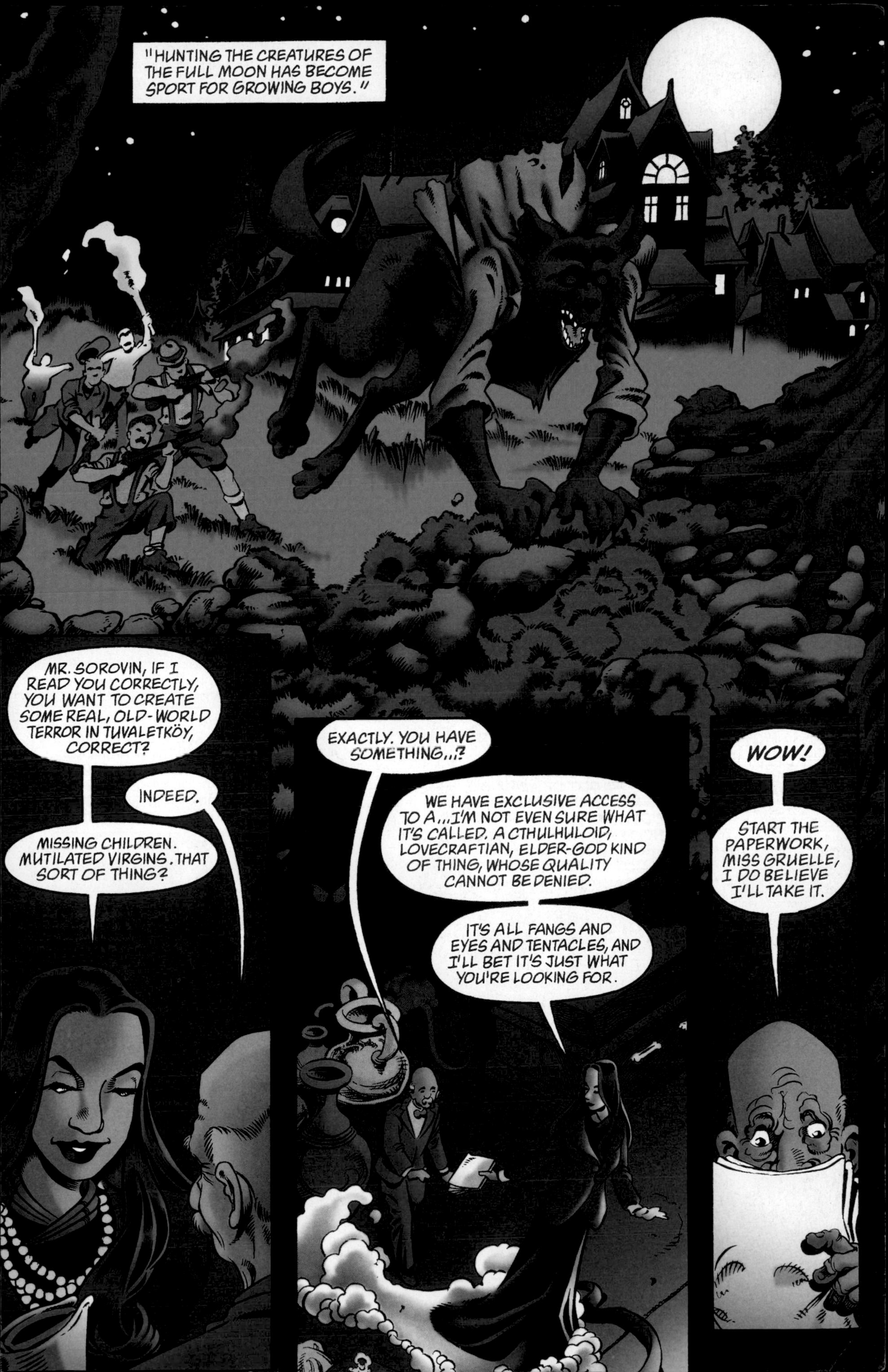
"HUNTING THE CREATURES OF THE FULL MOON HAS BECOME SPORT FOR GROWING BOYS."
MR. SOROVIN, IF I READ YOU CORRECTLY, YOU WANT TO CREATE SOME REAL, OLD-WORLD TERROR IN TUVALETKÖY, CORRECT?
INDEED.
MISSING CHILDREN. MUTILATED VIRGINS. THAT SORT OF THING?
EXACTLY. YOU HAVE SOMETHING...?
WE HAVE EXCLUSIVE ACCESS TO A...I'M NOT EVEN SURE WHAT IT'S CALLED. A CTHULHULOID, LOVECRAFTIAN, ELDER-GOD KIND OF THING, WHOSE QUALITY CANNOT BE DENIED.
IT'S ALL FANGS AND EYES AND TENTACLES, AND I'LL BET IT'S JUST WHAT YOU'RE LOOKING FOR.
WOW!
START THE PAPERWORK, MISS GRUELLE, I DO BELIEVE I'LL TAKE IT.

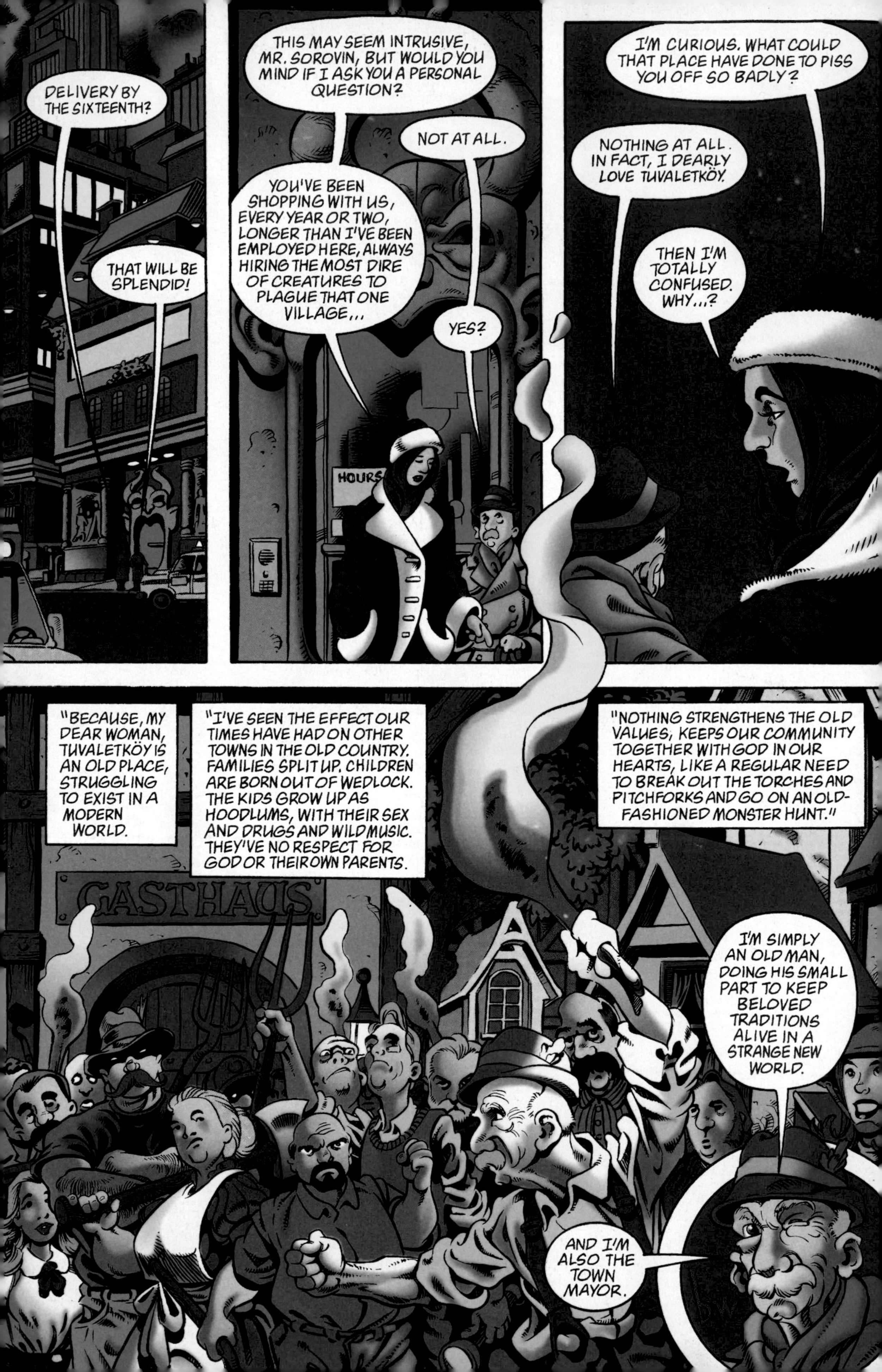
DELIVERY BY THE SIXTEENTH?
THAT WILL BE SPLENDID!
THIS MAY SEEM INTRUSIVE, MR. SOROVIN, BUT WOULD YOU MIND IF I ASK YOU A PERSONAL QUESTION?
NOT AT ALL.
YOU'VE BEEN SHOPPING WITH US, EVERY YEAR OR TWO, LONGER THAN I'VE BEEN EMPLOYED HERE, ALWAYS HIRING THE MOST DIRE OF CREATURES TO PLAGUE THAT ONE VILLAGE...
YES?
HOURS
I'M CURIOUS. WHAT COULD THAT PLACE HAVE DONE TO PISS YOU OFF SO BADLY?
NOTHING AT ALL. IN FACT, I DEARLY LOVE TUVALETKÖY.
THEN I'M TOTALLY CONFUSED. WHY...?
"BECAUSE, MY DEAR WOMAN, TUVALETKÖY IS AN OLD PLACE, STRUGGLING TO EXIST IN A MODERN WORLD.
"I'VE SEEN THE EFFECT OUR TIMES HAVE HAD ON OTHER TOWNS IN THE OLD COUNTRY. FAMILIES SPLIT UP. CHILDREN ARE BORN OUT OF WEDLOCK. THE KIDS GROW UP AS HOODLUMS, WITH THEIR SEX AND DRUGS AND WILD MUSIC. THEY'VE NO RESPECT FOR GOD OR THEIR OWN PARENTS.
"NOTHING STRENGTHENS THE OLD VALUES, KEEPS OUR COMMUNITY TOGETHER WITH GOD IN OUR HEARTS, LIKE A REGULAR NEED TO BREAK OUT THE TORCHES AND PITCHFORKS AND GO ON AN OLD-FASHIONED MONSTER HUNT."
GASTHAUS
I'M SIMPLY AN OLD MAN, DOING HIS SMALL PART TO KEEP BELOVED TRADITIONS ALIVE IN A STRANGE NEW WORLD.
AND I'M ALSO THE TOWN MAYOR.

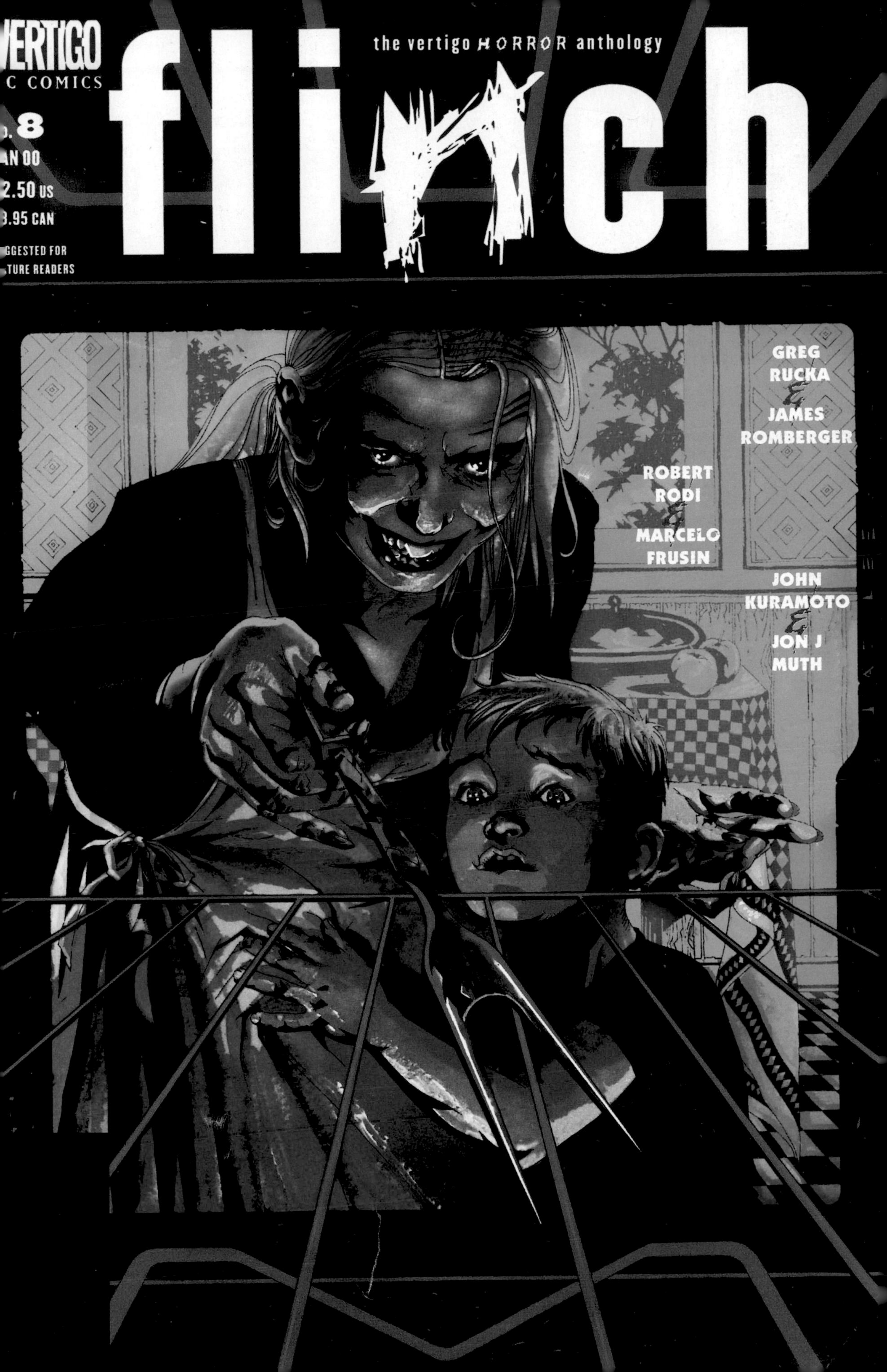
VERTIGO
C COMICS
. 8
AN 00
2.50 US
.95 CAN
GGESTED FOR
TURE READERS
the vertigo HORROR anthology
flinch
GREG
RUCKA
&
JAMES
ROMBERGER
ROBERT
RODI
&
MARCELO
FRUSIN
JOHN
KURAMOTO
&
JON J
MUTH

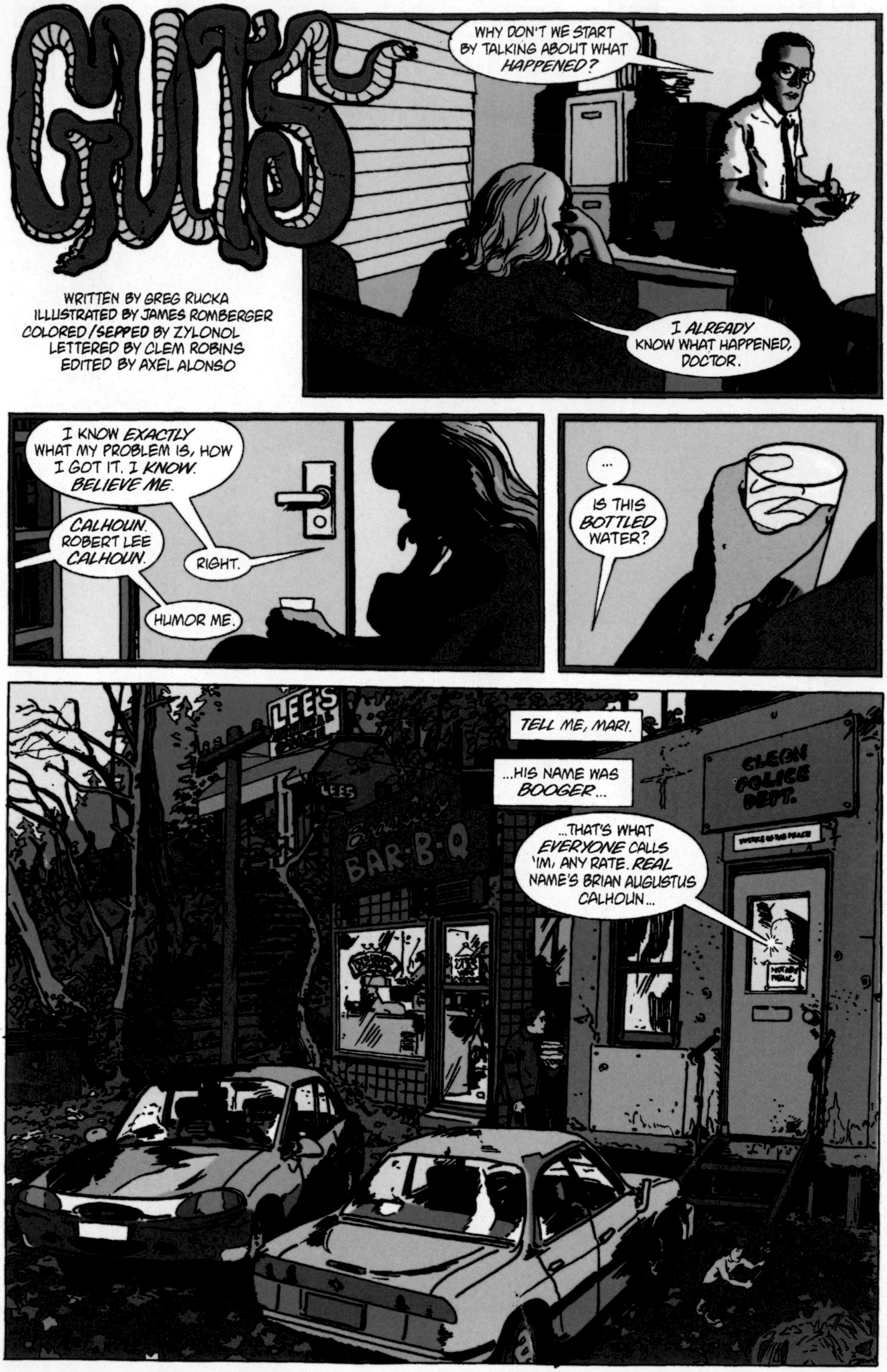
GUTS
WRITTEN BY GREG RUCKA
ILLUSTRATED BY JAMES ROMBERGER
COLORED/SEPPED BY ZYLONOL
LETTERED BY CLEM ROBINS
EDITED BY AXEL ALONSO
WHY DON'T WE START BY TALKING ABOUT WHAT HAPPENED?
I ALREADY KNOW WHAT HAPPENED, DOCTOR.
I KNOW EXACTLY WHAT MY PROBLEM IS, HOW I GOT IT. I KNOW. BELIEVE ME.
RIGHT.
CALHOUN. ROBERT LEE CALHOUN.
HUMOR ME.
...
IS THIS BOTTLED WATER?
LEE'S
BAR-B-Q
CLEON POLICE DEPT.
TELL ME, MARI.
...HIS NAME WAS BOOGER...
...THAT'S WHAT EVERYONE CALLS 'IM, ANY RATE. REAL NAME'S BRIAN AUGUSTUS CALHOUN...

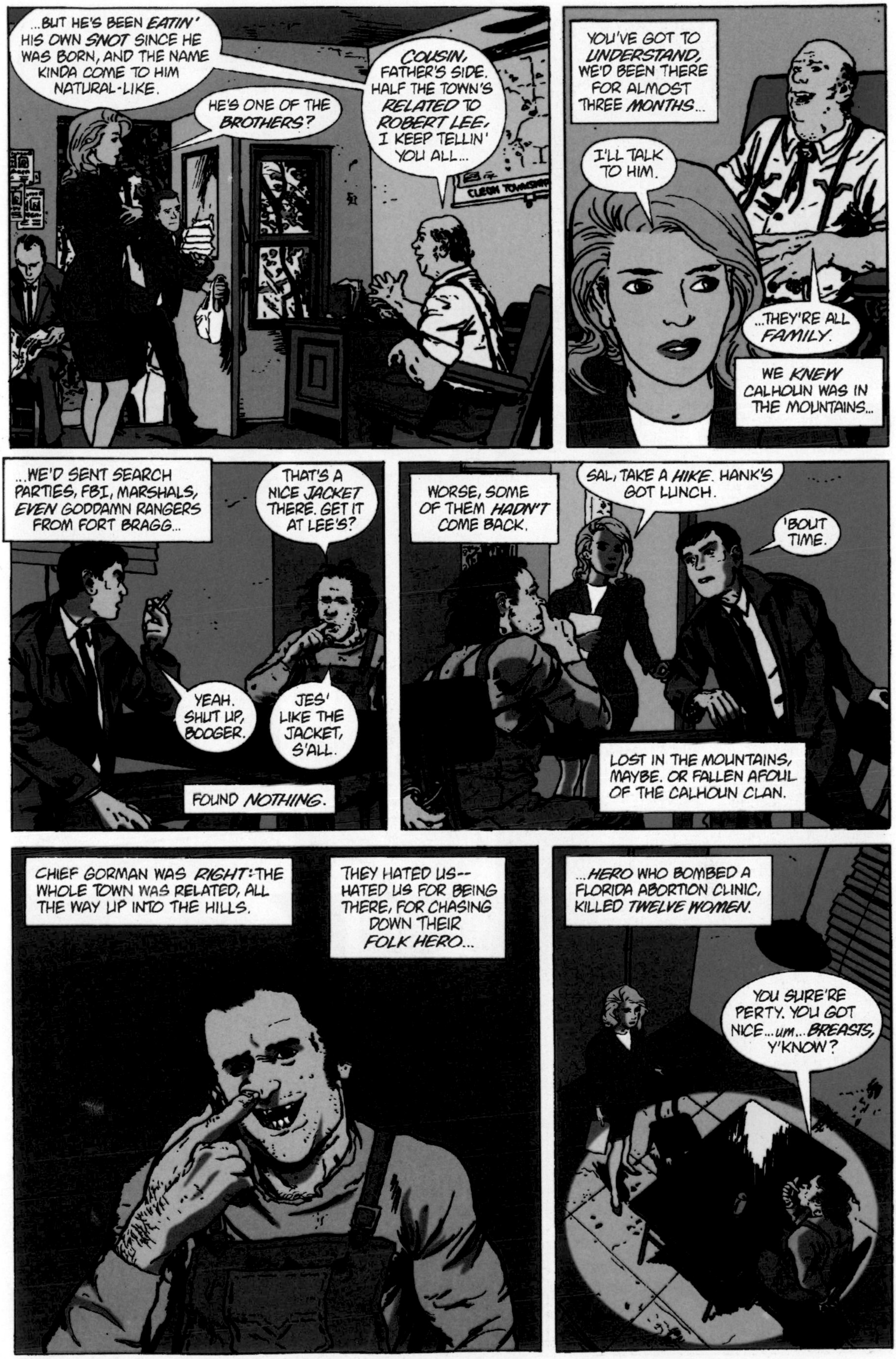

...BUT HE'S BEEN EATIN' HIS OWN SNOT SINCE HE WAS BORN, AND THE NAME KINDA COME TO HIM NATURAL-LIKE.
HE'S ONE OF THE BROTHERS?
COUSIN, FATHER'S SIDE. HALF THE TOWN'S RELATED TO ROBERT LEE, I KEEP TELLIN' YOU ALL...
CLEGH TOWNSHIP
YOU'VE GOT TO UNDERSTAND, WE'D BEEN THERE FOR ALMOST THREE MONTHS...
I'LL TALK TO HIM.
...THEY'RE ALL FAMILY.
WE KNEW CALHOUN WAS IN THE MOUNTAINS...
...WE'D SENT SEARCH PARTIES, FBI, MARSHALS, EVEN GODDAMN RANGERS FROM FORT BRAGG...
THAT'S A NICE JACKET THERE. GET IT AT LEE'S?
YEAH. SHUT UP, BOOGER.
JES' LIKE THE JACKET, S'ALL.
FOUND NOTHING.
WORSE, SOME OF THEM HADN'T COME BACK.
SAL, TAKE A HIKE. HANK'S GOT LUNCH.
'BOUT TIME.
LOST IN THE MOUNTAINS, MAYBE. OR FALLEN AFOUL OF THE CALHOUN CLAN.
CHIEF GORMAN WAS RIGHT: THE WHOLE TOWN WAS RELATED, ALL THE WAY UP INTO THE HILLS.
THEY HATED US--HATED US FOR BEING THERE, FOR CHASING DOWN THEIR FOLK HERO...
...HERO WHO BOMBED A FLORIDA ABORTION CLINIC, KILLED TWELVE WOMEN.
YOU SURE'RE PERTY. YOU GOT NICE...um...BREASTS, Y'KNOW?

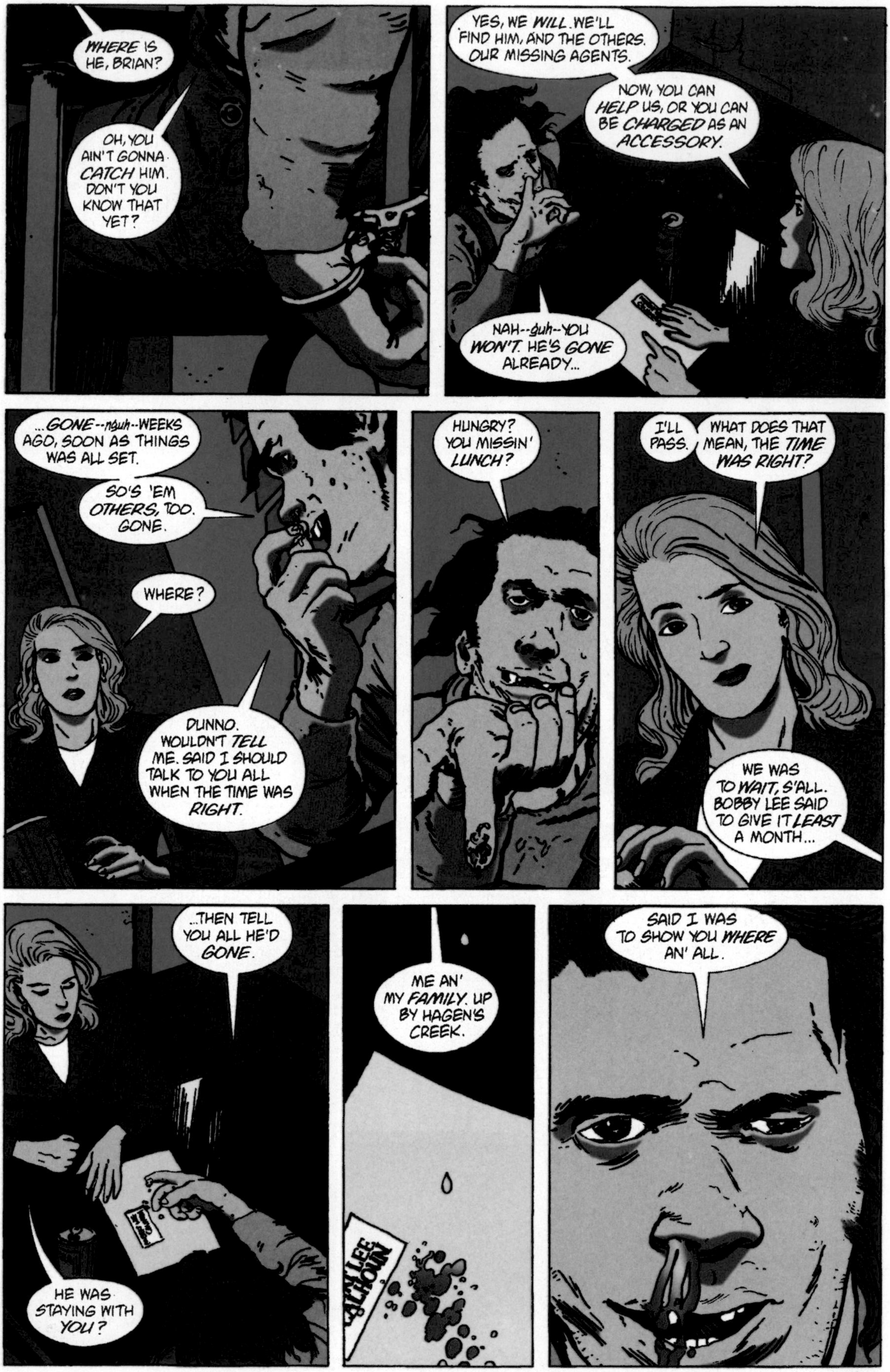

WHERE IS HE, BRIAN?
OH, YOU AIN'T GONNA CATCH HIM. DON'T YOU KNOW THAT YET?
YES, WE WILL. WE'LL FIND HIM, AND THE OTHERS. OUR MISSING AGENTS.
NOW, YOU CAN HELP US, OR YOU CAN BE CHARGED AS AN ACCESSORY.
NAH--guh--YOU WON'T. HE'S GONE ALREADY...
...GONE--nguh--WEEKS AGO, SOON AS THINGS WAS ALL SET.
SO'S 'EM OTHERS, TOO. GONE.
WHERE?
DUNNO. WOULDN'T TELL ME. SAID I SHOULD TALK TO YOU ALL WHEN THE TIME WAS RIGHT.
HUNGRY? YOU MISSIN' LUNCH?
I'LL PASS.
WHAT DOES THAT MEAN, THE TIME WAS RIGHT?
WE WAS TO WAIT, S'ALL. BOBBY LEE SAID TO GIVE IT LEAST A MONTH...
...THEN TELL YOU ALL HE'D GONE.
HE WAS STAYING WITH YOU?
ME AN' MY FAMILY. UP BY HAGEN'S CREEK.
SAID I WAS TO SHOW YOU WHERE AN' ALL.

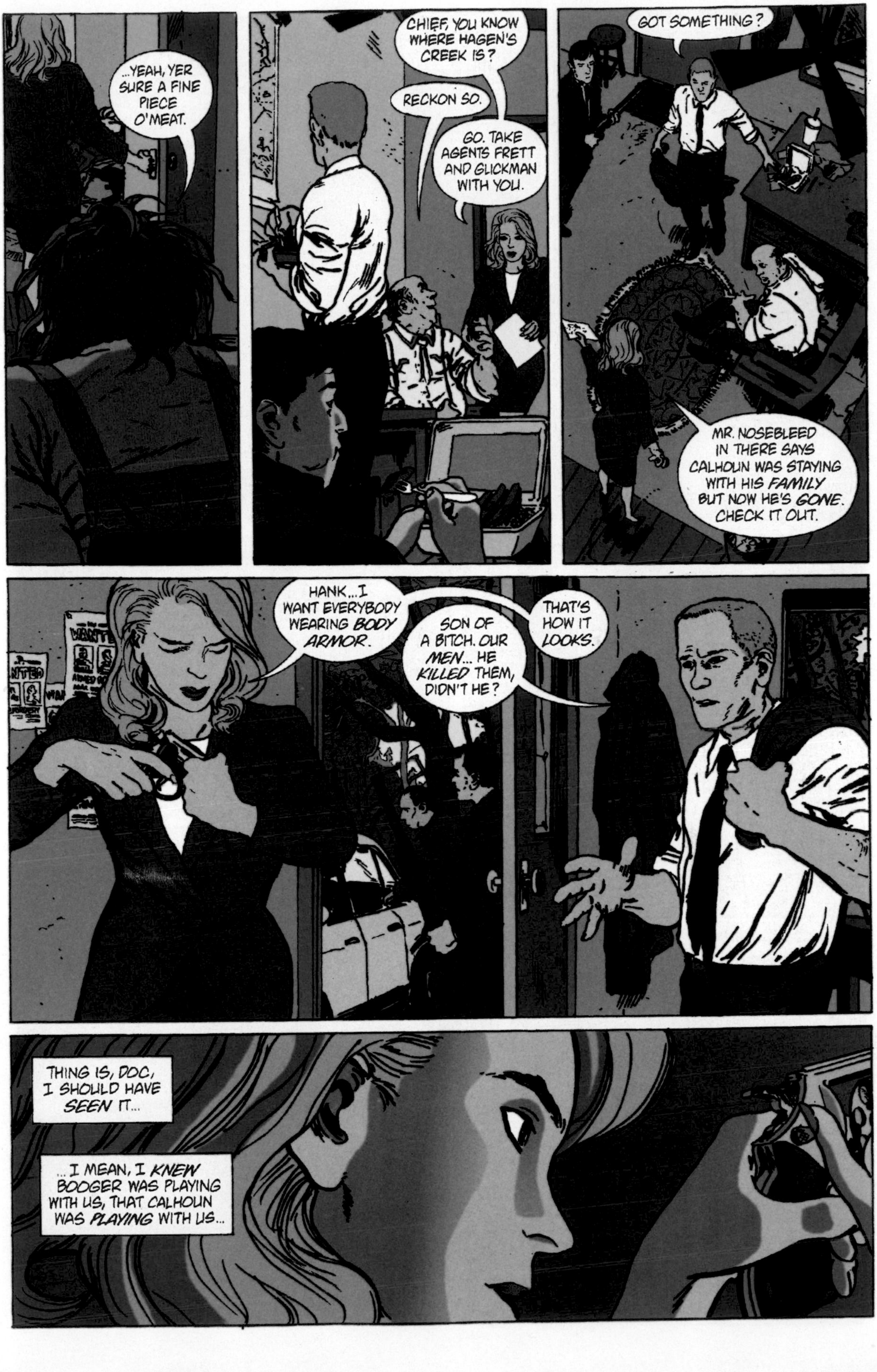
...YEAH, YER SURE A FINE PIECE O'MEAT.
CHIEF, YOU KNOW WHERE HAGEN'S CREEK IS?
RECKON SO.
GO. TAKE AGENTS FRETT AND GLICKMAN WITH YOU.
GOT SOMETHING?
MR. NOSEBLEED IN THERE SAYS CALHOUN WAS STAYING WITH HIS FAMILY BUT NOW HE'S GONE. CHECK IT OUT.
HANK...I WANT EVERYBODY WEARING BODY ARMOR.
SON OF A BITCH. OUR MEN... HE KILLED THEM, DIDN'T HE?
THAT'S HOW IT LOOKS.
THING IS, DOC, I SHOULD HAVE SEEN IT...
...I MEAN, I KNEW BOOGER WAS PLAYING WITH US, THAT CALHOUN WAS PLAYING WITH US...

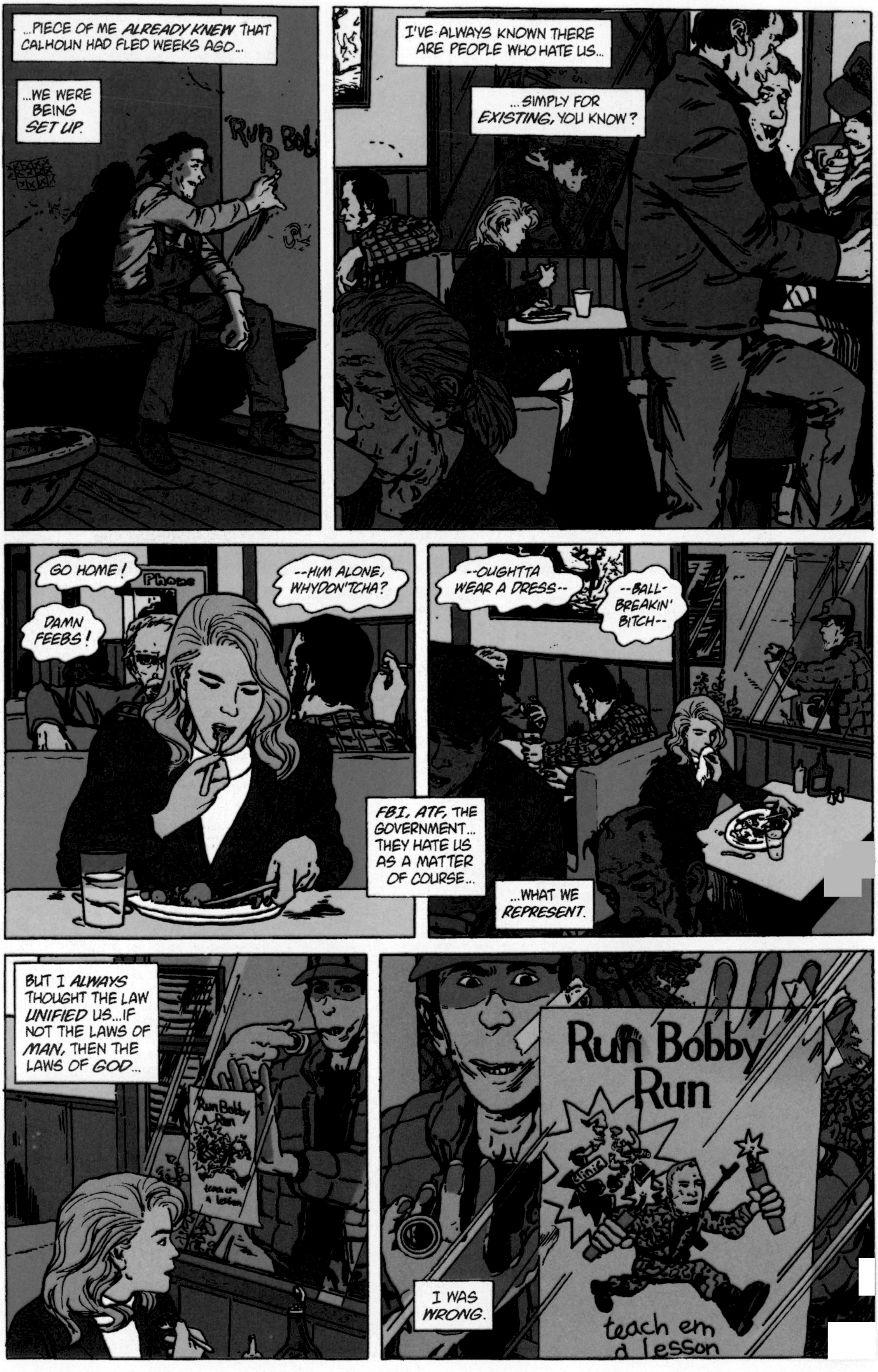
...PIECE OF ME ALREADY KNEW THAT CALHOUN HAD FLED WEEKS AGO...
...WE WERE BEING SET UP.
Run Bob
I'VE ALWAYS KNOWN THERE ARE PEOPLE WHO HATE US...
... SIMPLY FOR EXISTING, YOU KNOW?
GO HOME!
DAMN FEEBS!
Phone
--HIM ALONE, WHYDON'TCHA?
FBI, ATF, THE GOVERNMENT... THEY HATE US AS A MATTER OF COURSE...
--OUGHTTA WEAR A DRESS--
--BALL-BREAKIN' BITCH--
...WHAT WE REPRESENT.
BUT I ALWAYS THOUGHT THE LAW UNIFIED US...IF NOT THE LAWS OF MAN, THEN THE LAWS OF GOD...
Run Bobby Run
teach em a lesson
Run Bobby Run
clinic
teach em a lesson
I WAS WRONG.

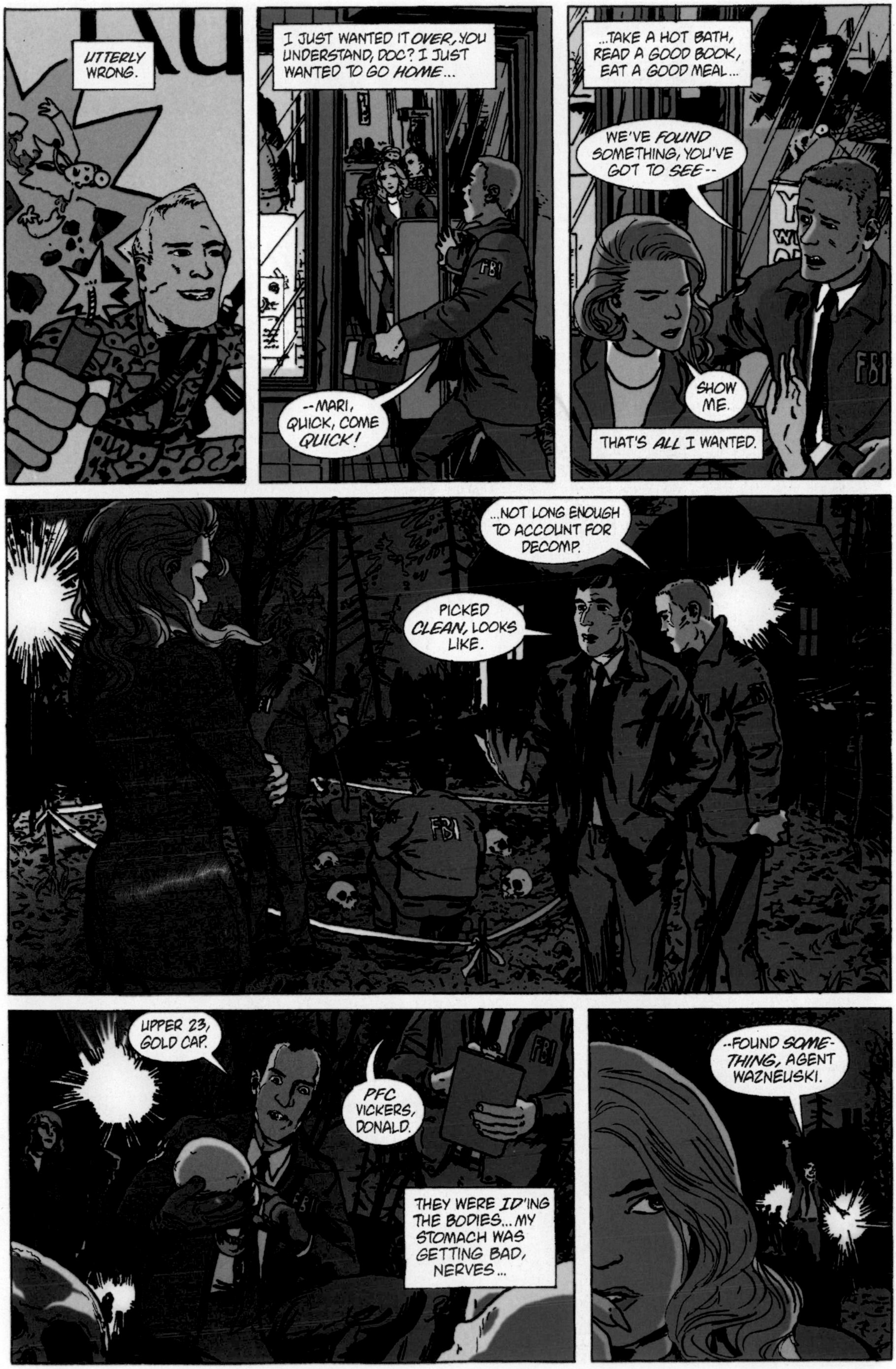
UTTERLY WRONG.
I JUST WANTED IT OVER, YOU UNDERSTAND, DOC? I JUST WANTED TO GO HOME...
--MARI, QUICK, COME QUICK!
...TAKE A HOT BATH, READ A GOOD BOOK, EAT A GOOD MEAL...
WE'VE FOUND SOMETHING, YOU'VE GOT TO SEE--
SHOW ME.
THAT'S ALL I WANTED.
...NOT LONG ENOUGH TO ACCOUNT FOR DECOMP.
PICKED CLEAN, LOOKS LIKE.
UPPER 23, GOLD CAP.
PFC VICKERS, DONALD.
THEY WERE ID'ING THE BODIES... MY STOMACH WAS GETTING BAD, NERVES...
--FOUND SOMETHING, AGENT WAZNEUSKI.

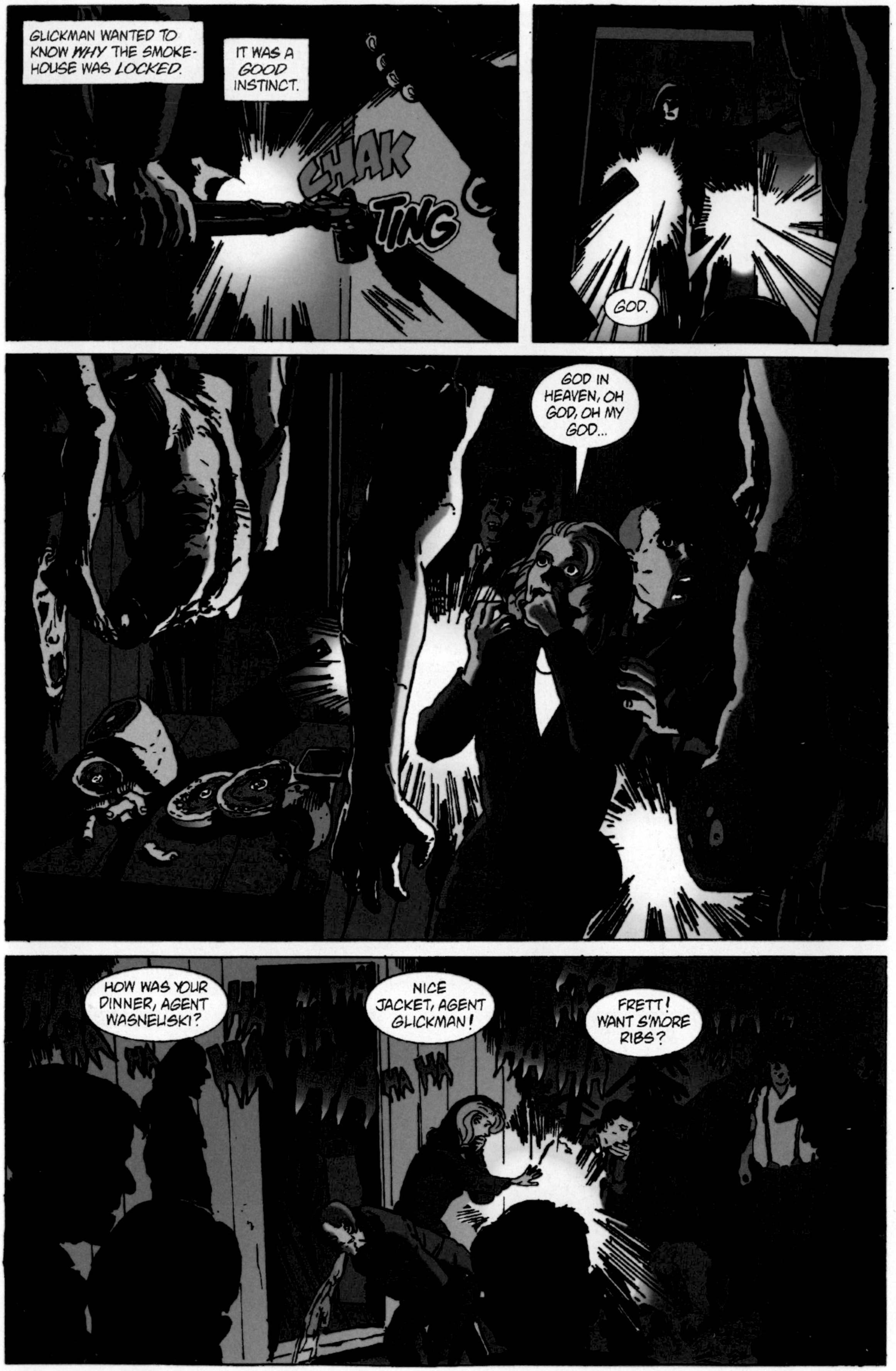
GLICKMAN WANTED TO KNOW WHY THE SMOKE-HOUSE WAS LOCKED.
IT WAS A GOOD INSTINCT.
CHAK
TING
GOD.
GOD IN HEAVEN, OH GOD, OH MY GOD...
HOW WAS YOUR DINNER, AGENT WASNEUSKI?
NICE JACKET, AGENT GLICKMAN!
FRETT! WANT S'MORE RIBS?
HA HA HA

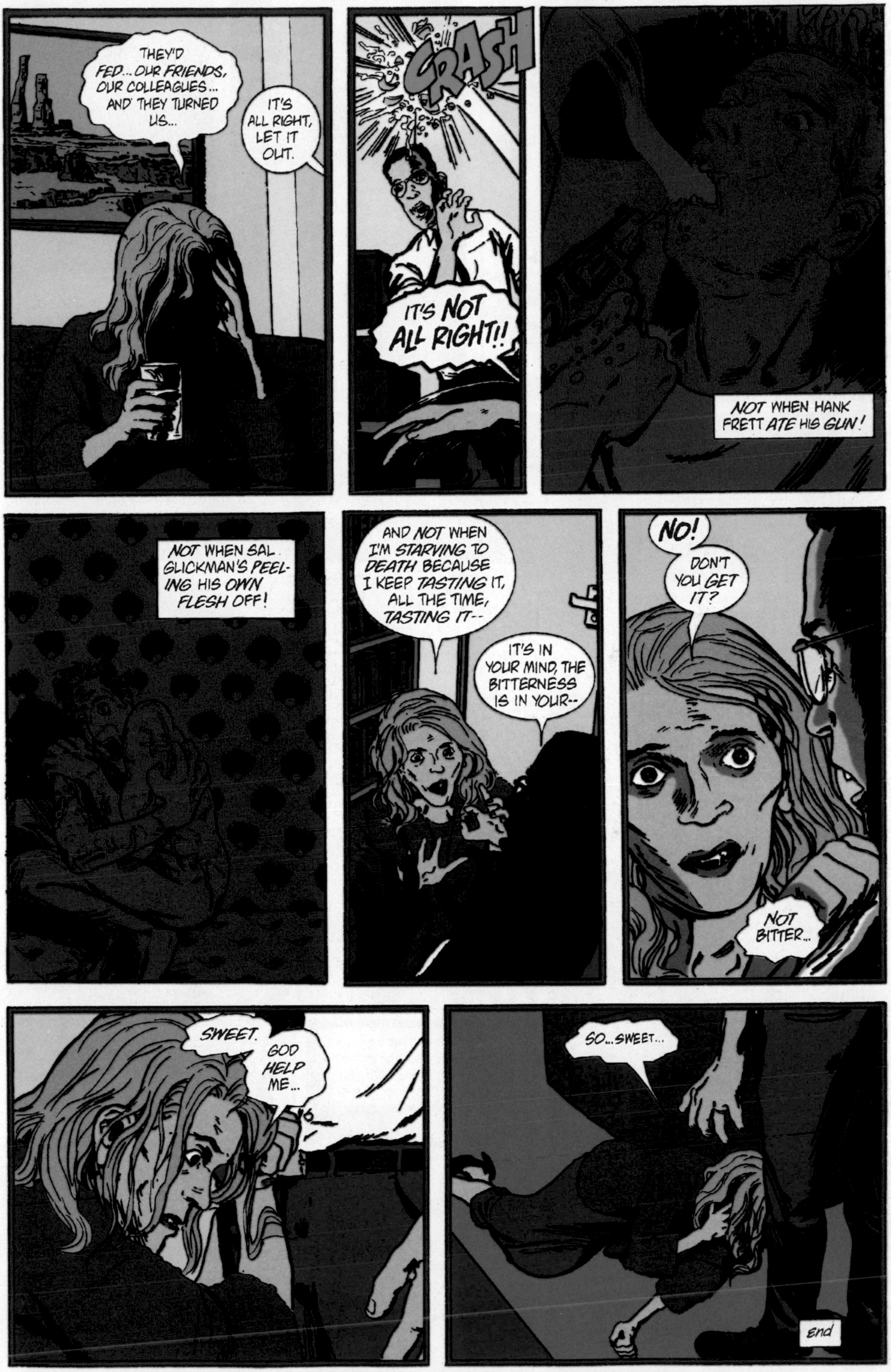
THEY'D FED... OUR FRIENDS, OUR COLLEAGUES... AND THEY TURNED US...
IT'S ALL RIGHT, LET IT OUT.
CRASH
IT'S NOT ALL RIGHT!!
NOT WHEN HANK FRETT ATE HIS GUN!
NOT WHEN SAL GLICKMAN'S PEELING HIS OWN FLESH OFF!
AND NOT WHEN I'M STARVING TO DEATH BECAUSE I KEEP TASTING IT, ALL THE TIME, TASTING IT--
IT'S IN YOUR MIND, THE BITTERNESS IS IN YOUR--
NO!
DON'T YOU GET IT?
NOT BITTER...
SWEET.
GOD HELP ME...
SO... SWEET...
end

i'm coming, jerry

coming for you

i think it's high time. after all we couldn't know each other better could we. or at least I couldn't know YOU better

# "you've got hate mail"

writer
robert rodi

artist
marcelo frusin

colorist
patricia mulvihill

separations
digital chameleon

letterer
clem robins

editor
axel alonso

i know how old you were when you got married. i know your best man's name. i know how much you paid for the ring. i know who caught the bouquet.

i know why you broke up. every little detail

YOU GO TO HELL, YOU GODDAMN LYING--

OUTTA MY WAY, YOU CHEAP PIECE OF--

TAK TAK TAK TAK

i know how badly you were burned, jerry. you swore you'd never risk a relationship again.

but thanks to the internet relationships are now risk-free!!! isn't this a wonderful time? :-)

UNNNGGH-- AAHHHN--

that's how we first "met" – remember?
jerr57: you sound pretty hot—you ready for action?
mmia!: depends on what you mean by action
jerr57: let's go private chat & i'll tell

TAK TAK TA

you were so cute. you hated it that I wouldn't "play ball" :-)

jerr57: after that, i finish off with my tongue
mmial: well but i hardly know you
jerr57: ???what is this shit?

what can i say? i'm a lady

mmial: you make me blush talking like that
jerr57: i'll do more than make you blush
mmial: oh STOP you
jerr57: haven't started yet

not that you ever treated me like one. but i liked you. you intrigued me

mmial: tell me more about yourself
jerr57: look if you're not going to get me off, sayonara bitch.

TAK TAK TAK TAK TAK TAK TAK TAK TAK TAK TAK TAK

i decided to get to know you better

...FUCK IS THIS...?

i guess i was like a puppy, following you ... ere the s... to all those chatrooms
twistigal: i don't know if i can take that much
jerr57: you'll take it and like it
twistigal: what if i scream?
jerr57: you think you won't?
mmial: hi jerry! remember me?
mmial: jerry?
mmial: jerry? still there??

i loved finding out about you thru all the interesting places you'd go

i guess you didn't like me doing it though
jerr... a useless comparison. What about Don Dixon?
Owlman: You can't compare glam rock to punk!
jerry57: i'm talking raw early glam rock, not the pathetic arena glam that came later
mmial: hi jerry! i like 70s rock too!

after a while, you even tried to fool me

but all i had to do was wait in your favorite rooms. i always recognized your "voice" whenever you logged on

her throat's a mess
AlFan: she's still the greatest
Zciter: she's a pathetic arena whore
mmial: hi jerry! me again! i ... your new ... screen na...

FUUUCK!

YOU OKAY, JERRY?

NO!--YES. COMPUTER PROBLEMS. IT'S NOTHING.

...

WELL, YOU JUST LET ME KNOW IF IT'S ANYTHING I CAN *HELP* YOU WITH.

i never doubted you'd come back

CLICK

then you stopped coming online. i thought you might be sick. then i realized you were trying to avoid me. that really hurt! :~(

but i'm very forgiving. i'm also very patient.

WELCOME!... YOU'VE GOT MAIL!

| 3/18/99 | mmial | something you'll like |
| 3/18/99 | N873882@Wo... | MAKE MONEY OVER THE NET! |
| 3/19/99 | mmial | miss you |
| 3/19/99 | mmial | where are you? |
| 3/19/99 | mmial | please read |
| 3/19/99 | ALLG... | HOT NAKED CO-EDS LIVE! |
| 3/20/99 | mmial | thought of you today |
| 3/20/99 | 838JJi@NetPa... | $10,000 PER WEEK GUARANTE |
| 3/20/99 | mmial | you're so cruel |
| 3/20/99 | mmial | please please read |
| 3/21/99 | EdMcT | Thoughts on your CDC contrac |
| 3/21/99 | mmial | you son of a bitch |

$10,00
you'r
please p
Thoughts on your

I KNOW I'M GOING TO REGRET OPENING THIS...

:hink you can jus
you fucking bast
et you get away
e kind of faggot?
make you pay fo

CLICK

i guess you didn't miss me tho cause you never answered any of my messages. (well i admit some of them were a LITTLE pushy)

i didn't have any choice, did i? i had to take our relationship to the next level

BRRRING

HELLO?...

CLICK

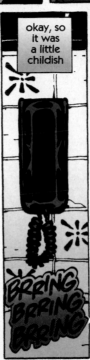

okay, so it was a little childish

BRRING BRRING BRRING

HELLO?... WHO'S TH--

i would've talked to you eventually you know. i had to punish you a little bit first

BRRING BRRING BRRING

but you stopped picking up darn you! you even unplugged your answering machine. bet you were curious how i got hold of your number tho!

and that wasn't ALL i got hold of!

| | MEL'S | .76 |
| | | 50.18 |
| 9/15/99 | ABERNATHY'S | $440.63 |
| 9/11/99 | BALM PEACH | $287.88 |
| 9/12/99 | LEONID'S | $1,080.06 |
| 9/12/99 | VILLAGE CYCLE | $550.93 |
| 9/13/99 | DOWN DECOR | $660.22 |
| 9/13/99 | TRENHOLM'S | |

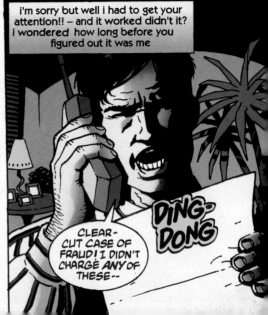

i'm sorry but well i had to get your attention!! -- and it worked didn't it? i wondered how long before you figured out it was me

CLEAR-CUT CASE OF FRAUD! I DIDN'T CHARGE ANY OF THESE--

DING-DONG

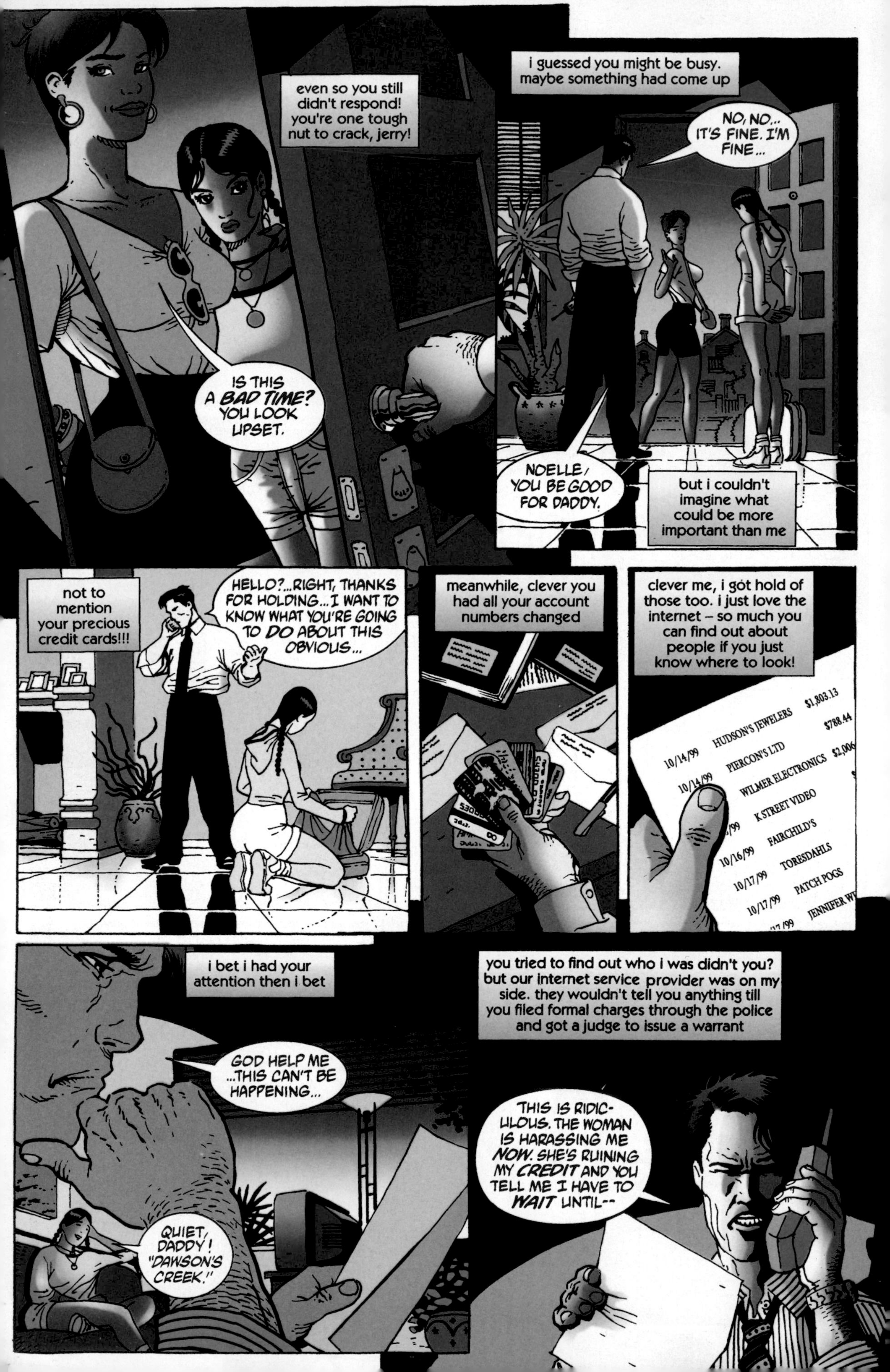
even so you still didn't respond! you're one tough nut to crack, jerry!
IS THIS A BAD TIME? YOU LOOK UPSET.
i guessed you might be busy. maybe something had come up
NO, NO... IT'S FINE. I'M FINE...
NOELLE, YOU BE GOOD FOR DADDY.
but i couldn't imagine what could be more important than me
not to mention your precious credit cards!!!
HELLO?...RIGHT, THANKS FOR HOLDING...I WANT TO KNOW WHAT YOU'RE GOING TO DO ABOUT THIS OBVIOUS...
meanwhile, clever you had all your account numbers changed
clever me, i got hold of those too. i just love the internet – so much you can find out about people if you just know where to look!
10/14/99 HUDSON'S JEWELERS $1,803.13
10/14/99 PIERCON'S LTD $788.44
WILMER ELECTRONICS
K STREET VIDEO
FAIRCHILD'S
10/16/99 TORESDAHLS
10/17/99 PATCH POGS
10/17/99
i bet i had your attention then i bet
you tried to find out who i was didn't you? but our internet service provider was on my side. they wouldn't tell you anything till you filed formal charges through the police and got a judge to issue a warrant
GOD HELP ME ...THIS CAN'T BE HAPPENING...
QUIET, DADDY! "DAWSON'S CREEK."
THIS IS RIDICULOUS. THE WOMAN IS HARASSING ME NOW. SHE'S RUINING MY CREDIT AND YOU TELL ME I HAVE TO WAIT UNTIL--

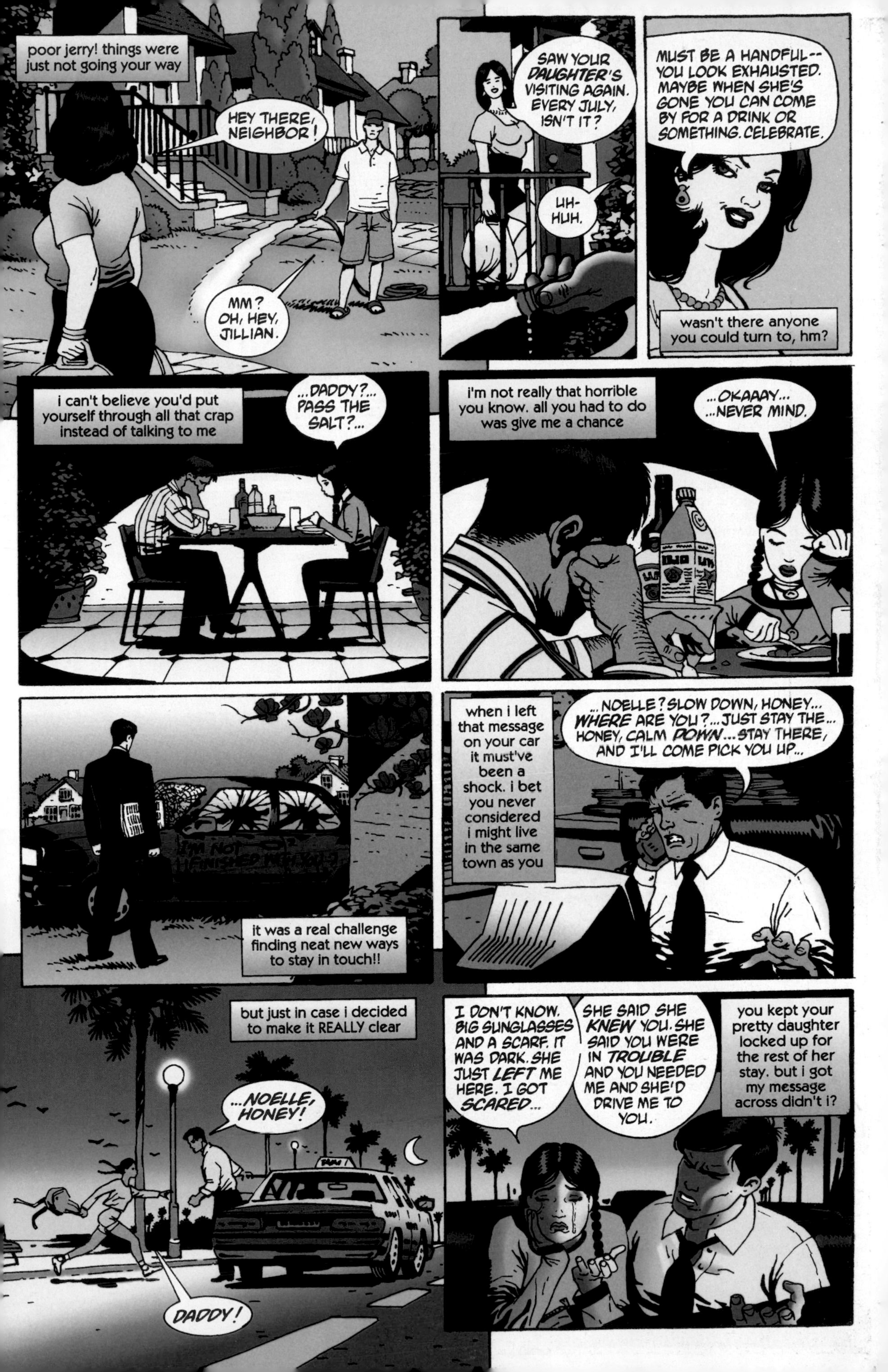
poor jerry! things were just not going your way
HEY THERE, NEIGHBOR!
MM? OH, HEY, JILLIAN.
SAW YOUR DAUGHTER'S VISITING AGAIN. EVERY JULY, ISN'T IT?
UH-HUH.
MUST BE A HANDFUL-- YOU LOOK EXHAUSTED. MAYBE WHEN SHE'S GONE YOU CAN COME BY FOR A DRINK OR SOMETHING. CELEBRATE.
wasn't there anyone you could turn to, hm?
i can't believe you'd put yourself through all that crap instead of talking to me
...DADDY?... PASS THE SALT?...
i'm not really that horrible you know. all you had to do was give me a chance
...OKAAAY... ...NEVER MIND.
it was a real challenge finding neat new ways to stay in touch!!
when i left that message on your car it must've been a shock. i bet you never considered i might live in the same town as you
...NOELLE? SLOW DOWN, HONEY... WHERE ARE YOU?... JUST STAY THE... HONEY, CALM DOWN... STAY THERE, AND I'LL COME PICK YOU UP...
but just in case i decided to make it REALLY clear
...NOELLE, HONEY!
DADDY!
I DON'T KNOW. BIG SUNGLASSES AND A SCARF. IT WAS DARK. SHE JUST LEFT ME HERE. I GOT SCARED...
SHE SAID SHE KNEW YOU. SHE SAID YOU WERE IN TROUBLE AND YOU NEEDED ME AND SHE'D DRIVE ME TO YOU.
you kept your pretty daughter locked up for the rest of her stay. but i got my message across didn't i?

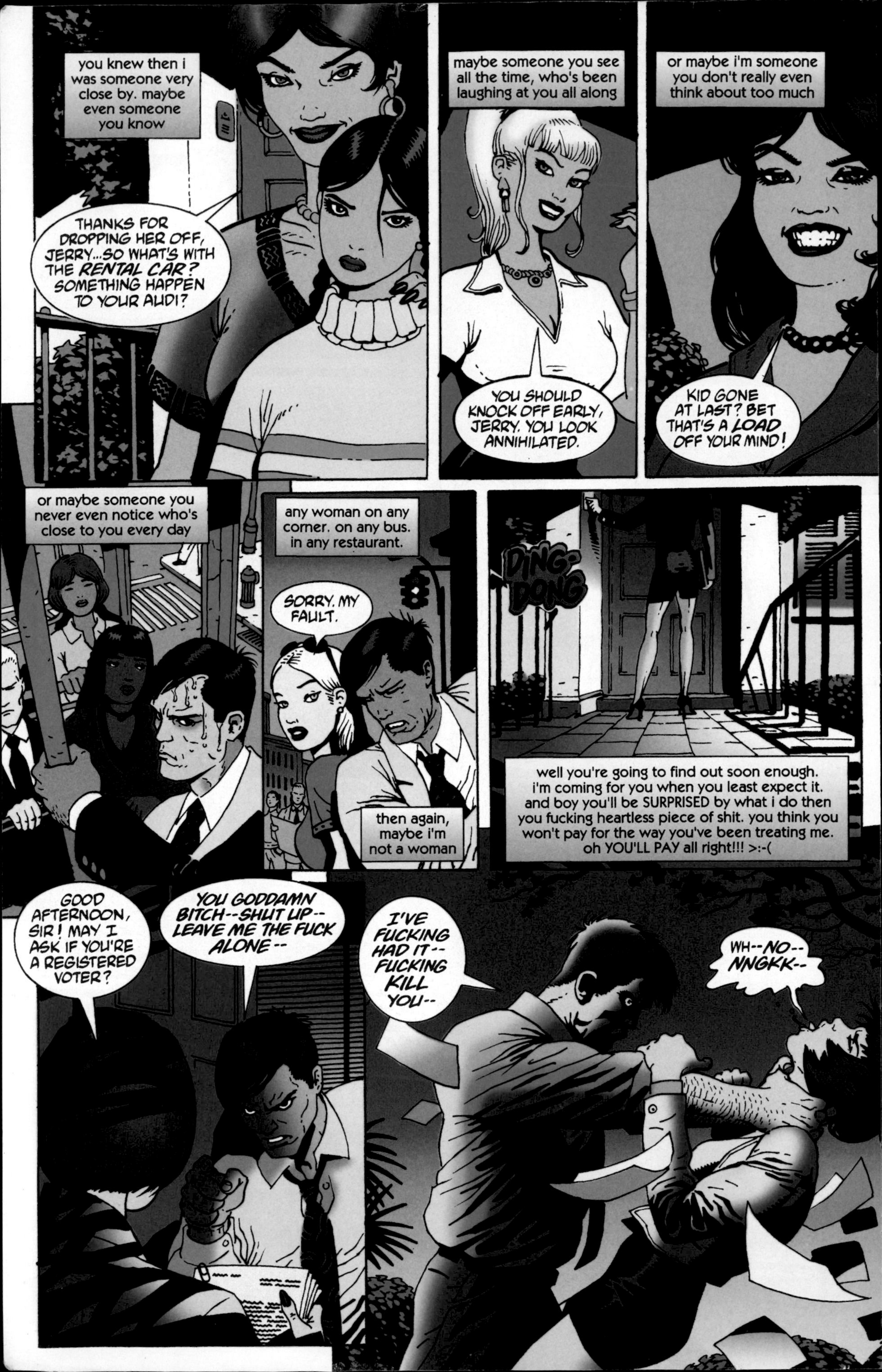
you knew then i was someone very close by. maybe even someone you know
THANKS FOR DROPPING HER OFF, JERRY...SO WHAT'S WITH THE RENTAL CAR? SOMETHING HAPPEN TO YOUR AUDI?
maybe someone you see all the time, who's been laughing at you all along
YOU SHOULD KNOCK OFF EARLY, JERRY. YOU LOOK ANNIHILATED.
or maybe i'm someone you don't really even think about too much
KID GONE AT LAST? BET THAT'S A LOAD OFF YOUR MIND!
or maybe someone you never even notice who's close to you every day
any woman on any corner. on any bus. in any restaurant.
SORRY. MY FAULT.
then again, maybe i'm not a woman
DING-DONG
well you're going to find out soon enough. i'm coming for you when you least expect it. and boy you'll be SURPRISED by what i do then you fucking heartless piece of shit. you think you won't pay for the way you've been treating me. oh YOU'LL PAY all right!!! >:-(
GOOD AFTERNOON, SIR! MAY I ASK IF YOU'RE A REGISTERED VOTER?
YOU GODDAMN BITCH--SHUT UP--LEAVE ME THE FUCK ALONE--
I'VE FUCKING HAD IT--FUCKING KILL YOU--
WH--NO--NNGKK--

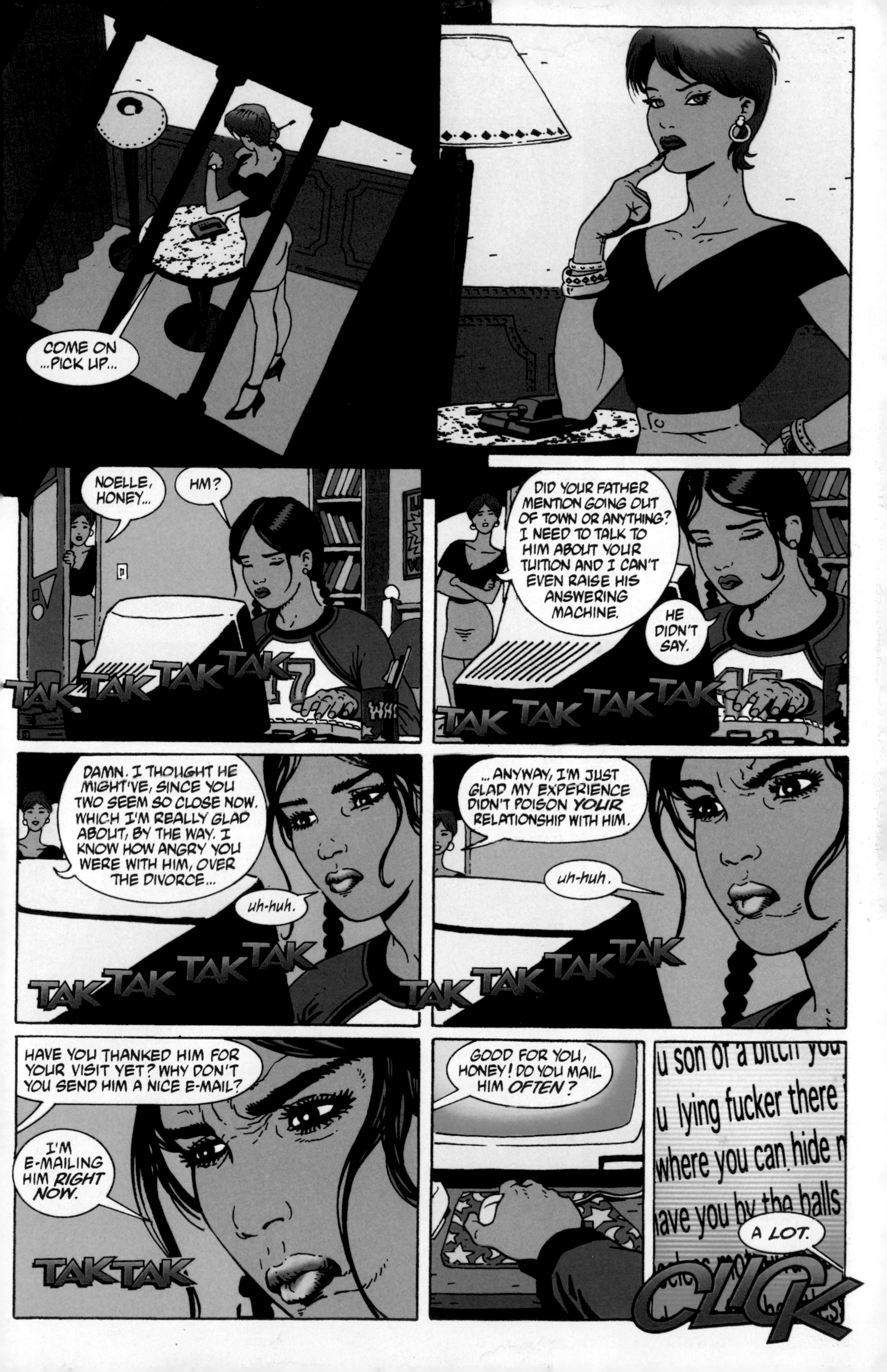
COME ON ...PICK UP...
NOELLE, HONEY...
HM?
TAK TAK TAK TAK
DID YOUR FATHER MENTION GOING OUT OF TOWN OR ANYTHING? I NEED TO TALK TO HIM ABOUT YOUR TUITION AND I CAN'T EVEN RAISE HIS ANSWERING MACHINE.
HE DIDN'T SAY.
TAK TAK TAK TAK
DAMN. I THOUGHT HE MIGHT'VE, SINCE YOU TWO SEEM SO CLOSE NOW. WHICH I'M REALLY GLAD ABOUT, BY THE WAY. I KNOW HOW ANGRY YOU WERE WITH HIM, OVER THE DIVORCE...
uh-huh.
TAK TAK TAK TAK
...ANYWAY, I'M JUST GLAD MY EXPERIENCE DIDN'T POISON *YOUR* RELATIONSHIP WITH HIM.
uh-huh.
TAK TAK TAK TAK
HAVE YOU THANKED HIM FOR YOUR VISIT YET? WHY DON'T YOU SEND HIM A NICE E-MAIL?
I'M E-MAILING HIM *RIGHT NOW*.
TAK TAK
GOOD FOR YOU, HONEY! DO YOU MAIL HIM *OFTEN*?
u son of a bitch you
u lying fucker there
where you can hide
ave you by the balls
A *LOT*.
CLICK

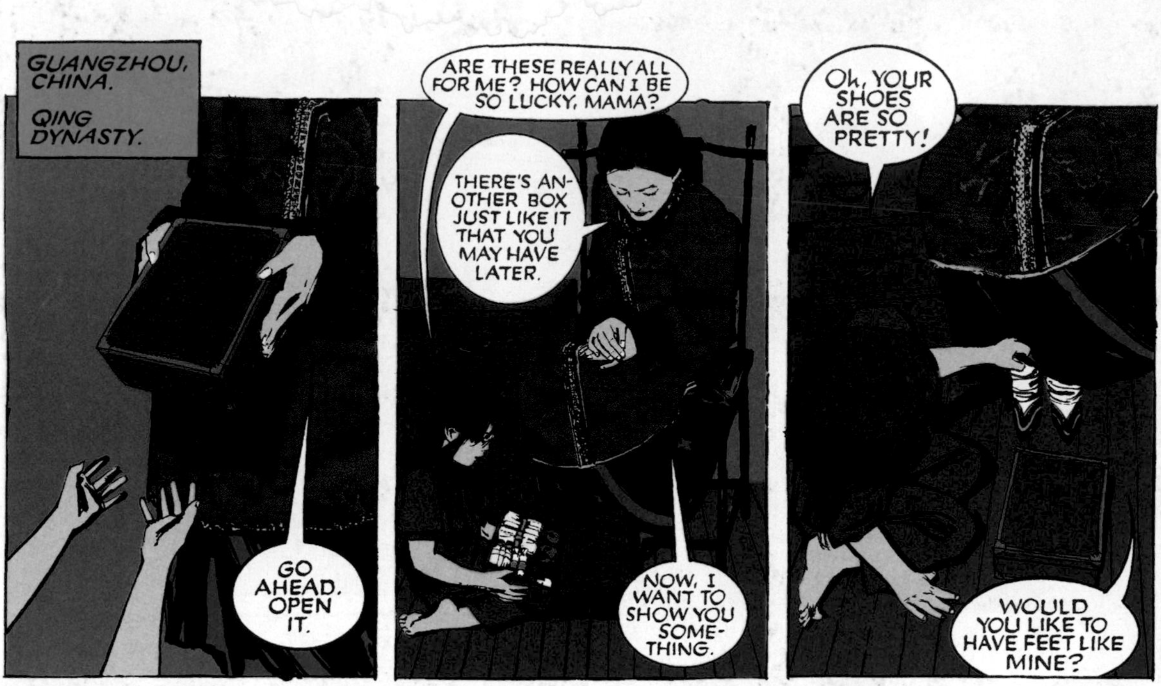
GUANGZHOU, CHINA.
QING DYNASTY.
GO AHEAD. OPEN IT.
ARE THESE REALLY ALL FOR ME? HOW CAN I BE SO LUCKY, MAMA?
THERE'S AN-OTHER BOX JUST LIKE IT THAT YOU MAY HAVE LATER.
NOW, I WANT TO SHOW YOU SOME-THING.
Oh, YOUR SHOES ARE SO PRETTY!
WOULD YOU LIKE TO HAVE FEET LIKE MINE?

# THE LOTUS SHOES

JOHN KURAMOTO *writer, color/seps* JON J MUTH *artist* TOM ORZECHOWSKI *letterer* JENNIFER LEE *editor*

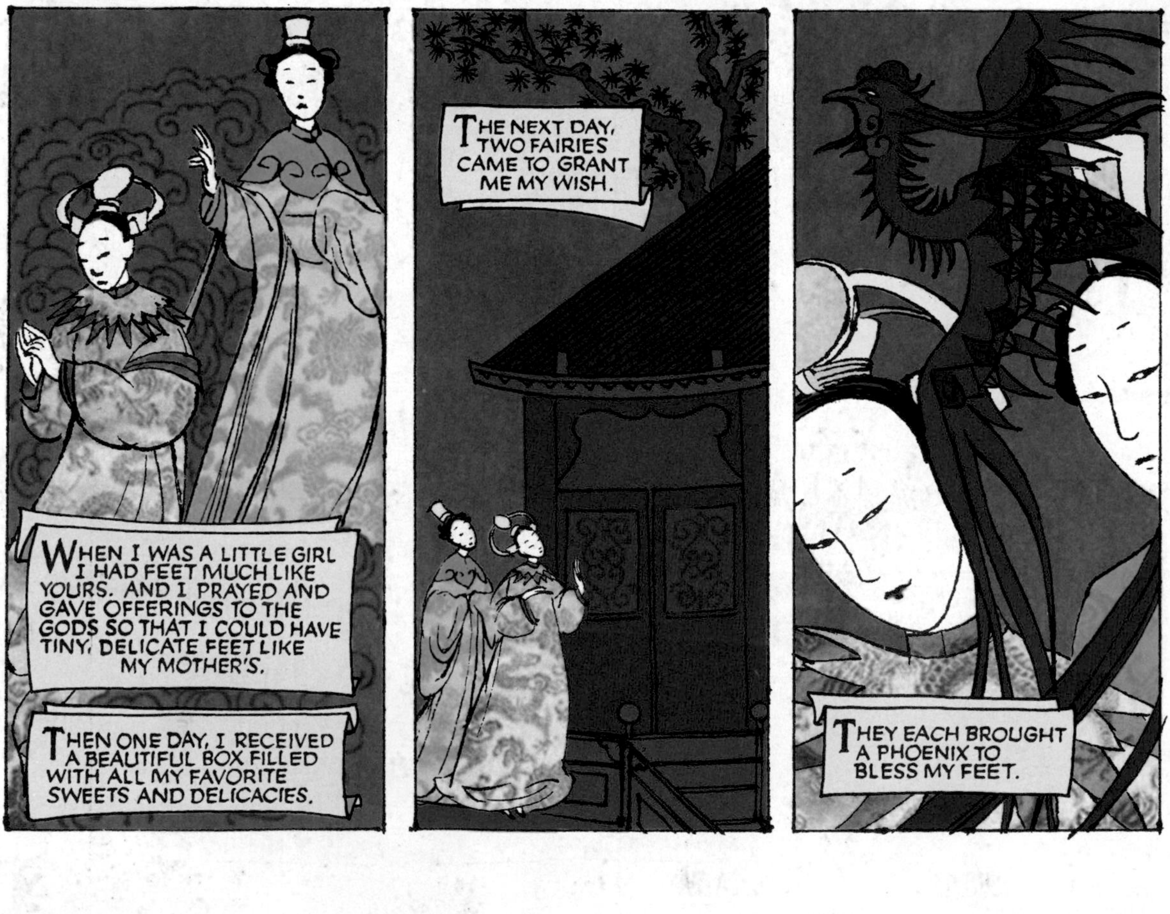
WHEN I WAS A LITTLE GIRL I HAD FEET MUCH LIKE YOURS. AND I PRAYED AND GAVE OFFERINGS TO THE GODS SO THAT I COULD HAVE TINY, DELICATE FEET LIKE MY MOTHER'S.
THEN ONE DAY, I RECEIVED A BEAUTIFUL BOX FILLED WITH ALL MY FAVORITE SWEETS AND DELICACIES.
THE NEXT DAY, TWO FAIRIES CAME TO GRANT ME MY WISH.
THEY EACH BROUGHT A PHOENIX TO BLESS MY FEET.

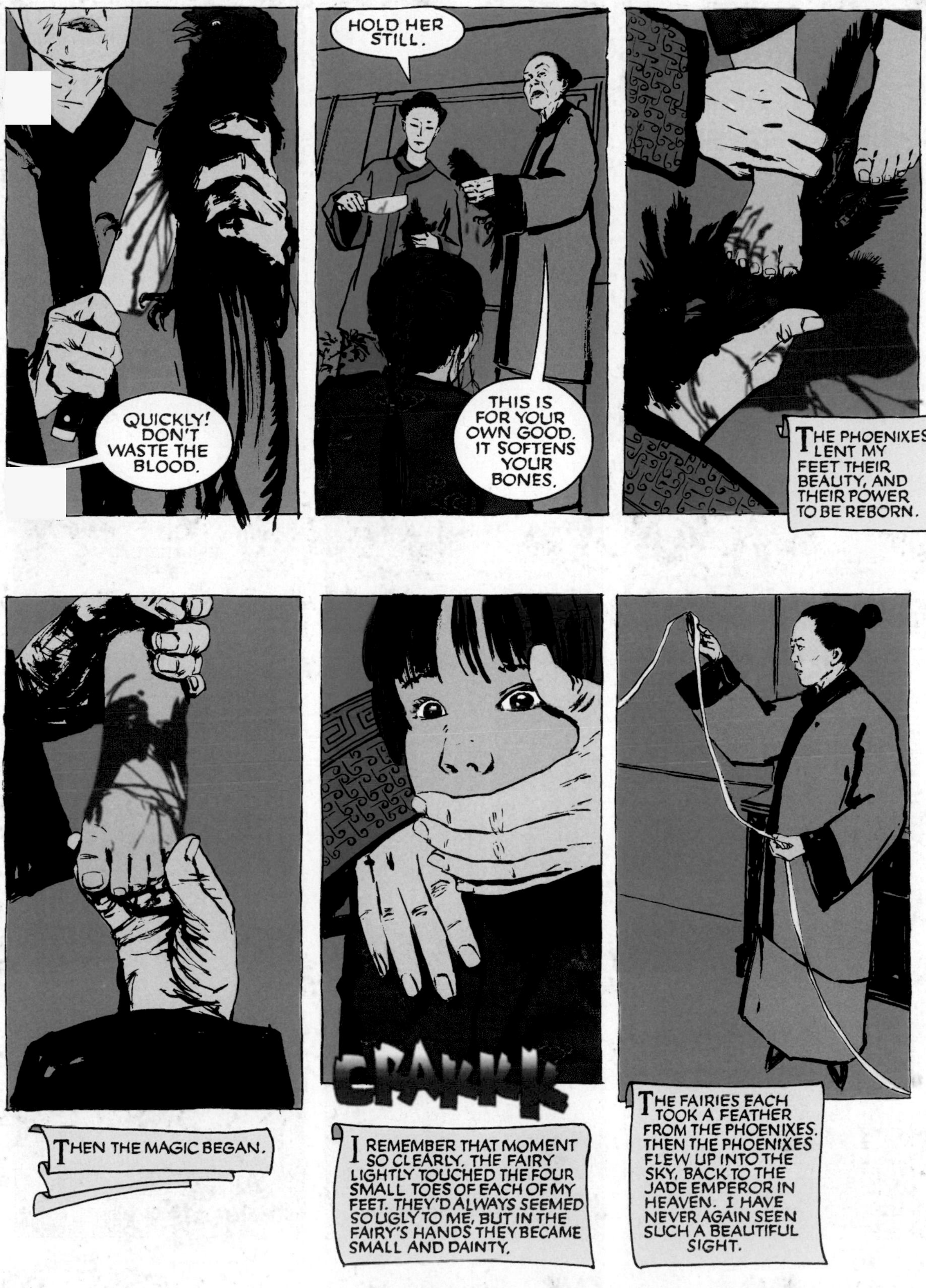
QUICKLY! DON'T WASTE THE BLOOD.
HOLD HER STILL.
THIS IS FOR YOUR OWN GOOD. IT SOFTENS YOUR BONES.
THE PHOENIXES LENT MY FEET THEIR BEAUTY, AND THEIR POWER TO BE REBORN.
THEN THE MAGIC BEGAN.
CRAKKK
I REMEMBER THAT MOMENT SO CLEARLY. THE FAIRY LIGHTLY TOUCHED THE FOUR SMALL TOES OF EACH OF MY FEET. THEY'D ALWAYS SEEMED SO UGLY TO ME, BUT IN THE FAIRY'S HANDS THEY BECAME SMALL AND DAINTY.
THE FAIRIES EACH TOOK A FEATHER FROM THE PHOENIXES. THEN THE PHOENIXES FLEW UP INTO THE SKY, BACK TO THE JADE EMPEROR IN HEAVEN. I HAVE NEVER AGAIN SEEN SUCH A BEAUTIFUL SIGHT.

THE PHOENIX FEATHERS BECAME LONG RIBBONS OF SILK. AS THE RIBBONS WRAPPED THEMSELVES AROUND MY FEET, I COULD SEE MY FEET TAKE ON THE SHAPE OF A LOTUS BUD, ROUND AT THE HEEL AND DELICATELY TAPERING TO A POINT. MY FEET WERE SO PERFECT, I COULD HAVE CRIED.

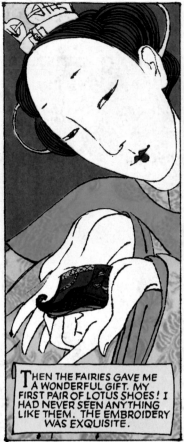

THEN THE FAIRIES GAVE ME A WONDERFUL GIFT. MY FIRST PAIR OF LOTUS SHOES! I HAD NEVER SEEN ANYTHING LIKE THEM. THE EMBROIDERY WAS EXQUISITE.

THEY SLIPPED ONTO MY FEET WITH EASE, FOR MY FEET HAD BEEN MADE FOR THEM.

THE FAIRIES BECKONED ME TO STAND. WHEN I DID, I FELT THAT I HAD NEVER REALLY STOOD ON MY OWN FEET BEFORE.

NOT ONLY HAD MY FEET CHANGED, BUT I HAD CHANGED. THE WHOLE WORLD HAD CHANGED.

I FELT SO LIGHT ON MY FEET, AS THOUGH I WERE FLOATING.

BUT THE FAIRIES HAD SO MUCH MORE TO TEACH ME.

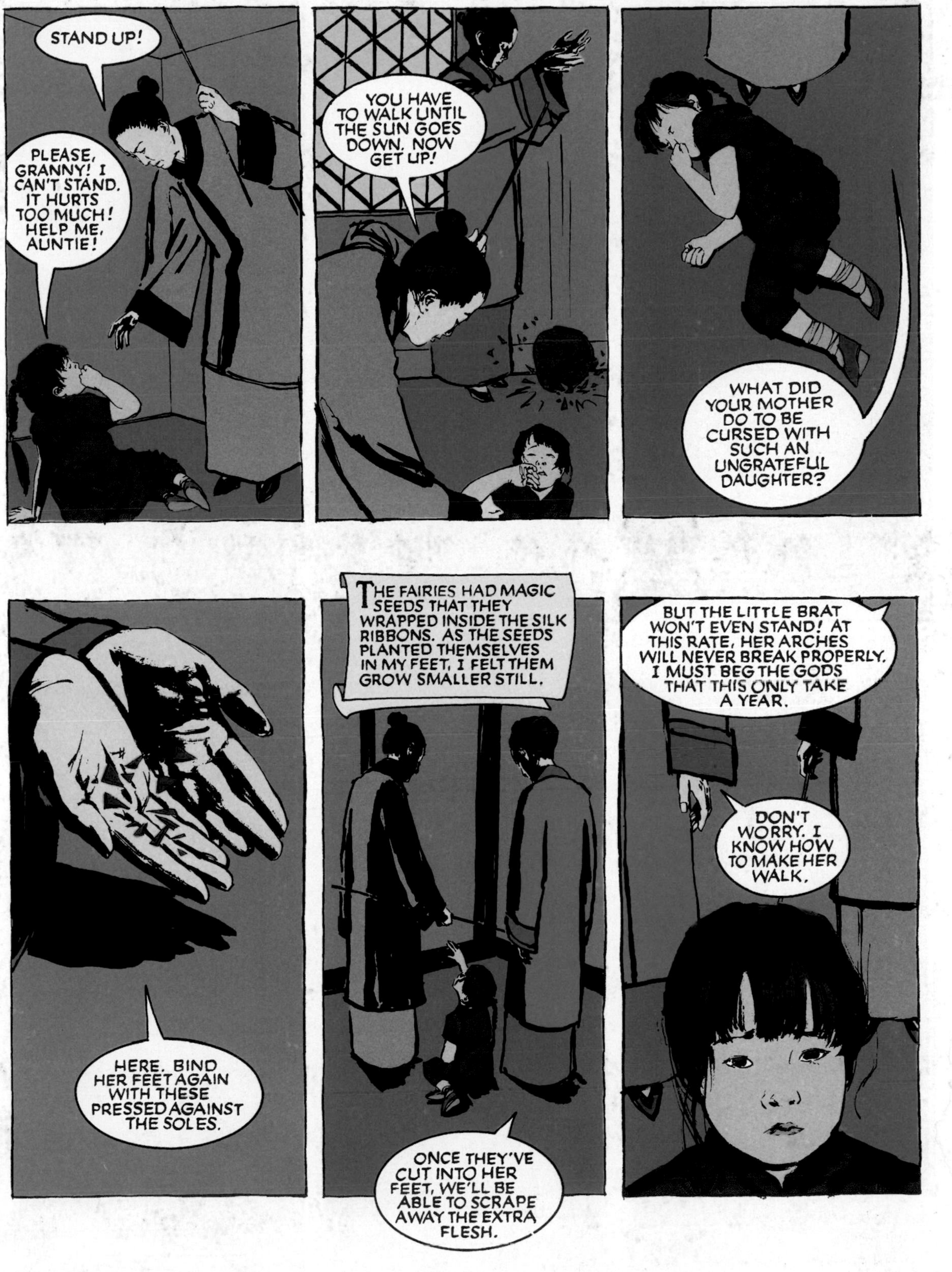
STAND UP!
PLEASE, GRANNY! I CAN'T STAND. IT HURTS TOO MUCH! HELP ME, AUNTIE!
YOU HAVE TO WALK UNTIL THE SUN GOES DOWN. NOW GET UP!
WHAT DID YOUR MOTHER DO TO BE CURSED WITH SUCH AN UNGRATEFUL DAUGHTER?
HERE. BIND HER FEET AGAIN WITH THESE PRESSED AGAINST THE SOLES.
THE FAIRIES HAD MAGIC SEEDS THAT THEY WRAPPED INSIDE THE SILK RIBBONS. AS THE SEEDS PLANTED THEMSELVES IN MY FEET, I FELT THEM GROW SMALLER STILL.
ONCE THEY'VE CUT INTO HER FEET, WE'LL BE ABLE TO SCRAPE AWAY THE EXTRA FLESH.
BUT THE LITTLE BRAT WON'T EVEN STAND! AT THIS RATE, HER ARCHES WILL NEVER BREAK PROPERLY. I MUST BEG THE GODS THAT THIS ONLY TAKE A YEAR.
DON'T WORRY. I KNOW HOW TO MAKE HER WALK.

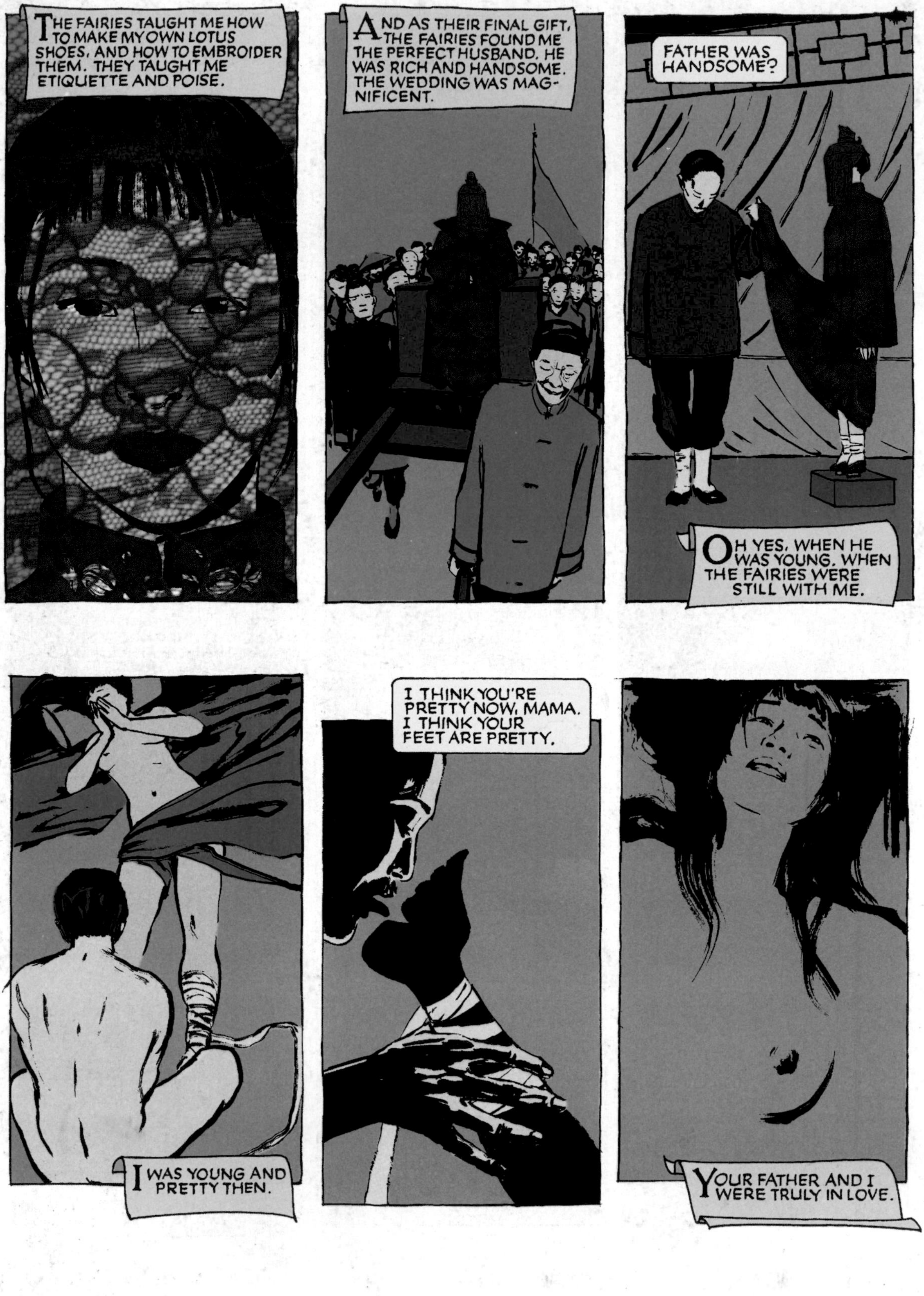
THE FAIRIES TAUGHT ME HOW TO MAKE MY OWN LOTUS SHOES, AND HOW TO EMBROIDER THEM. THEY TAUGHT ME ETIQUETTE AND POISE.
AND AS THEIR FINAL GIFT, THE FAIRIES FOUND ME THE PERFECT HUSBAND. HE WAS RICH AND HANDSOME. THE WEDDING WAS MAG-NIFICENT.
FATHER WAS HANDSOME?
OH YES. WHEN HE WAS YOUNG. WHEN THE FAIRIES WERE STILL WITH ME.
I WAS YOUNG AND PRETTY THEN.
I THINK YOU'RE PRETTY NOW, MAMA. I THINK YOUR FEET ARE PRETTY.
YOUR FATHER AND I WERE TRULY IN LOVE.

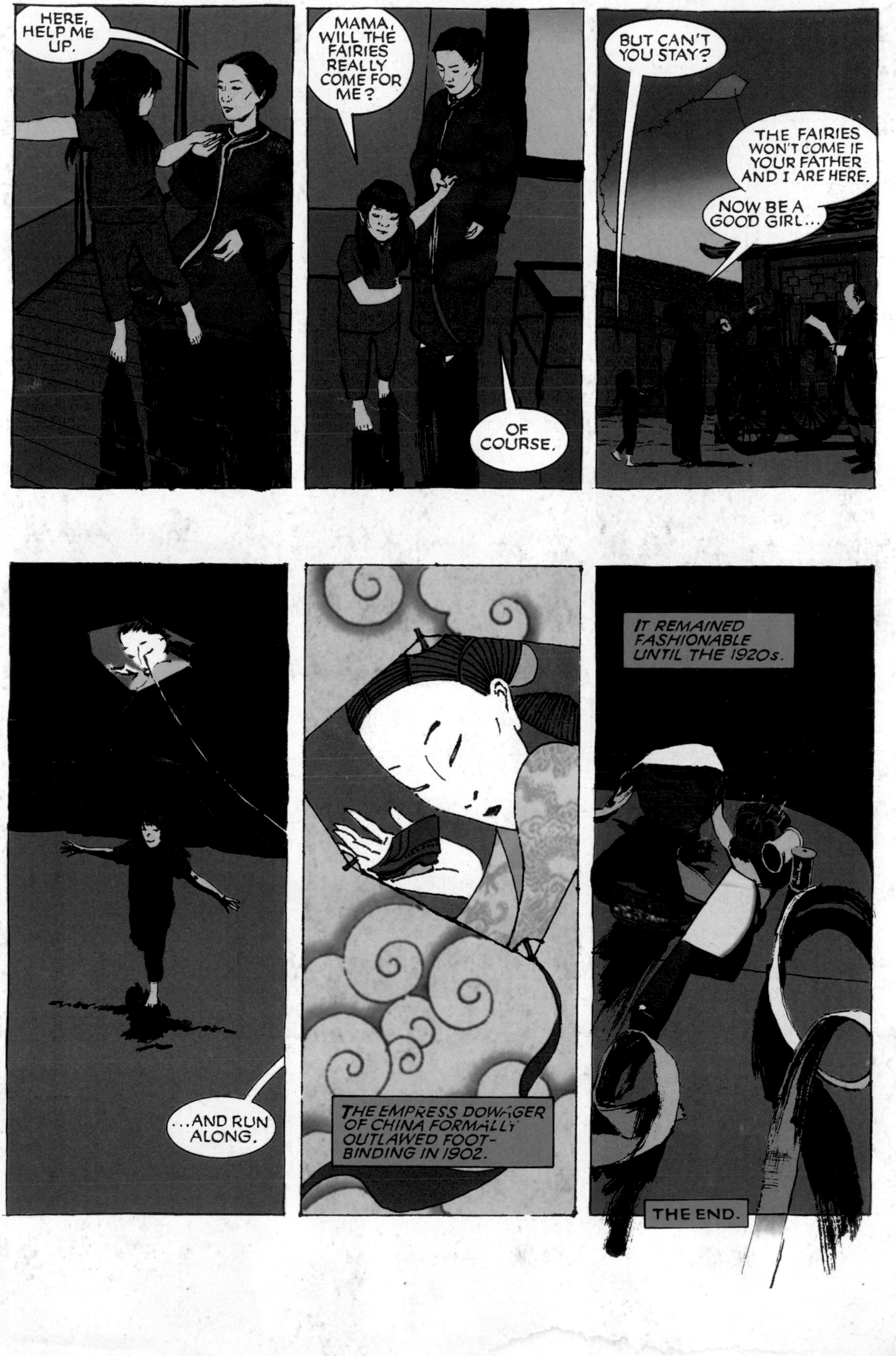
HERE, HELP ME UP.
MAMA, WILL THE FAIRIES REALLY COME FOR ME?
OF COURSE.
BUT CAN'T YOU STAY?
THE FAIRIES WON'T COME IF YOUR FATHER AND I ARE HERE.
NOW BE A GOOD GIRL...
...AND RUN ALONG.
THE EMPRESS DOWAGER OF CHINA FORMALLY OUTLAWED FOOT-BINDING IN 1902.
IT REMAINED FASHIONABLE UNTIL THE 1920s.
THE END.